CHRIST
our righteousness

CHRIST
our righteousness

J.W. "BILL" LEHMAN

Editing by Dwight Turner
Transcription by Debra Pigeon
and Dwight Turner
Graphic Design by MCM Design Studio, LLC

Editor's Note: In this manuscript,
every effort has been made to preserve the original content
of the audio recordings from which each chapter is taken.

ADDITIONAL COPIES
Additional copies of this book may be obtained
by contacting your nearest Adventist Book Center
or other Christian bookseller (refer to the ISBN number
below or on the back cover of this book).

INFORMATION
Additional information about this book and other resources
by J.W. "Bill" Lehman are available on the Internet at the
Sermons of Hope web site - www.sermonsofhope.org

*All Scripture quotations are from the Kings James version
unless otherwise noted.*

ISBN: 0-9742647-0-9

Contents

Abbreviations

AA	*The Acts of the Apostles*	MCC	*The Matchless Charms of Christ*
BC	*The Seventh-day Adventist Bible Commentary* (1BC, 2BC...etc., for volumes 1-7)	MH	*The Ministry of Healing*
		MLT	*My Life Today*
COL	*Christ's Object Lessons*	MM	*Medical Ministry*
COR	*Christ Our Righteousness* (by E. G. Daniels)	MYP	*Messages To Young People*
DA	*The Desire of Ages*	PP	*Patriarchs and Prophets*
CG	*Child Guidance*	QD	*Questions on Doctrine*
CS	*Christian Service*	RH	*Review and Herald*
Ed	*Education*	SC	*Steps to Christ*
EW	*Early Writings*	SD	*Sons and Daughters of God*
FE	*Fundamentals of Christian Education*	SG	*Spiritual Gifts* (1SG, 2SG...etc.)
FLB	*The Faith I Live By*	ST	*Signs of the Times*
GAG	*God's Amazing Grace*	1SM	*Selected Messages,* Book 1
GW	*Gospel Workers*	1T	*Testimonies for the Church* (1T, 2T...etc., for volumes 1-9)
MB	*Thoughts From the Mount of Blessing*	TM	*Testimonies to Ministers*

Foreword

THIS BOOK WAS TRANSCRIBED from a series of sermons preached by the late J.W. "Bill" Lehman. The series was titled Christ Our Righteousness, and was conducted during the middle 1970s at the Campus Hill Seventh-day Adventist Church in Loma Linda, California. We believe that God in His providence has brought this material to light once again, for it deals with a topic that is of utmost importance to those living in the last days of earth's history. Bill Lehman's presentation of this most controversial subject is done in a way that puts Christ at the very center of righteousness. Those who read this book will go away with a higher appreciation for the Christ who loved them so much that He endured the shame and agony of the cross.

As we near the end of time, Satan will unleash all his weapons against the church and its individual members. As in the desert of ancient Egypt when deadly serpents visited the children of Israel, God's people today are falling victim to the modern serpents of doubt, worldly and sensual pleasures, substance abuse, false doctrine, and many other snares of Satan. Those who would be saved must follow the divine remedy and look unto Jesus. Once we have applied the remedy to our own souls, we must then go help others to look unto Jesus as their only hope.

Lifting Jesus before the world is the work to be done by God's people in the last days. This fact is made clear by one who spoke for God: "The end is near!...Light is to shine forth from God' people in clear, distinct rays, bringing Jesus before the churches and before the world...One interest will prevail, one subject will swallow up every other—Christ Our Righteousness." SD 259. As the end draws near and increasing spiritual darkness engulfs the world, the attention of a small remnant will focus more and more upon Christ and His righteousness.

In 1888, the Lord sent through Waggoner and Jones a message that was to empower God's people to finish the work. That message was for the most part rejected; and since then the subjects of justification by faith and Christ our righteousness have for short periods of time returned to the forefront of discussion amongst Seventh-day Adventists. During those times, books were published and multiple theories were presented; but after a few years people would lose interest and the message would fade back into the shadows. However, Ellen White predicted that before the end, this subject will not only rise again, it "will prevail." This means that much of the confusion that has surrounded this subject in the past will be cleared away, and many will see perhaps for the first time the wonderful truths of this glorious message. If this subject is so important that it will swallow up every other subject, should we not now set our minds to discovering the important aspects of this message?

This book contains a sound theological foundation for the subject of Christ our righteousness and offers amazing insight into those aspects of the message that have often been misunderstood and misinterpreted. If prayerfully studied, this book will prove to be invaluable to all who truly hunger and thirst after righteousness. The message in each chapter will endear the heart of the reader to Christ in a special way.

—Dwight Turner, Editor

CHRIST OUR RIGHTEOUSNESS— TODAY'S MESSAGE

THERE ARE SOME TODAY who minimize the message of Christ our righteousness, believing there are other topics far more important, such as the second coming of Jesus, some of the prophecies, our personal needs in the Christian life, and the law and the Sabbath. Some even say that Christ our righteousness is a fad that will soon pass away; and it might be that, but not because God planned for it to be that way.

All of these comments demonstrate a terrible ignorance of the scope and meaning of the topic of Christ our righteousness. Such a depreciation of the message often causes many to not see its true worth, value, and importance in their lives; and therefore they fail to experience Christ as their righteousness.

The following quote is one of the most significant things Ellen White wrote regarding the third angel's message: "Several have written to me inquiring if the message of justification by faith is the third angel's message, and I have answered, 'It is the third angel's message in verity.'" COR 64. There are several other statements like this. "The Lord in His great mercy sent a most precious message to His people through Elders Waggoner and Jones....It presented justification through faith in the Surety; it invited the people to receive the righteousness of Christ, which is made manifest in obedience to all the commandments of God.... This is the message that God commanded to be given to the world. It is the third angel's message, which is to be proclaimed with a loud voice, and attended with the outpouring of His Spirit in a large measure." TM 91,92. The terms "justification by faith" and "Christ our righteousness" are used interchangeably; therefore, Christ our righteousness is the third angel's message, which we know to be the final message from God to the world in the last days.

"The time of test is just upon us, for the Loud Cry of the third angel has already begun in the revelation of the righteousness of Christ, the sin pardoning Redeemer. This is the beginning of the light of the angel whose glory shall fill the whole earth." COR 56.

Throughout the Spirit of Prophecy we find that the terms third angel's message, the Loud Cry of the third angel, justification by faith, and Christ our righteousness are all closely interrelated, and in fact synonymous. This message is unique in that, even though you can apply Christ our righteousness to a personal experience at any time in the Christian era, it has a special quality in the last days. Most will agree that these are the last days. The Loud Cry of the third angel is the last message according to the book of Revelation. There will be no greater message sent from God than this precious truth—the message of Christ our righteousness. This final message will lighten the earth with the glory (character) of God, bringing to a close God's final work upon the earth.

There are so few people who understand anything about this subject. We who proclaim to be ready for the coming of Jesus, and to be preparing the world for that event, sometimes depreciate the message that will finish God's work; and therefore think that we are finishing His work without it. If there is any message today that is "present truth," it is the message of justification by faith in the righteousness of Christ. It is our terrible ignorance of the scope and meaning of this topic that perhaps has kept us here so many years, when we thought He would come a long time ago. If this is the third angel's message, it is not only timely, but extremely urgent; for the alternative is for millions to be lost. Some people object to that, but you can object all you want. That is the way it is according to the Scriptures. You can argue with God, but I doubt that you will win.

In the stream of time, we live in a day of extreme emergency; yet somehow many who used to sense that have forgotten all about it. We do not like to be pressured anymore, or pushed; but time is pressing us and urging us. To sleep in this day and time is as dire as Christ painted it where He said, "in such an hour as ye think not the Son of man cometh." Matthew 24:44. This message is vital to our correct understanding of the issues of our day and age. Without Christ our righteousness, we will misunderstand those issues and pervert them, and they will not mean to us what they should.

Many understand last day events and the third angel's message through a legalistic viewpoint, which brings about terrible misunderstandings for the third angel's message is Christ our righteousness in verity. To look at this message through legalism is to corrupt the message that God intended would finish the work. When we see all the issues of our day through the eyes of Christ and His righteousness, suddenly we will understand where we are in time and how urgent these days are. We will also have a clearer vision of Christ and His righteousness

The teeth in the Sabbath that makes it very urgent is the mark of the beast; and the teeth in Christ our righteousness is the fact that it is the third angel's message in verity—the Loud Cry. It is not something we can toy with like a cat with a mouse and say, "Well, I will decide later." Later may be too late. The urgency of the times prods us on to make a choice now and not tomorrow!

There are many similarities between Christ our righteousness and the third angel's message that we often do not see. The Loud Cry declares that "Babylon is fallen." Revelation 18:2. You must study about Babel and Babylon. Babylon is the symbol of self-righteousness—do it yourself in your own efforts and your own strength. As Nebuchadnezzar said, "Is not this great Babylon, that I have built...by the might of my power, and for the honour of my majesty?" Daniel 4: 30. Babylon fell because that same spirit persisted in his grandson Belshazzar during the feast that night as described in Daniel chapter 5. Daniel reviews to Belshazzar the experience of his father, and he states there in verse 22, "And thou his son, O Belshazzar, hast not humbled thine heart, though thou knewest all this." That is, you knew all the experience of your grandfather, how he was humbled down to be like an animal because of his terrible pride and because of his contesting with God; though you knew all of this, you have not humbled yourself. Babylon is like that, and the Bible declares its fall.

The third angel's message has to do with commandment keeping, and Daniel 7:25 predicts a power that "thinks to change times and laws." Babylon prefers to have man made laws. In addition to this, in Revelation chapter 13, it says that all will be caused to worship this power and its commands. This is accomplished first of all by deceiving the masses with its miracles, and then forced by a decree prohibiting buying or selling for all who do not submit to their commands.

In Revelation 14:12, we are told that God's people keep His commandments. Why do they keep them? Are they forced to? Jesus said, "If ye love Me, keep My commandments." John 14:15. What a difference there is between causing them to worship, and wooing or winning them so that they love and obey Him.

Jesus taught that the law was supreme love for God and to love our neighbors as ourselves. In Revelation 18:3, in the loud cry of the third angel, we are taught that Babylon has an intimate love affair, not with Christ, but with "the kings of the earth." She loves, but not Jesus. In addition, she does not keep the second half of the Ten Commandments because she causes those that would not worship the beast to be killed, which is not exactly loving your neighbor as yourself. The mistreatment of human beings, the unkindness to others, is a part of the activities of the enemy of Christ; and yet they claim to be commandment keepers. They claim to obey God and to rightly represent Him in the earth. This is just a little birds-eye view of some of the aspects of the third angel's message and the loud cry, and it helps us see how different it is from Christ our righteousness.

In opposition to this power will be those who will shine for Christ. Those who love God will truly obey Him; and they will also love their neighbors as themselves. This will be made manifest to the world.

We will be digging into the meaning of the third angel's message from the one viewpoint of Christ our righteousness (or justification by faith as we more often call it).

Here is the entire text of the message: "And after these things I saw another angel come down from heaven, having great power; and the earth was lightened with his glory. And he cried mightily with a strong voice, saying, Babylon the great is fallen, is fallen, and is become the habitation of devils, and the hold of every foul spirit, and a cage of every unclean and hateful bird. For all nations have drunk of the wine of the wrath of her fornication, and the kings of the earth have committed fornication with her, and the merchants of the earth are waxed rich through the abundance of her delicacies. And I heard another voice from heaven, saying, Come out of her, My people, that ye be not partakers of her sins, and that ye receive not of her plagues. For her sins have reached unto heaven, and God hath remembered her iniquities." Revelation 18:1-5. This is what we call the "Loud Cry" of the third angel. It seems that as the third angel's message is going forth, another angel comes with power to make the message more effective.

Notice that "the earth was lightened with his glory." What is the glory that lights up the earth in this message? It is not literally the angel. In the Greek language, the word for "angel" means "messenger." This is a symbol of a message that sweeps the earth, like an angel encircling the globe. But it is not the glory of the angel. It is the glory of the message.

What is the glory that lights up the earth? "Arise, shine; for thy light is come, and the glory of the Lord is risen upon thee. For, behold, the darkness shall cover the earth, and gross darkness the people: but the Lord shall arise upon thee, and His glory shall be seen upon thee. And the Gentiles shall come to thy light, and kings to the brightness of thy rising." Isaiah 60:1-3. This is a command to stand up and shine. Why should we shine? Because "thy light is come." Your light and my light; and the glory of the Lord is risen upon us just like the sun coming up in the morning. This is the prophecy of the light of Revelation 18:1 that something tremendous would happen to lighten the whole earth.

Jesus taught that "Ye are the light of the world." Matthew 5:14. You! In Isaiah it says you are to rise and shine for your light is come. Jesus also said, "Let your light so shine before men, that they may see your good works, and glorify your Father which is in heaven." Matthew 5:16. Through good works light is to shine out to the world, and the result is that your Father will be glorified. The light spoken of here is good works, not just good words (although they might be pleasant, too). It is talking about good actions that the world will appreciate.

Literally, the people involved in the Loud Cry will shine. In the book Early Writings, there are several places where it mentions this. "The work of this angel comes in at the right time to join in the last great work of the third angel's message as it swells to a loud cry." "I saw a great light resting upon them [God's people], and they united to fearlessly proclaim the third angel's message." "The glory of God rested upon the patient, waiting saints, and they fearlessly gave the last solemn warning...." "The light that was shed upon the waiting ones penetrated everywhere...." "Servants of God, endowed with power from on high with their faces lighted up, and shining with holy consecration, went forth to proclaim the message from heaven." "God's people were strengthened by the excellent glory which rested upon them in rich abundance and prepared them to endure the hour of temptation." EW 277-279.

These quotations tell us that these people will literally shine in the radiance of God's glory that rests upon them. When Jesus spoke about people seeing our good works and glorifying God, He was speaking about the light, or glory, streaming from the right kind of good works; and I hope you have not set your mind in a mold as to what those good works are. Too often our definitions are incorrect, compared to those Christ gives us.

How do the saints become so glorious that they shine like the sun? "So the followers of Christ are to shed light into the darkness of the world. Through the Holy Spirit, God's word is a light as it becomes a transforming power in the life of the receiver. By implanting in their hearts the principles of His word, the Holy Spirit develops in men the attributes of God. The light of His glory—His character—is to shine forth in His followers. Thus they are to glorify God...." COL 414. In other words, the world is to see God in His saints by seeing God's character in them. This is what it is talking about when it says the earth is lightened with His glory.

You can get some idea about God's glory being His character in the story of when Moses asked to see God's glory. "And he said, I beseech Thee, shew me Thy glory. And He said, I will make all My goodness pass before thee, and I will proclaim the name of the Lord...." Exodus 33:18,19. "And the Lord passed by before him, and proclaimed, The Lord, The Lord God, merciful and gracious, longsuffering, and abundant in goodness and truth, keeping mercy for thousands, forgiving iniquity and transgression and sin...." Exodus 34:6,7. This is the character of God; and His character is love. Our God is love. When He proclaimed His character, He proclaimed these attributes described here. Our God is love, and His love (His character) will be seen like glory; like the sun coming up in the morning, covering the whole earth.

The day when the earth will be lightened with His glory was prophesied in the Old and New Testaments. God will be seen as He really is, not as people suppose He is. There is a vast difference. Human beings will show the world what God is like.

This light is needed because Isaiah tells us that "darkness shall cover the earth, and gross darkness the people: but the Lord shall arise upon thee, and His glory shall be seen upon thee." Isaiah 60:2. Into this darkness God's glory will shine, and the world will see God as He is, manifested in His people.

"It is the darkness of misapprehension of God [we fear Him] that is enshrouding the world. Men are losing their knowledge of His character. It has been misunderstood and misinterpreted." COL 415. That does not mean only the people in other churches. There are many of us that are fearful of God. We say, "But I have been sinning." He knew that everyone had been sinning before He ever came to this world. "But God commendeth His love toward us, in that, while we were yet sinners, Christ died for us." Romans 5:8. He knows you are a sinner, but that does not chase Him away, or He would have never come in the first place. He takes the sins that separate God and man out of the way. He is the only one who could do that. He is the sin bearer who carries them all away. They have all been laid upon Him; therefore they no longer separate. Why? Because Christ took them out of the way. There is no wall of partition dividing God and man anymore, which is misunderstood Old Testament theology that causes people to fear God. The Pharisees fled from Jesus in the temple, but the little children and the mothers stayed there. It is possible to become comfortable in the presence of God.

There is a gross misunderstanding about God. In fact, one of the largest tasks for the church to accomplish today is to gain a right understanding of God. Many of our students do not understand Him well. The same is true of many parents, church members, and pastors. We often present Him in a vastly different way than He really is. No wonder people are afraid of the God they imagine Him to be. Therefore people do not feel accepted because He seems to be so tyrannical, dictatorial, oppressive, and demanding. We always present Him as pointing the finger at us, so we cringe in our guilt. God is not like that. There is a darkness in the world, a misapprehension of God; and we must go back and present Him as Christ did when He walked this earth; for as Jesus said, "he that hath seen Me hath seen the Father." John 14:9.

The Bible says that into this darkness light will shine—the light of the glory of God. "At this time [when there is darkness in the earth] a message from God is to be proclaimed, a message illuminating in its influence and saving in its power. His character is to be made known [that is the message]. Into the darkness of the world is to be shed the light of His glory, the light of His goodness, mercy, and truth." COL 415. Someone must do more than just speak about this. It is more than a proclamation. It is a demonstration, a manifestation, so that the world sees God in His people. His character is to be demonstrated in our lives.

The quote on page 415 continues on: "The children of God are to manifest His glory. In their own life and character they are to reveal what the grace of God has done for them. The light of the Sun of Righteousness is to shine forth in good works—in words of truth and deeds of holiness." He is counting on us to manifest Him to the world, to demonstrate what God's true character is really like—that He is truly a God of love.

He will make us like that. His goal for you is to make you a light of His glory—of His character—so that you might glorify Him in your good works. He is able to accomplish that, is He not? That should be our goal.

Isaiah wrote about this in slightly different language: "O Zion, that bringest good tidings, get thee up into the high mountain; O Jerusalem, that bringest good tidings, lift up thy voice with strength; lift it up, be not afraid; say unto the cities of Judah, Behold your God!" Isaiah 40:9. Behold your God.

"Those who wait for the Bridegroom's coming are to say to the people, 'Behold your God.' The last rays of merciful light, the last message of mercy to be given to the world, is a revelation of His character of love." COL 415. The world has not yet, apart from Jesus, seen God. Jesus was the only One who has truly revealed Him to the world; and now we understand there will be a message that will lighten the whole earth that will say, "Behold God in His people; and God is love." They will see that. There will be no last plagues until the world sees that God is love. There will be no return of Jesus until the world sees that God is love. This is the last message—the revelation of God's character of love.

We preach that Christ is coming back soon. Too often we only present a Christ that will be taking vengeance on those who know Him not. We teach a Judgment going on, and you had better be ready or you will burn. Is that revealing a God of love? We are trying to frighten people into being ready, and that does not reveal God's love at all. God hates the sin, but He certainly loves the sinner. There is a great deal of difference between hating acts of sin and hating people. You and I might have some trouble making distinctions, but God does not. He does not hate the sinner. He loves the sinner; although He despises some of the things we do. Your parents do not like some of the acts you do, but they love you. You may not like some of the actions of your spouse, but you love your spouse. God makes the same distinctions. God is love, but how often we present Him as threatening us if we do not line up. God is a God of love and He is not like that. He woos us to His side. He does not drive us as the beast power does.

How is it that God's people will be like God in character? "For God, who commanded the light to shine out of darkness, hath shined in our hearts, to give the light of the knowledge of the glory of God in the face of Jesus Christ." 2 Corinthians 4:6. God shines light that gives us knowledge and understanding about His character. As we behold Jesus, we behold our heavenly Father, and a light, an understanding, comes into us; and the glory of His character becomes a glory to us, just as to Moses in the mount when he beheld the glory of God in the law and the sacrifice. The face of Moses shined so brightly that the people could not look upon him. This was a human being who had walked so closely with God that he literally glorified God physically as well as spiritually; for he was a reflector of that brilliance, of that light that he had beheld there in the mount.

This is a creative act. God who commanded the light to shine out of darkness hath shined in our hearts. As He created light and darkness, so He creates light in the darkened minds of His people and the people of the world. He shines into their hearts.

Paul said that when the old man is put off, you are to be "renewed in the spirit of your mind; and that ye put on the new man, which after God is created in righteousness and true holiness." Ephesians 4:24. That new creature, or creation, is a creative act. God makes a new person. And just like He caused the light to shine out of darkness back in the beginning, so He does now in you and in me. He wants to do this in the whole world in the last days.

Paul wrote about beholding His glory. "But we all, with open face beholding as in a glass the glory of the Lord [His character], are changed into the same image from glory to glory, even as by the Spirit of the Lord." 2 Corinthians 3:18. As we fall in love with Him and become enraptured with Him, as we adore Him, as we are devoted to Him, we see His glory—His character—and we are changed into the same image; even from glory to glory, or from one degree to another, until we shall shine as the stars in their beauty.

Paul wrote that "we have this treasure [this glory, this character, this beauty] in earthen vessels [in corrupt human bodies], that the excellency of the power may be of God, and not of us." 2 Corinthians 4:7. Everyone knows that fallen human beings are not like God. Everyone knows that in our corrupt bodies we cannot possibly produce a character like His. The entire world knows that for we have demonstrated it for six thousand years. Therefore, all the praise is to Him if men become like Him. When He shines into our hearts and changes us, and by beholding His glory we are changed from glory to glory, everyone will know that God has brought this about, and not man. The world will praise Him and not us, because the message is Christ our righteousness, not we our righteousness.

The first angel's message says that we are to "worship Him that made heaven, and earth, and the sea, and the fountains of waters." Revelation 14:7. Worship the Creator. He is the only One who can make light shine out of darkness; and the minds of many today are darkened. That is why the Bible does not make sense to many people. That is why God's commands seem unreasonable. That is why we have so many frustrations and so many problems. Our minds are beclouded and dead in trespasses and sins. They must be "quickened by the Spirit." 1 Peter 3:18. He says He will shine into our minds, so that the darkness and mystery would be taken away; and you will say, "Oh, now I see!"

Just as God accomplishes the rising of the sun every day, He accomplishes the rising of the Sun of Righteousness in our lives. He accomplishes the glory of God in human beings—earthen vessels—in all their weakness and sinfulness. He accomplishes this until we are changed into vessels of beauty and of honor.

We become like Him while the others worship the beast and his image, which are man-made powers, and obeyed in man's strength; not transformed by the Divine One. What a difference. And so many of us, as we attempt to make ourselves better in our own strength, are joining with those who worship the beast and his image. It is all man made unless it is Christ our righteousness.

The distinctions have become wide between those who love Him and those who are being forced, or who are trying to force themselves, to love Him. One group trusts only Him and His righteousness, and not their own. They are recreated by His power and not their own. They are transformed by His glory until all praise is to Him and not to themselves. The other group will take the praise to themselves for their own efforts to satisfy God's laws.

God's goal for you and for me is not to be good enough to be saved. This is one misunderstanding that must be taken away. Our goal is not to be good enough to be saved. It never has been that. God's goal for every human being is to be like Him. He wants to be seen in the world through us. The world understands us but they do not understand Him. It is that darkness that must be taken away. The world will see God in human beings before Jesus comes back. Christ our righteousness tells us that His glory is to be seen, and not ours. Ours is all contaminated, corrupt, and vile.

The goal of Christ our righteousness and justification by faith is not simply just to be good enough to get to heaven. That is an erroneous concept. It is not striving to be obedient. It is to be like Him. God does not want to come and pat us on the back and say, "You have done a good job." He wants to say, "You have honored Me; I will honor you. You have glorified Me, I will glorify you." The world cannot be saved by seeing us become better and better and better. It does not matter how good we become because the world will not be saved by our becoming good. The world will be saved by God. They must see Him, they must love Him, they must adore Him, they must receive His Person; but they do not know Him until they see Him in us. We will be a revelation of God to a dying world.

John told us in very simple words that "when He shall appear, we shall be like Him." 1 John 3:2. Some people listen to this and become very discouraged. They say, "I can never become like Him." But the One who made something out of nothing, the One who made light to shine out of darkness, can make something out of nothing in you, too. If you understand the Creator, and the power of God unto salvation, which Paul defines as the gospel, it is not what you can do, but rather what He will do with you when He is permitted to do that.

"It is His glory to pardon the chief of sinners." MH 161. And His glory is His character. He says, "I don't care how bad you are. That doesn't bother Me or prevent Me from doing something for you. My character is manifested when I pardon the chief of sinners and transform them. Then the world truly sees that I am God; and a God of love and of might and power who loves humans so much that He can change the vilest of sinners." Then God is seen! Yet all the time we keep saying, "I am too bad!" So what! That is no problem to Him. He has been working with the bad for six thousand years. It is His glory to take care of the worst sinners. It does not bring praise to Him to take care only of fine, upstanding citizens who never had a sin in their lives; although there are not any like that—they just think they are. The ones who really bless Him are the ones that everyone thinks is lost—the hopeless cases. They really honor His name when He converts them, do they not?

The Lord is capable. What do you think of God? Is He too small to accomplish His plans? We are everlastingly looking at weak self and becoming discouraged. He tells us to look to Him and be saved and to be transformed. It is His glory that is to be seen in our transformation, not ours.

When does the light of the angel come to lighten the earth? It is made clear in the Old Testament by the gospel prophet Isaiah. "Then shall thy light break forth as the morning, and thine health shall spring forth speedily: and thy righteousness shall go before thee; the glory of the Lord shall be thy rereward [rear guard]." Isaiah 58:6. This verse begins with "Then." When is "then"? It is referring back to two previous verses. "Is not this the fast that I have chosen? To loose the bands of wickedness, to undo the heavy burdens, and to let the oppressed go free, and that ye break every yoke? Is it not to deal thy bread to the hungry, and that thou bring the poor that are cast out to thy house? When thou seest the naked, that thou cover him; and that thou hide not thyself from thine own flesh?" Verses 6,7. When this happens, "Then shall thy light break forth as the morning: and thy righteousness shall go before thee." Then God will be seen.

"Thus in the night of spiritual darkness God's glory is to shine forth through His church in lifting up the bowed down and comforting those that mourn. All around us are heard the wails of a world's sorrow. On every hand are the needy and distressed. It is ours to aid in relieving and softening life's hardships and misery. Practical work will have far more effect than mere sermonizing. We are to give food to the hungry, clothing to the naked, and shelter to the homeless. And we are called to do more than this. The wants of the soul, only the love of Christ can satisfy. If Christ is abiding in us, our hearts will be full of divine sympathy. The sealed fountains of earnest, Christlike love will be unsealed." COL 417.

Christ wants to give each of us a tender heart that sympathizes with people, that has compassion as He had, that is sensitive to the needs of those around us. He will supply all their needs according to His riches in glory, no matter what those needs are. This goodness of God will be reflected and manifested in humanity. God will be seen in the person of His saints. This is what He is waiting for.

The Bible says the result of this light is that "the Gentiles [or unbelievers] shall come to thy light, and the kings to the brightness of thy rising." Isaiah 60:3. A tremendous ingathering, or harvest of souls will take place. Multitudes came in at Pentecost. We are told that the Latter Rain will be even greater.

An Old Testament writer prophesied that "the earth shall be filled with the knowledge of the glory of the Lord, as the waters cover the sea." Habakkuk 2:14. Here is Ellen White's comment on this Bible text: "Another angel comes down from heaven having great power, and the earth is to be lightened with his glory. The Spirit of the Lord will so graciously bless consecrated human instrumentalities that men, women, and children will open their lips in praise and thanksgiving, filling the earth with the knowledge of God, and with His unsurpassed glory as the waters cover the sea." 7BC 984. It will be so extensive there will be millions of people shining for God, filled with His glory and manifesting His character, and the whole earth will be full of His glory. Human beings, multitudes in every land, will shine for God, saying, "Behold your God. He is like us, and we are like Him."

We are to proclaim His glory and grace, not by sermons, but every moment and every hour of every day, wherever we live, wherever we go. We cannot preach the Loud Cry in words. We will live the Loud Cry.

It is God's glory to pardon the chiefest of sinners. It does not matter how vile you have been or how far you have gone. God will manifest Himself in you, He will glorify Himself in you, and the world will be amazed as they behold God in humanity. And then Jesus will come.

How He longs to come into your heart. How He longs to rise like the sun in the morning with light, warming us on the inside and the outside; and glowing in us, shining in us, until the whole life is so transformed that our very lips, our every act, manifests His love and His goodness; until we cannot contain and constrain ourselves. We must shine for Him. "Let your light so shine before men, that they may see your good works, and glorify your Father which is in heaven." Matthew 5:16.

It is our privilege to have that transformation, not tomorrow but this very day. God has been waiting many years to shine out into the darkness of this world through our lives. May His will be done for you and for me is my prayer in His precious name.

THE STARTING
POINT OF
RIGHTEOUSNESS

MUCH HAS BEEN WRITTEN by Seventh-day Adventist authors on the subject of Christ our righteousness. Beginning in 1888 and onward, there has been a great deal of difficulty with this subject. Our denomination faced a major crisis when in 1888, the finest leaders we had disagreed about this subject. Christ our righteousness has become such a volatile topic that when I first learned about it, my advisors in college told me to leave this subject alone, saying it would chase me out of the church. Yet I read in the Spirit of Prophecy and the Bible that this message is fundamental to the salvation of all who hear the gospel. A few people claim to know what it is all about; but there are some aspects of it that many apparently do not understand, for we as a people do not agree about this subject at all.

In order to understand why some have fought violently against the message of Christ our righteousness, you must go back and look at what took place in 1888. There was an emphasis on the subject of justification by faith in Minneapolis that has almost never been presented since then. It is the negative side of justification by faith. You may think there is nothing negative about it. It is positive and hopeful, but there is a side to it that can be looked upon as very negative. I do not like to talk about negative things, but you will never understand unless I do. There is an aspect to this subject that, as first presented in 1888, some people detest.

This somewhat negative theme is the most basic element of the subject of justification by faith. Leaving out this theme prevents us from experiencing it. Justification by faith is not to be simply a theory, but an experience. It is not enough to just understand it. It is something you must practice every day. We must put it into effect in our lives. It must do something for us, otherwise it is just an abstract theory that does no one any good. And we do not necessarily practice it just because we can preach about it or talk about it to our friends and neighbors.

This negative aspect to Christ our righteousness and justification by faith is the starting point for true righteousness. It was this aspect that brought so much opposition to the message of Jones and Waggoner in 1888. There was a lot of argument and debate over subjects like the Trinity, but those subjects did not intimidate people. This negative aspect that we are discussing caused much opposition, even though it was not argued or debated, or in fact even discussed to any significant degree.

This negative aspect is found in Ellen White's definition of justification by faith. "What is justification by faith? It is the work of God in laying the glory of man in the dust, and doing for man that which it is not in his power to do for himself." TM 456. We like the last part of that sentence where it talks about God doing for man that which we cannot do for ourselves. But many do not like the part about laying the glory of man in the dust. It is the work of God to lay the glory of man in the dust—those things about which we could boast. You cannot have the last part without also having the first part. You cannot have God do for you that which you cannot do for yourself unless first of all He lays your glory in the dust. So the negative part of justification by faith is having the Lord lay our glory in the dust.

How would you like to have been a prominent person living back in the days when this message was first taught? Imagine two messengers sent by God standing up and telling you that all your righteousness is "filthy rags." The implication is that, if Christ is your righteousness, then you do not have any. If He must be my righteousness, I cannot produce it of myself. Worse still, it says to me that all the righteous deeds I have been trying to do are not righteous. All the Sabbath-keeping, all the tithe paying, all the missionary work, all the preaching, all the Bible work—none of these are righteousness. If Christ must be your righteousness, then all of your righteousness is nothing. We must admit that we do not hear much about this. The reason is that preachers do not like to talk about it. The reason we preachers do not like to talk about it is because it condemns us as well as you. No one can escape, for it does not make any exceptions, except for Jesus.

We like to talk about the positive aspects of justification by faith—how Christ is my righteousness, how righteousness is a free gift, imputed and imparted to me; but we almost always leave out the part about laying my glory in the dust. Many just do not like it. But we cannot teach Christ our righteousness and justification by faith without putting this in. We have been trying to do it for a long time, and all we are doing is tickling our ears and not changing our hearts.

You can be as lost teaching and believing Christ our righteousness as you can by being a legalist and a Pharisee. There were some pretty prominent people in the 1888 movement (and afterwards) who believed this doctrine and yet who are lost. The two most prominent men, Jones and Waggoner, went out, not because they were wrong about the subject, but apparently they got lost some place, didn't they? This is why people warned me that this is a dangerous subject.

14

The devil would like us to distort this subject. Why? Because when Christ our righteousness is correctly taught and preached, it deprives me of all that past righteousness that I thought was my ticket to heaven! When I almost had heaven in my grasp, some preacher comes along and tells me I am not going to make it because I do not have any righteousness of my own. I must have the Lord's righteousness to be saved. Therefore, our natural inclination will be to omit this from the subject, and only talk about the positive aspects.

When those men whom Ellen White called the "leading brethren" listened to Jones and Waggoner talk about this, they cringed to imagine themselves standing in the pulpit before the audience that had literally thought that they were faultless. Church members do often expect our ministers and leaders to be faultless; and I am amazed at how many young people think that preachers are a different order of being. When they discover we are not, they are greatly let down and almost depressed. How can we follow such failing leaders, they ask?

Ministers and church leaders have a terrible hang-up about this subject because we have to put up a façade to please the members. Imagine some well-known church leader in 1888 standing up and saying, "Brethren, I am sorry but I have to confess that I have been a very selfish man, a very proud person." That never happened. Some leaders feared that the people thought they were too perfect; and the people would wonder how that person ever got into such a high office. They would feel like they had been deceived. So those leading brethren imagined themselves being castigated and evicted by the members of the church—if they confessed their weaknesses and sins. Would you be big enough to do that? There were not many who were big enough then, and there are not many who would today. That is why we do not have altar calls in most of our churches anymore. That is why we do not require people to come down front and give their heart to Christ. That is degrading to some people, not elevating. Why do you require them to do that?

The correct preaching of justification by faith intimidates people, at least at the beginning. The Bible teaches us that we must be righteous. The teaching of justification by faith says that we are not righteous, and if I am not righteous, I do not satisfy the Bible requirement. Therefore, I am a condemned, lost soul. That is the negative side of it. It turns people off when we preach the truth about justification by faith.

The Jews had the same problem. "For they, being ignorant of God's righteousness, and going about to establish their own righteousness, have not submitted themselves unto the righteousness of God." Romans 10:3. This ignorance was willing. They learned about the righteousness of God in Christ Jesus, but they rejected it. They were seeking to establish their own. Therefore they did not submit themselves to His. The next verse tells us "For Christ is the end [the fulfillment] of the law for righteousness to everyone that believeth." To those who believe that Christ is their righteousness, He is the fulfillment of the law for them. But if I am seeking to establish my own righteousness—even just a tiny bit of my own righteousness—will I ever accept His? It is impossible.

Somehow there must come an awareness of my condition before I will ever look for righteousness elsewhere. As long as I am satisfied with my own righteousness, or any portion of it, I will never seek righteousness from Him, because I am content. If my Sabbath-keeping is good enough for me, if my tithe paying is good enough for me, if my work for the Lord is good enough for me and I am satisfied with it (rich and increased with goods and have need of nothing), I do not have need of His righteousness. I already have it, I have already attained. I can go to church every Sabbath and go home feeling very happy and content thinking I have got it made. I think that I literally do not need Christ as my righteousness. And if as a pastor I tell you that you do need it, many would say, "Why are you criticizing me? I am just as good as you are [and you are]; and therefore what right do you have to tell me I am not righteous?" We can rise up on our high horse and be intimidated by the whole thing, and go along accepting only our own righteousness. You would be amazed at how easily we can do this. We just automatically fall into this rut and go our own way, thinking we are not that bad and do not have to worry about any other righteousness. I have the truth, and I have been following it, have I not? So as far as I am concerned, that is righteousness, and that is good enough.

We like anything that elevates self, but we dislike anything that depreciates self. Nowadays preachers like to talk about "self worth." It has a nice ring to it. You are somebody. Be proud of yourself. We talk about self-love, and we take that marvelous text "Love your neighbor as yourself," and conclude that if you do not love yourself you cannot love your neighbor. And we say, "Oh, goody! I always wanted to love myself, and now I am told it is alright." We have sensitivity sessions where we discover that the things we feared about ourselves, other people have, too. And since they are not afraid of them, why should I be? Maybe I am not so bad after all. We like all these things that enhance self, but don't tell us any more about the things that depreciate self.

Jones and Waggoner did not avoid the negative side of Christ our righteousness. In fact, Waggoner made it very prominent. Here are a few statements he made to the not-so-appreciative crowd there in Minneapolis. He used several texts from the Psalms. "When I consider Thy heavens, the work of Thy fingers; the moon and the stars, which Thou hast ordained; what is man, that Thou art mindful of him? And the son of man, that Thou visitest him?" "My heart was hot within me; while I was musing the fire burned: then spake I with my tongue. Lord, make me to know mine end, and the measure of my days, which it is; that I may know how frail I am. Behold, Thou hast made my days as an hand-breadth; and mine age is as nothing before Thee: verily every man at his best state is altogether vanity." "Put them in fear, O Lord: that the nations may know themselves to be but men." "Put not your trust in princes, nor in the son of man, in whom there is no help." Psalms 8:3,4; 39:3-5; 9:20; 146:3.

Ecclesiastes 3:19,20 is another text he dwelt upon. "For that which befalleth the sons of men befalleth beasts; even one thing befalleth them: as the one dieth, so dieth the other; yea, they have all one breath; so that a man hath no pre-eminence above a beast; for all is vanity."

There were two texts from Isaiah. "All nations before Him are as nothing; and they are counted to Him less than nothing, and vanity." "The voice said, Cry. And he said, What shall I cry? All flesh is grass, and all the goodliness thereof is as the flower of the field: The grass withereth, the flower fadeth: but the word of our God shall stand for ever," Isaiah 40:17; 40:6-8. All of these verses were put into Waggoner's preaching of justification by faith. He said these texts show that God is everything, and that man is nothing.

Before I chase you away, I must pause and say that in all of the preaching by Jones and Waggoner about the nothingness of man, they were always pointing out that God loved man and counted him so precious that He gave for man the most valuable thing in all heaven—the Lord Jesus. And the reason why sinners are valuable is because of the price paid for them, and because originally they were made in the image of God. It is not because we are so good, but rather because of what God made us in the beginning, and because of what God thought about us when He gave Jesus for us. It is God's estimation of man that makes us good and valuable, not our estimation of ourselves. In Christ we are valuable. In ourselves we are nothing.

You need to ponder for a long time that we, like the flowers and grass, are nothing. We do not worry when a blade of grass or a flower dies. It is here for a short while and then gone. Our goodness is like flowers that are here for a few days, and then gone. Can you put your trust in that? No, of course not. We must put out trust in something far better than that.

Waggoner also used some New Testament texts. "I am the Vine, ye are the branches: He that abideth in Me, and I in him, the same bringeth forth much fruit: for without Me ye can do nothing." John 15:5. "For I know that in me dwelleth no good thing." Romans 7:18. Can you imagine the apostle Paul, who did so much for the Lord at all times, saying this about himself?

Paul also wrote in Philippians 3:3 that he counted "all things but loss for the excellency of the knowledge of Christ Jesus my Lord: for whom I have suffered the loss of all things, and do count them but dung, that I may win Christ." Those things included monetary loss, losing his position in the Sanhedrin, and the prestige he once held amongst his brethren; but there was something else that Paul lost. He said he was a Pharisee of the Pharisees. A Pharisee is proud of his own righteousness. Paul had to discard his own righteousness. Paul had to look upon himself as having nothing but filthy rags, in and of himself, prior to the time of his conversion. Paul is talking about the willing death of self. What is good in self that it should be enhanced, or fostered, or that you should take credit for?

I have had people say to me, "Elder Lehman, you do terrible things to us. All my life I've looked forward to some kind of success or achievement, and now you come along and with one swoop you wipe me out and say I cannot have it." This was not my idea. I did not invent it. It has always been in the Bible and the Spirit of Prophecy. Friend, if we have missed it, we have been deceived, and we have grossly neglected the things that will get us to the kingdom. These days I fear we are willingly neglecting some of these things. We keep hoping that there is some other way that we can circumvent the death of self, that some way we can have self and Christ as our righteousness at the same time. We keep hoping and praying that some magnificent pastor will come along who has deciphered the Bible correctly and can show us how to have both. Or perhaps someone will write a book that says we can have both, and that will allow self to be inflated all it wants, yet still have the righteousness of Christ.

Only needy souls will ever plead for the righteousness of Christ. Only those who see themselves as unrighteous will sense a need for that. Only the ones who hunger and thirst for righteousness will request it. As long as you are content for self to do what it wants to, and call that righteousness, you will never hunger and thirst after His righteousness. Self must be cast into the dust. This is the beginning point for true preaching of justification by faith—the laying the glory of man in the dust, which is the work of God, and not the work of the preacher or anyone else. It is the work of God. He does it, which is a good thing for us; and we must accept it.

When the children of Israel came out of Egypt, they had many distortions of the truth. They lived in a heathen land where they had come to believe that God was angry with them, and that they must somehow appease Him and court His favor. They attempted to become righteous in their own energy and works. The Lord had to change that attitude. I sense that today He has the same job to do with many of us. The Lord gave them something called the old covenant, but they could not be saved under the provisions of that old covenant. God gave them that covenant to teach them lessons that they must learn, or they would never need Him. They would always be content in their own ways and in their own righteousness.

Ellen White explained the old covenant and why God gave it to the nation of Israel at Sinai. "Another compact—called in Scripture the 'old' covenant—was formed between God and Israel at Sinai…The Abrahamic covenant…is called the 'second,' or 'new,' covenant….But if the Abrahamic covenant contained the promise of redemption, why was another covenant formed at Sinai? In their bondage the people had to a great extent lost the knowledge of God and of the principles of the Abrahamic covenant....Living in the midst of idolatry and corruption, they had no true conception of the holiness of God, of the exceeding sinfulness of their own hearts, their utter inability, in themselves, to render obedience to God's law, and their need of a Saviour. All this they must be taught [emphasis supplied]. God brought them to Sinai; He manifested His glory; He gave them His law, with the promise of great blessings on condition of obedience....The people did not realize...that without Christ it was impossible for them to keep God's law...Feeling that they were able to establish their own righteousness, they declared, 'All that the Lord hath said will we do, and be obedient.' Exodus 24:7....yet only a few weeks passed before they broke their covenant with God, and bowed down to worship a graven image....now, seeing their sinfulness and their need of pardon, they were brought to feel their need of the Saviour....Now they were prepared to appreciate the blessings of the new covenant." PP 371,372.

God gave the old covenant to teach His people some crucial lessons. In the process of learning those lessons, they "were prepared to appreciate the blessings of the new covenant." Many today need to be taught those same lessons. They essentially come into the church under the old covenant. They hear the law and realize that it is good. They vow to keep it (go read your baptismal vows). Yet soon they realize that they cannot keep it in their weak flesh. So this next quote applies not only to the ancient Israelites, but to modern Israel as well: "Before there could be any permanent reformation, the people must be led to feel their utter inability in themselves to render obedience to God...While they trusted in their own strength and righteousness, it was impossible for them to secure the pardon of their sins; they could not meet the claims of God's perfect law, and it was in vain that they pledged themselves to serve God. It was only by faith in Christ that they could secure pardon of sin and receive strength to obey God's law. They must cease to rely on their own efforts for salvation, they must trust wholly in the merits of the promised Saviour, if they would be accepted of God." PP 524. That is good news. We often do not like its implications, but it is good news.

Keeping these quotes in mind, look at these words from the gospel prophet. "Comfort ye, comfort ye My people, saith your God. Speak ye comfortably to Jerusalem, and cry unto her, that her warfare is accomplished [no more strife, no more struggle, no more battling], that her iniquity is pardoned: for she hath received of the Lord's hand double for all her sins." Isaiah 40:1,2. Why does He say that? When Christ is your righteousness, what about the struggles? What about the wars? What about the battles? When Christ becomes my righteousness, the struggle to become righteous in myself ceases. The warfare stops. I am righteous only in Christ, never in myself. He is my righteousness. The struggle, the warfare, stops the instant I accept Him as my righteousness, as my justification. "Her warfare is accomplished...her iniquity is pardoned." Therefore, "speak comfortably to her." You can take it easy now, for the warfare is over. Comfort the people with Christ our righteousness. You do not have to struggle to attain righteousness. In Christ you have attained. In Christ you have achieved. He is our victory. He is our success. He is the victor for all humankind. He is our King, and in Him we are accepted. We must cease to rely on our own efforts for salvation, and must trust wholly in the merits of the promised Savior, if we would be accepted of God.

"Come with humble hearts, not thinking that you must do some good work to merit the favor of God, or that you must make yourself better before you can come to Christ. You are powerless to do good, and cannot better your condition. Apart from Christ we have no merit, no righteousness. Our sinfulness, our weakness, our human imperfection make it impossible that we should appear before God unless we are clothed in Christ's spotless righteousness. We are to be found in Him not having our own righteousness, but the righteousness which is in Christ." "The righteousness of Christ is presented as a free gift to the sinner if he will accept it. He has nothing of his own but what is tainted and corrupted, polluted with sin, utterly repulsive to a pure and holy God. Only through the righteous character of Jesus Christ can man come nigh to God." 1SM 333,342.

This next quote is one to be treasured: "None but God can subdue the pride of man's heart. We cannot save ourselves. We cannot regenerate ourselves. In the heavenly courts there will be no song sung, To me that loved myself, and washed myself, redeemed myself, unto me be glory and honor, and blessing and praise. But this is the keynote of the song that is sung by many here in their world. They do not know what it means to be meek and lowly in heart; and they do not mean to know this, if they can avoid it. The whole gospel is comprised in learning of Christ, His meekness and lowliness." TM 456.

This subject is not a difficult one to understand, but it is a difficult one to accept. The proud heart rises up against it. A man in his late sixties who was a member of my church comprehended the thoughts of all this in a sermon I gave one Sabbath. He was usually a talkative man, but that day he was as silent as could be. At home while eating Sabbath lunch, he sat sullenly at the table with his wife and a lady who was a resident in their home. He did not touch a bite of food although his wife was an excellent cook. He just sat there and moped. After ten or fifteen minutes, he finally uttered, "If that preacher is right, everything I've been doing for the last forty years is no good." The two ladies, like a chorus that had rehearsed for years, responded, "That is right!" If you had hit him in the head with a ball bat, it would not have hurt as much.

That man literally did not speak for six straight weeks. He could speak, but he did not. After prayer meetings he would usually hang around outside and talk to everyone. He was an elder in that church. He had been after his son for over twenty years to go back to church. The son told me later that for some strange reason his dad had stopped nagging him. The man was in absolute misery. It was complete torture for him, night and day. He was distressed, frustrated, confused. He was completely upset, because he had lost his ticket to heaven; but it was a supposed ticket that would never get him there. His dear wife, who loved him very much, had longed for the day when he would discover that all his righteousness is as filthy rags. For years he had treated her like many legalists and self-righteous people treat others who do not live up to their standards.

By observing others and myself, I have found that when you discover the negative side of justification by faith, it can be a most unpleasant experience. Some hang on the fence, vacillating back and forth. The Lord very patiently and kindly tries to comfort us, tries to help us make a decision. But until we turn our backs on vile self, we can never have Christ as our righteousness. I do not care how well you know this topic or how well you can teach it, or how much you say you believe it; until we turn our backs on self, Christ is not all in all, and we really do not need His righteousness. Ours is good enough.

The Lord wants us to have an experience where Christ is supreme, where He is unto us both salvation and righteousness. When Seventh-day Adventists in all walks of life become filled with the glory of this subject, when they make their decision for Jesus completely as their righteousness, as well as their Savior, the work will be finished in a hurry. We will see revivals everyplace. And then the Lord Jesus can say to us, "Well done, good and faithful servant."

May God help us to realize that the only thing we are going to lose is something very bad, which is sinful self; and that the Giver of every good and precious gift will take away no good thing from us. He will only take away the bad things. May we trust Him and look to Him for our righteousness, for this will make us extremely happy, and we will find tremendous comfort. "Speak ye comfortably to My people," the Lord says.

3

JUSTIFIED HOW?

REVELATION 3:17 DESCRIBES THE last church of the seven churches of Revelation: "Because thou sayest, I am rich, and increased with goods, and have need of nothing; and knowest not that thou are wretched, and miserable, and poor, and blind, and naked." There is a terrible deception pictured here. They say one thing while they are actually the opposite.

We say that we are not that group of people, but our best-known writer says we are. As an individual you probably say, "I am not deceived." I am sure that if you are a minister you will say, "It's not possible! I teach too much truth to be deceived." But because we say we are not deceived, it is difficult to convince us that we are. In fact, we will hardly look at it; and the first problem in accepting Christ our righteousness is to realize the fact that we might be deceived. In fact, there are millions of Christians who must be deceived because they are so disagreeable. We are all so many miles apart from one another. Even in the confines of any individual church congregation, we are certainly not going down the road side by side in our theology. We are vastly different in many ways, and we cannot all possibly be right. When everyone says, "I am right," then that positively guarantees deception.

The Spirit of Prophecy comments on what this deception is all about. "What is it that constitutes the wretchedness and nakedness of those who feel rich and increased with goods? It is the want of the righteousness of Christ [they don't have it]. In their own righteousness they are represented as clothed in filthy rags; and yet in this condition they flatter themselves that they are clothed upon with Christ's righteousness. Could deception be greater?" RH, August 7, 1894. They insist they have Christ's righteousness, but the True Witness says, "No, you do not. You have your own filthy rags." Yet all the time they insist that they have His righteousness. Could deception be greater?

We can go on for years accusing others of being deceived, but someday we must come face to face with Revelation 3:17. We must confront ourselves with this text. We should be willing to ask, 'Lord, is it I? Can I be a Laodicean?" I know all the arguments people use to wiggle out of being Laodicean, but we all must ask, "Lord, is it I?" During that last supper with Jesus, the disciples asked that question, each one wondering if it would be he that betrayed Jesus. Of that elite group of disciples, all could betray Him. They all forsook Him and fled, and denied Him in some way. It was not only Judas who denied Him. Peter certainly did. The others ran frightened, although they were sure they never would. Are you and I better than they? We must take a hard, careful look at this.

This deception was so great in 1889 that Ellen White had this to say: "There is not one in one hundred who understands for himself the Bible truth on this subject [justification by faith] that is so necessary to our present and eternal welfare." COR 87. Not even one percent understands. Are we better than those to whom she wrote this?

By 1904, things had not improved very much. "For the last twenty years, a subtle, unconsecrated influence has been leading men to look to men, to bind up with men, to neglect their heavenly Companion. Many have turned away from Christ. They have failed to appreciate the One who declares, 'Lo, I am with you always.' Let us do all in our power to redeem the past." RH, February 18, 1904. They had not improved very much over the "one in one hundred" of 1889, had they? They were still turning away from Christ.

Why is it so difficult to understand this? Why is it so easy to be deceived about it? "The enemy of man and God is not willing that this truth [justification by faith] should be clearly presented; for he knows that if the people receive it fully, his power will be broken." COR 54. Is his power broken in your life? Then have you received it fully?

This quote continues on: "If the enemy of truth and righteousness can obliterate from the mind the thought that it is necessary to depend upon the righteousness of Christ for salvation, he will do it. If Satan can succeed in leading men to place value upon his own works, as works of merit and righteousness, he knows he can overcome him by his temptations and make him his victim and prey. Lift up Jesus before the people. Strike the door posts with the blood of Calvary's Lamb."

Somehow in days gone by we have argued and debated about this subject more and more, yet understood it less and less. By 1924, this topic seemed so extremely important and so relevant to the ministerial department of the General Conference that they requested Elder Daniels, a former General Conference president, to write a book on the topic. So Elder Daniels wrote the book Christ Our Righteousness. In the foreword of that book he describes the condition of the people in 1924. He wrote: "In our blindness and dullness of heart, we have wandered far out of the way, and for many years have been failing to appropriate this sublime truth—Christ our Righteousness. But all the while our great Leader has been calling His people to come into line on this great fundamental of the gospel—receiving by faith the imputed righteousness of Christ for sins that are past, and the imparted righteousness of Christ for revealing the divine nature in human flesh." It was hoped that by this book the Lord would bring us back to a correct understanding of this fundamental truth of the gospel.

Apparently, many back then were missing this marvelous truth; and to say it cannot mean us today is to suffer with the pride of the Pharisees who went on and on until they could crucify the Son of God, and still believe that God was with them, even as late as 70 AD when the temple was being destroyed. When God departed from the temple, Christ said, "Behold, your house is left unto you desolate" (Matthew 23:38); but they still worshipped God as though He were there. But He was not there. And friend, it is possible that we can come and go to church for decades and never meet God. They did, and they were as human as we are. Like them, we can go on and on with gross assumptions and just be totally deceived, walking in darkness and thinking we are the children of light. We can criticize them greatly, but we really only criticize ourselves. Too often we are unimpressed. We cannot remember five minutes later anything about the worship service. Somehow we can go about as blind and deceived as they. The Lord is begging and pleading with us to learn what He has for us that we might have missed, and about which we might be deceived.

With all this warning concerning deception and misunderstanding, the least we can do is to take an honest look at ourselves, and ask, "Is it possible that I am deceived concerning Christ and His righteousness and justification by faith?" Preachers have the most difficult task of all, because they will point to all the good they have been doing for years, and all they have been preaching about it, and that leads to many assumptions.

Is there any possibility that, while I think I understand justification by faith, I really do not? I know that most people have some kind of a belief in justification by faith, but is it the complete Bible teaching on that subject? Or is it your own interpretation of it? Which is it? The Lord is not accusing us of not having a belief in justification by faith. He is saying we do not know what it is and we have not experienced the real article. It is not the lack of some teaching on it. It is the right teaching and the right understanding and right experience of it. We must compare different theories of justification by faith—yours and the true Bible teaching concerning it. Is yours completely in accordance with the Bible? If it is not, you need to come in line with the Scriptures. God knows more about this than we do, so we need to line up with what He has to say. It is not a deficiency in a belief of it, but rather the deception as to what the genuine article really is. Do we have that which the Bible teaches?

We want to look into those vulnerable areas where we are prone to deception and misunderstanding, and also into those areas we disagree on. You may not agree with me, but at least let me ask you: Is it possible that you are deceived about justification by faith? Do you completely understand it? It should be our prayer: "Lord, open our eyes that we may see." Let us examine our own hearts and ask, "What do I believe about this and how does it compare with what the Bible teaches?" We will be looking at what the Bible and the Spirit of Prophecy say concerning it; and we will discover that the areas of dispute on this subject are areas of misunderstanding.

The most obvious deceptions and misunderstandings are in the area of faith and works. This is at the heart of all the problems. It has been so for hundreds of years in the Christian church; and it is amazing how we can get so tangled up in the subject of faith and works.

What is justification by faith? In *Webster's Collegiate Dictionary*, the definition of "just" is: "Conforming to spiritual law, or righteous, especially before God." To be just is to be righteous before God and to conform to spiritual law. So the act of justification is the act of making us just or righteous before God. Justification is to make us righteous.

Ellen White understood that "Righteousness is right doing...." COL 312. Do not shudder at that. Some seem to have had a different interpretation of righteousness. Righteousness is right doing. Some say it is right relationships. Yes, it can be; but do right relationships bring right actions? Yes, they do. Ultimately we come back to right doing. True justification by faith is right doing before God.

The problems confronting us concerning justification by faith include these: How does a sinner who is not just before God become righteous in God's sight? How do those who are wrong become right in God's sight? How do sinners become saints in God's sight? How do those who are disobedient become obedient to the law?

Is it accomplished by attempting to do good works? The Lord lays His requirements before us, and we say, "Okay, I will do it." That seems to be the obvious response, but sometimes the obvious answer is not the right answer. To say "I will do it" is old covenant mentality. There is more than one way to get inside a house, and it is not always through the front entrance. In fact, the front door may be locked and barred. It may be much faster to go in the back door, or through a window. The most obvious way is not necessarily the right way. It could be the wrong way, or an impossible way.

Is this righteousness before God accomplished by obedience to the law? Is it accomplished by trying to obey or by praying to be obedient? Is it accomplished by a life-long struggle of trying to obey? We can go on and on with the ideas people have about this.

This problem must be answered clearly, and we must use all the information available in order to channel our minds down the right highway. Otherwise we will wander all over the place in our own thinking. "Let no one take the limited, narrow position that any of the works of man can help in the least possible way to liquidate the debt of his transgression. This is a fatal deception [and we are talking about deceptions]. If you would understand it, you must cease haggling over your pet ideas, and with humble hearts survey the atonement. This matter is so dimly comprehended that thousands upon thousands claiming to be sons of God are children of the wicked one, because they will depend on their own works." 1SM 343. This is a deadly deception. While professing to be children of God they are really children of the devil, because they will depend on their own works just that much! We need to either throw the inspired books away or begin to agree with them.

The quote continues on: "God always demanded good works, the law demands it, but because man placed himself in sin where his good works were valueless, Jesus' righteousness alone can avail." There is one good reason why you cannot obey the law to satisfy God and become just in His eyes, and that is that we are born in sin and therefore our good works are "valueless." Therefore, only one Person's righteousness, or obedience to the law, is of any value. That is why she says, "Jesus' righteousness alone can avail." Our own righteousness will never avail.

Immediately many have a thousand fears and want to argue that we are trying to do away with the law. We must dispel those fears and outline the sequence that God outlines for us, or we will be as lost as anyone else (even while keeping the Sabbath). We must never forget that "because man placed himself in sin where his good works were valueless, Jesus' righteousness [His good works] alone can avail."

"Man cannot possibly meet the demands of the law of God in human strength alone. His offerings, his works, will always be tainted with sin....The law demands righteousness, and this the sinner owes to the law; but he is incapable of rendering it." COR 116.

All of these quotations tell us two things as to why man can never be justified by his own works. First, he is incapable of producing good works. Second, everything that he does is valueless because it is tainted with the sins of his past life. No matter how perfect your background, everything you do is tainted with sin and self. Everything. We must never trust our own righteousness. We are incapable of producing true righteousness, and all we do is tainted with sin.

Here lies another deception. Because we obey certain requirements of God's law, because we avoid certain sinful acts that others commit, we then assume that we are obeying and are therefore righteous. Seventh-day Adventists are in more jeopardy in this area than any other group of people I know of. It is because we can prove by the Bible that what we teach is truth that we say we are conforming and are therefore righteous. We have to be most careful about that because it might be a total deception.

There is an inherent weakness in this type of obedience. "It is true that there may be an outward correctness of deportment without the renewing power of Christ. The love of influence and the desire for the esteem of others may produce a well-ordered life. Self-respect may lead us to avoid the appearance of evil. A selfish heart may perform generous actions." SC 58. If I do what is right because I am afraid of what the neighbors will think, is that righteousness? No, that is fear. If I do what you think I should do in order to get your esteem, is that righteousness? No, that is ego, or self being inflated by the approval of others. Many appear to be crude, uncultured or uneducated, and one of the most terrible criticisms today is to accuse others of being that way; and intellectuals seem to indulge in this greatly. Without any logic whatsoever, they say, "You are not well educated—you just don't understand." They used that on Jesus, too, did they not? How, having never gone to school, could He ever understand? Be careful whose club you join with your criticisms. I might have an outward correctness of deportment but be without Christ in my heart.

Certain pressures will accomplish this. Those pressures are listed for us: "Education, culture, the exercise of the will, human effort all have their proper sphere, but here they are powerless. They may produce an outward correctness of behavior, but they cannot change the heart. They cannot purify the springs of life. There must be a power working from within, a new life from above, before men can be changed from sin to holiness. That power is Christ." SC 18. Many think that the heart can be changed by education, culture, human effort, and the exercise of the will. They have almost totally left out Jesus in this process. Outward performance can be the greatest deception; and many are prone to point to their performance most of the time.

Paul put forth the same argument when he wrote: "Therefore we conclude that a man is justified by faith without the deeds of the law." Romans 3:2. We are justified by faith only, and not by any of our efforts at obeying the law.

This causes many disputes. Some say that we are not using all the Scriptures and thus you are trying to deceive us. If you do not believe that a person is justified by faith alone without the deeds of the law, if you do not accept this just as it is, without thinking that certain verses in the book of James disagree with it, if you do not accept it by faith alone, then you do not have justification by faith, nor do you understand it. And until you understand that James does not disagree with Paul (for the same Holy Spirit inspired both men), you can never be justified by faith. We must harmonize both Paul and James. They are both talking about Abraham in the context of faith and works.

James did not disagree with Paul at all. James was simply discussing faith, not justification. James said that even the devils believe; therefore, your faith is nothing special unless it is different from what the devils believe. He argues that there is a difference between true faith and false faith (or presumption). He tells us how to tell the difference between the two. "Seest thou how faith wrought with his works, and by works was faith made perfect?" James 2:22. Faith was at work in his actions, and thus the integrity of his faith was proved. Abraham established his faith by his works. And it was by his faith that he was justified.

"Genuine faith will be manifested in good works, for good works are the fruits of faith....Those who are justified by faith must have a heart to keep the way of the Lord. It is an evidence that a man is not justified by faith when his works do not correspond to his profession. James says, 'Seest thou how faith wrought with his works, and by works was his faith made perfect?' (James 2:22). The faith that does not produce good works does not justify the soul. 'Ye see then how that by works a man is justified, and not by faith only' (James 2:24). 'Abraham believed God, and it was counted unto him for righteousness' (Rom. 4:3)." 1SM 397.

All that James was saying is that we are justified by faith alone, but we are not really justified unless that belief produces good works. His argument is not that we are justified by works. He only says that we are justified by faith providing it is genuine faith. If it is genuine faith, good works will follow. The sequence is genuine faith, justification, and then works, in that order. It is not works, justification, and then faith. We are justified by faith alone, and the result of that is good works. James was apparently dealing with some people who thought they were justified and professed that. He asked, "Are you really? Have you really had the faith that justifies? Then why do I not see the good works?"

James and Paul are in total agreement. James is arguing for genuine faith, for genuine faith will truly justify; and that in turn will make us accomplish good works for God. He is examining faith and saying that works are the result, not the cause, of justification. When we speak of justification by faith, we are talking about the cause—how and for what reason are we justified? Not by my works, but by my faith.

The biggest question here is: Who accomplishes justification? Is it something I do for God, or something that He does for me? How is it accomplished? Paul talks about Abraham and how God did something for him. "What shall we say then that Abraham our father, as pertaining to the flesh, hath found? For if Abraham were justified by works, he hath whereof to glory; but not before God. For what saith the scripture? Abraham believed God, and it was counted unto him for righteousness. Now to him that worketh is the reward not reckoned of grace, but of debt. But to him that worketh not, but believeth on him that justifieth the ungodly, his faith is counted for righteousness." Romans 4:1-5.

It comes across even more clear in the Good News Version: "What shall we say then of Abraham our racial ancestor? What did he find? If he was put right with God by the things he did, he would have something to boast about; but he cannot boast before God. The Scriptures say that Abraham believed God, and because of his faith, God accepted him as righteous. A man who works is paid. His wages are not regarded as a gift but as something that he has earned. As for the man who does not work, however, but simply puts his faith in God, who declares the guilty of the innocent, it is his faith that God takes into account in order to put him right with Himself."

Justification is an act of God, and not of man. Man simply believes what God does for us. There are other texts that will help us understand this. "It is God that justifieth." Romans 8:33 (last part). "And by Him all that believe are justified from all things, from which ye could not be justified by the law of Moses." Acts 13:39. God does for us what the law could not do. By Him we are justified, and not by ourselves. "That He might be just, and the justifier of him which believeth in Jesus." Romans 3:26. He is the Justifier; I am not; nor do I earn His justification, for it is by grace. "Being justified freely by His grace...." Romans 3:24. "Much more then, being now justified by His blood, we shall be saved from wrath through Him." Romans 5:9. Not by our activity, but by belief in His sacrifice. "...even so by the righteousness of One the free gift came upon all men unto justification of life." Romans 5:18 (last part). By one Person's righteousness, justification came unto all men. It is something from outside man coming upon him and unto him. Is that what your Bible says? And it is by one Person's obedience, not by many people's obedience. There is one more text to see. "Even the righteousness of God which is by faith of Jesus Christ unto all and upon all them that believe." Romans 3:22. Again, it is something that comes "unto" us and "upon" us. It is not what I achieve or am doing for Him.

There are many places in Scripture where it is taught that justification comes from outside, and not from inside of us. We are all familiar with a parable found in Luke chapter 18 where Jesus taught this truth. A Pharisee and a publican were in the temple praying. The Pharisee said he was thankful that he was not like other men, doing the terrible things they do. He listed the good things he did, and thus he thought he obeyed the law and was right (or just) before God. The publican came along and it is said he would not lift up his eyes to heaven. He said, "God be merciful to me a sinner." Verse 13. He had no good works to plead. Christ's conclusion is found in verse 14. He said, "this man [this publican] went down to his house justified rather than the other." The man who said he had no good works was justified.

This seems to be a contradiction to many of us. That is, when you seek to be righteous by right doing, you do not obey the law. When you seek it by faith and not by right doing, you do obey the law. Have you ever seen anything so puzzling? This is the most radical logic we have ever heard of. But Paul taught that very thing when he wrote: "What shall we say then? That the Gentiles, which followed not after righteousness, have attained to righteousness, even the righteousness which is of faith. But Israel, which followed after the law of righteousness, had not attained to the law of righteousness. Because they sought it not by faith, but as it were by the works of the law." Romans 9:30-32. Paul is saying that the obvious approach of trying to do right because the law and God ask you to do right is not the right way. The Jews tried that and it did not work. They were not obedient. We can try it and it will not work, either. But the ones who did not seek after it [try to obey] but sought it by faith became righteous. They literally did what the law requires of them. They were not attempting to obey the law; but rather attempting to put their faith in God. This led to righteousness and to true justification. This is very difficult to understand. People ask, "How can that be? Many do not understand this at all.

There are two texts that help us understand this better. "But the scripture hath concluded all under sin...." Galatians 3:22. This includes the fine, upstanding citizens like the mayor and the pastor of the church. "What then? Are we better than they? No, in no wise: for we have before proved both Jews and Gentiles, that they are all under sin; As it is written, There is none righteous, no, not one. There is none that understandeth, there is none that seekest after God. They are all gone out of the way, they are together become unprofitable: there is none that doeth good, no, not one." Romans 3:9-12. Do you want to argue with Paul?

We see an upstanding person saying, "Lord, let me try." God steps back and says, "Alright, go ahead." So he tries and tries for fifty years. Then God comes back and asks, "Well, how good are you?" And the person says, "Well, I've done lots of good things." And the Lord replies, "I know that, but let's ask your wife how good you are." "Oh, don't talk to her!" "Let's ask your children." "Oh, no." "Let's ask those who work for you." "No, don't ask them." It is that way with many. You can seek righteousness by the law, but it can not be attained that way. All our righteousness is as filthy rags; and it does not matter how hard we try.

All of our good works are valueless. They are tainted with sin because we have all been sinners. We do not climb out of that miry pit by trying to do good. It is like quicksand—the more you try, the more you sink. You might think you are out, but everyone close to you knows by your attitude toward them and treatment of them that you are still in the muck.

It does not matter how much you try to do good. You are incapable of doing good because all you do is tainted with self and with past sins. "Can the Ethiopian change his skin, or the leopard his spots? Then may ye also do good, that are accustomed to do evil." Jeremiah 13:23. If it is impossible for them, it is impossible for you. We must look at this as it is, and not as we would like to make it. It does not matter how good you are, or how good you have been, or how good you would like to be, or how good you try to be. All our righteousness is ultimately as filthy rags.

Job asked the question and also provided the answer: "Who can bring a clean thing out of an unclean? Not one." Job 14:4. Who can bring righteousness out of a sinner? No one can. Someone from outside of us who is righteous must come in and clean up the sinner and make him just. The sinner cannot do it for himself. He must believe that someone wants to do that for him. "Surely, shall one say, in the Lord have I righteousness and strength." Isaiah 45:24. All our righteousness is of Him. I have none. I must go to Him as the only source of righteousness. That is the only place I can find it. Paul prayed, "And be found in Him, not having mine own righteousness, which is of the law, but that which is through the faith of Christ, the righteousness which is of God by faith." Philippians 3:9.

When we put all these texts together, we have a startling message. If you are a proud person, as so many of us are, you will hate it. You will hate the person who brings this message to you for he has destroyed all your hopes. And I am just as prone to dislike it as anyone because I like to be proud of myself, don't you? But we are told that this topic of justification by faith is laying the glory of man in the dust and doing for man what he cannot do for himself. There goes my pride in the dust, and I don't like it down there. I want it up on a pinnacle somewhere with everyone worshipping it.

On the other hand, to those who have been struggling for years and years to do what is right, only to discover that they are incapable, this is a most precious, most hopeful, most enlightening message. It is glorious, because the good news is that God will do for you what you cannot do. The thing we desire to do, the thing we need most, the thing that is the most precious in all of life, He says He will give to us. He does this because He is so good. Do you believe God is that good? This is the big question. Do you believe that God so loved sinners that He gave His Son for them? That Jesus so loved sinners that He died for them? That He has interceded all these two thousand years for them? Is He that good? Or are you always trying to prove how good you are in comparison to other people?

The nice thing about all this is that the praise will go to Him, not to me. He can handle it, but I cannot handle praise. Friend, if you will really look at this subject, and really look at yourself in the light of the Bible, you will find out that the truth on this subject is glorious! It is just wonderful. And if you are a believer in this, it will make you want to jump and shout for joy. Once this truth gets hold of you, you cannot keep quiet about it. You will just radiate it. Our spiritual stupor is evidence that we are quite a long way from understanding and accepting this message. In our lukewarmness, we just cannot get excited about what God does for humans. It is so wonderful, so real; and it is mine if I will by faith reach out and grasp the goodness of God to sinners.

May God help us by lifting this gloom, this dullness, this blindness that keeps us from accepting what He has tried to show us. May He illumine our minds until we praise Him from Whom all blessings flow.

GRACE
OR MERIT?

ARE WE JUSTIFIED COMPLETELY by grace, completely by merit, or by both grace and merit? There is a constant warfare in which we are engaged concerning this topic.

We can quickly understand how we are pardoned, or forgiven, by God's grace entirely. That seems to cause us no difficulty. But whether or not this makes us just, or right, and that this is accomplished by grace, is where the problem is. I can accept the fact that I am pardoned by His grace, but that I am just by His grace is a different thing. When a criminal is released from prison, having paid his penalty to society, is he just? He is free. He no longer has to pay a penalty. But is he just? *Just* means he is right and you can depend on him. He will do right from then on. Will he? We reason that, before we can be just or righteous, we must prove by our actions that we are that way. We must prove it for a long time. When we have not committed these sins for many years, then we may be regarded as righteous. But until that time, many people think we are simply kidding ourselves. Most Seventh-day Adventists call this justification by faith—that you are pardoned and forgiven completely by His grace, but that you must establish by your actions and behavior that you are just or righteous; and it does not matter what people think about it, you are not righteous until you prove you are. We go on thinking this is justification by faith. God might *count* us righteous because our sins are forgiven, but we are not truly righteous because we have not established it.

This is an assumption we make as we study the subject superficially. It appeals to us. I used to think that by praying, by trying, by seeking to better understand, by much Bible study, that someday I would truly be righteous, and therefore justified. God would know it, I would know it, and everyone else would know it. When someone disagreed with my understanding of this theory of justification, I usually branded them as quite permissive and of omitting human effort, which I knew the Bible taught; and therefore they must be wrong and I was certainly right. I also thought they were like those "Christians" who would eliminate the law and all obedience to it; and I could not believe them. They seem to think that grace eliminates the law and obedience, but that did not seem right to me. I did not believe in that kind of grace.

I would always argue strongly for my theory of justification, certain that I was right and others were wrong. But frequently, something would trouble me; and I hope it also troubles you. I was forced to think that all was not well in my own heart because many of my sinful habits were still with me; and with too many of them, there had been no improvement. Sometimes they had worsened. What made me think that I was on the road to righteousness? Sometimes I felt very guilty, and the harder I seemed to try do right the more I failed. You don't have that trouble, do you? I tried to find a different interpretation of Romans 7 to suit my sinfulness, as many have succeeded in doing. I seemed to find very little love in my heart for people. When I mistreated people, I could justify that mistreatment by the fact that I was right and they were wrong. I did not like myself for some of these things; and time did not seem to help me. I waited and waited for time to improve my condition, but I could not see very much growth and progress. Yet I was sure I understood justification by faith. Do you find yourself in that kind of dilemma?

Then I read the following quotation: "They have not been instructed as they should have been that Christ is unto them both salvation and righteousness." RH, September 3, 1889. Salvation means pardon from my sins, and I believed that; but I did not know what it meant to have Christ "unto" me as my righteousness. In fact, I was trying to do that for myself, and I believed that God wanted me to do that, that He demanded it, and that I must strive for righteousness. And since I was trying to do this myself, I had not received His righteousness. I did not even know He wanted to give it to me, until I had proven I was righteous. Then I would be good enough to receive it, meriting the acclaim of God and the title He placed upon me. I did not have His righteousness although I believed in His pardon.

More and more I began to see a duality in this message that I had missed before. "The repentant soul realizes that his justification comes because Christ, as his substitute and surety, has died for him, as his atonement and righteousness." COR 67. Notice the duality of this. Atonement means He died for my sins, thus pardoning me. I believed that, but I did not believe He was my righteousness.

A two-fold action is also brought out here: "Through Christ, restoration as well as reconciliation is provided for man." COR 95. I believed that Christ had taken my sins away, reconciling me, but I surely had not been restored, for I was deep in my sinful habits. I looked for restoration and thought it would come some day, if I lived long enough; but I did not have it.

"Genuine faith appropriates the righteousness of Christ, and the sinner is made an overcomer with Christ." COR 96. I definitely was not an overcomer, although it took me a few years to recognize that. I thought that overcoming would take time, but eventually I would be righteous. But lots of time had gone by, and I was not an overcomer. Apparently I did not know what it was like to have Christ as my righteousness.

"Through faith in His name, He imputes unto us His righteousness, and it [that righteousness] becomes a living principle in our life." COR 98. His righteousness becomes a "living principle"—something active in me, functioning in me. And, of course, if His righteousness is functioning in me, it produces righteousness in my life. He imputes it to me—He gives it from Him to me. It becomes a living principle in my life. That bothered me terribly.

"The righteousness of Christ is not a cloak to cover unconfessed and unforsaken sin; it is a principle of life that transforms the character and controls the conduct." COR 99. The righteousness of Christ transforms the character and controls the conduct. I was trying to be a different person. I was trying to control my sins, but was not succeeding. Yet the quotes I was reading say that His righteousness transforms my character when given to me. It controls my conduct. It was evident that this was not happening to me.

"Christ imputes to us His sinless character and presents us to the Father in His own purity. There are many who think that it is impossible to escape from the power of sin [and I was finding that], but the promise is that we may be filled with all the fullness of God [and that includes His righteousness]." COR 99. We aim too low. God wants to fill us with all His fullness. We escape the power of sin, not by our striving, but by His giving. He gives us His sinless character.

These quotes made me realize that I did not understand justification by faith, even though I had assumed I did. And it was definite that I had not experienced it. If the Spirit of Prophecy quotes were correct (and I knew they were), then my theory was wrong. But sad to say, I still could not give up my theory. Have you found that to be true? I found that these statements disagreed with me, but I could not give up my theory. The new way seemed too easy, like I was just lying down and He was doing it all for me. That is the way it appeared to me. Where was the striving? How could I be counted righteous when I had not established it by a righteous life? These are the arguments I used upon myself. I was more confused than ever. My theory seemed to be wrong, but I did not know how to find the truth concerning justification by faith; nor did I know how to experience it. Often I would defend my old theory because I just did not grasp the truth. Mine was the only theory I knew and I would cling to it.

Much of my confusion was an unwillingness to believe that God would do it for me by His grace. There is one thing we have never emphasized sufficiently, and that is God's goodness to sinners—His grace that is wholly undeserved. There is almost no denomination in the whole world today that emphasizes God's grace sufficiently. The consequence is that we try to do it ourselves. If God is not that gracious, then somebody must do it. I was sure I had to do something to deserve or establish justification. When I finally admitted my theory was wrong, and I began searching for a better way.

Many of you reading this have had exactly the same experience. If you had to speak from a pulpit on this subject, we could figure it out it in five minutes. Almost anyone who understands it could tell.

Is justification by grace or by merit? Or by both? And especially the aspect of being accounted just or righteous. Do I establish righteousness by my actions, or does it come completely by God's grace to me? Justification is more than pardon. It is being accounted just. It is predicting a future performance; and it tricks us that way.

The Bible teaches it very clearly in several texts. "Being justified freely by His grace through the redemption that is in Christ Jesus." Romans 3:24. "That being justified by His grace, we should be made heirs according to the hope of eternal life." Titus 3:7. We are justified by grace, and in no way are we justified by works. "Therefore by the deeds of the law [by my own obedience to that law or my actions to it] there shall no flesh be justified in His sight: [why not?] for by the law is the knowledge of sin." Not justified by the law but justified by Christ. Any activity in obedience to the law will not justify. "Not by works of righteousness that we have done, but according to His mercy He saved us…" Titus 3:5. Verse 7 talks about "being justified by His grace." It is not our works that we have done that justifies. It is His mercy and His grace. "Who hath saved us, and called us with an holy calling, not according to our works, but according to His own purpose and grace, which was given us in Christ Jesus before the world began." 2 Timothy 1:9. The Bible teaches this repeatedly. We cannot escape from it.

One of the finest texts is one we seldom hear about. "And if by grace, then is it no more of works: otherwise grace is no more grace. But if it be of works, then is it no more grace: otherwise work is no more work." Romans 11:6. Works and grace, in this context, are opposites; for if righteousness is by grace, it cannot be of works. Work earns, or deserves, or merits something. Grace is unmerited. They are not similar. It is impossible to have it by grace and also by works. The righteousness of the righteous is of God, and not of man.

There are more texts we need to see. "Surely, shall one say, in the Lord have I righteousness and strength." Isaiah 45:24. In the Lord, not in myself. "This is the heritage of the servants of the Lord, and their righteousness is of Me, saith the Lord." Isaiah 54:17, last part. Where do they obtain it? From Him. "…and this is His name whereby He shall be called, THE LORD OUR RIGHTEOUSNESS." Jeremiah 23: 6 (the last four words are capitalized in the Bible!). The life He lived, which was a righteous life, was not for Himself. It was for me. He is the Lord, our righteousness. So the righteousness of the righteous is not of man; it is of God. Therefore, if you try to establish your own, you are definitely not receiving His.

The Bible teaches us that, in justification, this righteousness comes from God to us, "Even the righteousness of God which is by faith of Jesus Christ unto all and upon all them that believe." Romans 3:22. It comes from Him to us. This is the process of justification.

The Bible teaches that it is a gift. "For if by one man's offence death reigned by one; much more they which receive abundance of grace and of the gift of righteousness shall reign in line by One, Jesus Christ. Therefore as by the offence of one, judgment came upon all men to condemnation; even so by the righteousness of One the free gift came upon all men unto justification of life." Romans 5:18,19. By one Person's righteousness, the free gift came unto all men. There is no way you can change these texts without destroying the truth. It is *never* our righteousness that makes us righteous. It is always and everlastingly His righteousness. And it comes from Him unto us in justification. I do not make myself just by trying to be righteous, by trying to be obedient. It is not accomplished that way. I accept by faith that He wants to give it to me. I believe it in my heart and it comes unto me. I claim it as my very own. This is righteousness by faith. His righteousness literally becomes mine, as we will study in a later chapter.

Here is a precious gem of truth that should never be forgotten: "The righteousness of God is embodied in Christ. We receive righteousness by receiving Him." MB 18. The righteousness that Romans 3:22 speaks of as coming unto us, is embodied in the person of Jesus. We receive righteousness by receiving Him. Righteousness is not striving and praying for patience, and then getting it. I receive patience in Jesus, in His person. I say, "Jesus, be my patience. Take away my impatience and my irritability. Live in my life and be patience for me." This is called appropriating the righteousness of Christ, which we will study later. It is something He has that I lack and that I can never produce. It is impossible for me to satisfy the claims of the law. I cannot be patient. I cannot avoid those things the law forbids. I was born in sin, and I am prone to do them unless He comes in and lives His life in me. Then I receive Christ as my righteousness, and He performs in me that which is well pleasing to Him and to His Father.

Justification is always a dual blessing. It never merely pardons or forgives. That is only part of it. If you really understand pardon, then that is enough; but unfortunately we think pardon is different. We will clarify that later on.

According to the quotes we have seen, justification is both salvation and righteousness, atonement and righteousness, and it not only forgives but it transforms the life and controls the actions. I am forgiven, and then He gives me His righteousness; and this righteousness is something I receive, not something I produce by trying. It is a gift. Therefore it is all of grace.

The dual action that is involved in justification is described and illustrated in a parable that Jesus gave; and most of these complicated things we have been discussing are found in the parables. Parables are nice because they clarify mysterious, difficult topics. You probably never thought it was talking about this subject, but it very definitely is; and I learned it years ago reading the Spirit of Prophecy. "When the unclean spirit is gone out of a man [that is my sinfulness], he [the unclean spirit] walketh through dry places, seeking rest, and findeth none. Then he saith, I will return into my house from whence I came out; and when he is come, he findeth it empty, swept and garnished. Then goeth he, and taketh with himself seven other spirits more wicked than himself, and they enter in and dwell there: and the last state of that man is worse than the first." Matthew 12:43-45. This is the empty house experience, or the casting out of a devil. He returns to the same house (or person) after he has been cast out. This has to do with pardon and righteousness.

The Spirit of Prophecy comments upon this parable: "The parable of the man from whom an evil spirit had been cast out, who did not fill the soul with the love of Christ, illustrates the necessity of not only emptying the heart [getting rid of the sins], but of supplying the vacuum with a Divine Occupant. The demon desired to return to the heart from which he had been expelled. He came, and though it was swept and garnished, he found it still empty and entered in with seven other spirits more evil than himself, so that the last state of the man was worse than the first. The man in His parable refused to do the work of Satan, but the trouble with him was that, after the heart was swept and garnished, he failed to invite the presence of the heavenly Guest. It is not enough to make the heart empty. We must have the vacuum filled with the love of God. The soul must be furnished with the graces of the Spirit of God. We may leave off many bad habits and yet not be truly sanctified [and that means set apart initially and not the whole experience] because we do not have a connection with God. We must unite with Christ. There is a reservoir of power at our command, and we are not to remain in the dark, cold, sunless cave of unbelief; or we shall not catch the bright beams of the Sun of Righteousness." RH, January 24, 1893.

We have to think about this for a while. Picture sin as being on the negative side of zero, zero as neutral, and all the positives on the opposite side of zero from the negatives. When I receive pardon, I take away all the negatives. But this only gives me an empty house experience, and puts me at zero. There is no sin there, but neither is there righteousness. Righteousness is not an empty house, a life void of sins. Righteousness is a positive. It is a *doing*. Somehow that house must be filled, and the house is you and I. We must be filled with the presence and graces of God—His righteousness. It is not sufficient to have pardon; I must also have righteousness. Too many are content with an empty house, and the devil comes back with sins that were once there and finds it empty; and he brings worse devils and comes back to live in you; and you ask, "How did I become so evil while going to church every Sabbath?" It is because your heart was never filled with the Divine presence and with the love of Christ. Far too many of us are content to just remain empty. We say, "I am so thankful the Lord took my sins away." But what did He do in place of them? Christ is not our righteousness until positives come into our lives. Then we begin to live like Jesus, which is what He wanted to accomplish in the first place.

All of this is explained in this marvelous quote: "We must be emptied of self [or move from the negative side to zero]. But this is not all that is required; for when we have renounced our idols, the vacuum must be supplied. If the heart is left desolate, and the vacuum not supplied, it will be in the condition of him whose house was 'empty, swept, and garnished,' without a guest to occupy it. The evil spirit took unto him seven other spirits more wicked than himself, and entered in and dwelt there; and the last state of that man was worse than the first. As you empty the heart of self, you must accept the righteousness of Christ [which is the positive]. Lay hold of it [the righteousness of Christ] by faith; for you must have the mind and spirit of Christ, that you may work the works of Christ. If you open the door of the heart, Jesus will supply the vacuum by the gift of His Spirit, and then you can be a living preacher in your home, in the church, and in the world." COR 119.

This is justification by faith in its truthfulness. All other versions are deceptions and misunderstandings. Somehow we must come to the place where we begin to realize how good and filled with grace is our God. He knew we could not perform, and He gave us dozens of texts in the Bible to show this. He loved us and made us in the beginning, and He knew that in order to save us, He must come and do for us what we could not do for ourselves. He came to offer that to us. He so loved that He came and provided in Jesus all these necessities. Yet somehow we go on and try to eliminate Christ in His fullness by seeking to do for ourselves what He came to do for us.

Always remember that in justification, there is a dual action: both an emptying and a filling. It is not enough to be forgiven or to be emptied of self. Christ in His righteousness must abide in my heart. He must be a full, complete God to me. His presence must come into this emptied, pardoned, cleansed house.

The Spirit of Prophecy describes this same experience in another illustration that is very simple, especially if you like gardening. "The garden of your heart must be cultivated. The poisonous, Satanic plants must be uprooted. The soil must be prepared, thoroughly ploughed by the Word of God; and the precious seeds of truth must be sown and tended by a wise and skillful Gardener." RH, January 24, 1893. You are not the gardener. There is not one parable about a husbandman that calls us the gardener. He is always the Gardener. It is not only tearing out the old weeds and preparing the soil (which is pardoning); somebody must plant the right seed and tend and cultivate the garden; and that Somebody is Jesus. The seed is Christ and His righteousness. Jesus is called the "seed" in Genesis 3:15, in Genesis 12:7, and in Galatians 3:19.

Christ must be planted because He will bring forth the fruits of righteousness in my heart. He must cultivate, He must water; He must brighten us with the sunshine of His love. He is the wise, skillful Gardener. I am not. I receive this by receiving Christ Jesus. When I try to do it myself, you can tell right away that I am a foolish gardener, and a very poor one when it comes to cultivating righteousness. I must be submissive and yielding, allowing Him to break up the fallow ground of my heart and to plant the seed of righteousness in my heart. This He longs to do for me. Forgiveness and pardon is the uprooting of the Satanic plants. The planting of new seed is putting Christ into my life; and then He begins to produce after His kind.

"I am the Vine, ye are the branches: he that abideth in Me, and I in him, the same bringeth forth much fruit: for without Me ye can do nothing." John 15:5. If you are not attached to Jesus, there is no life in you. Without Jesus we are utterly helpless. Jesus must do the work. He is the living vine. We live only as we are attached to Jesus.

While I can do nothing without Him, Philippians 4:13 tells us the converse: "I can do all things through Christ which strengtheneth me." Without Him I am helpless; with Him I can do all things.

If we do not accept this, if we do not receive Christ as our righteousness, we will do exactly as the Jews did. "For they being ignorant of God's righteousness, and going about to establish their own righteousness, have not submitted themselves unto the righteousness of God." Romans 10:3. There is a righteousness that is better than yours or mine. It is the "righteousness of God" that He wants to give to us. But if I will not receive His righteousness, and accept it or believe that it is by grace, then I will go about to establish my own as though I were ignorant of His. And that is a sad plight. While you think you are becoming better as you try to clean up the outside of the cup, you leave the inside dirty, as Jesus said, being like a white-washed sepulcher—beautiful on the outside but full of dead men's bones. While you think you are a sweet-smelling Christian, everyone holds their nose when you come around, including your children and your spouse and your neighbor. Because the person who seeks to establish his own righteousness always has an "I" and a "me" problem; and people get tired of a two-note song. Our lives become a monotone, and a disgusting and boring one. And it is very apparent to others that Christ is not my righteousness; and we wonder why we have so few friends. We chase them away with our pride of self-attainment and self-achievement.

"For Christ is the end of the law for righteousness to every one that believeth" Romans 10:4. He is the perfect fulfillment of the law. He establishes the law by His achievements. He perfectly obeyed the law and is the fulfillment of it for righteousness to everyone that believes. That is why He became a man. He could not give to us the righteousness of God while remaining away from us as another Being. Only when He became a human being and was identified with the human family could He give righteousness to us.

Elder Daniels quoted in his book what Martin Luther wrote about the difficulty in trying to establish our own righteousness, and this is what Luther wrote: "If the article of justification be once lost, then is all true Christian doctrine lost....He then that strayeth from this 'Christian righteousness,' must needs fall into the 'righteousness of the law;' that is to say, when he hath lost Christ, he must fall into the confidence of his own works....For if he neglect the article of justification, we *lose it altogether*. Therefore most necessary it is, chiefly, and above all things, that we teach and repeat this article continually." COR 90. It is true that we need to go over and over these truths so that we never resort back to our own righteousness.

Luther's quote continues: "Yea, though we learn it and understand it well, yet is there not that taketh hold of it perfectly, or believeth it with his heart....Therefore I fear lest this doctrine be defaced and darkened again, when we are dead. For the world must be replenished with horrible darkness and errors, before the latter day come." COR 91. How right he was. If once neglected, while we think we are children of light we might be children of darkness, because Christ is not our righteousness. We may have some truth, but that becomes darkness in us when Christ is not our righteousness. We distort truth and pervert it by self-efforts, by contaminating it with sinful self; and its glory, its unselfishness, its love, its grace are all gone! Why? Because man becomes so prominent in his doing of truth that you cannot find the real truth any longer. The Sabbath doctrine easily becomes a perversion of the Sabbath when it is not the Sabbath as Jesus kept it. It is merely the correct twenty-four hours. The how and why of keeping it and what blessings are found in it get lost in our arguing and debating. We distort everything by self unless Christ operates in us.

We must receive Christ as our Savior for pardon, and as our righteousness for right doing (obedience). And it is all done by grace and not by merit. Christ is both salvation (pardon) and righteousness to me. All my hope is in Him, every bit of it. There is that marvelous text: "Christ in you, the hope of glory." Colossians 1:27. If He is not in me, I have no hope. He must be in me; and there is no way He can come into me without being my righteousness. There is no way He can abide, or stay there, unless He can do His will. And His will is His Father's will, which is the keeping of the law. He can perform that law flawlessly. He is the fulfillment of it. He is the epitome of righteousness. As Christ comes into my heart by faith and by love for Him, as I receive Him and know that He is a God of grace, then, low and behold, for me to live is Christ.

The world today wants to see Jesus, not you, not me. The world is tired of weak human beings. We do not perform flawlessly. They say as the Greeks did, "We would see Jesus," but they will never see Jesus in us until He is both salvation and righteousness. This very moment, He is waiting to bestow the treasures of heaven, in the righteousness of Christ, to you and to me. He stands with His hands outstretched, filled with His righteousness, and He asks us, "Why will you die? Why do you try to establish your own righteousness when Mine is so freely given and completely available. When I am knocking and trying to get in, you won't let Me in with My righteousness. Instead of going about with your own filthy rags, won't you let Me take them off and put on the spotless robes of My righteousness? Won't you trust Me? Don't you believe I am that good? Why do you diminish My goodness? I am the mighty One."

Friend, why will you go on in a miserable existence, trying to be good enough to be accepted when you are already accepted in Christ? All you have to do is receive Him. May God help us this day to see the truth of justification by faith—that Jesus is both salvation and righteousness. What a marvelous truth. May God help us to understand it and receive Him in the fullness of our hearts, in the fullness of His grace.

5

RIGHTEOUS RECORDS OR RIGHTEOUS LIVES?

THERE ARE SEVERAL AREAS of justification by faith that are misunderstood and misinterpreted. If you do not agree with me on some of the things I have to say, that would be quite natural. If you have an open mind and a teachable spirit, I would like to present some material that I believe will help us to understand some of these things that are so difficult.

"For what saith the scripture? Abraham believed God, and it was counted unto him for righteousness." Romans 4:3. Let's look closer at the word "counted." Abraham's belief was counted unto him for righteousness. Verse 5 says: " But to him that worketh not, but believeth on him that justifieth the ungodly, his faith is counted for righteousness.' These words and others like them elsewhere in the Scriptures cause people a great deal of confusion about justification by faith. Because of these words, they say that justification by faith is only a change in the records. The theory is that there is really no change in the life. It is just an accounting system where, though I am counted righteous, I really am not righteous. Many believe that this is justification by faith. Is God merely keeping books in justification by faith, or is He changing lives? Is there a literal change in the life from sin to righteousness; or does God just enter into the book of accounting that we are righteous, even though we continue to practice sin?

There is evidence in the Spirit of Prophecy that would lead us to believe He is keeping good books. "By faith he [meaning the sinner], who has so grievously wronged and offended God, can bring to God the merits of Christ, and the Lord places the obedience of His Son to the sinner's account. Christ's righteousness is accepted in place of man's failure." COR 19. People read this and say God is keeping books in justification by faith.

"Therefore being justified by faith, we have peace with God through our Lord Jesus Christ." Romans 5:1. Ellen White, in the book *Christ Our Righteousness* quotes this verse on page 20, and inserts a bracketed note after the word "justified." The note reads "accounted righteous." So she defines justification as being accounted righteous. This would make you think that God is doing bookkeeping.

This next quote says essentially the same thing: "By faith he can bring to God the merits of Christ, and the Lord places the obedience of His Son to the sinner's account [just like that other statement]. Christ's righteousness is accepted in place of man's failure, and God receives, pardons, justifies, the repentant, believing soul, treats him as though he were righteous [treats him not as he is, but as though he were righteous], and loves him as He loves His Son. This is how faith is accounted righteousness." 1 SM 367. God treats him as though he is righteous, and this is how faith is accounted righteousness. It does not say he is righteous. It says He treats him as though he is; and that causes trouble.

Another quote expands on this: "In ourselves we are sinners; but in Christ we are righteous [this is talking about justification]. Having made us righteous through the imputed righteousness of Christ, God pronounces us just, and treats us as just." 1SM 394. He pronounces us just and treats us as just. But, again, He does not say we are just. In ourselves we are sinners and in Christ we are righteous; and He pronounces us just and treats us as just.

Most understand this to mean that it is as if I were just, or as if I were righteous, but that I am really still a sinner. They say that this is what these statements mean. It is only bookkeeping. This theory holds that I am really not righteous at all, and God is not saying that I am.

"When God pardons the sinner, remits the punishment he deserves, and treats him as though he had not sinned, He receives him into divine favor, and justifies him through the merits of Christ's righteousness." 1SM 389. God treats him as though he had not sinned, but he has sinned. With all this evidence, most people say, "Well, justification by faith is bookkeeping. It is just God accounting us righteous, but in no way does it make me righteous." It is merely accounting, keeping the records of heaven straight; and Adventists are more prone to this idea than others because we teach so much about the record books of heaven and the Judgment.

Before you accept this completely (and many already have accepted it and taught it), you need to pause for awhile and meditate about what you are saying; because you might be saying some things you don't want to say. What kind of a bookkeeper is your God? Does He falsify the records to make you look good? I shouldn't say that, should I? That shoots holes in your ideas about accounting. Is God an unjust accountant? Does He makes the records say one thing when our lives reveal something else? Are His books kept in that fashion, the ones that are going to judge us? No, we don't want to think that about God, do we? Be very careful what you assume the Bible is teaching about bookkeeping when it comes to accounting us righteous, for you might make God look like a falsifier of records. Does He not know our lives? And are the records not compatible with our lives? Are they not one and the same thing? I think so. Be careful that you don't charge God about this.

There is another aspect in looking at this accounting system that is something we almost never think about concerning God's words, accounting, or promises. "For all the promises of God [and I would like to say accounting there], in Him [in Christ] are yea, and in Him Amen, unto the glory of God by us." 2 Corinthians 1: 20. Whatever God promises or accounts, it is as though they were, as though they had already been done or taken place. All His promises are yea (yes) and amen (so be it). For when God speaks, things take place, do they not? His speaking is reality. It cannot be otherwise. He creates by His words. And so His accounting is as if it has already happened. He does that with His words.

There is another side to this problem. In justification by faith, is God only keeping books, or is He changing lives? We must come to understand how it is that God is able to justify guilty sinners and why He can do this without being unjust. That is, how can He take sinful people and call them righteous and still be called fair and just? That is exactly what He is doing, isn't it? How can you do that? God, because He is supreme, cannot bypass His own regulations of justice. We get lost in a quandary and confusion about God's justice and doing an unjust thing, which is making sinners righteous. How does He do this? We must deal with this, especially when it comes to accounting.

How and why He does this is explained by Paul. He assumes you understand it well, so he just races through it, barely covering the high points. "And therefore it [Abraham's faith] was imputed to him for righteousness. Now it was not written for his sake alone, that it was imputed to him; But for us also, to whom it shall be imputed, if we believe on Him that raised up Jesus our Lord from the dead; Who was delivered for our offences, and was raised again for our justification." Romans 4:22-25. What Paul is saying here is that there is a just reason why God can call the sinful righteous. He does this by laying all our sins on Christ. Christ was punished for your sins and mine. He was delivered for our sins, was punished and died for them, and buried. And the Bible says He was resurrected (there in the last phrase) for our justification. What does that mean? Well, it is so obvious and so simple that you run right by it and miss it. The important thing about the death, burial, and resurrection of Christ is that they were sufficient to pay the penalty for all the sins of all mankind.

When Jesus was being punished for our sins, and when He lay in that grave, the Father determined a time when He would send the mightiest angel from heaven to the tomb where Jesus lay. This angel said to the dead Jesus, "Thy Father calls Thee." DA 780. At those words, Christ resurrected Himself. The disciples had heard Him say that He would raise up the temple of His body in three days. When the Father, the divine Judge, called Him, He (the Father) had determined that justice was satisfied. When all the penalty for all our sins had sufficiently been paid for, then sinners could all be justified.

"Jesus refused to receive the homage of His people until He had the assurance that His sacrifice was accepted by the Father. He ascended to the heavenly courts, and from God Himself heard the assurance that His atonement for the sins of men had been ample, that through His blood all might gain eternal life." DA 790. The death of the one Person, the punishment of this Lord Jesus Christ, was enough to pay for the sins of all mankind, for all time. The Judge of heaven said the punishment was ample.

This is what the angel who came down from heaven was conveying when he said, "Thy Father calls Thee." His atonement for our sins had been ample. Ellen White said that He was in that stony prison house as a prisoner of divine justice. He was held captive for our sins, just like in a penitentiary. The devil claimed Him because He was contaminated with our sins, not His own sins. But the Father said it was sufficient. He called Him to come forth from the grave.

"Now He declares: Father, it is finished. I have done Thy will, O My God. I have completed the work of redemption. If Thy justice is satisfied, 'I will that they also, whom Thou hast given Me, be with Me where I am.'....The voice of God is heard proclaiming that justice is satisfied. Satan is vanquished. Christ's toiling, struggling ones on earth are 'accepted in the Beloved.' Eph.1:6. Before the heavenly angels and the representatives of unfallen worlds, they are declared justified." DA 834. Justified by whom? Justified by the Father.

All of this was made possible when Jesus died for all our sins. When He was resurrected, He was raised for our justification. After He came out of the grave, the Father Himself assured Him that the atonement had been ample. Man, if he accepts the provision made for his salvation, does not have to be punished for his sins, for Christ has already been punished. "There is therefore now no condemnation to them which are in Christ Jesus." Romans 8:1.

This is enlarged upon in the Spirit of Prophecy in several places. "Justice demands that sin be not merely pardoned, but the death penalty must be executed [justice demands that somebody must die]. God, in the gift of His only-begotten Son, met both these requirements. By dying in man's stead, Christ exhausted the penalty and provided a pardon." 6BC 1099. When you exhaust something, how much remains? Nothing. He exhausted the penalty and provided a pardon. God provided both the pardon and the death. The penalty is all gone in Jesus. He is able to justify sinners and still be just, because Christ took all our sins and paid a price sufficient for the penalty—the punishment for every sinner. It is all accomplished in Jesus.

It is by His death, burial, and resurrection that I am justified, as Paul elaborates in Romans 4 so nicely. His sacrifice and His resurrection have earned Jesus the right to justify you, and still be a just God. He has the right to do that. This is how He can do it and why He can do it. If He had not done that in the death, burial and resurrection of Jesus, we could never be justified. Therefore, God is fair. He is just when He says He will forgive sinners and call the sinful "righteous." The wise and omniscient One says this.

If this was accomplished two thousand years ago, how do I receive what He has done for me? I receive it by the description that Paul gives in Romans 6 where there is a succession of ideas. He first describes how Christ accomplished it: "Know ye not, that so many of us as were baptized into Jesus Christ were baptized into His death? Therefore we are buried with Him by baptism into death: that like as Christ was raised up from the dead by the glory of the Father, even so we also should walk in newness of life. For if we have been planted together in the likeness of His death, we shall be also in the likeness of His resurrection: Knowing this, that our old man is crucified with Him, that the body of sin might be destroyed, that henceforth we should not serve sin. For he that is dead is freed from sin." Romans 4:4-7.

Paul said you are justified by the death, burial and resurrection of Jesus. You receive that justification and it becomes personal, individual, when you follow Him in this experience of the old man of sin dying, buried in the watery grave and coming up to the new life. We call this the new birth. I have done what some would call a strange thing. I have put justification by faith and the new birth together, all in the same package. You are justified by the death, burial and resurrection according to Romans 4. You receive it in the experience of Romans 6 (the new birth) where following Him in death, burial and resurrection, you come up to a new life.

When you put these two together, you have some unique thoughts and ideas. You cannot separate justification by faith and the new birth without doing damage to one or the other. You must keep them together; and when you put them together you get an unusual answer to that question: Is God only keeping records or changing lives? Justification is identified with the new birth. He is obviously changing lives, right? That is what new birth means, and I must remind you of that. He justifies all in His death, burial, and resurrection. We enter into that experience by following Him in the same experience—in the new birth and the death of the old man of sin.

These similarities and their connection are described in the Spirit of Prophecy. "The righteousness by which we are justified is imputed, the righteousness by which we are sanctified is imparted." COR 98. The first is our title to heaven; the second is our fitness for heaven. I am justified by faith in Christ's righteousness as imputed to me. This is my title to heaven. The Bible does not use the word title, to my knowledge. Instead, it uses another word. It is called "birthright," an old-fashioned term we seldom think about. A title is a right. It is authority.

When I am born again as a child of God in the new birth, I have a title, or a birthright, to heaven, because I am now a son of God. I am one of His relatives. Relatives have certain rights. If you don't believe it, try to probate a will and you will find out. Try to leave out the relatives with no mention of their names and see what happens to the will. Every relative's name must be mentioned whether he gets something or not. He has a right by law. The Bible honors relationships, and as I become a child of God, I have a right called a "birthright" or a title to heaven. Birthright is another word for imputed righteousness or justification by faith. The birthright gives you the right to justification by faith, and justification by faith gives you the title to heaven. You cannot separate them or you will do damage to either one or the other.

We can see some of these similarities between the new birth and justification in a few quotations. "In order to obtain the righteousness of Christ, it is necessary to know what that repentance is which works a radical change of mind and spirit and action." 1SM 393. The radical change of mind is a new heart, the new birth. In order to obtain the righteousness of Christ, it is necessary to know this "radical change of mind and spirit and action."

"As he [the sinner] beholds the righteousness of Christ in the divine precepts, he exclaims, 'The law of the Lord is perfect, converting the soul.'" COR 116. How is it that the sinner says that? When he beholds the righteousness of Christ in the law. If you do not see the righteousness of Christ in the law, of course, it does not convert you. When he beholds the righteousness of Christ there in the law, he exclaims, "The law of the Lord is perfect, converting the soul." This is talking about conversion and the righteousness that is of faith.

Continuing with the quotation: "As the sinner is pardoned for his transgression through the merits of Christ [which is His righteousness], as he is clothed with the righteousness through faith in Him, he declares with the psalmist, 'How sweet are Thy words unto my taste! yea, sweeter than honey to my mouth.' 'More to be desired are they than gold, yea, than much fine gold: sweeter also than honey in the honeycomb.' This is conversion." Ellen White talks about being justified by the merits of Christ, and being clothed with His robe of righteousness. This is conversion, and you cannot separate it from justification by faith. It is impossible.

Elder Daniels, as he studied through this and wrote his book, gave his own thoughts on this in the introductory chapter, page 21: "Righteousness by faith is a transaction, an experience. It is a submitting unto the 'righteousness of God.' It is a change of standing before God and His law. It is a regeneration, a new birth." That is what it is, and we must not change it.

As soon as you have accepted that justification by faith and the new birth are connected, realizing that you cannot separate them, then you have the answer to that problem about whether justification is merely bookkeeping or changing lives. In the new birth it is quite obvious that certain things happen to the life, not merely something to the books. In Romans 6:4, we read that in the new birth, we are to "walk in newness of life." In 2 Corinthians 5:17, it says that those who are in Christ are new creatures, and that "Old things are passed away, behold, all things have become new." There is something new, right?

Best of all is that there is righteousness in the new birth. "And that ye put on the new man, which after God is created in righteousness and true holiness." Ephesians 4:24. Can Jesus, the righteous One, in a creative act make someone righteous? It doesn't say a person evolves righteous. It doesn't say that someday he will get better and better until he is righteous. Creation is not evolution. Creation is an instantaneous action. He spoke and there it was! Therefore, in the new man, the new birth, I am created in righteousness and true holiness. I do not get it by trying or wishing for it. I do not get it by praying for it. I get it by believing that He does it for me, that He has achieved it, and He wants to give it to me. He makes me righteous.

The same thoughts are found a little differently in Romans chapter 3 where it talks about declaring us righteous. God created all things by the word of His mouth. When God declares something by the words of His mouth, it is creative act! He declares us righteous. He creates us righteous. And the new birth is a creative act. God is making new life. I am created in righteousness and true holiness. He does it for me as I believe it and expect it and anticipate it, and know that He wants to do it. It is not because of any goodness on my part. He made everything out of nothing and I am nothing. The Lord can make something out of nothing, but He does not make something out of something. It depreciates His creative ability to make something out of something. Then He is obligated or indebted to pre-existent matter. This is Pantheism. God is not indebted to you for righteousness or re-creation. It is all His power. It is a gift. He does it for you and for me. This takes place in this marvelous thing called conversion.

"When a man is converted to God, a new moral taste is created." COR 101. "Holiness is the gift of God through Christ. Those who receive the Saviour become sons of God. They are His spiritual children, born again, renewed in righteousness and true holiness. Their minds are changed." 6BC 1117.

Here is a quote that talks about what we are like as a result of being born of Adam: "Since we are sinful, unholy, we cannot perfectly obey the holy law. We have no righteousness of our own with which to meet the claims of the law of God. But Christ has made a way of escape for us. He lived on earth amid trials and temptations such as we have to meet. He lived a sinless life. He died for us, and now He offers to take our sins and give us His righteousness. If you give yourself to Him and accept Him as your Saviour, then, sinful as your life may have been, for His sake you are accounted righteous [the first part—the accounting]. Christ's character stands in place of your character, and you are accepted before God just as if you had not sinned. More than this, Christ changes the heart." SC 62. This changing of the heart is the other half. He accounts me righteous, He pardons me, but more than this, Christ changes the heart. He not only changes the books and the pages, He changes the heart. Something happens to me, and it is much more than good bookkeeping.

How does He do this? "He abides in your heart by faith. You are to maintain this connection with Christ by faith and the continual surrender of your will to Him; and so long as you do this, He will work in you to will and to do according to His good pleasure...Then with Christ working in you, you will manifest the same spirit and do the same good works—works of righteousness, obedience. Our only ground of hope is in the righteousness of Christ imputed to us, and in that wrought by His Spirit working in and through us." SC 62,63. More than the accounting, more than the pardoning, He changes the heart. He functions inside of you as you receive Him by faith, as you respond to His love. As you love Him, He permeates your mind and takes control of you. You become obsessed with Him, and He possesses you. Then He operates His own good will and pleasure in you. His pleasure, of course, is to do His Father's will, which is obedience to the law. This is what happens in the new birth, and it is a marvelous thing. We must never depreciate all that God offers us.

In the new birth we actually become partakers of the divine nature. God Himself comes to live in man. Immanuel means God with us. He did not cease to be Immanuel when He went back to heaven, for He sent His Spirit, who is also God, and who can be in every one of us. Jesus said His Spirit shall abide with you, and He shall be in you. The heavenly presence abides in us and we are changed. He works out His will inside of us as well as on the record books for us.

"Genuine faith appropriates the righteousness of Christ and the sinner is made an overcomer with Christ; for He is made a partaker of the divine nature and thus divinity and humanity are combined." "In the religion of Christ there is a regenerating influence that transforms the entire being, lifting man above every debasing, groveling vice, and raising the thoughts and desires toward God and heaven. Linked to the Infinite One, man is made a partaker of the divine nature." COR 96. "When the soul surrenders itself to Christ, a new power takes possession of the new heart. A change is wrought which man can never accomplish for himself. It is a supernatural work, bringing a supernatural element into human nature." COR 99,100. Imagine combining divinity with humanity. This happens in the new covenant where God writes His law in our minds and hearts. Christ is the very personification of the law of God. He is God's character perfectly lived out.

We have come back for the third time to this two-fold aspect of justification by faith—that it is both salvation and righteousness. Not only does He take care of records, He takes care of hearts and lives. He does both. The thing I like the best is that He takes care of the life. We are changed by Christ. I cannot change my life, but by faith in Him and His precious love and sacrifice for me, I may have a justified, a converted life that He will accomplish in me.

These questions are answered so nicely in this one quotation: "The atonement of Christ is not a mere skillful way to have our sins pardoned [in other words, God did not just scheme and devise how to get around the law and be just]. It is a divine remedy for the cure of transgression and the restoration of spiritual health. It is the heaven-ordained means by which the righteousness of Christ may be not only upon us but in our hearts and characters." 6BC 1074.

In this marvelous experience of justification by faith, Christ comes into me. He does not just take care of some books somewhere. He does do this, but He also comes inside my heart and changes my very character. What happens when the mighty One gets inside of this poor, weak human being? Suddenly the weak say, "I am strong through Christ who strengthens me." Suddenly the weak have become mighty. The Bible has many texts about the weak saying they are strong. God comes to abide in me and suddenly I do things that I never knew I could do. Christ is able to do that.

At the time of the new birth and justification, we are only babes in Christ. We are not mature Christians. After the new birth we must grow to maturity. There are many texts that state this. "Till we all come in the unity of the faith, and of the knowledge of the Son of God, unto a perfect man, unto the measure of the stature of the fullness of Christ." Ephesians 4:13. "For every one that useth milk is unskillful in the word of righteousness: for he is a babe. But strong meat belongeth to them that are of full age, even to those who by reason of use have their senses exercised to discern both good and evil." Hebrews 5:13,14. There is a growth that takes place after the new birth and after justification.

In this immature child of God, or babe in Christ, it will not be obvious or prominent that righteousness is there. It will not protrude, no more than the skills, talents, abilities and capabilities are obvious in a baby. The baby looks so helpless, so weak. But when you see that baby a few years later, a young fellow, husky and strong and 6 feet tall, talented and capable, you ask, "Where did he come from? I never anticipated all this from that little package." But in that little package were all the potentials, right? The whole thing was there. God did not add new things. There was learning, there was experience, there was growth and development; but the package was there. And that package is Christ in me the hope of glory. The righteousness was there. As you grow and mature, that righteousness becomes obvious. Your neighbors begin to see it; your family begins to see it. It becomes prominent, until finally you have grown to the fullness of the stature of Christ. We shall be like Him, John teaches.

Righteousness by faith, or justification, is a seed experience. Christ and His righteousness are planted in my heart when I am born again—born of the Seed of the word, born of the Spirit. He comes to live in my heart and He is both the Seed and the Gardener. He watches over the seed and makes sure it germinates. He watches that tender little plant when it is so vulnerable in its babyhood. He gives it just the right food, the right amount of sunshine and the rain that it might grow; and as it grows He tends it, He cares for it, He plans for it. He is always the divine Gardener watching over His plants and making sure they will grow up.

What do I do? Every morning I say, "Lord I am not righteous, and I cannot be righteous; but You are the mighty One, you are the righteous One. I submit my whole life to you. Take care of me today. Guide me today. Plan for me today. Control me today. Use me today." And little by little His righteousness begins to flourish as I submit and give Him all the controls of my life. And that plant grows and grows and grows. Soon the neighbors ask, "How did you get that way?" And I can say, " I really don't know too much about it. Somebody else was doing it for me." Isn't that true? Someone else does it for us. If people say, "You really are a righteous person," you will say, "Me? I haven't seen it." For in our humility and self-distrust we do not notice that we are righteous.

The book *The Great Controversy* talks about this at length. We never brag of what we are like. We only say, "Lord, be merciful to me a sinner." And as we yield to the mighty One, He works mighty works in the weak one; and the world marvels and takes knowledge that we have been with Jesus. Does this mean we become more righteous as we grow? Does it mean I am more perfect? More mature, yes, but more perfect? All the righteousness I have when I am a born-again Christian in my babyhood is all of Jesus. When I have lived fifty or sixty years, all by His grace, all the righteousness I have then is all of Jesus. All my works have been wrought by Him; and whether you take me as an infant in Christ or as a mature Christian in Christ, the righteousness in me is all of Christ; and we will say, "The Lord our righteousness!" All our righteousness is of Him. I have all of Him in the beginning and I have all of Him in the end. I might not know all about Him in the beginning. I might not have reached out and claimed all of His righteousness. But the fullness of the Godhead dwells in Him completely, and when He has come to live in me, it is all there. I might have to learn much more about Him. Over time, I will learn to love Him much more and trust Him much more and distrust self more. But the fullness of the righteousness of Christ abides in me from the day I am born again as a Christian.

This is a marvelous experience. It really is. What God wants to do for us is not to just take care of pages of books, even marvelous heavenly pages, for He is an accurate bookkeeper. He also wants to take care of hearts. What does He write down in those books? He writes: "This is My adopted child who is forgiven and righteous. I know because I am making him that way. This is a just thing to do because Christ died and was resurrected for his sins."

There are two texts that so uniquely describe this. "But of Him are ye in Christ Jesus, who of God is made unto us wisdom, and righteousness, and sanctification, and redemption." 1 Corinthians 1:30. You are in Christ who was made unto us righteousness. As you hide in Christ, and He in you, He becomes your righteousness. "That Christ may dwell in your hearts by faith; that ye, being rooted and grounded in love..." As you respond to His love, by loving Him you will love others. You literally take root in love, and that heavenly plant of righteousness is a plant of love; for love is the fulfilling of the law, and the keeping of the law is righteousness, so love is righteousness. You are being rooted and grounded in love when Christ lives in you, that you "May be able to comprehend with all saints what is the breadth, and length, and depth, and height" of God's love; and "to know the love of Christ, which passeth knowledge, that ye might be filled with all the fullness of God.' Ephesians 3:17-21.

You see, friend, justification by faith is a marvelous, intimate love affair. He comes down and becomes intimate with the human family, and new children are born in that intimacy—children of God. And as I respond to His love, I say, "O Lord, take possession of me, live in me, fill my mind, possess me, control me, be my Lord and Master, consume me, fill me with the fullness of God." And as He does that, lo and behold you will see in me, the sinner, the Lord my righteousness.

May God grant you this glorious experience. He has been waiting for years and years to give it to every person He wants us to become missionaries to go out and offer this to everyone and convince them that God wants to do it for them. And the world will stand amazed as they look at us, and they will ask, "Isn't this man from a sinful place? Didn't he use to be a terrible and proud person? Why is He so righteous? How did He get that way?" And God will be praised as they see the righteousness of Christ perfectly reproduced in us. What a glorious experience is ours. Let us claim it today.

6

THE OTHER HALF
OF FORGIVENESS

OUR PROBLEM TODAY IS that there is a great hindrance in understanding the twofold aspect of justification—that God both forgives us and makes us righteous. It is easy to believe we are forgiven, but we have trouble believing that we are made just because so often after conversion, we find ourselves committing the same sins as we did before. It becomes very obvious to us that we are not righteous or we would not do the same things that we did before that are so wrong. We reason that, since so many are like us and continue doing the same sins they did before conversion, justification must not include being made righteous. It only means that I am forgiven. Everyone cannot be wrong. We all seem to go on and on in our weaknesses and sins, thinking that justification must not include making us righteous. We assume that. This is quite a roadblock in understanding the twofold aspect of justification by faith.

Are we truly justified by faith in Christ and His righteousness when we go on in the same old sins? I am not talking about new ones, but just the old ones. Are we really justified by faith? This has much to do with your understanding of the subject, and it has caused some to invent their own understanding or ideas about it, and all in order to accommodate their own experience.

To understand this we must go back and study pardon and forgiveness. Then the other aspect of the new life will be much easier to understand. As soon as you read the next quotation, you are going to think I have been deceiving you so far. I have been presenting how justification is more than merely forgiveness, and also includes being made righteous or just. After you read this next quote, you are going to think I am contradicting myself.

"As the penitent sinner, contrite before God, discerns Christ's atonement in his behalf, and accepts this atonement as his only hope in this life and the future life, his sins are pardoned. This is justification by faith." 6BC 1070. His sins are pardoned, which is justification by faith. In case you did not understand, at the bottom of the same page it says: "Pardon and justification are one and the same thing. Justification is a full, complete pardon of sin. The moment a sinner accepts Christ by faith, that moment he is pardoned. The righteousness of Christ is imputed to him, and he is no more to doubt God's forgiving grace."

Why did I tell you that justification was more than pardon, more than forgiveness, when she says they are the same thing? Because I was dealing with your understanding of forgiveness and pardon. Many believe that forgiveness is simply gaining peace with God again, or reconciliation as it is called in the Bible. Forgiveness is where all the wrongs are set right and there is no more guilt or condemnation, and that is all there is to it. This is what happens as we deal in our affairs with one another. If two people are alienated because one offends the other, and if one asks for forgiveness, the alienation is gone. There are no more ill feelings; and we assume that forgiveness with God is identical to that. But the Bible and the Spirit of Prophecy teach a forgiveness much greater than this human understanding of this topic. I was dealing only with your understanding of the words forgiveness and pardon. In this study you will understand what the Bible says about it and you will see that I was teaching you the truth about justification; for it includes pardon and all of its ramifications, which includes making us right.

Ellen White tells us that in David's prayer, we find the correct understanding of pardon. We need to learn how to confess and seek forgiveness as did David. You might not brand yourself with his type of sinning, but this is the pattern of prayer for those who confess. "Have mercy upon me, O God, according to Thy lovingkindness: according unto the multitude of Thy tender mercies blot out my transgressions. Wash me thoroughly from mine iniquity, and cleanse me from my sin. For I acknowledge my transgressions: and my sin is ever before me [he could not forget about them]. Against Thee, Thee only, have I sinned, and done this evil in Thy sight: that Thou mightest be justified when Thou speakest, and be clear when Thou judgest. Behold, I was shapen in iniquity; and in sin did my mother conceive me. Behold, Thou desirest truth in the inward parts: and in the hidden part Thou shalt make me to know wisdom. Purge me with hyssop, and I shall be clean: wash me, and I shall be whiter than snow. Make me to hear joy and gladness; that the bones which Thou hast broken may rejoice. Hide Thy face from my sins, and blot out all mine iniquities. Create in me a clean heart, O God; and renew a right spirit within me." Psalms 51:1-10.

That last verse (10) is unique in confession. Most of us use some of the other thoughts, but very few people use verse 10 in their confession of their sins. It is a whole different perspective of confession, a whole new dimension. David said he saw something inside of him that needed correcting, it was not just the vile sins he had committed with Bathsheba and having her husband killed. It was far more than that. The reason he did those things was that there was something corrupt inside him. He knew he needed a new heart and a renewed spirit that would change him so that he would never again conceive of such things. "Create in me a clean heart." This is confession, and the forgiveness that results is genuine forgiveness. This is the true picture of pardon. Everything else is only partial. In this plea for a new heart, we see the other half of forgiveness.

The book of Isaiah, we are told, also contains a picture of God's forgiveness and genuine confession. "Let the wicked forsake his way, and the unrighteous man his thoughts: and let him return unto the Lord, and he will have mercy upon him; and to our God, for he will abundantly pardon. For My thoughts are not your thoughts, neither are your ways My ways, saith the Lord. For as the heavens are higher than the earth, so are My ways higher than your ways, and My thoughts than your thoughts." Isaiah 55:7-9.

In genuine forgiveness, where there was sin there will be righteousness, where there was a sinner there will be a saint. God who can give new life to a parched land by the showers of rain that come down from heaven can, by His grace, send showers of His Spirit to transform your life so there will be no more thorns in your life. This He can do by creating in us clean hearts.

"But forgiveness has a *broader meaning* than many suppose. When God gives the promise that He 'will abundantly pardon,' He adds, as if the meaning of that promise exceeded all that we could comprehend: 'My thoughts are not your thoughts [and she quotes Isaiah 55]. God's forgiveness is not merely a judicial act by which He sets us free from condemnation. It is not only forgiveness for sin, but reclaiming from sin. It is the outflow of redeeming love that transforms the heart. David had the true conception of forgiveness when he prayed, 'Create in me a clean heart, O God; and renew a right spirit within me.' And again he says, 'As far as the east is from the west, so far hath He removed our transgressions from us.' Psalm 103:12." MB 114.

How far is the east from the west? The earth is about twenty-five thousand miles in circumference. Is that how far it is from east to west? No, for when you go around twenty-five thousand miles, east and west are still just as far apart as when you started. East and west never meet. As far as the east is from the west, this is how far He has separated our sins from us. They can never be found again.

The Spirit of Prophecy includes the new heart in the true conception of forgiveness; but we seldom include these thoughts in our limited understanding of forgiveness. That is why I have added the other dimension in previous discussions about justification and pardon. Now we will put all the pieces together.

Pardon includes a reclaiming from sin, a transformation of the heart that removes sin as far away as the east is from the west. In true pardon, you can never find those sins in God's books, and they no longer reside in your heart. They become non-existent. God has a different idea about forgiveness than we usually anticipate or expect when we come asking for forgiveness. Justification includes a conversion experience, which David called a clean heart and a right spirit.

In His forgiveness, God is making it so I will not sin. Is God able to do that? We of ourselves cannot stop sinning, but He can stop us. How able is your God? "Now unto Him that is able to do exceeding abundantly above all that we ask or think." Ephesians 3:20. If He is that able, can we gain victory over besetting sins? When John the Baptist saw Jesus coming to the Jordan River, he said "Behold, the Lamb of God which taketh away the sin of the world." John 1:29. What does Jesus do? He takes sin away. How far? As far as the east from the west.

"The religion of Christ means more than the forgiveness of sin; it means taking away our sins....It means divine illumination, rejoicing in God. It means a heart emptied of self, and blessed with the abiding presence of Christ." COL 419,420. When I receive Christ, I receive His righteousness. The abiding presence of Christ must come into me. Continuing on with the quotation: "When Christ reigns in the soul, there is purity, freedom from sin. The glory, the fullness, the completeness of the gospel plan is fulfilled in the life. The acceptance of the Saviour brings a glow of perfect peace, perfect love, perfect assurance. The beauty and fragrance of the character of Christ revealed in the life testifies that God has indeed sent His Son into the world to be its Saviour."

If you are going to include Christ in the life, there must be a transformation. If He becomes your Master, He produces different activity than was found before when you were the master or the devil was the master of your life. The new Master produces different works. If you have accepted Christ as your Supreme Master, saying as did Thomas, "My Lord and my God," then God produces different actions and behavior in you. This is what Christianity is.

Please don't get negative on me and think that I am criticizing you. I am not trying to be critical. I am trying to help us to understand what God is offering us, and that we have been satisfied with too little. The world no longer is buying our Christianity. In fact, they are tired of Christians because they are so ineffective, so weak. They are very critical of us and I am happy they are. You know why? It might prod us into looking at our Christianity to see whether we have the genuine article or if we are a farce of some kind. We will not take criticism from fellow Christians, but we might take it from the world when they tell us how ineffective we are, how helpless we are to ourselves, and how little we help other people. Maybe we will find fault with ourselves when we begin to accept their faultfinding.

Our concept of forgiveness reminds me of a house we lived in when I was a young boy. We rented an old house and we were a very poor family with quite a few children in the home. Every time it rained the roof would leak. Not one or two leaks, but dozens. It leaked in the bedroom, and the living room, and the kitchen and everywhere else. Our routine at that time was to bring out a bunch of pails, kettles, and pans to catch the dripping water. When it stopped raining and the sun came out, we would put away the pans and pails after we emptied them, and save them for the next rainstorm. There were many neighbors just like us. In fact, that was the normal routine in my neighborhood.

Some people use forgiveness like those pails. Every time they get a leak in their life—their character—they run and get the bucket of forgiveness and say, "O Lord, please forgive me for this terrible sin." Then they feel better. Empty the pail, and then wait until the next time to sin. Every time it rains, and sometimes it pours, we run and get the buckets of forgiveness and say, Lord forgive me for this or for that. A very sensible person would find some shingles, and wherever there was a leak he would put on a new shingle. What could you do with the pails then? You could probably throw them away. Are you understanding me? The leaks are sin in our lives requiring the pails of forgiveness; but if you start patching up the roof (and I don't mean to imply that the Lord does a patch job), when He plugs up the leaks of the sin in our lives, you don't need the forgiveness, do you? No. If you do not commit the sin anymore, do you have to ask forgiveness for it? Not at all. Don't you think the Lord would like to plug up the leaks? Does He always want us to have a bucket brigade of forgiveness? Much of what we teach about forgiveness is just that. Our prayers are structured to catch the leaks in our lives. And we say, "Oh, if I only ask enough times for forgiveness, the Lord will forgive me and I will be saved." We have taught that so many times.

It is almost inconceivable of what we have done to the Investigative Judgment and to God's character with this attitude of forgiveness. Under this concept, if I lose my temper eighteen thousand and twenty times in a life time, in order to be judged righteous in the Judgment, I must ask God to forgive me for my temper eighteen thousand and twenty times. If I only ask for forgiveness for my temper eighteen thousand and nineteen times, God says, "Ha! I caught you! You missed one and you are going to burn." That is the way some people picture God. They think God is out to trap us. We have left this concept with our children and with people we teach about the Judgment. People go away thinking that God is some kind of spy, watching their character to see if it is flawless; and if we goof up one time too many, we won't make it. With all the array of sins we have, just imagine all the times we have to ask for forgiveness for all those sins. People come to me and say, "Elder Lehman, I am worried. I am afraid there are sins that I've forgotten all about, and if I don't confess them I will be lost." I have difficulty answering them because their understanding of forgiveness and God's pardon is so meager and so perverted that it takes a long time to get them straight. God is not like that with forgiveness. He is able to abundantly pardon our sins, the Bible says, and take it all away, as high as the heavens are above the earth, as far as the east is from the west, He removes them from us. Yet we think we must confess every act to be declared righteous in the Judgment. God's bookkeeping is not like that at all. I cannot find that concept in the Scriptures or the Spirit of Prophecy. This is an invention of ours because of a wrong concept of forgiveness.

In addition to making the Investigative Judgment a perversion, we have also done the same thing to repentance. Repentance is almost a farce with this understanding of forgiveness that so many of us believe in. Supposedly we are sorry when we offend someone because we love them, and therefore repentant, which is sorrow for that sin. Can you imagine yourself going to a dear friend whom you have offended and saying to that person, "I am very sorry I offended you. I really love you very much and I don't want to harm you. I hope you will forgive me, but I will probably do it again before long." If you were that person's friend you would say, "I, really wonder how much you love me if you are planning on offending me again tomorrow or next week." But that is exactly what we do with God. We say, "I love you very much, Lord, and I hope you will keep on forgiving me even though I might offend you for the rest of my life." And we hope that He believes we love Him. But we ourselves really wonder if we do with that kind of repentance. That is a farce. That is not sorrow for sin. If we are sorry for sin, we do not plan, or even make allowances, for offending again that person whom we love so dearly. So our concept of repentance is not Biblical, either. You must go back into this whole picture and discover the true understanding of forgiveness and confession.

Repentance is described in this fashion: "Repentance includes sorrow for sin and a turning away from it. We shall not renounce sin unless we see its sinfulness; until we turn away from it in heart, there will be no real change in the life." SC23. There is no real sorrow for sin until we really see how bad it is. The Lord can do that for us, for both forgiveness and repentance are gifts.

Much of our problem concerning all of these aspects revolving around the one word "pardon" is that most of our understanding about repentance and confession and forgiveness are all verbal transactions. I go through the motions of saying the words, "Lord, I am sorry I was mean this morning. I hope you will forgive me." And we imagine God, like a great High Priest of some kind, gets on His hot line to the recording angel and says, "Bill Lehman has confessed his sin of being mean this morning, so mark pardon next to that sin." And I feel relieved. It is all taken care of. Is that right? This is what many have invented about confession and forgiveness. The Bible does not teach that kind of confession.

In Hebrews 9:22, the apostle Paul brings out a key thought about forgiveness and confession: "And almost all things are by the law purged with blood; and without shedding of blood is no remission." Ellen White quotes this verse, then says: "Remission, or putting away of sin, is the work to be accomplished." GC 417. Remission for sin is the putting away of sin; and you cannot take sin away without the shedding of blood.

We are only forgiven because Christ died on Calvary. There is no other reason why. He earned the right by shedding His blood to cleanse us from sin, and forgiveness is only offered at Calvary. Christ has gone to heaven as our High Priest, and He ministers His precious blood in our behalf, does He not? That is what He is doing there. His sacrifice, His atonement for us is what He offers in our behalf there in heaven. When I come confessing my sin I must never leave out the death and the blood of Jesus. Many have gone so far today that they do not even like this subject. There are many among us who criticize this and call it a bloody religion, meaning it is unsophisticated, non-intellectual, crude. Believe me, if you have trouble even thinking about your sins, you will have a terrible time adding the blood of Jesus to that sin. You will stay a thousand miles away from what caused the shedding of Christ's blood and never look back.

If those who are frightened about the mere mention of their sins and sinfulness would go to the cross, it would really do something to them. Some have come to the place where they have invented a sophisticated religion that is a crossless Christianity; and if it is crossless, it is Christless. The heart of all the ministry of Jesus was His death on Calvary. You leave it out and you have no gospel. You can use all kinds of Bible texts, but you have no gospel without the cross. None! There is no gospel, there is no good news, for the Bible is not good news without the cross. It is bad news, it is all condemnation, and it is all law and no mercy without the cross. I don't care how many texts you use, if you leave out the cross of Jesus you have left out all the good news, and all of us are a hopeless people.

The Jews believed the Scriptures and preached them very prominently, and even memorized great portions of them, but they killed the Savior. It is not enough to be Bible Christians. Somebody must be a gospel, Christ-filled, cross-preaching Christian. There is no salvation and no forgiveness apart from the cross. We have learned how to use the Bible without the cross and without Jesus. We are satisfied as long as it is Bible. That is not enough. It must be the cross and the gospel and Jesus in the Bible, from cover to cover. Without this we are hopeless people practicing an imaginary religion.

Forgiveness in the Old Testament was far more than some kind of a verbal communication or transaction. I know that some people do not like this and what the Old Testament had to say about this as a symbol or a type. Often it says more in that picture than you can read in the words in the New Testament. Come with me back to the Old Testament and look at the words and the picture there.

Leviticus chapter 4 talks about how priests are to do this, how rich people are to do it (or rulers), and how common people are to do this; and since we consider ourselves common, let's read what it says about us in verses 28 and 29: "Or if his sin, which he hath sinned, come to his knowledge: then he shall bring his offering, a kid of the goats, a female without blemish, for his sin which he hath sinned. And he shall lay his hand upon the head of the sin offering, and slay the sin offering in the place of the burnt offering." And the "he" is the sinner, not the priest.

This is confession in the Old Testament, which was meant to be an example, or picture, of confession in the New Testament. In olden days, when sin comes to your knowledge, there was only one way you could confess it. You had to bring a sacrifice, an animal, to slay. You brought the animal and the priest helped you tie it down so it could not get away; and then he hands you the knife, and if you like to quibble about it he would say to you, "I didn't do the sin. You did. It is your sacrifice, not mine. This animal is not dying for me, it is dying for you." You hold onto the knife and take a good look at it, and you take a good look at that animal.

Have you ever seen a young lamb, or ever have one as a pet? Suppose you had one that was one year old that you raised up yourself; and this is the animal you are going to offer. How do you feel? You gulp, and your heart does flip-flops and ends up as a knot in your throat. And you wish there was some other way. We always wish there were some other way, but the Bible says that without the shedding of blood there is no putting away of sin. I am just as capable as you are when it comes to inventing other ways, and I am just as sure as you that they do not work. They have never worked in my life at all; and I like to invent them by the hundreds, because I just don't like to do the job, do you? It makes me miserable to think that my sins are like that. It isn't very pleasant to think that an animal should die for me. All I can see is its innocence. Why should it die? The ceremonial law said the sinner must put his hand on the animal's head, which to that person meant that he was transferring his sins to that innocent animal. He must die because I sinned, not because it sinned.

Friend, there was no other way to find forgiveness in the Old Testament except this way. Some people think it has changed for the better. In reality, it changed for the worse. In the place of the lamb, it is the Lamb of God now. In the place of an animal, it is Jesus, the priceless Son of God. Our sins crucify Him afresh. Does that make you feel better? It is as though you are right at Calvary watching Him die for your sins when you come confessing in the Biblical fashion. This is why there are so few righteous people. We hate Calvary. We will not linger there a thoughtful hour, and some people cannot stand it for two seconds. Our minds want to evade that place, and the thoughts we have while there. So we hop the next jet plane (not a boat like Jonah) and go in the opposite direction, and we never look back. We say, "I never want to see that horrible place again." And we go on indulging our own ways and inventing new ways to say that we are justified. We even pick the Scriptures like Romans chapter 7 and misinterpret them to allow for our lack of a just life. We fix it up beautifully so it sounds logical and sensible. We say, "Well, Paul said you can keep on sinning after you are converted." Did he really? The same old sins, is that what he really said? That makes God very small in my estimation, and incapable of changing my heart. That makes the converted heart a heart that loves sin and still indulges it. I really believe that when we spend that thoughtful hour at the cross everyday, it will change our whole concept of justification and forgiveness and righteousness. I am not criticizing anybody. I can look at myself and see how seldom I bring my sins to the foot of cross.

Ellen White said there is no higher place that you can ever reach than kneeling at the foot of the cross. And believe me, when you have been there a little while and experienced the saving grace of Christ, and the beauty of Jesus and His tremendous love in dying for us, you will never want to leave. At first you are miserable, then you do not want to get away. You always want to stay there. It is a strange thing that happens at the cross. This is a different concept than what we have usually had, and we must go back and live the experience of forgiveness and confession, not just mouth a few words. We must go back and see the sacrifice in our mind's eye.

"Jesus has said, 'I, if I be lifted up from the earth, will draw all men unto Me.' John 12:32. Christ must be revealed to the sinner as the Savior dying for the sins of the world; and as we behold the Lamb of God upon the cross of Calvary, the mystery of redemption begins to unfold to our minds, and the goodness of God leads us to repentance." SC 26,27. Repentance was given at Calvary. The goodness of God seen there in that love gift, with all that agony, leads me to repentance. Continuing on with the quote: "In dying for sinners, Christ manifested a love that is incomprehensible; and as the sinner beholds this love, it softens the heart, impresses the mind, and inspires contrition in the soul....And as Christ draws them to look upon His cross, to behold Him whom their sins have pierced, the commandment comes home to the conscience. The wickedness of their life, the deep-seated sin of the soul, is revealed to them. They begin to comprehend something of the righteousness of Christ, and exclaim, 'What is sin, that it should require such a sacrifice for the redemption of its victim? Was all this love, all this suffering, all this humiliation, demanded, that we might not perish, but have everlasting life?' The sinner may resist this love, may refuse to be drawn to Christ; but if he does not resist, he will be drawn to Jesus; a knowledge of the plan of salvation will lead him to the foot of the cross in repentance for his sins, which have caused the sufferings of God's dear Son."

Do you understand what is happening? He is trying to woo us. He is trying to lead us there. He wants you to see the magnitude of His love. Why? So you will love Him. If you stay away you can never see that love, you can never comprehend it. It is there that you find it, and not from just talking about it or reading about it. It is coming there with your own sins right down in the front of the cross.

The Spirit of Prophecy enlarges on this: "We may have flattered ourselves, as did Nicodemus, that our life has been upright, that our moral character is correct, and think that we need not humble the heart before God, like the common sinner: but when the light from Christ shines into our souls, we shall see how impure we are; we shall discern the selfishness of motive, the enmity against God, that has defiled every act of life. Then we shall know that our own righteousness is indeed as filthy rags, and that the blood of Christ alone can cleanse us from the defilement of sin, and renew our hearts in His own likeness. One ray of the glory of God, one gleam of the purity of Christ, penetrating the soul, makes every spot of defilement painfully distinct, and lays bare the deformity and defects of the human character. It makes apparent the unhallowed desires, the infidelity of the heart, the impurity of the lips. The sinner's acts of disloyalty in making void the law of God, are exposed to his sight…He loathes himself as he views the pure, spotless character of Christ." SC 28,29.

When you come to that condition, you really find yourself at the bottom. The temptation for depression is terrible. You want to flee from that place. So to encourage us, the author continues: "As you see the enormity of sin, as you see yourself as you really are, do not give up to despair. It was sinners that Christ came to save. We have not to reconcile God to us, but—O wondrous love!—God in Christ is 'reconciling the world unto Himself.' 2 Corinthians 5:19. He is wooing by His tender love the hearts of His erring children. No earthly parent could be as patient with the faults and mistakes of his children, as is God with those He seeks to save. No one could plead more tenderly with the transgressor. No human lips ever poured out more tender entreaties to the wanderer than does He. All His promises, His warnings, are but the breathing of unutterable love." SC 35.

We thought He was criticizing us as He shows us how bad we are. He is only showing us how much we need Him. He is saying, "Come unto Me all ye that labor and are heavy laden and I will give you rest. I will take away the load of burdens and the fear. I will bless you. Come unto Me." All His warnings, all His promises, all His entreaties are the breathings of unutterable love, a love that is beyond our understanding. This is what He is doing to us as He makes plain to us our sinfulness and brings about repentance at the cross.

The last of this is the consequences of it: "Confession will not be acceptable to God without sincere repentance and reformation. There must be decided changes in the life; everything offensive to God must be put away." SC 39. Don't get too upset with me. The next sentence is a jewel: "This will be the result of genuine sorrow for sin."

Now let's go back and clear it up, shall we? Confession will be acceptable to God with sincere repentance and reformation. But I cannot change my life, and I cannot even produce sorrow for sin. "There must be decided changes in the life; everything offensive to God must be put away." How? This will be the result of genuine sorrow for sin; and the sorrow for sin is found at Calvary. As I come there, it breaks my heart that I could do all this to Jesus; and as I sorrow for sin, the result is genuine repentance and genuine reformation, and a change in my life—the putting away of everything offensive to God. How can I hurt the One who loves me so much? But you see, I will never comprehend that love, nor my offense, until I am at the cross. Never. There it is all taken care of; and the natural result of being at the cross is true heart-sorrow for sin and a radical change in the life. This is the natural result. When I see myself going the same old way, I may be certain that it has been a long time since I have been to Calvary, and I did not stay very long then. When I find myself crushed with a load of sin and bringing out the bucket of forgiveness a hundred times a day or more, I have almost totally forgotten Calvary. Just one time in confession, if I had come to the cross and knelt there, and recognized I am forgiven because He died for me, then suddenly there are changes in my life. Suddenly I want a new heart like David and I loathe myself; and I ask God to create in me a clean heart and renew a right spirit in me. I don't want to be anymore like I used to be! Is that what Davis said? I never want to see that old sinful fellow again. Make me a new David. I don't like that old fellow. I don't care how nice you have been, when you come to the cross you will find the other half of forgiveness. This is what John meant when he wrote, "If we confess our sins, He is faithful and just to forgive us our sins and to cleanse us from all unrighteousness." This is what it is all about. If we truly confess, He forgives and He cleanses.

"By every sin Jesus is wounded afresh; and as we look upon Him whom we have pierced, we mourn for the sins that have brought anguish upon Him. Such mourning will lead to the renunciation of sin." DA 300. Renunciation—I will never do it again. And friend, this works a marvelous transformation. It is only at the cross that I see myself and want to be somebody different. There He makes me different. I do not make myself different. He makes me different; and as I leave that place I do not want to leave, because there is peace at the cross. You can criticize me all you want. He has taken care of it all. You can find out all of my failures. He has taken care of all of them. You can reject me all you wish. He accepts me just like I am, without even one plea. I do not care what you find wrong with me. At the cross it is all taken care of. I find perfect rest, perfect freedom in Christ at the cross. And there I am safe ever more, and I do not want to leave that place. I just want to linger in that place of quiet rest. How nice and pleasant it is there.

You know, friend, we have been struggling for years to be good enough for God to accept us. We have been struggling for years thinking about how much praying, and how much striving, how much studying or something else we must do so that we can be good enough. And all the time we have been going around the cross, a thousand miles away from it. All the time we have been running in the opposite direction and never looking back. And all the time we came confessing our sins, but left out the blood and the precious love of Jesus. And all the time we acted as if we did not care if Jesus ever lived or died for our sins. And all the time we go unforgiven. Yet we keep on thinking we are forgiven and that we must be a Christian because we go to church, because we keep the right day, because we pay tithe. And Jesus says, "Why do you stay so far from Me if you love Me? And how can you avoid Me at the very place where I expressed supreme love." Greater love hath no man than He that lays down His life for His friends.

God is waiting for Seventh-day Adventists to not only be forgiven for sin, but to be reclaimed from sin. The world is looking for a Christian who is displaying and demonstrating a God like this. For they long to have this peace, this joy, this freedom. They do not know where to find it. They come to our churches and go away empty. They come to our homes and go away empty; and they have gone other places, also. Jesus has been waiting and longing to make us a different people. He wants to give us total forgiveness, which includes a changed life. May God help us to realize how much He really loves us.

WHAT IS RIGHTEOUSNESS?

THE SUBJECT OF RIGHTEOUSNESS is as controversial as the subject of perfection. What is righteousness? Some people say it is just doing your best and God does the rest; and many think they can establish this by certain quotations and texts in the Bible. Some say it is total sinlessness, and they are striving very diligently to be that way. If you believe in situational ethics, then righteousness depends on the circumstances. Therefore, you have many theories to choose from.

Most of us realize that righteousness has some connection with obedience to God's law, for "Righteousness is right doing." COL 312. Also, "All unrighteousness is sin." 1 John 5:17. If unrighteousness is sin, then righteousness must be obedience; and sin is the transgression of the law. Therefore, from these definitions, we are correct in attaching the concept of righteousness to obedience to the law.

When you begin to study this topic of righteousness in connection with the law, you immediately begin to check yourself by the law. Am I breaking the Sabbath by my actions or behavior? Or is something I said lying? Is taking a particular thing stealing? Is using certain expressions and words taking God's name in vain? And so forth. We have a long checklist of thou shalt nots, and we examine ourselves in this light. If we find something in our lives that seems to be a violation, we launch a campaign against it. We begin to pray and study and ask God to bless us. Finally, if by His grace we believe it, suddenly that sin disappears and we cannot see it in our lives anymore. Then we can say, "I am more righteous because one more sin is gone." And hopefully, if we live long enough, they will all be gone. Is that righteousness?

There are many of us who have been trying to do this for years. Is the absence of sins righteousness? If you cannot find any sin in your life, are you righteous? Is righteousness established by not killing, not stealing, not lying, not committing adultery, not taking God's name in vain? Is that righteousness? Many of us have thought so for a long time. If not doing all those things is righteousness, then we would all do well to join the hermits and the monks and leave society and give

67

our minds to holy things. You will find out that you are not terribly tempted to be dishonest in a monastery. There are no temptations to steal there. There are many ways that man has devised to keep himself from the temptation to sin. But is that righteousness? If it is, why stay where you are. Let's all join a monastery immediately. Most of us have thought that the absence of sin in our lives is righteousness.

We ask again: What is righteousness? When Christ looked at obedience to the law as being righteousness, He discussed the law as He understood it. He knew it very well because we understand He was the Giver of the law. A lawyer once came to Jesus and asked, "Master, which is the great commandment in the law?" Matthew 22:36. "Jesus said unto him, Thou shalt love the Lord thy God with all thy heart, and with all thy soul, and with all thy mind. This is the first and great commandment. And the second is like unto it, Thou shalt love thy neighbor as thyself. On these two commandments hang all the law and the prophets." Verses 37-40. Jesus taught that a right concept of the law is embodied in supreme love for God and loving your neighbor as yourselves. This is a right concept of righteousness.

To Jesus, the keeping of the law was not simply the omission of sin. It was the doing of good. Most of us think it is the elimination of sin in our lives. But we often forget what Jesus said in Luke 11:24 about devils being cast out, and leaving the person empty. The devils came back in and filled the void. Just because the sin was gone did not mean there was any righteousness there. When all the sin is gone, a person is only empty. There is nothing good there; the life is just empty of sin. Righteousness is more than the elimination of sin in our lives. Righteousness is not a negative (not killing, not stealing) but a positive. It is love for God and love for our fellow man; and it is doing acts of love with an unselfish motive.

This is more than a profession. The Lord talked about those who professed but did not do. He talked about the two men where one said he would do it but he did not do it; the other fellow said he would not but he did. Jesus said the one who did it was blessed. "Not every one that saith unto Me, Lord, Lord, shall enter into the kingdom of heaven; but he that doeth the will of My Father which is in heaven." Matthew 7:21. The doers are blessed. It is not enough to eliminate wrongdoing. Into my life there must come this loving, this right doing, or I am not righteous. It is not the discontinuance of acts of transgression, but the doing of acts of love for God and for man.

Suppose I have an automobile I wish to sell to you. You are my brother or sister in the faith, and as we are talking a deal, there is a good possibility that if I just deceive you a little bit about the mileage that you would pay me three hundred dollars more. So here is the temptation to lie to you and receive extra money on the deal. Why should I not lie to you? Should I not lie to you because it is against my principles? Should I not lie because liars will be lost? Or should I not lie to you because I love you? If I find myself in that situation, I can say to myself, "If I just told him the speedometer is off, that isn't too bad, is it? I don't want to be lost, but I would sure like to have that money." I find myself torn between two desires: more money and the desire to be saved. Nothing wrong with that, is it? I choose between two desires, and I weigh it back and forth (the gears are grinding in my head), and I find myself wanting to have my cake and eat it too. I finally conclude that this fellow is a member of the church, so I should not lie to him; so I don't lie to him. I go away and say, "Thank God I am not like other people are…I didn't lie." When I kneel for prayer that evening, I say, "You are sure doing good things for me because I did not lie today." But in my heart, I am still dreaming about what I could have done with the extra three hundred dollars. Is that righteousness? I did not lie! I told the truth. Isn't telling the truth righteousness? We have told our children this, haven't we? But if we understand correctly, this is not righteousness.

"The love of God is something more than a mere negation. It is a positive and active principle, a living spring ever flowing to bless others. If the love of Christ dwells in us, we shall not only cherish no hatred towards our fellows, but we shall seek in every way to manifest love toward them." MB 58. In other words, if I really love you because of the love of Christ in my heart, it is not just avoiding doing wrong to you, it is taking every opportunity to do good things for you. That is a different kind of righteousness, is it not? Yet all the time we have been praying, "Lord, keep me from doing wrong things."

Righteousness is very much different than most of us suppose; and I want to show you some quotations about our inability to be righteous, and how different righteousness is from what most of us believe it to be. "Because of his [Adam's] sin, our natures are fallen. We cannot make ourselves righteous. Since we are sinful, unholy, we cannot perfectly obey the holy law. We have no righteousness of our own with which to meet the claims of the law of God." SC 62. We are ill equipped, and we cannot do it. All our attempts at obeying the law are destined to failure.

"Because the law of the Lord is perfect, therefore changeless, it is impossible for sinful men in themselves to meet the standard of its requirement." MB 50. In other words, it is too holy for me to meets its requirements. "The law of God is as holy as He is holy, as perfect as He is perfect. It presents to men the righteousness of God. It is impossible for man, of himself, to keep this law, for the nature of man is depraved, deformed, and wholly unlike the character of God." MB 54. It is natural for us to do the opposite of what the law requires.

Paul talked about this in the book of Romans: "What then? Are we better than they [are the Gentiles better than the Jews?]? No, in no wise: for we have before proved both Jews and Gentiles, that they are all under sin; as it is written, There is none righteous, no, not one." Romans 3:9,10. Neither Jew nor Gentile is righteous. This might discourage those who are trying to be righteous. If you are trying to be righteous of yourselves, you won't like what I am saying. If you have failed and are about to give up, you will like everything I am going to say.

If you read on in Romans chapter 3, it continues talking about our unrighteousness and our inability to keep God's law. After verse 20 comes a transition where a very unique thing takes place. In the first twenty verses, Paul discusses the non-righteous; then it changes in verse 21 with the little word "but." "But now the righteousness of God…." It first talks about the unrighteousness of man and all of man's attempts to be righteous; then it says, "but now" something else has happened—"the righteousness of God without the law is manifested." This righteousness is for us. "Even the righteousness of God which is by faith of Jesus Christ unto all and upon all them that believe." Verse 22. Paul is talking about people who try to be righteous, and he said none of them are. We all try to be and sometimes we think we are, but we are not. He said that this does not mean that all is lost in the pursuit of righteousness. He said there is a better kind—the righteousness of God which is unto all and upon all that believe, and it comes by the faith of Jesus Christ.

This righteousness of Christ is not the righteousness of some person billions of miles away. If you read Philippians 3:9 and put it with Romans 3, you will understand a little about this. Paul prayed about what he might possess when he finished his life: "And be found in Him [Christ], not having mine own righteousness, which is of the law [my attempts to keep it], but that which is through the faith of Christ, the righteousness which is of God by faith." Paul says a human being can have that. It is unto to all that believe. He said he did not want his own righteousness. He only wanted the righteousness of God, which is found in Jesus and comes by faith in Him.

The righteousness of God in Christ is righteousness in a human. The righteousness of God is in divinity. But as Christ lived that Godly life, righteousness was found in a human being who lived just like we live. And that means this righteousness can be for us! And it comes to us in the Person of Jesus.

Paul is saying in Romans 3 that God is asking why we strive to keep the law when all are sinners and unrighteous. God is standing there waiting to give you His righteousness in the person of Jesus. Would you trade one for the other? Why do you try to achieve your own righteousness when He offers you something so much better?

Did you know that Jesus did not claim that His righteousness was His own. "Jesus saith unto him [Philip], have I been so long time with you, and yet hast thou not known me, Philip? He that hath seen me hath seen the Father; and how sayest thou then, Show us the Father. Believest not that I am in the Father, and the Father in Me? The words that I speak unto you I speak not of Myself: but the

Father that dwelleth in Me, He doeth the works." John 14:9,10. The words and righteous works seen in Jesus were not His but the righteousness of the Father in Him.

There are other texts that state this, such as: "When ye have lifted up the Son of man, then shall ye know that I am He, and that I do nothing of Myself; but as My Father hath taught Me, I speak these things." John 8:28. "Then answered Jesus and said unto them, Verily, verily, I say unto you, The Son can do nothing of Himself, but what He seeth the Father do: for what things soever He [the Father] doeth, these also doeth the Son likewise." John 5:19. Therefore, the words He spoke and His acts of righteousness were not His. They were the righteousness of God the Father in Jesus. And this is what is offered to us!

I want you to look at this righteousness of God much more closely, because we have imagined righteousness to be many things. Again, what is righteousness? What is the righteousness I may have, and must have? What is the righteousness that gets us into heaven?

Ellen White wrote: "The righteousness of God is absolute. This righteousness characterizes all His works, all His laws. As God is, so must His people be." 1SM 198. What does the word "absolute" mean? We know basically that it has a high and exalted meaning. Here is what the dictionary says: "Free from imperfection or perfect; positive or certain; free from limit, from restriction or qualification." In other words, it is unlimited righteousness. There is no restriction on it. It is as high as high can be. The definition of absolute is: "determined in itself, and not by anything outside itself." In other words, God's righteousness is not judged by someone or something else. It is determined in itself. It is not dependent or relative. It is ultimate and intrinsic as absolute moral law! There is nothing more exalted or inherent in itself, and in Himself.

One final definition of the noun absolute: "All reality considered as the final or total fact or existence." It is the final, total fact of righteousness. There is nothing after it, and there is nothing more complete.

When you put all these definitions together, the righteousness of God is all of that. That word "absolute" characterizes all His works and all His laws, too. The law is absolute. There is nothing greater, and nothing more perfect.

Do you think you can keep that law? You have to be a good Pharisee and totally deceived to think you can keep that kind of a law. One bad thing about many of us is that we thought we exalted the law when we really depreciated it. We have deprived the world of a correct view of the law, for we have not presented it correctly as the epitome of righteousness. And so people think that they can keep it. Any attempt of a depraved, degraded sinner to keep that law degrades that law. We have been degrading it for years. It is ridiculous to think that sinners can keep that law. It is too perfect, it is too high; and you are only depreciating God and His marvelous law and His government by thinking that you can do it. We must put the law back where it belongs—as absolute.

"His law is a transcript of His own character." COL 315. Any obedience to God's law must be a likeness to God, right? If the law is God's character written down, then obedience to that law makes you like Him, right? Yes, obedience to His law is likeness to Him. Therefore, true obedience is God-likeness. John talks about this: "Beloved, now are we the sons of God, and it doth not yet appear what we shall be: but we know that, when He [Jesus] shall appear, we shall be like Him; for we shall see Him as He is." 1 John 3:2. If we are like Jesus, and Jesus said, "If you have seen me you have seen the Father" (John 14:9), then if we are like Jesus, we are like the Father; and law keeping is having the character of God, or God-likeness. This character, this law, is absolute; and this righteousness, this obedience to God's law, is God-likeness.

Now let's look at it from another viewpoint lest we misunderstand what the righteousness of God really is. John taught that "God is love." 1 John 4:8. As the beloved prophet thought of describing God (and he knew God well because He knew Jesus so well), he proclaimed that God is love. In that one word he described His whole character, of which the law is a more lengthy description. As Moses asked to see God, he saw God's character there in Exodus chapter 34 where in verse 5 He talked about His love. God is love, and since the law is a transcript of His character, His law has to be love. That is why Jesus said: "Love the Lord thy God with all thy heart...and thy neighbor as thyself." Matthew 22:37.

Christ, who knew His Father and in whom the Father dwelt, knew that God's character was in that law. He knew that God was love and so He knew the law was love. Therefore, Paul tells us that "love is the fulfilling of the law." Romans 13:10. Love is perfect obedience to the law. It is supreme love for God and love for your neighbor. That fulfills the law!

I want to come to one conclusion: Love is righteousness, and righteousness is love. If God is love, and the law describes His character, and the law is the character of love, and obedience to that law is love, and obedience is righteousness, then righteousness is love. Do you agree with me? Righteousness is love.

This means that all those years I had been trying to do something else that I called righteousness. Somehow I was totally deceived and missing the boat. Righteousness, if it is love, is not trying avoid hurting you. Righteousness is doing good things for you and blessing you in every way I can think of. That is righteousness, because righteousness is love.

"Blessed are they that hunger and thirst after righteousness, for they shall be filled." Matthew 5:6. Here is Ellen White's comment on this beatitude: "Righteousness is holiness, likeness to God; and God is love (1 John 4:16). It [righteousness] is conformity to the law of God, 'For all Thy commandments are righteousness,' (Psalm 119:172); and 'love is the fulfilling of the law.' (Romans

13:10). Righteousness is love, and love is the light and the life of God. The righteousness of God is embodied in Christ [that love is, you see]. We receive righteousness by receiving Him." MB 18. "Righteousness is love," and never forget that.

If "righteousness is holiness to God...and God is love," then righteousness is love. I am amazed that we have lived so long pursuing righteousness and so few of us have discovered that righteousness is love. If there is love in my heart, planted there by Jesus, then there is love for you, because He loves you tremendously. When there is love in my heart for you, I find it difficult to lie to you or cheat you; and I surely don't have any trouble loving the Lord with all my heart and strength and mind. It is not an attempt to make the outside look perfect or flawless. It is goodness coming out of the heart that embraces and loves humanity. That is Christianity.

There are people in the world dying for lack of real Christianity because they can find so little of it. It is becoming worse and worse because the churches do not offer the love of Christ that will change our lives. We offer all kinds of other things, but we do not offer this. This is a different understanding of righteousness than most of us follow in our lives. It is obedience to the law, but it is far more that that. It is a law of love; so obedience is loving people.

Another statement in the Spirit of Prophecy teaches that righteousness is love: "But notice here that obedience is not a mere outward compliance, but the service of love. The law of God is an expression of His very nature; it is an embodiment of the great principle of love, and hence is the foundation of His government in heaven and earth. If our hearts are renewed in the likeness of God [talking about the new birth], if the divine love is implanted in the soul, will not the law of God be carried out in the life? When the principle of love is implanted in the heart, when man is renewed after the image of Him that created him, the new covenant promise is fulfilled, 'I will put My laws into their hearts, and in their minds will I write them.' And if the law is written in the heart, will it not shape the life? Obedience—the service and allegiance of love—is the true sign of discipleship." SC 60.

Obedience is the service and allegiance of love. That is a different kind of obedience. Don't you like that? If we have someone serving us and allegiant to us out of love, doesn't that make us feel good? Wouldn't you like to be sweet to someone else? If it is good to receive this love, how much more blessed to give it? Then it is a double blessing—you as the giver, they as the receiver.

If we go back to Romans 3:10 where we started, it says "There is none righteous." If you use the definition that righteousness is love, it says there are none who love. Paul said we are no better than the Jews. They did not love and neither do we. You say, now wait a minute, are you telling me that there are none that love? That seems quite extreme.

In the Bible we find the fall of Adam and Eve. After one sin—just one—and probably on the same day, by that one sin, Adam and Eve were estranged from each other. One sin in one day; because when God came that evening and asked, "Where are you?" Adam said, "Eve did it." And she said, "The serpent did it." Believe me, Eve knew that Adam did not love her anymore. They were birds of a feather in sin so they were hiding together; but not in affection. They were ashamed. Look at how little love remained after just one day from just one sin. And in only one generation, from a perfect place in perfect love, sin brought about the complete opposite of love; for Cain did the opposite of love—he killed his brother. In one generation we see love on one extreme and hatred and murder on the other. He hated his brother and killed him. Why? One sin brought about this degeneracy and love was gone.

What is it like after six thousand years of sin? We have been deceiving ourselves about this thing called love. If one sin brought about such estrangement and lack of love, think of what six thousand years has accomplished. Our understanding of love is extremely feeble; and remember that righteousness is love and love is righteousness. Our understanding of righteousness is very meager. When the Bible says there is none righteous, it means there is none loving. We find in our hearts this selfishness coming up all the time. The love that is of God is a self-renouncing love, a self-denying love, a self-sacrificing love. Love not only forgets itself, it does good things for other people. It plans good things for other people. That is genuine love that Christ demonstrated to us. This is a most unusual type of love, and righteousness is love.

Now do you understand why we cannot produce that kind of love? If one sin caused all that separation, all that estrangement, and caused that love to flee away from Adam's heart after one sin, just think how we have been chasing love out of our lives for years. We cannot produce it, and yet this love is the fulfillment of God's law. It is perfect righteousness. Where does it come from? It only comes from Jesus.

Jesus said: "A new commandment I give unto you, That ye love one another; as I have loved you, that ye also love one another." 1 John 13:34. Do you love like Jesus loved? I don't. I thought I did once in a while. All day long Jesus cared for people. The people His family hated and His nation hated, He loved. It did not matter who they were. He loved them all. He loved those people the Jews called "dogs," and taught His disciples to love them, also. And when He was hanging on Calvary's cross, He said, "Father, forgive them." Do you call that love? That is a different kind of love than I have. I cannot manufacture it; I cannot plan for it; I cannot conceive of it. I must receive it from God. God so loved the world that He gave to us His only begotten Son. His love for us was in Jesus. Righteousness is found in Christ. We receive righteousness by receiving Him. Love is found in Jesus. We receive love by receiving Jesus. I cannot do something that takes the place of it. I must receive it until it changes my whole life, and makes me love those I once hated. A whole transformation takes place. Why? Because the love of Christ has come into my soul.

"While the law is holy, the Jews could not attain righteousness by their own efforts to keep the law. The disciples of Christ must obtain righteousness of a different character from that of the Pharisees if they would enter the kingdom of heaven. God offered in His Son the perfect righteousness of the law. If they would open their hearts fully to receive Christ, then the very life of God—His love—would dwell in them, transforming them into His own likeness. And thus through God's free gift, they would possess the righteousness which the law requires." MB 54,55. Righteousness and love are in Jesus. When I open my heart and receive Him, the very life of God—His love—will abide in me; and He will change my life by that love until that very righteousness the law requires is in me and demonstrated in my life.

All that I am trying to say in defining righteousness is wrapped up in the Sermon on the Mount, and especially the conclusion of that sermon. What is righteousness? It is love. That is obedience to the law, for the law is love. It is the character of the Father, and that is love. It is likeness to God, and that is love. All of this is wrapped up in one very small statement in Matthew 5:48: "Be ye therefore perfect, even as your Father which is in heaven is perfect." He could have said, "Be ye therefore righteous" or "loving." We look at that and say, "I give up; I will never be that good." Stop looking at yourself. Who do you think you are? It does not say look at yourself. It says look at the Father; and look unto Jesus, the author and finisher of our faith. Is He able to do that? He did not say to look at yourself and see if you are as good as the Father. He did not say that at all!

"The Jews had been wearily toiling to reach perfection by their own efforts, and they had failed. Christ has already told them that their righteousness could never enter the kingdom of heaven [do you ever feel that way?]. Now He points out to them the character of the righteousness that all who enter heaven will possess. Throughout the Sermon on the Mount He describes its fruits [the fruits of righteousness], and now in one sentence He points out its source and its nature: be perfect as God is perfect. The law is but a transcript of the character of God. Behold in your heavenly Father a perfect manifestation of the principles that are the foundation of His government. God is love. Like rays of light from the sun, love and light and joy flow out from Him to all His creatures. It is His nature to give. His very life is the outflow of unselfish love…He tells us to be perfect as He is, in the same manner [not to the same degree]. We are to be centers of light and blessing to our little circle, even as He is to the universe. We have nothing of ourselves, but the light of His love shines upon us. We are to reflect its brightness. 'In His borrowed goodness good,' [not mine—I am only a steward of His goodness] we may be perfect in our sphere, even as God is perfect in His." MB 77,78. He has a huge circle. I have a small circle. He is saying I should be a center of light to my little circle. We can do that if He abides in us.

She goes on: "Jesus said, Be perfect as your Father is perfect. If you are the children of God you are partakers of His nature, and you cannot but be like Him." It isn't striving to be good. You cannot avoid it if you partake of His nature. "Every child lives by the life of his father. If you are God's children, begotten by His Spirit, you live by the life of God. In Christ dwells 'all the fullness of the Godhead bodily' (Colossians 2:9); and the life of Jesus is made manifest 'in our mortal flesh' (2 Corinthians 4:11). That life in you will produce the same character and manifest the same works as it did in Him. Thus you will be in harmony with every precept of His law; for 'the law of the Lord is perfect, restoring the soul.' Psalm 19:7, margin. Through love 'the righteousness of the law' will be fulfilled in us, who walk not after the flesh, but after the Spirit. Romans 8:4."

This is an amazing thing. What is righteousness? It is obedience to the law. What is the law? Love, a transcript of God's character, and God is love. Righteousness is love. God so loved that He gave. He gave me the Prince of love, did He not? He gave me the God of love. Jesus lived a life of love for me and for His Father. He loved me so much that He finally gave His life for me. Behold what manner of love! And by beholding that love, I am transformed into His likeness. I love Christ and I love you until I am like Jesus. And when I am like Jesus I am like His Father. But now is manifest the righteousness of God unto all and upon all them that believe. It comes by faith in Christ.

It is our misunderstanding of righteousness that has led us into a weary struggle. We have pled with God to stop us from sinning, and God has been saying all along that He wants to make us lovers. We get the cart before the horse. The power that enables a person to love other people is in Jesus. When you love them, you won't hate them, you won't lie to them, you won't cheat them, you won't kill them. But you cannot make yourself like that. He transforms all who will receive Him and He makes them right. It is His love—His righteousness—that comes into me. I can receive that. I can believe it with all my heart. I can reach out and embrace it. In fact, it is difficult not to embrace it because I want to so much. Don't you? It is so wonderful to be loved like this.

We have a problem understanding how He can love us so much when we can be so unloving and unrighteous. But He does. He loved David who was a murderer. He loved Peter who cut off the ear of that servant (he wasn't aiming at his ear). He loved Moses who was going to deliver Israel by killing the Egyptian. Does He love you? Surely He does. How much He wants that love to be in our hearts, so that the world will see God in all His love and all His righteousness and beauty. He is so precious to us that we can hardly wait for Jesus to come back;

and He will carry us up through the heavens and introduce us to His Father, the God of all love and light. And we will fall down and adore Him, this God who is love. And over and over we will sing "Hallelujah!" And we will never get tired of telling Him how much we love Him. And He will never get tired of listening, because He is a God of love.

Don't you want to be like Him? I do. And it is so easy to reach out and receive the gift of heaven—the perfect gift of love. God can make the hardest soul a loving Christian. May God help us to be holy, to be righteous, to be loving, even as He is righteous.

RIGHTEOUS— BY EXAMPLE OR BY A GIFT?

MANY BELIEVE THAT RIGHTEOUSNESS by faith is only following Christ as our example, and as we copy Him we become righteous. There are many quotations and Bible texts that seem to support this idea. Others believe that the Bible and Spirit of Prophecy present Christ as our substitute in righteousness as well as in death. They say that He lived a righteous life on our behalf, that His righteousness is offered in place of our sinfulness, and since I have no righteousness of my own and cannot produce it, He literally is righteousness for me, and not merely the example, or pattern, of righteousness.

It is apparent that these two ideas are in conflict, for if Christ is doing something for me and offers to give His righteousness to me, then I do not receive righteousness by copying Him. On the other hand, if I must copy Christ in order to be righteous, then righteousness is not something He has done for me, nor do I receive it as a gift.

Most people hold one or the other of these two views. Whatever philosophy you establish and accept is the way you will attempt to live Christ our righteousness. There are many conflicting ideas about Christ our righteousness, and many who hold a particular view fully believe that they are following the truth about this subject. Those who claim to follow Christ as their pattern say *that* is Christ our righteousness. Those who say we receive righteousness as a gift say *that* is Christ our righteousness. This is another one of those problem areas that cause us to misunderstand and misinterpret this subject.

Let us first examine Christ as our example. There are many texts in the Bible that seem to say this. "A new commandment I give unto you, That ye love one another; as I have loved you, that ye also love one another." John 13:34. Jesus seems to be saying here that we are to love as He loved.

Here is a similar test: "He that saith he abideth in Him ought himself also so to walk, even as He walked." 1 John 2:6. In other words, live just like He lived.

"For even hereunto were ye called: because Christ also suffered for us, leaving us an example, that ye should follow His steps: Who did no sin, neither was guile found in His mouth." 1 Peter 2:21,22. We are to follow in the steps of Christ who suffered, who did no sin, and who had no guile. He was righteous, and we assume we will be righteous if we follow Him by suffering, committing no sin, and by removing all guile from our hearts.

The wording in this next text is different but it says essentially the same thing: "Know ye not, that so many of us as were baptized into Jesus Christ were baptized into His death? There we are buried with Him by baptism into death: that like as Christ was raised up from the dead by the glory of the Father, even so we also should walk in newness of life. For if we have been planted together in the likeness of His death, we shall be also in the likeness of His resurrection: Knowing this, that our old man is crucified with Him, that the body of sin might be destroyed, that henceforth we should not serve sin." Romans 6:3-6. If you are like Him in death and burial, you will be like Him in resurrection. Do as I do is what it says to many people.

Now I want to ask you a question: Are we righteous because we do right things? If I flawlessly follow the pattern of Jesus, will I be righteous? Is the doing of right things righteousness? Many think it is, and have thought that for years. They have assumed that if they are doing everything just right, then they are going to be saved. They think that is righteousness.

There are a few quotations that seem to present Christ as our example and as our pattern. "Christ is our pattern; His life was an example of good works." 1T 505.

"How many imitate the great Exemplar? All who have professed to be followers of Christ have, in taking this step, pledged themselves to walk even as He walked." 2T 32.

"A pattern has been given you...If you turn from this correct, this perfect pattern, and take an incorrect one...your course of action will receive its merited reward; your life will be a failure." 2T 396. You have a correct pattern. If you turn from the correct one to follow an incorrect one, your life will be a failure and you will be lost.

"It is not by looking away from Him that we imitate the life of Jesus, but by trying through faith and love and by earnest, persevering effort to approach the perfect Pattern." 6BC 1098,1099.

"All should copy the Pattern as closely as possible." 5T 254.

"You are not excusable for not living a Christ-like life. Christ came to this world, subject to His Father's will, for one great purpose—to show men and women what God desires them to be and what they may be." MM 42.

If you go and look up these quotations, you will note that I omitted a few words in two of them. The reason I did that is because I wanted to show you how most people read them. Stay with me and I will come back to these quotations again later.

Now we will ask some difficult questions. Can we attain to righteousness merely by imitating, or copying the right pattern? If that is true, the best copycat is the best Christian, right? Did Jesus in His sermon on the mount say blessed are the copycats for they shall inherit the kingdom of heaven? If you can copy Jesus and be righteous, why could we not copy the law and be righteous? Isn't the law righteous? And isn't the law God's character written down? So why not just copy the law and be righteous? And what difference does it make if we are copying the law or copying Jesus?

Paul discussed our inability to copy the law when he wrote: "For what the law could not do, in that it was weak through the flesh, God sending His own Son in the likeness of sinful flesh, and for sin, condemned sin in the flesh: That the righteousness of the law might be fulfilled in us, who walk not after the flesh, but after the Spirit." Romans 8:3,4. There are some things the law cannot do. The law cannot cause us to be obedient to the law. Why? Because it is dependent on weak, human flesh. If I could not copy the law because of the weakness of my flesh, how can I copy Jesus with the same flesh? So it does not matter what the pattern is if you are dependent on man's inability. Something has to be done about that before we can do any copying of any kind. I am unable to copy the pattern of the law or of Christ because of my weak, human flesh.

Some will reason that justification is a gift of God, and following the Pattern is sanctification. That seems to be quite a logical concept, so I want to take a little detour and discuss sanctification in that context.

Concerning sanctification and righteousness, Paul wrote: "But of Him are ye in Christ Jesus, who of God is made unto us wisdom, and righteousness, and sanctification, and redemption." 1Corinthians 1:30. It does not sound like we copy Him to be sanctified, does it? It says He is "made" unto us sanctification. That is a vastly different thing than copying Him.

"And be found in Him, not having mine own righteousness, which is of the law, but that which is through the faith of Christ, the righteousness which is of God by faith." Philippians 3:9. In the context here, as Paul talks about his hope of resurrection, he seems to say that when he has finished his life, he does not want his own righteousness. He wants to have Christ's. Certainly when Paul finished his life, he was sanctified. Yet at that point (at the end of his life) he still does not want his own righteousness.

Some people say that in righteousness by faith there is a starting point where you have lots of Christ's righteousness, but as you go along in the Christian life and begin to grow, you need less and less of His righteousness until finally you have all of your own. Paul does not see it that way at all. He says that at the end of his life, he does not want any of his own righteousness. Sanctification, then, is not necessarily copying the pattern.

"You are powerless to do good, and cannot better your condition. Apart from Christ we have no merit, no righteousness. Our sinfulness, our weakness, our human imperfection makes it impossible that we should appear before God unless we are clothed in Christ's spotless righteousness. 1SM 333.

"The righteousness of Christ is presented as a free gift to the sinner if he will accept it. He has nothing of his own but what is tainted and corrupted, polluted with sin, utterly repulsive to a pure and holy God. Only through the righteous character of Jesus Christ can man come nigh to God." 1SM 342.

And one more: "In Him [Christ], is our hope, our justification, our righteousness." 1SM 351. It seems that all of righteousness is found in Jesus; that none is found in us, and that man is incapable of following the Pattern. Man cannot perform although he would like to. The things he wants to do he cannot do because of the weakness of the flesh.

Why does the Bible and the Spirit of Prophecy teach us to copy the Pattern? Why does Ellen White call Christ the Pattern and the Example and say we should imitate and copy Him? There are two very good reasons. When Jesus came to His people, the Jews, they were always discussing the law and righteousness. If asked to define righteousness, they would say it is to do what the law says (or at least their interpretation of the law). Jesus did not agree with them. Both Jesus and the Jews believed in the law, but they did not both agree on what obedience to the law is. They had two different opinions. The Jews thought they knew what the law said, but Jesus, as the great I AM, said He wrote the law. He essentially said that He was the law in human flesh and the standard of righteousness.

This was made clear in an article by Ellen White titled "Christ the Impersonation of the Law" where she wrote: "He came to live out the law, and His words and character were daily a correct exposition of the law of God…..Jesus was a living manifestation of what the law was…" ST, March 14, 1985. Jesus tried to convey to the Jews that what the law says is what He is. The Jews were confused as to what constitutes obedience to the law; and a dispute about what the law really says continues to this day. Jesus says you can argue all you want, but the righteousness of the law is what He is. If your ideas about righteousness do not agree with what He is, then your ideas are wrong.

Christ is the pattern of the standard of righteousness. We are to copy the standard. To be righteous you must be like Him. The Bible says when He comes we shall be like Him. He will be reproduced in us. He does not say that we are to copy Him in His actions, or try to mimic Him. He says that He is the standard of righteousness and that there is no other standard. He is the goal of righteousness. He is the goal to be attained. He is righteousness.

There is a second reason why He is called the Pattern, and it is a bit different than what many think it means. He is not only what righteousness is, but He is how righteousness is achieved. He is both the *what* and the *how* of righteousness. Of course, we have problems when we start talking about the *how* of righteousness. The method by which Christ lived that righteous life was by perfect faith and trust in His Father Therefore, Jesus could say that the words He spoke and the works He did were not His, but those of the Father. He said He lived by faith in the Father. And if we live by faith in Christ, we live righteously. We, by faith, receive righteousness by receiving Him. Christ is the pattern by the way righteousness is accomplished and by the standard of righteousness. There is no other righteousness, and there is no other way.

Paul discussed this when he talked about the righteousness of God that we receive: "Even the righteousness of God which is by faith of Jesus Christ unto all and upon all them that believe." Romans 3:22. Jesus was righteous because He lived by faith in the Father. If we live by faith in Christ, we may live by His righteousness and be righteous.

This is different than copying actions. Consider how when a man wishes to learn how to drive, he is given a driving instructor. They go through all the streets, up and down the freeways, practicing how to park and back up. Eventually the man can do everything the instructor does. Then he says, "Now I know how to drive like the instructor." Does he? Of course not. There is more to driving than mechanical movements of a wheel and turn signal and brakes and gas pedal. Good driving is more than going through the motions. The instructor has been driving for many years and has learned judgment by experience. You cannot teach judgment in a driving course. We see many foolish people who think they can drive well because they completed a driving course. I was like that when I went to flying school When I finished flying school, I could do all the things the instructor could do; but I was a flying fool. I could fly but I did not have any sense. The neighbors who lived close to where we used to fly knew that by the way we blew the shingles off their roofs. My instructor never did that. There were a lot of things he would not do that I did. He had better judgment.

There are a lot of things that Jesus will not do that Christians do, because Christians assume they can do like He does; but it is an assumption. The doing of certain actions is not being a righteous person. Righteousness is not simply doing what is right. Righteousness is being right. There is a vast difference. A fish does not swim to prove it is a fish. It swims because it is a fish. A Christian does not do righteousness to prove he is righteous. He does righteousness because he is righteous.

We can do the same thing with righteousness by faith as the Jews did with the ceremonial law. The Lord gave them specific instructions for the ceremonial law through a vision He gave to Moses. If you committed a sin you were to bring a sacrifice; and He told them what kind, where to bring it, and all the things to do. Over and over they would come with a sacrifice, kill the sacrifice, then say they are forgiven and righteous. By the time of Isaiah, the Lord said He was sick of their sacrifices. They thought their endless sacrificing was righteousness, but it was nothing but the bloodthirsty killing of thousands of animals. God tried to convey to them that it was not what they were doing (killing all those animals) that made them righteous. Those animals were only a symbol of Christ and His love and death for them. If they did not see Him dying for their sins, if they did not see the fulfillment of the symbol, they were as unrighteous as can be! They were doing everything right but they were lost!

The Jews thought that righteousness was merely the doing of right things. And we can copy the Pattern in much right doing and be as unrighteous as they were because our right doing can be just plain selfish and a way of trying to earn our way to heaven. It is not the doing. It is not what you do on the outside. If Christ were inside their hearts, they would become broken-hearted when having to kill that animal. The day must have come when they liked to kill animals, or they wouldn't have killed so many. The day must have come when they were hardened on the inside. How could they kill animals to the extent that they did and yet think they were righteous before God?

The Lord knew that the human heart did not like to kill. The system of animal sacrifices was to be a divine deterrent that would turn them around from habitual sin, and bring about repentance. The Jews fell into the deception of believing that they could be saved by following the pattern outlined by Moses in the ceremonial law. We can fall into the same trap by thinking that if we only imitate Jesus, we will be saved.

Righteousness is not achieved by trying to mimic Jesus. "Having made us righteous through the imputed righteousness of Christ…" 1SM 394. We are made righteous by something He puts into us or imputes to us. So it is not a mere following of a pattern. It is something that happens to us that He causes. We must be born again. In other words, we must receive new hearts that "are created in righteousness and true holiness." Ephesians 4:24. When I get a new heart, things are different. Righteousness is of the heart, not of the hand or the tongue or the eye or the appetite. It is of the heart. That is where righteousness is. If I do not have a new heart, my hands may do right things but for the wrong reasons. Righteousness is not something that I do on the outside, but something that comes from the inside of me which God has put there, which is the new heart.

Christ had much to say about that, especially in Matthew 25 where He talked about people who clean up the outside of the cup so nicely, but leave the inside dirty. He said that people like that are nothing but beautiful tombstones, but inside they are just filled with dead men's bones. They emphasize the outside and never worry about the heart. Righteousness is of the heart. All that right doing will accomplish nothing, no matter how right it is.

"Let this mind be in you, which was also in Christ Jesus." Philippians 2:5. "In order to serve Him aright [which is the doing], we must be born of the divine Spirit. This will purify the heart and renew the mind, giving us a new capacity for knowing and loving God. It will give us a willing obedience to all His requirements. This is true worship." DA 189. This "new capacity for knowing and loving God" is an unusual thing. When we are unconverted, we do not know what it is like to be converted; but we assume we do because we assume we are converted. We go on and on thinking we know and thinking we love; and all the time based on a wrong concept.

This righteousness the devil throws at us is a counterfeit, and a counterfeit looks very much like the real thing. A person might look like a Christian and not be a Christian because they lack that new heart. When you set out to copy the pattern, there is always the danger that you only have the appearance of righteousness. The Lord looks on the heart, but man does not see the heart. In fact, we do not even want to look at the heart. We prefer to judge by appearances. If you do not think so, listen to our gossip everyday. We are everlastingly judging by appearances. We like that. We indulge it. We swear up and down that we are right in how we judge people based on what appears to us as sins they commit; and thus we feel justified in telling the neighbors about what we saw another person doing. What did we see? Externals. What do we know about the heart? Nothing. Have you never been guilty of judging people by their external behavior? Our ignorance is abominable.

This matter of following the Pattern, if not properly put into perspective, can be a dangerous trap. When Christ is in my heart, I have a new capacity for knowing and loving Him. I begin to understand things I never saw before. Things that were obscure and dark before are now plain to me; and I marvel at how I could have misunderstood it before.

At the heart of all this is a statement of Jesus: "If ye love Me, keep My commandments." John 14:15. If you do not love Him, don't try, for all your trying is a counterfeit. If you love Him, then and only then copy the Pattern. Without the love, you need not bother trying.

This is the entire secret about following the Pattern. The Bible says that God is love, and Jesus taught that the law is love. And love is the fulfilling of the law (Romans 13:10). Obedience to the law is righteousness; therefore, the righteousness that is obedience to a law of love is also love. "Righteousness is love." MB 18. Love is not what I do with my hands necessarily, but what I have in my heart. Many people do nice things with their hands that seem to be acts of love, but something is missing. But when love is in the heart, then you know it is genuine love. You sense it, you perceive it, and you respond with love. Love is not something you can act out or put on. Love comes out of the inside of you—if Jesus is in the heart. God is love. His very Being is love. He does not love to prove that He is righteous. He loves because He is love.

Truly understanding that God is love does something for my heart. It changes me on the inside, and I begin to love Him in return. "When, as erring, sinful beings, we come to Christ and become partakers of His pardoning grace, love springs up in the heart. Every burden is light; for the yoke that Christ imposes is easy. Duty becomes a delight, and sacrifice a pleasure. The path that before seemed shrouded in darkness, becomes bright with beams from the Sun of Righteousness. The loveliness of the character of Christ will be seen in His followers. It was His delight to do the will of God. Love to God, zeal for His glory, was the controlling power in our Saviour's life. Love beautified and ennobled all His actions. Love is of God. The unconsecrated heart cannot originate or produce it. It is found only in the heart where Jesus reigns. 'We love because He first loved us.' In the heart renewed by divine grace, love is the principle of action. It modifies the character, governs the impulses, controls the passions, subdues enmity, and ennobles the affections. This love, cherished in the soul, sweetens the life, and sheds a refining influence on all around." SC 59. Not until Christ comes into the heart is there genuine love for God and for our fellow man; but when this love comes in, we are righteous. If love is righteousness, when Christ by His love is there, that love is righteousness.

"When Christ dwells in the heart, the soul will be so filled with His love, with the joy of communion with Him, that it will cleave to Him; and in the contemplation of Him, self will be forgotten [this is copying the Pattern]. Love to Christ will be the spring of action. Those who feel the constraining love of God, do not ask how little may be given to meet the requirements of God; they do not ask for the lowest standard, but aim at perfect conformity to the will of their Redeemer. With earnest desire they yield all, and manifest an interest proportionate to the value of the object that they seek. A profession of Christ without this deep love, is mere talk, dry formality, and heavy drudgery." SC 44,45. When He comes into the heart, the heart is filled with love.

When you love Him, you want to behold Him. You cannot take your eyes off of Him. The Bible talks about this in 2 Corinthians 3:18 where it says by beholding Him, we are transformed into the same image or likeness. But why do we behold Him? You only behold those things for a long time that you adore. This is why the disciple John looked to Jesus. "Even John, the beloved disciple, the one who most fully reflected the likeness of the Saviour, did not naturally possess that loveliness of character...But as the character of the Divine One was manifested to him, he saw his own deficiency, and was humbled by the knowledge. The strength and patience, the power and tenderness, the majesty and meekness, that he beheld in the daily life of the Son of God, filled his soul with admiration and love. Day by day his heart was drawn out toward Christ, until he lost sight of self in love for his Master. His resentful, ambitious temper was yielded to the molding power of Christ. The regenerating influence of the Holy Spirit renewed his heart. The power of the love of Christ wrought a transformation of character. This is the sure result of union with Jesus. When Christ abides in the heart, the whole nature is transformed. Christ's Spirit, His love, softens the heart, subdues the soul, and arises the thoughts and desires toward God and heaven." SC 73. I keep looking at Him, and I can never fill my soul with enough. He grows more lovely every minute I look at Him, and I am drawn out of myself until I can no longer see myself. All I see is the lovely Jesus. Then, copying the Pattern is fun; otherwise it is "mere talk, dry formality, and heavy drudgery."

To sit and behold Jesus, to meditate on Him, to be absorbed in Him, to revel in Him is a fantastic experience. And only those who love Him will do it. They will like to talk about Him, they will like to witness concerning Him, and not so much about cold, sterile doctrines. Jesus is not a theory. He is an intimate, living Being. He lived all those doctrines. Tell people about Jesus. Loving people is practical. We can do that. When we love the Pattern, we can copy Him and we can tell people about Him.

What is righteousness? Is it the following or imitating of a pattern, or is it loving Jesus (remember that righteousness is love)? As we love Jesus, there is righteousness in us. We do the right things because we love Him. But the righteousness is not what we do. Righteousness is Whom we have abiding in our hearts. God first implants this love in our hearts. As I behold that love and grace, I am transformed—I have a renewed heart with a greater capacity for knowing and loving God. As I comprehend more about forgiveness and how He first loved me, I understand even more. When we see ourselves forgiven, we know that not only are the sins of the past gone, we know that we belong to the family of God and that we are reinstated as though we had never sinned. We are treated as righteous because God has declared us righteous. I take in the fullness of what it means to be forgiven, and see that I am not only a sinner forgiven, but that now I am reinstated as a righteous person, belonging to the family of God. And God says to all the angels in heaven, "This man is righteous." And I say, "Glory to God in the highest! Praise His name!" Something has happened to me. Something is different. And what Jesus does for me in changing my life is a gift. I have not earned a thing. It is all by His grace. I copy the Pattern because the gift of love is in my heart. This loving Christ with all my heart is righteousness, and not the copying of the Pattern. Righteousness is the result of the love God has placed in my heart. After that love is there, there is the drawing of my mind and heart out to Him, and I cannot stay away from Him.

Let's go back to two previous quotes and add in the words we omitted. The first quote is used by those who teach that righteousness is achieved by copying Jesus: "Christ is our pattern; His life was an example of good works." 1T 505. But notice what follows: "He was a man of sorrows and acquainted with grief....Compare your course of life with that of your Master, who made so great a sacrifice that you might be saved. He frequently spent the entire night upon the damp ground in agonizing prayer. You are seeking your own pleasure. Listen to the vain, frivolous conversation...Is this imitating the pattern?" In other words, can you really imitate the Pattern? Or is your life so filled with selfishness that you could never come close to copying the life of Jesus?

Here is the second quote: "You are not excusable for living an un-Christlike life. Christ came to this world, subject to His Father's will, for one great purpose—to show men and women what God desires them to be and what they may be." When I quoted this originally, I left out three words. When I put them in, it shows how we *should* understand this quote: "...to show men and women what God desires them to be and what, *through His grace,* they may be." MM 42. Note that it is "through His grace" that we are to do what God desires us to do.

The next paragraph (on page 42) sheds even more light: "But I do not begin to write this letter to condemn you, but to encourage you to look away from sinful examples to the perfect Example, to point you to the path of peace and holiness. The Lord's merciful love is still for you. But He would have you follow a better way than you have followed in the past. This you are to do, not by keeping our eyes fixed on the defective lives of professing Christians, but by beholding Christ, the Sent of God, who in this world and in human nature lived a pure, noble, perfect life, setting an example that all may safely follow. The Lord is reaching out His hand to save you. I long to see you responding to His invitation."

This is so different from the way many view the idea of following the Pattern. Only if His grace and love abide in our hearts can we copy Him. If you love Him, copy Him. If that love and grace is not there, your efforts at copying Jesus are futile.

"It is not by looking away from Him that we imitate the life of Jesus, but by talking of Him, by dwelling upon His perfection, by seeking to refine the tastes and elevating the character, by trying *through faith and love* [not just by trying], and by earnest, persevering effort to approach the perfect Pattern. By having a knowledge of Christ, His words, His habits, and His lessons of instruction, we borrow the virtues of the character we have closely studied, and become imbued with the Spirit we have so much admired. Jesus becomes to us the Chiefest among ten thousand, the One altogether lovely." 6BC 1098,1099.

When Christ becomes the Chiefest among ten thousand to me, I won't even consider following self or Satan. There is no one like Jesus. I sit at His feet charmed, because no one ever cared for me like Jesus. Like John the beloved who leaned on Jesus' breast, we do not care what happens just as long as we can be with Jesus. And the Pattern becomes wonderful because He is altogether lovely. He is the epitome and standard of righteousness, and righteousness is love. Jesus so loved me, how can I help but love Him? And as I love Him, I behold Him. That is copying the Pattern.

But it is not the copying that makes me righteous. It is that wonderful love put into my heart to give me a new capacity for knowing and loving God and my fellow man. That is righteousness. I imitate Him because I love Him so much.

And I do the right things because the love I have in my heart is righteousness. I have the right spirit and motivation because the Spirit of Jesus and the love of God are in my heart.

I believe with all my heart that Christ is trying to touch your heart. He doesn't just worry about what your hands do, and your lips say, and what you eat. He is asking, "Do you love Me? Haven't I loved you. Don't I still love you? Haven't I forgiven you for a mountain of debts of sin? And haven't I imputed you My righteousness? Don't you have much to love Me for? Haven't I pronounced you righteous before the heavenly universe? Don't you know that you are accepted in Me as though you had never sinned? Don't you belong to My family? Aren't you overjoyed that I am so good to you? Why do you look elsewhere for righteousness? How can you reject so much love?"

This is what Christ wants to do for us. This will make us different. And the world will take knowledge that we have been with Jesus, because we are so different. We will possess that softening, sweetening influence. And the world will marvel that such sinners as we could become like Jesus. May God grant you this marvelous experience.

TWO MEN,
TWO ACTS,
TWO RESULTS

THE TERM CHRIST OUR righteousness implies that someone else is righteous for us, that we have substitutionary righteousness, that someone takes our place not only in death but also in righteousness. Most Christians can accept the idea that Christ died in their place, but it becomes a little more difficult to understand and accept the idea that He lived, or is righteous, on my behalf, and takes my place that way. So this topic in and of itself causes us uncertainty. This study deals with this idea that Christ is the One who takes my place to provide righteousness for me on my behalf.

There are two men who are involved in a proper understanding of Christ our righteousness. The first of these two men is identified by the apostle Paul: "Wherefore, as by one man [Adam], sin entered into the world, and death by sin; and so death passed upon all men, for that all have sinned" Romans 5:12. The other Man you will find in verse 15: "But not as the offence, so also is the free gift. For if through the offence of one many be dead, much more the grace of God, and the gift by grace, which is by one Man, Jesus Christ, hath abounded unto many." Here are the two men. I call them "men" because Jesus was called the "Man Christ Jesus"; and in no way do we deny or neglect His divinity by saying this. Paul also refers to them as the two Adams in 1 Corinthians 15 (the first Adam and the second Adam).

Paul is here explaining that condemnation and judgment came from the first Adam; and that from the second Adam there is life, justification, and righteousness. These are the results of the acts of the two persons. One brought death upon mankind, the other brought life.

Verse 18 is a unique verse in the Bible, and one which we want to look at very closely: "Therefore as by the offence of one judgment came upon all men to condemnation; even so by the righteousness of one the free gift came upon all men unto justification of life." Other translations have variations of this. In the Revised Standard Version it reads, "One man's trespass [singular]"; when in the King James Version it says "by the offence of one." In the American Standard Version it reads, "by one transgression and one act of righteousness." In the Good

News Version it reads, "one sin and one righteous act." These verses establish that there was one act performed by each of the two Adams, and each of those acts is very unique in that it had a major result upon the condition of mankind. By one act of Adam, certain things happen to us. By the act of the second Adam, certain things also happen to us. One of those acts was an act of sin, and the other act was one of perfect righteousness.

Paul described the results of those two acts: "For as by one man's [Adam's] disobedience many were made sinners, so by the obedience of One shall many be made righteous." Romans 5:19. Almost all translations agree with the fact that by one man's disobedience, many were made sinners. The disobedience, according to verse 18, is isolated to one act of sin; and then by one Man's single act of perfect righteousness, many are made righteous. Those two acts are what we want to discuss in detail.

Some people become alarmed about this because when we talk about the one act of Adam, we get very close to original sin, and many people do not know what to think about the idea of original sin. Remember that the genuine and the counterfeit are not total opposites. They are very similar. A counterfeit is something that can deceive us. Don't go too far away from the teaching of original sin or you might miss the truth entirely. Stay close to it for there is much there if we understand it correctly.

Note that verse 18 says that "judgment came upon all men to condemnation" by the offence of one man, and that "by the righteousness of One the free gift came upon all men unto justification." These are things that *come* to us. But verse 19 talks about something that it does *to* us. "For as by one man's disobedience many were made sinners, so by the obedience of One shall many be made righteous." By the sin of Adam, we were made sinners. By the obedience of Christ we are made righteous.

How can one person make another sinful? How can one person make another righteous? That is not easy for us to understand. Both of these two persons are called "Adam," and both the first and second Adam had unique qualities and positions. Adam was the father of all living. Every person who has ever lived has come from Adam.

Christ is also called "the everlasting Father." Isaiah 9:6. By redemption He is called a quickening Spirit in 1 Corinthians 15. All those who come to Christ He quickens, or gives life to. By His resurrection He has accomplished this. Therefore, He is the Life Giver. Thus, in a sense, He is the Father of all who live. He was the Creator originally, and He is the Re-Creator through His resurrecting power. So both Adams are fathers of the human race; and fathers and children have unique relationships. Fathers can influence their children by heredity; and there is spiritual heredity as well as physical heredity. We are here largely emphasizing the spiritual aspects in heredity rather than the physical.

Both are fathers and both can give something to their children, both by heredity and also by environment.

This is made obvious in Galatians 6:7 where it talks about the natural laws that govern us as human beings, and also plants and animals. The last part of the verse reads, "for whatsoever a man soweth, that shall he also reap." If you plant corn you never get potatoes. If you plant peas you never get oranges. Like always produces like. Therefore, Adam would produce after his kind, and Christ (the second Adam) would produce after His kind. This is true if you understand genetics, and this is true in the spiritual realm as well as in the physical.

Consider our first father Adam and our relationship to him. "As related to the first Adam, men receive from him nothing but guilt and the sentence of death." 6BC 1074. "I am lost in Adam." SD 120. Adam's sin causes me to be that way. "Because of sin, his [Adam's] posterity was born with inherent propensities of disobedience." 5BC, 1128.

This is discussed in the Bible. "This is the book of the generations of Adam [his offspring]. In the day that God created man, in the likeness of God made He him." Genesis 5:1. When He made Adam, He made him like God; but things changed by verse 3 because Adam had sinned. "And Adam lived an hundred and thirty years, and begat a son in his own likeness." Adam was made in the likeness of God. But now it says he begets a son in his own likeness. Adam had been changed because of sin, and Seth had become like Adam. He still had some of the image of God in him, but his nature had been changed.

"≠Yet he [Seth] was a son of Adam like sinful Cain, and inherited from the nature of Adam no more natural goodness than did Cain." 3SG 53. "While Adam was created sinless, in the likeness of God, Seth, like Cain, inherited the fallen nature of his parents." PP 80. There was a different likeness, a different image, than there was originally in Adam. "Christ redeemed man from the penalty of Adam's disgraceful fall." 6BC 1092. Not man's fall, but Adam's fall. Some penalty has come to us because of Adam's sin.

This gives you some idea of what has happened to us as human beings because of heredity. There are certain things that come to us about which we had no choice. All we had to do was to be born, and we had no choice about that. If I can inherit certain things from Adam, I can also inherit things from Christ. It functions the same way. Now we are going to the positive side.

The Bible discusses some of this inheritance from Christ. "And so it is written, The first man Adam was made a living soul; the last Adam was made a quickening Spirit. Howbeit that was not first which is spiritual, but that which is natural; and afterward that which is spiritual. The first man is of the earth, earthy: the second Man is the Lord from heaven." 1 Corinthians 15:45-47. Then skipping to verse 49: "And as we have borne the image of the earthy [of Adam], we shall also bear the image of the heavenly [of Christ]." We receive something from Adam by heredity, and we receive something from Christ the same way; and we will bear His likeness.

"As related to the first Adam, men receive from him nothing but guilt and the sentence of death. It places him [man] where, through accepting Christ as his Saviour, he becomes a partaker of the divine nature. Thus he becomes connected with God and Christ." 6BC 1074. By being born of Adam, man became a partaker of his human, sinful nature. By Christ becoming a human, and by my receiving Christ as my Savior, I can partake of His divine nature. So now, through Christ, there is a relationship established with God. "As many as have received Him, to them gave He power [which means the authority or the right] to become sons of God." John 1:12. If you are a child of God, you are born of God, and you take after the likeness of your heavenly Parent. God is reproducing Himself in His children. The purpose of the new birth is that God may dwell in man. That is what He wants to accomplish.

There are many texts about this. "And have put on the new man, which is renewed in knowledge after the image of Him that created him." Colossians 3:10. "And as we have borne the image of the earthy, we shall also bear the image of the heavenly." 1 Corinthians 15:49. "...but we know that, when He shall appear, we shall be like Him..." 1 John 3:2. "...until Christ be formed in you." Galatians 4:19. "My little children, of whom I travail in birth again until Christ be formed in you." Galatians 4:19. Christ is to be reproduced in us.

"In his relation to Christ, he will be bone of His bone, flesh of His flesh, one with Christ in a peculiar relationship, because Christ took the humanity of man." 7BC 926. We can be one with Christ in a peculiar relationship. What Adam has done to us by heredity, Christ comes along to undo by our being born again. Christ in you, that we may bear the image of the heavenly, even if we are born of the earthly.

We do not often realize why we are the way we are and what we can be by the work of Christ. This is so important. There are other influences and powers that the two Adams possess, besides being a father, that also have an influence upon us, that also have a control, and that also do something to us and for us. You cannot avoid being born of your parents. The next one is similar to it in many ways. Christ and Adam are both kings as well as fathers; and kings do things to their people, often about which the people have no choice. Just because you belong to that kingdom, the king can do something to you or against you. Adam was a king and Christ was a King.

After God made man, He said, "...let them have dominion over the fish of the sea, and over the fowl of the air, and over the cattle, and over all the earth, and over every creeping thing that creepeth upon the earth." Genesis 1:26. Adam and Eve were given dominion over every living thing. "While they remained true to God, Adam and his companion were to bear rule over the earth." PP

50. Unlimited control was given them over every living thing. They ruled the animals, they ruled the earth; but Adam never had the opportunity to rule man, because he was still only with his wife. Apparently at that point, others had not come along. When others had come along he would have ruled them; but he forfeited his kingship when he succumbed to Satan.

"At his creation Adam was placed in dominion over the earth. But by yielding to temptation, he was brought under the power of Satan. 'Of whom a man is overcome, of the same is he brought in bondage.' 2 Peter 2:19. When man became Satan's captive, the dominion that he held, passed to his conqueror. Thus Satan became 'the god of this world.' 2 Corinthians 4:4. He had usurped that dominion over the earth which had been originally given to Adam." PP 67. When Adam succumbed to Satan in the first act of sin, the devil then usurped the position of being our king, and he fashioned himself the king of this earth, and our king without our choosing, as did Adam. Christ came to undo that. When Jesus was tempted in the wilderness, Satan showed Him the kingdoms of the world and then said, "All these things will I give Thee, if Thou wilt fall down and worship me." Matthew 4:9. Satan professed to be the king, or the god, of this world. But those kingdoms were really not his; he only claimed them as his.

"After tempting man to sin, Satan claimed the earth as his, and styled himself the prince of this world. Having conformed to his own nature the father and mother of our race, he thought to establish here his empire." DA 114. Adam and Eve had become like the devil in that their natures were conformed to the devil's. If Adam gives you his nature, what nature are you really receiving? Isn't that a nice, pleasant thought? Through Adam the devil can pass on to me the nature conforming to that of Satan himself.

"Having conformed to his own nature the father and mother of our race, he thought to establish here his empire. He declared that men had chosen him as their sovereign. Through his control of men, he held dominion over the world. Christ had come to disprove Satan's claim. As the Son of man, Christ would stand loyal to God. Thus it would be shown that Satan had not gained complete control of the human race, and that his claim to the world was false. All who desired deliverance from his power would be set free. The dominion that Adam had lost through sin would be recovered." DA 114,115.

It is a unique thing that our first parents conformed to the image, or nature, of Satan. This happened by their act of sin. That is what Adam bequeathed to us. All of this is accomplished when Adam the king was conquered by another power.

This can best be explained by looking at king David before he was king. You remember how Goliath came out from the Philistines to challenge the Israelites. Instead of the armies engaging in a general war, they had devised a scheme where Goliath announced that if there was one Israelite who could defeat him, then all the Philistines would be defeated; but if he defeated that one man, then all the Israelites would be defeated. Day after day he came out and bellowed at the Israelites to send out their man; and day after day Israel was defeated by that one person. He looked enormous to the Israelites, didn't he? But he really wasn't that big. Then came David, a man not very large or experienced at warfare, and he asked, "Who is this uncircumcised Philistine, that he should defy the armies of the living God?" 1 Samuel 17:26. You know the story well, having learned it as a small child. When David defeated Goliath, every Israelite was victorious. David and Goliath never actually fought each other. But by one man's strength and by that one act, all the Philistines were defeated and Goliath was dead; and all of Israel was victorious and they *acted* victorious. Right away they started pursuing the Philistines and drove them out of the country. Before that they were cowardly. Now they were conquerors, and all because of one person. I am not only talking about David and Goliath. I am talking about the great controversy that all this symbolizes.

As in Adam all die, so in Christ shall all be made alive. They all conquer in Jesus. As in one man's disobedience all are defeated and disobedient, so in one Man all are righteous. Is Romans 5:19 true when it says that "by the righteousness of One the free gift came upon *all* men unto justification of life"? Many have trouble believing this is true.

"When man transgressed the divine law, his nature became evil, and he was in harmony, and not at variance, with Satan." GC 505. We had joined the devil's team. Adam started the whole thing rolling. Now, all of this has an effect upon us that is similar to heredity and by the fact that we did not choose it. It came about because our king was conquered, and therefore all his subjects were conquered with him.

Some people do not understand the kingship of Adam and that we are his subjects. In the Old Testament patriarchal system, the eldest son received the birthright. The birthright made him, first of all, priest in the clan. Second, it made him king; and thirdly, he received as an inheritance a double portion of his father's properties. The eldest son of all living on this earth is Adam. He is rightfully priest and king and has a double portion. No matter how you approach the problem, Adam was king, and all the younger brothers (the rest of us) are subject unto him. We do not understand kingdoms and monarchies very well because most of us have not lived in them; and we are talking about a typical, ideal monarchy and not the provisional type that they have in these days that are very much like a democracy. Adam was a true monarch, and when Satan overcame him, he overcame Adam's subjects as well; just as in the old days when a king was conquered or killed, the whole nation was enslaved.

We all are descendants of Adam and subjects of the kingdom that he once ruled in this world. Satan took over that kingdom and now we are all his subjects and are enslaved by him. He claims that we belong to him. This defeat, this captivity, and this harmony with Satan's nature are passed on to us. This happened when Adam, our first king, succumbed.

The opposite is also true. When Jesus came, He was a new King. Not many people recognized Him, but some of the heathen kings from the east knew that He was King. They knew He was God and they brought Him king's gifts, and they worshipped Him as King and as God. When Jesus came preaching, He talked about His kingdom, for He was King of the new kingdom—the kingdom of grace—that He established in His ministry.

Jesus came to undo our bondage to the kingdom of Satan, and to prove that Satan did not have that kind of control. When Christ overcame Satan in the wilderness and on Calvary's cross, He was setting every one of His subjects free! Every one of them! Satan is a dethroned king. He is no longer conqueror. He was defeated! Every one of Christ's subjects is a conqueror in Christ. Just as though we were defeated in Adam, so we are victorious in Christ.

These are two explanations of Romans 5:19 about how Adam made us sinners and how Christ makes us righteous. This is all accomplished by just one act of each of the two Adams. "So then as through one trespass *the judgment came* unto all men to condemnation; even so through one act of righteousness *the free gift came* unto all men to justification of life." Romans 5:18, ASV.

We understand Adam's one act of sin, but it is a little more difficult to understand Christ's one act of righteousness. What was that one act of righteousness? Since Christ did no sin, His whole life was righteous. What is that one act of perfect righteousness by which many are made righteous?

Recall the quote from page 18 of *Thoughts From the Mount of Blessing* that "righteousness is love." John taught that God is love, and since the law is a transcript of God's character, the law is love; and therefore the keeping of the law is love. For this reason, obedience is righteousness, and that is love. Righteousness is love. Therefore, the greatest act of righteousness is the greatest act of love. By that one perfect act of righteousness, or of love, He made many righteous.

I would like to suggest that Jesus defined that one, perfect act when He explained to His disciples that "Greater love hath no man than this, that a man lay down his life for his friends." John 15:13. You cannot conceive of a greater act of love than this, and therefore it is the greatest righteousness. Calvary was that one perfect act of righteousness where Jesus laid down His life for His friends. Therefore, the one righteous act is the death of Jesus on the cross. There is nothing else like it. It stands apart distinctly as does the sin of Adam in the garden. These two acts of the two Adams have an unusual quality in them.

First, look at Adam's quality, or problem. The serpent said to Eve, "ye shall be as gods." Genesis 3:5. Then she went to her husband after she had eaten and tempted him. Ellen White described how Adam and Eve felt: "She reasoned that this must be true [Satan's lie that they would not die], for she felt no evidence of God's displeasure, but on the contrary realized a delicious, exhilarating influence, thrilling every faculty with new life, such, she imagined, as inspired the heavenly messengers." PP 56. The quote continues speaking of Adam: "After all, he reasoned, might not the words of the wise serpent be true? Eve was before him, as beautiful and apparently as innocent as before this act of disobedience. She expressed greater love for him than before. No sign of death appeared in her, and he decided to brave the consequences. He seized the fruit and quickly ate. After his transgression Adam at first imagined himself entering upon a higher state of existence." PP 56,57. He thought he had become like God. This was part of the temptation, and this was part of his sin.

The Bible talks about the second Adam and His one perfect act of righteousness: "Who, being in the form of God, thought it not robbery to be equal with God: But made Himself of no reputation, and took upon Him the form of a servant, and was made in the likeness of men: And being found in fashion as a man, He humbled himself, and became obedient unto death, even the death of the cross." Philippians 2:6-8. The first Adam said, "I want to be like God," and he imagined himself as though he were. The second Adam, who is God, left His throne. He thought it not something to grasp at that He must attain to. He left heaven and made Himself of no reputation. He became a human being and a servant to mankind. And as a man He humbled Himself even lower "and became obedient unto death, even the death of the cross." Philippians 2:8.

Jesus' life was one of condescension where He went down and further down. Adam wanted to rise higher and higher and be like God. Which act is God-likeness? Which is the direction that leads toward God? God is righteousness. God is love. Adam was the opposite. He conformed to the nature of Satan when he aspired to be like God, for Satan said, "I will be like the most High." Isaiah 14: 14. Adam became just like Satan.

Jesus, who was God, became a man, and humbled Himself, even to the point of dying on a cross like a common criminal. In that one righteous act we see more of God's true character than perhaps in any other act of the Bible; for God is love, and God so loved the world that He gave His Son to do that. God was in Christ reconciling the world unto Himself. God was lowering Himself, way down even unto the death of the cross. The Father did not forsake His Son. He was with Him in all of that experience.

How do you imagine yourself to be God-like? Are there any of us who, like Adam, have not aspired to climb up to some more exhilarating position or experience? Jesus tells us by His condescension that if we want to rise higher, we must be like Him. To be condescending and humble is to be God-like. In God's kingdom, the law of self-renouncing love is the law of life. This love is self-sacrificing, self-denying, self-forgetful. God did not think of Himself. He thought of us. He did all this for us because He so loved us. He wanted to save us. By that one righteous act, many were made righteous. God was manifesting self-renouncing love, and that love does something to us.

Calvary is much more than dying for us. Calvary is righteous living at its most exalted level. Calvary is not dying. Calvary is living! Calvary is seeing God made manifest as a human in the fullness of His glory and love. There our God was living, showing us His love, doing for men what they cannot do for themselves. There you see the righteousness of God demonstrated right before your eyes in the magnificent glory of His character, radiating out to us. He does more than make up for the past where we failed. Calvary is the transforming power, for the power of His love comes down and changes our hearts. "We love him, because he first loved us." 1 John 4:19. And as day by day I come to Calvary and kneel there, it is doing something for me. It is more than one act of justification at the beginning of my Christian experience. Every day of my life His love is manifested in Calvary, and that has a molding influence. It is a power for good, a power of righteousness; and as I kneel there, the Potter still is working and the clay is still being molded. The pot is never finished until the life is over. It is not finished when I am justified. The Potter keeps on working, and He molds me by the one righteous act of Calvary, over and over again until my heart is melted and the clay is softened, and He is able to change the rough corners of my life, until I grow up to the fullness of the stature of Christ, and you behold Him in me.

The one righteous act made many righteous. Friend, we must never minimize Calvary. There was a good reason why Ellen White wrote that we ought to spend a thoughtful hour each day beholding those scenes, for only there do I truly comprehend the magnificence, the grandeur, the magnitude of the love of God for me.

By one man's disobedience many were made sinners. But those other verses say, where sin abounded, what happened? Grace did much more abound. The results of Adam's sin were tremendous, but that did not matter. The second Adam came and overwhelmed all those evil consequences. Grace much more abounded. The love of God can do more than take care of the past. He leads us into a more glorious experience so we would be higher—as though we had never fallen. That is where He leads us. And all by one righteous act of our Father, for Jesus is called Father; and of our King, the Lord Jesus Christ.

Will you receive Him as your Savior from all sin? Will you make Him the Ruler of your whole life and be subject unto Him? Will you say as did Thomas, "My Lord and my God. Rule me, dominate me, use me, mold me, make me righteous." This is the magnificence of the plan of salvation—Christ our righteousness. May God help us to know and understand and receive what Jesus has done for us in what the Bible calls the one act of perfect righteousness.

10

BUT WHAT
CAN I DO?

ONE PROBLEM AREA IN justification by faith is that of man's capabilities. What is our potential? What are we able to do and what are we not able to do? Where is the beginning place in our experience? Can man obey the law and thus become righteous? Will striving, self-discipline and strenuous effort produce a righteous life that God can accept and approve? Does not God command us to work and to strive?

There is much disagreement on these questions. There is also a deception involved in these questions concerning ourselves because it is so difficult for us to see ourselves as we really are. So often we judge ourselves by what other people are like, and if we are doing a little better than they, then everything must be all right. Our real concern should be: What does God think? Righteousness has to do with God and His concepts of righteousness; and His word and the Spirit of Prophecy contain much information about this. I want to survey several people in the Bible to give you some understanding of what we are like and how the Lord deals with us concerning these questions.

Among the most righteous people of Christ's day, at least as regarded by the general public, were the members of the Sanhedrin. They were the highest and the most elite. One of those men was Nicodemus who went to visit Jesus at night. At first, he did not ask Jesus a question. He only expressed his thoughts about who Jesus was. "There was a man of the Pharisees, named Nicodemus, a ruler of the Jews: The same came to Jesus by night, and said unto him, Rabbi, we know that Thou art a teacher come from God: for no man can do these miracles that Thou doest, except God be with Him." John 3:1-2. Either Christ did not hear him, or did not wish to hear him, because he steered Nicodemus in a different direction. He looked into his heart. Jesus had been thinking about this man for a long time. Jesus responds: "Verily, verily, I say unto thee, Except a man be born again, he cannot see the kingdom of God." Verse 3. He told Nicodemus about some things he cannot have and cannot do. This was a surprise to a man who seemed to be able to do so many things; and now he finds out there is something from which he is omitted.

"Nicodemus had heard the preaching of John the Baptist concerning repentance and baptism, and pointing the people to One who should baptize with the Holy Spirit. He himself had felt that there was a lack of spirituality among the Jews, that, to a great degree, they were controlled by bigotry and worldly ambition. He had hoped for a better state of things at the Messiah's coming. Yet the heart-searching message of the Baptist had failed to work in him conviction of sin. He was a strict Pharisee, and prided himself on his good works. He was widely esteemed for his benevolence and his liberality in sustaining the temple service, and he felt secure of the favor of God." DA 171. When Nicodemus went to the service on Sabbath, he was at perfect peace and in total complacency. He was a liberal giver, and secure in the pride of his own works. He felt he had gained the favor of God. There was nothing in his lifestyle to bother him.

The response of Jesus seemed to irritate Nicodemus. "He was startled at the thought of a kingdom too pure for him to see in his present state." His questions such as, "How can a man be born when he is old?" shows how flabbergasted this intellectual man was. He was startled out of his normal composure; and the Lord startled him on purpose for he wanted this man to see something that he could not see in his present condition. This was hard on Nicodemus, and it is hard on anyone who suddenly finds out that they have been falsely secure. Christ was not denouncing the man or being critical. He simply told him that unless you are born again, you cannot get inside heaven.

The words that Jesus spoke to Nicodemus apply to every person. "Many are not sensible to their condition and their danger...We may flatter ourselves, as did Nicodemus that our moral character has been correct and we need not humble ourselves before God like the common sinner. But we must be content to enter into life in the very same way as the chief of sinners. We must renounce our own righteousness and plead for the righteousness of Christ to be imputed to us. We must depend wholly upon Christ for our strength. Self must die. We must acknowledge that all we have is from the exceeding riches of divine grace." 5T 219.

Nicodemus was a very unusual and gifted person. He was an esteemed leader in the eyes of the people. If he were alive today, he might be elected General Conference President. Everyone back home would say, "Amen, they elected the right man." They would be happy about it because there would be nothing discernable about him that would seem to say that he was not ready for heaven. But Jesus told this capable man that unless he is born again, he would not make it.

The Bible has more to say on this that I would like to put together with the thoughts about Nicodemus. "For I say unto you, that except your righteousness shall exceed the righteousness of the scribes and Pharisees, ye shall in no case enter into the kingdom of heaven." Matthew 5:20. Just as Jesus told Nicodemus that he would not make it unless he was born again, He says to the rest of us that if we are not better than the Pharisees, we will not get there, either. He does not mean to be discouraging. He means for us to discern the true meaning of righteousness, and to judge righteousness by different criteria than we have in the past.

Another man who appeared very righteous and who felt that God had approved of him was Isaiah the gospel prophet. Isaiah felt approved of God until he saw the purity of the Lord high and lifted up in the temple: "Then said I, Woe is me! for I am undone; because I am a man of unclean lips." Isaiah 6:5. Isaiah knew himself to be a prophet of God; therefore he thought he was blessed of the Lord and spiritually safe.

"As the prophet Isaiah beheld the glory of the Lord, he was amazed and overwhelmed with a sense of his own weakness and unworthiness; and he cried, 'Woe is me!' Isaiah had denounced the sin of others; but now he sees himself exposed to the same condemnation he had pronounced upon them. He had been satisfied with a cold, lifeless ceremony in his worship of God. He had not known this until the vision was given him of the Lord. How little now appeared his wisdom and talents as he looked upon the sacredness and majesty of the sanctuary…His view of himself might be expressed in the language of the apostle Paul, 'O wretched man that I am! Who shall deliver me from the body of this death?'" FLB 190.

Here is an apparently righteous man, a prophet whom God had called to tell other people what was wrong with them, and now as he sees the purity of the Lord in the temple, he himself finds that there are many defects in his character. He felt totally undone. Just like Nicodemus, he was amazed and upset by this revelation; and he began to sense that there was something in him that he thought was only to be found in the people. He thought he was home safe, but now he had these suspicions that he was in the same sinful condition as the people he was sent to warn.

Another man of whom the Jews were greatly envious was Moses. He had a marvelous deliverance from the time he was born, trained by his mother, a very godly person, and raised up in the home of Pharaoh. This man who seemed to have such an excellent beginning thought that he was qualified to deliver God's people and that it was a righteous act to go out and start killing Egyptians; and so he did just that. When he found out he had been discovered, he became frightened and fled for his life. Pharaoh found out and determined to take the life of Moses. Then Moses, who seemed to be so righteous, spent forty long years herding sheep in the wilderness in order to eradicate some deeply imbedded problems in his life.

Can you imagine taking forty years to get rid of some negative things in your character? We admire Moses for having led God's people out of Egypt and for those forty years he spent dealing with all manner of trials in the desert. But just imagine spending forty years with a flock of sheep. What kind of education is that? At the beginning, Moses attempted to lead God's people as a general.

That's the way many people try to lead, commanding and manhandling, dictating and using weapons of all kinds. Some generals tell people what to do, and if they don't do it, he might have them shot. But the Lord had to take Moses by the hand and teach him a better way. Moses realized that he could not use the techniques of a general when tending after sheep. When he got mad at the sheep, he realized he could not afford to kill too many sheep or he would starve to death after awhile. The sheep were his livelihood. His job was to keep them alive, not kill them off. It took forty years for Moses to learn God's way to deal with people. He was a godly person and we think highly of him, but we never stop to think that God spent a long time getting him ready. There were character traits he had to get rid of before he could become the leader of Israel.

Another great man in Israel, at least at the beginning, was Saul. We usually remember only the bad things about this man, but the Bible tells some good things about him, and I would like you to see those first, and then put the bad things in perspective with them. "And the Spirit of the Lord will come upon thee, and thou shalt prophesy with them, and shalt be turned into another man....And it was so, that when he had turned his back to go from Samuel, God gave him another heart: and all those signs came to pass that day." 1 Samuel 10: 6,9. I left out the signs that were mentioned there. He became another man with a new heart—a converted person. God took care of that. When he was finally proclaimed king, these are the words that were said about him: "Therefore they enquired of the Lord further, if the man should yet come thither. And the Lord answered, Behold, he hath hid himself among the stuff [he was a humble person]: and when he stood among the people, he was higher than any of the people from his shoulders and upward. And Samuel said to all the people, See ye him whom the Lord hath chosen, that there is none like him among all the people? And all the people shouted, and said, God save the king." Verses 22-24.

Saul was at one time a born-again believer. God said to Saul that He would make him another man, and He gave him a new heart. This was King Saul! How long has it been since you have read those words? He had an amazing beginning and was considered by all the people as most righteous. That is why God chose him. He was a special leader and a godly man. Yet this is the man who for all those years tried to kill David because he was jealous of him. How could a man of such stature and prestige have any peer pressures? He came to the point in his life where he was envious of David and tried to kill him.

Worse still, Saul was for a while a prophet. This is significant when you put that in the context of the rest of his life. "And when they came thither to the hill, behold, a company of prophets met him; and the Spirit of God came upon him, and he [king Saul] prophesied among them. And it came to pass, when all that knew him beforetime saw that, behold, he prophesied among the prophets, then the people said one to another, What is this that is come unto the son of Kish? Is

Saul also among the prophets?" 1 Samuel 10:10,11. This must be put in context with the last acts in his life when he went to the witch of Endor, to the devil's messenger or false prophet, to find out what God would tell him to do. The man who with his own eyes had seen the visions and heard the voice of God as a prophet, turned his back on that years later and went to the devil's spokesman to ask what God wanted him to do. If his experience had not been that of a prophet, if he had not witnessed it with his own senses, his own mind, it might not have been so bad to go down to the witch of Endor. But prophets of God have certain responsibilities and accountabilities. Imagine him going to the devil's prophet. It is unbelievable.

What was there in Saul's heart—that new heart—that could cause him to do these things? Did he know his own heart? If someone ten years prior had told him he would go to the witch of Endor, he would have laughed. If someone had told him he would try to kill David, he would deny it over and over again. He would never believe that. None of these men we have mentioned would have believed some of the things the Bible tells about them in retrospect.

Israel's greatest king was David, whom God called "a man after Mine own heart." Acts 13:22. Surely David must have been a righteous man. He was God's own man for that time; yet lurking inside of him was the potential to commit adultery with Bathsheba, and then plan to have her husband murdered to cover up his own sin. There was no one who thought that David could do things like that. Had you tried to tell him before that time, he wouldn't have believed it at all. Yet there was something in David, in that righteous person, that brought on those problems. There was an inward corruption, and he seemed to sense this perhaps more than any other Bible writer as he wrote about his own experience: "Create in me a clean heart, O God; and renew a right spirit within me." Psalms 51:10. He knew that on the inside he must have been defiled or those thoughts and deeds could never have emanated from him. He asked the Lord to change him entirely from the inside.

Similar situations may be found in the disciples of Jesus. The three most prominent of the disciples were Peter, James, and John. Ellen White said they were with Him at all the miracles he performed. For Christ's entire ministry, they had a most intimate relationship with Him. Yet we find among them some of these same problems with self. Imagine seeing and eating and walking with Jesus day after day for years. Yet what were these men like?

You find out some things about James and John when their mother went to see Jesus. "Then came to Him the mother of Zebedee's children with her sons, worshipping Him, and desiring a certain thing of Him. And He said unto her, What wilt thou? She saith unto Him, Grant that these my two sons may sit, the one on Thy right hand, and the other on the left, in Thy kingdom. But Jesus answered and said, Ye know not what ye ask. Are ye able to drink of the cup that

I shall drink of, and to be baptized with the baptism that I am baptized with? They say unto Him, 'We are able.'" Matthew 20:20-22. Tell us what to do and we will jump. How foolish they were. They did not understand their own hearts. They did not understand the trials that were about to come upon them, or they would never have said they were able.

As we learned in the previous chapter, the greatest act of righteousness was the death of Jesus on the cross. There was more love in that one act than you can find anywhere else in the whole Bible. And remember that love is the fulfilling of the law. God is love and His character is written down in that law; and righteousness is obedience to the law. The sufferings of Christ on Calvary were the greatest act of obedience you can possibly find. When you put those sufferings together with the sacrifice of His life, you get a totally different concept of righteousness. Righteousness is not merely trying to avoid telling lies about somebody, or trying not to covet what other people have. That is such a juvenile understanding of righteousness.

Righteousness is most perfectly embodied in that one act of Jesus. In the death of Jesus we see the ultimate example of righteousness. The disciples were righteous because of the things they suffered for Christ and for us. We say we are willing to bear much for the Lord, but many baulk at the idea of suffering physical pain or humiliation. Many stand around in their pride and say, "My, I am so thankful I am not like other people." And they call that righteousness. How different was Jesus' demonstration of righteousness. Somehow we must go back and see how wrong the disciples were when they said, "We are able." Jesus told them they did not know what they were saying. They did not know what they were asking for and what was going to happen to them. They were not able. How little they knew their own hearts.

The most obvious and glaring case was that of Peter. Peter was an amazing person and some of us identify with him because he was so much like us. "And Jesus saith unto them, All ye shall be offended because of Me this night: for it is written, I will smite the Shepherd, and the sheep shall be scattered. But after that I am risen, I will go before you into Galilee. But Peter said unto Him, Although all shall be offended [meaning the other disciples], yet will not I. And Jesus saith unto him, Verily I say unto thee, That this day, even in this night, before the cock crow twice, thou shalt deny Me thrice. But he [Peter] spake the more vehemently, If I should die with Thee, I will not deny Thee in any wise. Likewise also said they all." Mark 14:27-31.

How could Peter say this so strongly? How could he dispute with the God of heaven? Peter, like many of us, would defend himself whenever anyone talked about his deficiencies. We automatically defend our own righteousness.

"When Peter said he would follow his Lord to prison and to death, he meant it, every word of it; but he did not know himself. Hidden in his heart were elements of evil that circumstances would fan into life." DA 673. Have you ever noticed how everything can be going along fine in your life and then the wrong set of circumstances come about? Some simply collapse. Have you ever found yourself in a social environment, laughing at all the jokes you thought you would never laugh at again? Some people fold up under certain circumstances. We give in and all our righteousness goes flying out the window.

Continuing with the quote: "Unless he was made conscious of his danger, these would prove his eternal ruin. The Savior saw in him a self-love and assurance that would overbear even his love for Christ." These days we teach people you must have self-love. Christ said that was Peter's most dangerous, vulnerable point. We say that you must love others as much as you love yourself, but you cannot love others unless you love yourself. Have you heard that preached lately? We talk about self-worth, self-achievement, pride, and self esteem. This was Peter's hang-up. The Lord saw in him a self-love and assurance that would overbear even his love for Christ.

Continuing on: "Much of infirmity, of unmortified sin, carelessness of spirit, unsanctified temper, heedlessness in entering into temptation, had been revealed in his experience. Christ's solemn warning was a call to heart searching. Peter needed to distrust himself, and to have a deeper faith in Christ." He needed to distrust himself, but he did not. What was his response? If you continue reading in that same paragraph on page 674, you find that "Peter felt that he was distrusted, and he thought it cruel. He was already offended, and he became more persistent in his self-confidence." He became more self-confident than he was before, and he was already too self-confident. Now he becomes more extreme than ever. Peter was like that; and sometimes the best help the Lord gives us only exaggerates our weak points. You can see it in others, but you cannot see it in yourself. The best help He gives us sometimes entrenches us as we seek to defend ourselves, our pride of opinion, our justification of self and all our acts.

We are so certain so often. We, like James and John, say we are able. How reluctant we are to say we are unable. The Lord said, "Except ye be converted, and become as little children, ye shall not enter into the kingdom of heaven." Matthew 18:3. The little child is always saying, "Mommy, I can't do it. Show me how." But we say we are able and that we can do what the Lord requires, and thus fulfill all righteousness.

Some sense their terrible inability and do not even want to try; while others always say they are able. Many who think they are quite able to do things right do not like us to speak to their loved ones, for those close to them know all about their hypocrisy and phoniness, and how they are different at church than at home. They know about these things. They listen to them pray at church but know that they almost never pray at home. There are many things in our characters that are understood very well by our children and spouses.

The Bible has many examples of people who did not know themselves. The Lord, in His divine grace, tries not to expose our hypocrisy to other people, but rather tries to reveal to our innermost soul the corruption that is there and the changes He would like to make on our behalf. The question is: Will we let Him? We have such pride. There are thousands, even millions, who are just like Peter, and James and John, and David, and Saul, and Moses, and Nicodemus, and Isaiah. Some of them learned about themselves by the revelation of God to their souls. Some of them never learned. And some of us will never learn, not because the Lord does not try, not because He does not love us, not because He has not tried repeatedly, for He never gives up. It is just that we will not let self be exposed. And we take it as extreme criticism when people begin to discuss with us very kindly about what's inside us that protrudes to the outside for everyone around us to see. We never seem to outgrow this. One of the marks of a healthy Christian is an honesty with self, when we take every negative statement about self and carefully meditate upon it, pondering if what people say is really the truth. A well-adjusted Christian does not get hung-up because there is something wrong on the inside. They expect to find something wrong on the inside.

Is that a new idea? Do you think you are so holy and perfect that you never find anything wrong? Are you so afraid of what's wrong that you think you could be lost? You know that the Lord knew all these things about us before He died for us; yet He still died for us. It does not matter how bad you are; He still would have died for your sins. There is nothing in your life so horrible that it is going to cause you to be lost, if you let Him take care of it.

I know of people who take personality tests and falsify the answers so they cannot find out what they are like on the inside. This doesn't make sense. There is nothing so terrible or startling there. We are just human beings and human beings are like us; and being like us is being sinful and having a lot of problems, like Moses had, like Saul had, and David and the others. They were apostles and prophets. How can you get any higher than they are? And the Lord came to expose to *them,* not to others, their innermost souls. We need to know the truth about ourselves, and then we will not think ourselves so righteous. And this will be a great blessing to us when that happens. Instead, we chase the blessing away. We think we are different.

Watch how in Sabbath school classes or during Bible studies people will try to prove the other fellow wrong. We want to advertise that we are right, and that we have a greater Bible knowledge than anybody else in the class. Adventists love to do this. We do it with non-Adventists and then wonder why they don't like us and come to our churches. But I showed them the truth! Yes, but how did you show them? By every time proving they were wrong. And then we think we love our brother as Jesus loved us. In this I detect a spirit like that of James and John—a desire to be preeminent in the kingdom.

Somehow we feel safe when we can always prove we are right. The Jews could prove they were right but they were lost, and they were even wrong about the Messiah. We must be careful about being right and calling that righteousness. We must be careful about adopting any attitude that would make us first in the kingdom. That is not the way. The first in the kingdom are those who serve. They are the meek and lowly ones.

In all of this we are certain that we believe in Christ as our righteousness, and that we live according to that truth; and yet Christ our righteousness teaches that I live by faith in the rightness and righteousness of another and not by the faith in myself. In my self-confidence I am establishing that I do not have faith in His righteousness, but am trying to have faith in my own. We might even claim that we are believers in Christ as our righteousness, but be a thousand miles from it.

In Romans, Paul spoke about those who go about establishing their own righteousness, being ignorant of God's righteousness. As soon as you try to make yourself righteous, you are ignorant of His. Righteousness comes by faith in another and not by confidence in self. It always has been that way.

The greatest truth we have to discover is the truthfulness about self. "But we are all as an unclean thing, and all our righteousnesses are as filthy rags; and we all do fade as a leaf; and our iniquities, like the wind, have taken us away." Isaiah 64:6. I have always believed this to be true for those in the world, haven't you? But I did not believe it for me, that my righteousness is nothing more than dirty rags. That is a different truth, isn't it? It is easy for you to apply it to your spouse or your children or somebody else; but does this mean you? Some people will answer, "No!"

There is another statement like this that is just as difficult to accept in a personal way: "The heart is deceitful above all things, and desperately wicked: who can know it?" Jeremiah 17:9. Your heart does not deceive me. My heart does not deceive you. But my heart deceives me and your heart deceives you. We make many assumptions that are a thousand miles from the truth about self. Distrust of self can be a healthy thing. We are always suspicious of the other person and think that they do not do us right. When I get into problems with several different people, I never realize that something may be wrong with me! Instead I become paranoid. All those people are not mistreating me. There is something wrong with my attitude.

The heart is deceitful and I do not understand my heart. It deceives me, and I go along assuming that since other aspects of my life are okay, there is nothing wrong in my heart. We fail to see our deceptions because we are prone to look at our outward actions and almost never take a look at our motives. Why do we go to church on Sabbath? Why do we pay tithe? Why do we feel we ought to do missionary work? Why do we feel we ought to stop doing that particular activity or sin or what ever it is? Why do you feel guilty about doing or not doing certain things?

As long as we are content with external activities that seem right to us, we go along quite complacent. We do not see our own selfishness because we do not look at our motives. The Lord is constantly trying to bring us to a realization of what we are like inside. But we keep fending Him off. It seems that we are desperate for Christian survival in our justification of self. We are frightened that something terrible is going to happen to us if something is found wrong with us. Why do we assume nothing is wrong with us; or why do we assume everything will be all right if we do not hear about it?

The Bible writer with the greatest understanding of this, and the one who has written the most about it, is the apostle Paul. He had the greatest difficulty because, while trying to kill off the Christian church, he thought he was serving God. What greater deception could there be? This is the man who wrote these strange words: "For if a man think himself to be something, when he is nothing, he deceiveth himself." Galatians 6:3. If we think ourselves to be something when we are nothing, we deceive ourselves.

A man of great understanding, of tremendous experience, and who had a close walk with God was inspired to write those words. He had already applied it to himself for he said, "I am the chief of sinners." 1 Timothy 1:15. This was not an idle boast. Paul was a humble, meek man, and he was utterly amazed that God would use him after all the terrible things he did in persecuting the church. He knew from experience that "where sin abounded, grace did much more abound." Romans 5:20. He believed himself to be the worst of all sinners. Who could do the terrible things he had done? He had no confidence in the flesh.

Why do we trust ourselves? Why do we have confidence in what we think or what we can do or what we can say? When we understand what self is like, we will have no confidence in the flesh. When God reveals your true self to you, you will not place much confidence in self. You will put your confidence in Him and His righteousness.

This was the emphasis back in 1888 when Christ our righteousness began to be preached. In the book *The Glad Tidings,* Waggoner over and over wrote about having no confidence in the flesh. He emphasized the nothingness of man, a concept that today many abhor.

Ellen White wrote: "When men see their own nothingness, they are prepared to be clothed with righteousness of Christ." COR, 104. This is preparation. "The burden of our message should be the mission in the life of Jesus Christ. Let there be a dwelling upon the humiliation, self-denial, meekness and lowliness of Christ, that proud and selfish hearts may see the difference between themselves and the Pattern, and may be humbled." COR, 38. We should say amen to that. Many do not like to think very much about the humiliation and self-denial of Jesus.

Remember this important definition: "What is justification by faith? It is the work of God in laying the glory of man in the dust, and doing for man that which it is not in his power to do for himself." TM 456. This can be a humiliating experience.

But in our distrust of self, we find great hope. "Nothing is apparently more helpless, yet really more invincible, than the soul that feels its nothingness and relies wholly on the merits of the Saviour. God would send every angel in heaven to the aid of such an one, rather than allow him to be overcome." 7T 17. He would empty heaven just for one person who senses his own nothingness.

In the Bible there is an experience that I almost never hear talked about. "And there shall ye remember your ways, and all your doings, wherein ye have been defiled; and ye shall lothe yourselves in your own sight for all your evils that ye have committed." Ezekiel 20:43. Someday, all of us will have a revelation of self. The Lord does not want to put our weaknesses and sins on display. That is not His way. He has a tender, loving, compassionate way. He is more long suffering than we can imagine. He understands that we are but flesh. He is able to succor us because He became human and understands us. He knows the problems we have in dealing with self. He knows how defensive we can be; but He knows we must see ourselves before we really want Him. Do you know that? Some think they are too good to need Him. And some think they are too bad to ever have Him.

This problem in Christ our righteousness is the most severe in the Adventist church today that it has ever been. As older members see how young people are lacking, they become even more critical. The young retaliate by criticizing the older ones. Neither believes the other. The credibility gap in our denomination is one of the widest. Somehow a strong emphasis on legalism—that you must do this or you are not accepted—has permeated our churches, our homes, and our schools for many years. We have lacked the knowledge of Christ and His righteousness and saving grace. A lack of emphasis on that has put every child in a dilemma. How do you perform without Jesus? How do you live these standards without Christ? The strong-willed can at least give an external appearance of righteousness; but there are many weak-willed among us and they cannot. There is a tremendous difference between strong-willed and weak-willed. The strong-willed cannot change the heart. They can just polish the outside; but don't step on their toes because they bite. They are still the same on the inside. Therefore, it does not matter whether you are strong-willed or weak-willed. On the inside they are both still the same. And as you see in your life these many failures that parents and teachers and pastors have taught you for years, you become more and more discouraged and you want to quit; and you feel condemned over and over and over again. Why would anyone want to be condemned all the time? No one does! You don't like Sabbath school, you don't like church, and you don't like Bible class because they are always sticking you. When you go home, you retaliate by finding fault with those who find fault, or against the establishment.

There is a reaction to this critical attitude and this legalistic emphasis. We find young people justifying their sins to protect themselves; and this is a defense measure, by the way. Then the older ones say, "Horrors! They are not only doing what is wrong but they justify what is wrong." Then they become even more extreme in their legalistic criticism, and more conservative, if you want to call it that. So old and young part ways, farther and farther away, both believing themselves to be right, and neither one believing that there is anything wrong with self. You cannot criticize if you grow up in our homes anymore. You cannot even tell people that there is anything wrong with them, because they have been told that so many, many times that they want to fight with you. In fact, they would like to punch you in the nose. Therefore, we don't talk about sin anymore. We have other names for it. And to protect ourselves and to find some hope, we join groups where they tell each other how good they are and where they emphasize self-love and self-achievement. We try to pick people up off the floor like gum that has been there for twenty years. And they like that. They don't want to go home, they don't want to go to church, and they don't want to go to school because everybody is telling them what is wrong with them. They cannot bear to see the nothingness of self. Dads and mothers, the preacher, the teacher told them that for many years. The older people say, "Don't go join those groups because they believe in ultimate promiscuousness. They say that everything wrong is okay." The older ones believe they are right and the young ones believe they are right. And the devil laughs and laughs and laughs when we all say we are right.

Friend, I honestly believe that is happening everyday, and it has been going on for a long time. How can the Lord tell us that He wants to bless us and that He has tremendous righteousness to give us as a free gift? He wants to take care of all the deficiencies, all the weakness, all the inadequacies, all the ineffectiveness. But not until you acknowledge your need and your nothingness will you ever depend upon Him. He must tell you that you are needy, and you must accept it. We have become so defensive. God has never been involved in this credibility gap. It has always been our misunderstandings, our misrepresentations, our misinterpretations. He is not critical like we are. He does not point the finger and denounce and exact performance. He has never done that; but we have done it as pastors and parents and teachers.

God has a still, small voice. He speaks to us like He did to Nicodemus, and to Moses, and to David. See how delicately He pointed it out to them. He is very careful that He does not crush out the only spark of hope we have, as He points out our deficiencies. He is literally asking, "Why will you die in your sins? Why will you die with all those things when I can take them away and make you like

Jesus?" Why do we go on and on perpetuating these problems? I believe with all my heart that the Lord this very day wants to bridge all these credibility gaps. He wants to look into every heart, not just the young. He wants to look into the preacher's heart; He wants to look into the administrator's heart; He wants to look into the teacher's heart. He wants to show us our sham, our phoniness, our corruptions. He wants to show us how we have misled people. He wants to look into parent's hearts, but he doesn't want them to give up. He doesn't want them to commit suicide. He does not want them to go around blaming themselves.

He wants us to turn to Him and depend on Him for the strength and the righteousness we do not have in self. He has been waiting all these years to bless us with His power and His Spirit, with His love and His righteousness. And we go on defending ourselves as though there was nothing wrong with us.

Forget the voices of many humans who find fault and who excuse and justify self. We are accountable for one voice: the voice of God's Spirit. He is speaking to us as He did to Nicodemus, telling us we must be born again, and have the blemishes and cancers taken out of our lives. Unless we become new persons, wholly dependant on God, we cannot enter the kingdom. He wants us there. That is why He died for us. He wants you to give Him your heart, to trust Him, and to lean on Him. It doesn't matter how useless you think you are, He can make you mighty. He can bless you and even make you like Jesus. He wants to say to you someday, "Well done good and faithful servant; enter thou into the joy of thy Lord."

May the Lord by His sweet grace somehow penetrate into our hearts and minds and take away all this defensiveness, all this self-justification; and may we see what Christ is really trying to do for us. This is my prayer for you in Jesus' name.

11

RIGHTEOUS— BY TRYING OR BUYING?

MANY CHRISTIANS BELIEVE THAT righteousness is a state or condition to be attained to, or a goal to be achieved by diligent effort. This is a foregone conclusion of many and a concept we have fostered. As a result, there is much striving to achieve this pinnacle that we call success. Attending this is frequent examination of ourselves to determine how we are doing. Am I progressing or not progressing? Most of the time we are looking at ourselves for personal victory over sin to give us some evidence as to whether we are on the road, climbing the ladder to that condition or status we are seeking.

It is true that there is much in the Spirit of Prophecy and the Bible that can be interpreted to mean that it is a climb to a condition; but there is also to be found texts and quotations that seem to indicate that it is not something to be attained to; that it is not a condition or status that we arrive at by much striving or trying.

I would like to give you an example of one of the opposite views. Jesus gave this marvelously simple parable: "Again, the kingdom of heaven is like unto a merchant man, seeking goodly pearls: Who, when he had found one pearl of great price, went and sold all that he had, and bought it." Matthew 13:45,46. You may want to know what that has to do with righteousness.

The inspired commentary teaches that "Christ Himself is the pearl of great price....The righteousness of Christ, as a pure, white pearl, has no defect, no stain." COL 115. "The righteousness of Christ as a pure, white pearl has no defect, no stain, no guilt. This righteousness may be ours." 1SM 399. "The righteousness of God is embodied in Christ. We receive righteousness by receiving Him." MB 18.

It does not matter if you call the pearl "Christ" or the "righteousness of Christ," you receive righteousness by receiving Him. It is all found in Him. In another place it calls salvation the pearl; but salvation is found in Christ. However you say it, it does not matter. You must receive the pearl in order to receive righteousness or salvation or Jesus. It is all wrapped up in one package—the Person we call Christ.

How did the merchantman obtain the pearl (or the righteousness)? He bought it. That is the way you get hold of righteousness. It is something you procure or acquire; not something you attain to or something you produce. I buy righteousness. I acquire it. I do not attain, I obtain. It is purchased rather than produced.

Some might think this is an isolated case, but the Bible has many other things to say about this. Here is one more example: "I counsel thee to buy of Me gold tried in the fire, that thou mayest be rich; and white raiment, that thou mayest be clothed." Revelation 3:18. What is the white raiment? "The white raiment He invites the soul to wear is His own robe of righteousness." COR 113. "The white raiment is the righteousness of Christ." 5T 233. How do you obtain that righteousness? "Buy of Me." The one who tells us this is the True Witness, which is Jesus according to Revelation 1:5. Jesus says, "Come to Me and buy righteousness." This is the way it comes to be in your life. You buy it.

That is a different concept. In fact, very few of us spend much time thinking that we obtain it by buying. Nearly all of us have been taught the concept that it is something I must produce out of myself; that it is something I must develop; that I must grow and attain to a condition called righteousness; that I do not go out and buy it from someone else who has it. I try to produce it myself. Therefore we get many misconceptions of Christ our righteousness or justification by faith. Life can become most discouraging with a perverted understanding of this subject.

In two places the Bible says, "Buy it!" The Spirit of Prophecy presents this same concept with a variety of terminology. "We can do this only as we grasp by faith the righteousness of Christ." 1SM 395. So righteousness is also something to be grasped.

Here is a similar idea: "Living faith enables its possessor to lay hold on the merits of Christ." 1SM364. This is a little different, but similar to the idea of grasping it.

"Through faith in Christ, he may claim the righteousness of the Son of God as all sufficient." COR 96. If you go out and put a claim on some land, it belongs to you.

"By faith he can bring to God the merits of Christ." 1SM 367. He can carry it there as if it were his very own.

"Genuine faith appropriates the righteousness of Christ, and the sinner is made an overcomer with Christ." 1SM 364. According to the dictionary, appropriate means "to take exclusive possession of." I like your suit. Take it off and let me put it on; and I walk away with it. I have appropriated your suit. I go to your house and ask, "Do you have keys to your house?" And you say, "Yes." And I say, "Would you please give them to me?" You put the keys in my hand, and I say, "I think I will keep the house." By faith we appropriate the righteousness of Christ.

"You must know Christ and appropriate the gift of His righteousness." COR 60. "The only way in which he [the sinner] can attain to righteousness is through faith. By faith he can bring to God the merits of Christ, and the Lord places the obedience of His Son to the sinner's account. Christ's righteousness is accepted in place of man's failure." COR 117.

In all these quotations, we *obtain* righteousness. We grasp it. We lay hold of it. We claim it. We appropriate it. None of those give the idea that it is something I climb to reach; not something I produce but something I take from another for myself.

The question is: How do I buy it? We need to spend a lot of time thinking about this because it will run out of your brain so fast it is worse than trying to hold on to mercury. We all have leaky containers when it comes to retaining thoughts like these. And we will go right back trying to attain, or produce, when the Lord is trying to teach us different thoughts. You have to spend time saturating yourself with these concepts or they will quickly leave you.

Here is an excellent text on buying: "Ho, every one that thirsteth, come ye to the waters, and he that hath no money; come ye, buy, and eat; yea, come, buy wine and milk without money and without price." Isaiah 55:1. He says if you do not have money, come anyhow; and come buy without money and without a price. What does this mean? How can you buy without money, without price?

The Bible and Spirit of Prophecy are filled with seeming contradictions that make you think, such as: "Salvation is a free gift, and yet it is to be bought and sold. In the market of which divine mercy has the management [a market that God operates], the precious pearl is represented as being bought without money and without price. In this market all may obtain the goods of heaven...The poorest are as well able as the richest to purchase salvation; for no amount of worldly wealth can secure it. It is obtained by willing obedience, by giving ourselves to Christ as His own purchased possession." COL 116,117. We need to keep these thoughts lingering in our minds.

What is this price that we pay to possess Christ and His righteousness? It is explained on page 116: "He is a gift, but only to those who give themselves, soul, body, and spirit, to Him without reserve." It is a two way street. He gives Himself to us when we give ourselves to Him; and it is a complete gift on our part as well as on His part. Continuing on: "We are to give ourselves to Christ, to live a life of willing obedience to all His requirements. All that we are, all the talents and capabilities we possess, are the Lord's, to be consecrated to His service. When we thus give ourselves wholly to Him, Christ, with all the treasures of heaven, gives Himself to us. We obtain the pearl of great price."

I am not in any way trying to make you feel worse or condemned or deficient. I am trying to tell you how we receive righteousness. The Bible asks, "Who can bring a clean thing out of an unclean? Not one." Job 14:4. And it also says we are all as an unclean thing. Therefore, you cannot get clean things out of unclean things. We cannot produce righteousness of ourselves. It is utterly impossible.

Yet over and over we continue to try to produce righteousness out of ourselves. The Lord says you cannot. We insist, and He says that is okay; you may have your choice, but you cannot produce righteousness. The Bible teaches that only God is righteous; and therefore you must go to Him to find it. There is no other place. All righteousness is found in Jesus. When God gave us Jesus He gave us righteousness to be ours. I must buy that righteousness at the price of giving myself to Him. Then I receive His righteousness. I give Him all that I have. It is a total consecration or commitment.

This concept of giving oneself bothers people today. You ask, "Why would anyone give themselves to someone else? I don't understand this." Ladies, why did you give yourselves to your husbands? I hope you took the right vows when you got married because there are vows today that are nothing like marriage. In marriage, you literally become the property of another person. If you don't believe it, go look at the legal involvements. When you get married, the property you own becomes your spouse's (half of his or hers). If you own a thousand acres and you get married, five hundred becomes your wife's or your husband's. Just like that, as soon as you sign on the dotted line, you gave away half your property. Worse still (to some people), you promise to love, honor, obey, and cherish. That is where the old-fashioned vows used to go. It is almost like slavery. And much marriage is just drudgery unless there is just one quality, and what's that? Love. Without that quality, this business of obeying is just downright slavery.

I have had many married people come to me and say they are slaves. The husband or wife demands this and that. I have seen many others whose lives look like slavery because of the demands of their spouse; but they do not seem to think it is slavery. The Psalmist wrote, "I delight to do Thy law." Psalms 40:8. Why is it so much fun obeying the law? Because of love. Without love, any obedience is just a demand or exaction from a dictator. With love, husbands can tell you that it is even fun to wash the dishes. Why do you give yourself to someone? Only because you love them. There is no other reason why. And we love Him because He first loved us and gave us abundant evidence of His love. Therefore we give ourselves to Him. It is so nice to be in love with Jesus.

If you do not understand that, and you try to do all those things required of you without that love, the Christian life is the most miserable life I can think of. The day has come when we have a mixture in all denominations of miserable people and happy people. Some people vacillate between being the two—once in a while they are happy and once in a while they are miserable. They keep forgetting how much the Lord loves them and how they really love Him. You do not give yourself to someone unless, by their marvelous love, that person has earned you. They purchase your affections, don't they? They are deserving of your esteem and affections. When they do that for you, it is wonderful.

We have read in Matthew 13:46 about the admirer of pearls; and you need to understand more about these connoisseurs of pearls or you will miss something in this parable. I was stationed in India during World War II in a place now called Bangladesh. This is the major city in the world for pink pearls. There are very few pearls like these. Those fellows would spend days and weeks with their little magnifying glasses examining pink pearls. They would squat on their haunches (no chairs) and just look and look at pearls all day long. I have gone back to those shops and seen the same fellow there every day for a week, just looking over all the pearls. Apparently it was somewhat like that in the area where Christ lived, so they knew what He was talking about. The man in the parable found one pearl of great price. There was no other like it. He had probably looked for years, and now he found one. What did he do? He sold everything he owned and bought it. Why? Nothing else was so precious. He could look at his house, his job, his education, his wife, his children, his cattle, his land, and say, "You can have it all; just give me this pearl." He walked away with that pearl knowing in his heart that giving up all he had was worth it.

Some people might think he had lost his mind. But he would say, "Oh, if you only knew what pearls are like. You just don't understand pearls." Jesus taught us not to put our valuable treasures out there for people who cannot appreciate them. The devil has said that God has cast His Pearl before swine; and sometimes it looks like the devil is right. The devil says that God wasted the Treasure of heaven by giving Him to people who cannot appreciate Him. This man appreciated that one pearl, and nothing was so precious. Nothing! He said, "I will gladly give everything I own if I can only have that one pearl." Why? Because of his esteem for that one pearl. He placed supreme value on that pearl. He knew what he was getting, and that was all he wanted. Forget everything else. When we give ourselves to Jesus, we forsake everything else and cling only unto Him. He is so precious. He is symbolized by that pearl of great price.

"We cannot earn salvation, but we are to seek for it with as much interest and perseverance as though we would abandon everything in the world for it." COL 117. Take everything I have, but give me Jesus. This is how you procure, how you obtain, how you buy, how you acquire righteousness. There is no other way. You can try to prove there is another way, but eventually you will come back to the conclusion that you must buy it like this. It might take you a lifetime to discover that, but you will find out that what you have tried to achieve was really not righteousness; and you will find out that all our righteousness is as filthy rags—when you really see His. By comparison, you have nothing of your own.

"The price we are required to pay is not gold or silver…God calls for your willing obedience. He asks you to give up your sins." COL 117. If this disturbs you, then read on; for now we come to the next logical question concerning this: Suppose I do not like pearls? Suppose they are not precious to me? Is that possible? It is possible, and the chapter on "The Pearl" in *Christ's Object Lessons* discusses that. How will I ever find an appreciation for the Pearl of great price—for Christ and His righteousness—if I just do not have an attraction for it? "It is the Holy Spirit that reveals to men the preciousness of the goodly pearl." COL 118. The Holy Spirit reveals to me the preciousness of Jesus. He tells me something I have not seen. There is a revelation from God to my soul that takes place.

You may ask, "Then why hasn't He told me about how precious the Pearl is? He is to blame if I don't think the Pearl is so precious. That is why I have not surrendered my all to possess Jesus. Why doesn't He tell me about it?" The quote continues there on page 118: "The time of the Holy Spirit's power is the time when in a special sense the heavenly gift is sought and found." He comes in great power to reveal Jesus when He is sought and found. The *seeking* of Jesus has something to do with this revelation. Continuing on: "In Christ's day many heard the gospel, but their minds were darkened by false teaching, and they did not recognize in the humble Teacher of Galilee the Sent of God. But after Christ's ascension His enthronement in His mediatorial kingdom was signalized by the outpouring of the Holy Spirit. On the day of Pentecost the Spirit was given. Christ's witnesses proclaimed the power of the risen Saviour. The light of heaven penetrated the darkened minds of those who had been deceived by the enemies of Christ [those who did not appreciate the Pearl]. They now saw Him exalted to be 'a Prince and a Saviour, for to give repentance to Israel, and forgiveness of sins.' Acts 5:31. They saw Him encircled with the glory of heaven, with infinite treasures in His hands to bestow upon all who would turn from their rebellion. As the apostles set forth the glory of the Only-Begotten of the Father, three thousand souls were convicted. [Before that, they were not convicted and did not have an appreciation of Jesus.] They were made to see themselves as they were, sinful and polluted, and Christ as their friend and Redeemer. Christ was lifted up, Christ was glorified, through the power of the Holy Spirit resting upon men. By faith these believers saw Him as the One who had borne humiliation, suffering, and death that they might not perish but have everlasting life. The revelation of Christ by the Spirit brought to them a realizing sense of His power and majesty, and they stretched forth their hands to Him by faith, saying, 'I believe.'" The Spirit brought about awareness and conviction. Now the Pearl was precious.

The quotation goes on to tell about the results of their awareness and conviction: "The Spirit of Christ animated the whole congregation; for they had found the pearl of great price." Why have some not yet found Him? What's wrong? The answer is stated right there on page 121: "The Spirit awaits our demand and reception." Something takes place when I seek Him. Those who sense their need, their deficiency, their lack, are to seek the Holy Spirit in the time of the Latter Rain. They will pray, "Lord, something is wrong. Come and bless me. Enlighten my darkened mind. Take away the Laodicean cobwebs out of my mind. Take away the numbness, the insensibility. Quicken my senses so I can perceive, so I can realize, so I am aware."

I have heard hundreds of Adventists asking the same question as the rich young ruler: "What lack I yet?" There is some suspicion, some doubt, something lurking in our minds that all is not right. Young and old ask the question: "What should I do?" We go around from this camp meeting to that camp meeting, listening to one speaker after another, looking for the thing to supply what we yet lack. If we would only seek, if we would only come with a demand, if we would only receive the faith, if we would only come in a special sense seeking Him, He would be found; and an awareness would come over the church and individuals that we have never had before.

There is a lack of awareness among us in general. There is a lack of responsiveness because our senses do not react to eternal truth. This deficiency is not criticism, for we are all aware of it. Why do we not seek the One who can supply all our needs according to His riches in glory? Why do we not beseech Him to open the windows of heaven and pour us out the blessing that will fill the vacuum? Seek the Lord in the time of the Latter Rain. When we do this, not only will a realization come to us but to all those round about us. Our own families, our neighbors, our friends, and all whose minds have been darkened by false teachings will be enlightened when the Spirit of truth comes down to convict. In the days of the apostles, He touched so many that three thousand were convicted in one day.

We are to seek God to supply this need. This seeking is the result of an awareness of a deficiency, and then a seeking to compensate for that. This brings about two realizations: the preciousness of the Pearl; and a genuine realization of ourselves. "They [those who were converted on the day of Pentecost] are made to see themselves as they were, sinful and polluted..." COL 120. They not only saw Jesus and how precious He was, they also saw themselves as vile sinners.

"All who have a sense of their deep soul poverty, who feel that they have nothing good in themselves, may find righteousness and strength by looking unto Jesus. He bids you exchange your poverty for the riches of His grace...Whatever may have been your past experience, however discouraging your present circumstances, if you will come to Jesus just as you are, weak, helpless, and despairing, our compassionate Saviour will meet you a great way off, and will throw about you His arms of love and His robe of righteousness." COR 115.

"When men see their own nothingness, they are prepared to be clothed with the righteousness of Christ." COR 104. What happens to us? We become frightened when we see our spiritual destitution. We think we are in a terrible condition and are going to be lost! That is not why the Lord told us we are spiritually poor. He tells us He has plenty to take care of all our spiritual poverty. He does not want us to stay like we have been. If we go to Him, He will supply all our needs and give us strength and righteousness. There is no reason for us to remain miserable and naked and blind. He delights to take care of His children. But we always think He is criticizing us when we discover our poverty, our destitute condition and spiritual nakedness.

There is a trade, or exchange, to be made. As you see His glorious purity and how priceless is the precious Pearl, you begin to see that you are in a pretty bad condition. Sometimes He does not come too close to you in all His purity because you would be crushed and feel hopeless by seeing yourself as you really are. You might want to give up or take your life. He draws near enough to tell you that you have misunderstood Him, that He is not trying to chase you away, that He wants you to come buy without money and without price, and that He has all that you need and is waiting and willing to give it to you. But you, in all your spiritual poverty, must go to Him! When you discover how poor and helpless you are, that is when you must go to Him. By seeing His goodness in comparison to yourself, you begin to see yourselves as you really are, and then you begin to desire to be like Him; and He tells you that you may have His righteousness if you will make the trade.

"There are some who seem to be always seeking for the heavenly pearl. But they do not make an entire surrender of their wrong habits. They do not die to self that Christ may live in them. Therefore they do not find the precious pearl. They have not overcome unholy ambition and their love for worldly attractions. They do not take up the cross and follow Christ in the path of self-denial and sacrifice." COL 118.

Many people with preconceived opinions misunderstand everything in this quote. They think they must become perfect and overcome all their sins before they can have His righteousness. No, it does not say that; but we have read it that way for many years. Then what does it say? It says that God wants you. He bought you with a price, the precious blood of Jesus. Will you be His possession? He is not demanding that you be His possession. He loves you with an everlasting love! Do you love Him so much that you want to be His? If you will be His, He will give Himself to you with all He has, and you will have no more spiritual poverty. Jesus will love you until you love Him and give yourself to Him. And when you give yourself to Him to love, honor, obey, and cherish, you will forget those things that have alienated you from God. Won't you?

A couple separated because he had some very bad habits. He stopped working, but would come home often enough to get her money to sustain his bad habits. After a long while, she said, "I don't like that. I want you to leave and not come back." He said, "But I want to stay." She said, "You only want to stay for my money; but you don't want to stay because you love me. You want to hang around because you love those habits; and I don't want to work all my life taking care of your bad habits. I would be glad to have you back, and I love you, but leave your habits some other place."

Of course, the problem is that we cannot. He knows that, so He asks you to give yourself to Him. He paid the price for your sins. 'Behold the Lamb of God that taketh away the sin of the world.' (John 1:29). Will you let Him take your sins away? Will you give yourself to Him? We cannot overcome our sins but we can give ourselves to Him.

God is not asking us to overcome in the way we usually think about it. He is asking us to die, to forget those things. Our sins seem valuable to us and we cherish them; but when you begin to compare them with the Pearl of great price, you will find out that the things you once valued so much suddenly are not so great. It is like seeing a new, beautiful car next to yours and you say, "Hey, that old heap should be in the junkyard." That is the way it is with all these sins. God is not telling us how bad we are. He is asking us if we want something better. Do you want what He has? Do you still want to hang on to those sins when you can have what He has to offer you? Are you like the pigs that cannot appreciate the valuable things in life? Are you using your mind to think about what is valuable and what is not valuable? Are you using good judgment?

We have come to a peculiar time when we want to have our cake and eat it, too. In our love affair with Christ, we have become spiritual "swingers." At a certain time of day we want to be intimate with our Lord, but later in the day, we say, "I want to go now to my other lover—the world—and just have a little bit of spiritual adultery. After all, the Lord is broad-minded, isn't He? And very understanding and loving." So we keep two or three other lovers around—those cherished sins we cling to. And we wonder why we do not have Him and His righteousness.

Those who cheat on their spouse sense a coldness and remoteness when they return home. Somehow there is not that warmth they once felt. The conversations kind of fizzle and there is not much to talk about. This is exactly why the Bible and church become so dull to us. Our affections are elsewhere. We have alienated our Lover by our own choice, and our spiritual life is not as warm and affectionate as it once was. We become lukewarm lovers.

Friend, the Lord has paid a precious price for us; and Jesus was the most valuable thing that heaven had. If God could have found something or someone more valuable than Christ, He would have given it to us. He is asking us if we appreciate truly valuable things? We have come to a time in which we have appreciation for all kinds of things. I knew a king in Rhuanda who so loved a rifle that had been given to him as a gift that he would not allow another person to touch it. Some people love degrees, or prestige, or position, or jobs, and you can go on and on. Some people forsake everything else to have one possession.

Some people forsake home, livelihood, spouse, and friends, just to get something they very much desire.

I recall when I had that kind of obsession for flying, and I thought there would never be such a delightful time as when I had my wings in the Air Force. Then I finally achieved that one pearl of great price (according to my estimation). Now I had everything! But then the day came when I thought it was the most boring thing anyone could ever find to do. I was disgusted with what I had achieved.

I have met those with great wealth who told me the same thing. They said that because of all the fears and pressures and worries they had with wealth. It wasn't worth it. I have met those who worked a lifetime for a certain accomplishment in a job or profession, and they would come to me and say, "Pastor, I'm bored stiff. What do I do?" They say they are too old to change, and have too much money wrapped up in their careers. The Lord allows us to go along, and sometimes it takes a long time, until we find the end result of those things we count so precious. Sometimes we cannot attain to those things, but He allows us to pursue them until we have lost our health, or our family, or until our children can no longer stand us because we have no interest in them. He lets us continue until we lose everything but that one thing we strove so much for. The Lords then asks tenderly, "Are you happy?" And after a while, you answer, "Not really."

The parable of Jesus says there is only one Pearl of great price. There is nothing else as valuable. There is nothing else as satisfactory, nothing else that will help you to achieve. Everything else is secondary to the one Pearl. He does not ask you to strive first and then have His righteousness. He says, "Give me what I purchased. Love Me because I first loved you. Be Mine because I have given Myself for you. Give Me your sins because I want to take them all away. Don't overcome by trying. Overcome by dying. Make Me the King of your life. Am I not the King of glory? Am I not your Creator? Let Me dominate you, and all this marvelous treasure will be yours."

There is no other way. There is just one Pearl of great price, and the Bible calls Him One altogether lovely, the Lily of the Valley, the Desire of all nations, the bright and morning Star, the Pearl of great price. What do you count more valuable than Christ? What are you trying to hold on to? What are you grasping for? What are you seeking to achieve rather than Jesus?

The man in the parable sold everything he had. He said, "Take the world, take me, take everything, but give me that one pearl." This is the only way that righteousness is attained. Jesus has been waiting a long time for us to discover something that has been extremely obvious. It is almost embarrassing to admit that we haven't found it. He wants us to admit that there is no one else like Him. He wants us to discover that He is extremely precious.

Today the Spirit of God is telling you something. He is bringing to you a realization and a conviction that you would rather have Jesus than anything. All those other things that have seemed so valuable to you are in reality nothing. You have been desiring all that garbage when you could have traded those things for Christ, the most valuable treasure in the universe.

May God help us to see how valueless our cherished sins are and to understand how precious is Jesus who has been waiting to bestow on every one of us His marvelous righteousness. When we see Him, everything else grows dim in the light of His glory and grace.

FAITH, WORKS,
AND RIGHTEOUSNESS

THE GREATEST PROBLEM WE have concerning Christ and His righteousness, and the one most likely misunderstood, concerns the part of man's works in his righteousness and salvation. There are many ideas and questions about this.

In previous chapters we have attempted to eliminate the idea that people must perform some type of works in order to secure their own righteousness. We have tried to show how Christ is our righteousness. I am sure that, as we have been showing what Christ has done for us in righteousness and salvation, almost everyone has had at least one or two Bible texts or statements from the Spirit of Prophecy that causes them to have some reservation concerning what Christ does for us. Many want to cling to the idea that their works, at least to some degree, qualify them to be righteous.

There is no way to cover all the kinds of works that man does in Christian living, so we will limit our area of discussion to those works that have to do with victory over sin, and therefore are associated with righteousness. We are not talking about those works that are a consequence of grace and salvation, such as the works of appreciation and thanksgiving, the good deeds to others, and the like. We are talking primarily about the area of the works that lead to victory over sin. This is the area where we have the most difficulty and that we misunderstand so easily.

Certain texts are quite prominent when discussing this aspect of works. For example, Paul emphasizes that "Ye have not yet resisted unto blood, striving against sin." Hebrews 12:4. There is another like it where Paul makes a parallel with Christians and those running a race. "And every man that striveth for the mastery is temperate in all things. Now they do it to obtain a corruptible crown; but we an incorruptible." 1 Corinthians 9:25. Since they deny themselves so much to win in a race, we ought to strive for mastery in the Christian life. By the way, the word translated here as "striveth" is limited to a specific kind of working. Strive means to fight. There is an agonizing struggle, an attainment or achievement, which requires much effort; but it is mainly talking about a fight or warfare in which we are involved.

This is illustrated where Paul wrote that we are to "Fight the good fight of faith…" 1 Timothy 6:12. When you begin to conceive of Christian works as a battle or warfare, you get a different concept than when you talk about struggling for some kind of supreme attainment. It is true that victory in warfare is an attainment, but it is a little different type than struggling for Christian perfection. The Bible often talks about striving and the warfare of Christian soldiers in the battle of life. This is the aspect we want to study here.

This is a difficult subject because every time you seek to define or describe the works of man in the struggle against sin, you always come very close to the works of God. In fact, the two are so intertwined that you cannot easily discuss one without the other. If you persist in reading what the Bible says about the works of man, you will discover that it always talks about the working of God. They are both intertwined and interrelated. We get into some difficulties when attempting to talk *only* about the works of man.

Let me show you how they are intertwined. "Wherefore, my beloved, as ye have always obeyed, not as in my presence only, but now much more in my absence, work out your own salvation with fear and trembling. For it is God which worketh in you both to will and to do of His good pleasure." Philippians 2: 12,13. Most people stop reading after it says, "work out your own salvation with fear and trembling. But it goes on to say, "for it is God which worketh in you…" You cannot separate the two thoughts. When you try to separate the two ideas, you make a distortion of truth.

Here is another one: "Whereunto I also labour, striving according to His working, which worketh in me mightily." Colossians 1:29. I work, He works, and He works in me.

With these thoughts in mind, let us try to isolate what are the works of man in seeking victory over sin. Again, this is a dangerous area because there is the danger of leaving out God and His works. And most of us do. We say, "I must do this apart from Him." Be very careful when you come to that conclusion about any works of any person and at any time; because Jesus said that "without Me ye can do nothing." John 15:5. And that means not one thing.

Nearly all the texts about man's works in regard to victory over sin are essentially describing the same thing in a variety of ways. "If any man will come after Me, let him deny himself, and take up his cross, and follow Me." Matthew 16:24. This is talking about a unique type of effort, or struggle, or work in the Christian life. If you are going to be a disciple of Jesus, you must deny yourself, take up your cross, and follow Him.

The same thought is stated in a different way: "So likewise, whosoever he be of you that forsaketh not all that he hath, he cannot be My disciple." Luke 14:33. Here is that same denial which involves taking up your cross to follow Him. It is the same thought but differently expressed. Taking up your cross means you are going to die. Those who heard Jesus speak those words knew that when a person took up a cross, they were ready to be crucified on it.

All this is talking about the battle against self. We battle against Satan, and we battle against people; but our warfare is not with people. Some think that if they were married to a different spouse, or had a different job, or had different children, or lived in a different environment, they would not have the war. The Bible does not agree with that. Primarily the battle is with self.

Ellen White describes this warfare: "The warfare against self is the greatest battle that was ever fought. The yielding of self, surrendering all to the will of God, requires a struggle; but the soul must submit to God before it can be renewed in holiness." SC 43. Surrendering all to God is our work, but do you see where God's work comes into the picture? His work is in the renewing of man in holiness. The greatest war we must fight is not with Satan or other people, it is the submitting of the will to God.

This experience is well illustrated in the encounter that the rich young ruler had with Jesus; and we read it so casually sometimes that we miss the struggle and the unspoken aspect of it. There is much there that we leave out. "Good Master, what good thing shall I do, that I may have eternal life?" Matthew 19: 16. Jesus told him he must keep the commandments; and the young ruler asked which ones. Jesus named a few of the Ten Commandments to which the young man replied, "All these things have I kept from my youth up: what lack I yet?" Picking up in verse 21, Jesus said, "If thou wilt be perfect, go and sell that thou hast, and give to the poor, and thou shalt have treasure in heaven: and come and follow Me. But when the young man heard that saying, he went away sorrowful: for he had great possessions. Then said Jesus unto His disciples, Verily I say unto you, That a rich man shall hardly enter into the kingdom of heaven. And again I say unto you, It is easier for a camel to go through the eye of a needle, than for a rich man to enter into the kingdom of God."

This man desired to follow Jesus, and he desired to be saved. He was looking at the finer points in his experience. He came seeking. He did a lot of things. In sincerity, he said he had kept all the commandments, but apparently he did not understand the spirit of them. So Christ told him what to do; but he would not go that far. Could he have done what Jesus told him to do? Was it impossible for him to give up his treasures and follow Jesus? Or was it possible? Or was he unwilling? Did Christ ask the impossible of this man? He never asks the impossible, does He?

Why was it so difficult to follow Jesus under those circumstances? Because riches have an attraction to self to this degree and extent. Christ was not exaggerating when He talked about the difficulty of the rich entering the kingdom. The richer you get, the more fearful and insecure you become. There is no security in wealth, but we all think there is. The ones who say they do not think so establish by lifestyle that they do think so. We attempt in many ways to provide for our security by possessions and wealth. Self is being attacked when you seek to remove that which, in our concepts, provides security. We do not like it when self comes under attack. We are adamant that we need our wealth to live. We may think we have more than enough to live, but we do not act that way when someone tries to take it away from us.

You can see the same battle in the experience of the prodigal son. We all know it very well, but let's refresh our memories. "A certain man had two sons: And the younger of them said to his father, Father, give me the portion of goods that falleth to me. And he divided unto them his living. And not many days after the younger son gathered all together, and took his journey into a far country, and there wasted his substance with riotous living. And when he had spent all, there arose a mighty famine in that land; and he began to be in want. And he went and joined himself to a citizen of that country; and he sent him into his fields to feed swine. And he would fain have filled his belly with the husks that the swine did eat: and no man gave unto him. And when he came to himself, he said, How many hired servants of my father's have bread enough and to spare, and I perish with hunger! I will arise and go to my father, and will say unto him, Father, I have sinned against heaven, and before thee, And am no more worthy to be called thy son: make me as one of thy hired servants." Luke 15:11-19.

You have to put yourself in his place. This man was on an ego trip that would never end. It was self, running wild with riotous living. Just spend, spend, spend. Doing your own thing, we call it. Spending what we have, and what we can borrow; but please don't deny self. Take everything you want, even if someone else has to pay for it if you cannot, because self must be satisfied. How could that young man go so long and far in his selfishness? He reached the point where he would have gladly eaten the husks with the pigs. To a Jew, this was the lowest you could go. He had gone to the bottom of the gutter. How can you persist serving self until you arrive at the bottom? Why is it that we do not have more sense before we reach that point?

The answer is quite easy. Everyone says, "I want to do it. I want to achieve. Let me alone. I want to succeed." When many know we are failures, and it is almost impossible to reverse the trend, we still say, "Let me show you I can do it." We are everlastingly trying to show God we can do it in righteousness. We are not willing to admit that we are that much of a failure. We are still plunging headlong down into the gutter, waiting until we are disgustingly unfit for society. Yet we keep saying, "I am doing pretty well. Just give me time and I will show you."

When you start to think about home and come to your senses (and nothing brings us to our senses better than the gutter), it is like being struck by a bolt of lightening. It half kills you before you realize anything. But why do we not arrive earlier at the conclusion to go home?

The fellow in the parable decided to go home. Would you like to have gone home as he did? He was a fellow who had gone out to do everything his own way, and knew exactly what he was going to do; and now he is going to go home and say he is a total failure. He went running home in dirty clothes, hungry and with no place to stay. Most would not want to go home once they reached that point. They would prefer to wait until they are fixed up and more of a success, and then go home and say, "Look what I have done." What did this fellow have to brag about? He said to his father, "I have sinned against heaven, and before thee, and am no more worthy to be called thy son: make me as one of thy hired servants." Most humans do not say that after they have been off on a long ego trip without a great deal of meditation and tremendous humiliation. You have to be in great need before you say you are no longer worthy. This was a prideful fellow. He knew exactly what it was all about.

This problem with self, this trauma that faces us, is so threatening that we do not even want to think about it. We resent anyone telling us about it. It makes us angry to hear sermons about it. So we choose the churches where we never hear it; and we choose to read Bible texts and read books where we never have to hear about it. We like to pat ourselves on the back and think that things are better than they are.

Jesus described this defeat of self, and its trauma, in what some would call extreme terms. "And if thy right eye offend thee, pluck it out, and cast it from thee: for it is profitable for thee that one of thy members should perish, and not that thy whole body should be cast into hell. And if thy right hand offend thee, cut it off, and cast it from thee: for it is profitable for thee that one of thy members should perish, and not that thy whole body should be cast into hell." Matthew 5: 29,30. This is not so extreme when you understand and agree with what Jesus said.

Ellen White explains this nicely: "To prevent disease from spreading to the body and destroying life, a man would submit to part even with his right hand. Much more should we be willing to surrender that which imperils the life of the soul." MB 60,61. I used to visit a man who had very serious diabetes. To save his life, they first cut off a toe, then three toes, then a foot, then the leg at the knee, then a finger, then another finger, then some more toes, and finally a hand. This big, tough man who had been a carpenter and a truck driver talked to me about his fears and agonies. It is not easy to part with your right hand, or even a finger or toe. He said to me, "Elder Lehman, I can feel the hand six months after it was cut off. I want to scratch it." I had this man's funeral after he passed away from his disease.

The symbolism of what Jesus taught is explained, continuing with the quote on page 61: "In order for us to reach this high ideal, that which causes the soul to stumble must be sacrificed. It is through the will that sin retains its hold upon us. The surrender of the will is represented as plucking out the eye or cutting off the hand. Often it seems to us that to surrender the will to God is to consent to go through life maimed or crippled; but it is better, says Christ, for self to be maimed, wounded, crippled, if thus you may enter into life. That which you look upon as disaster is the door to highest benefit."

There are many things in life that are like cutting off your hand. I have heard some say they would rather commit suicide rather than give up their sin; and I have been with those who tried, and who still insist they are right in committing suicide rather than deny self. This is how severe the struggle really is, and how misunderstood it is.

The Lord is a little more specific with us, and Ellen White described some of these things like cutting off the hand or plucking out the eye. "In giving ourselves to God, we must necessarily give up all that would separate us from Him. Hence the Saviour says, 'whosoever he be of you that forsaketh not all that he hath, he cannot be My disciple.' Luke 14:33. Whatever shall draw away the heart from God must be given up. Mammon is the idol of many. The love of money, the desire for wealth, is the golden chain that binds them to Satan. Reputation and worldly honor are worshipped by another class. The life of selfish ease and freedom from responsibility is the idol of others. But these slavish bands must be broken. We cannot be half the Lord's and half the world's. We are not God's children unless we are such entirely." SC 44.

When you begin to look at some of these things in your own lives, you begin to see that self is under attack; and our first reaction is to rise up and say, "But it is not true! I do not love those things. They are not my idols." Well, if it is not so great to you, it should be easy to give it up; but that is a vastly different story, isn't it? The difficulty in giving up these things is an indication of how important they are to us. We fight to keep them, and we call it self-preservation, like a drowning person who flails out to destroy the one who is rescuing them.

This brings us to the very heart of most of our problems. This is exactly where our salvation hinges. The reason why Christianity (and Adventism) is what it is today is because we have never met this head on and adequately handled it. We can talk about every aspect of theology, and we can learn all kinds of doctrines, but this is where the problem is. Our warfare is with self—the greatest battle ever to be fought. I can blame you, or my spouse, my circumstances, and everything else, but I still have to deal with self. Right here you have to be most careful. I told you at the beginning that every time you talk about the struggles and the works of man, you run right into the works of God. There is no way you can separate the two, for they are intimately interconnected and related.

"In the work of redemption there is no compulsion. No external force is employed. Under the influence of the Spirit of God, man is left free to choose whom he will serve. In the change that takes place when the soul surrenders to Christ, there is the highest sense of freedom [there is no dictator forcing us to do it]. The expulsion of sin is the act of the soul itself [and too many of us stop there, which only talks about the works of man]. True, we have no power to free ourselves from Satan's control; but when we desire to be set free from sin, and in our great need cry out for a power out of and above ourselves, the powers of the soul are imbued with the divine energy of the Holy Spirit, and they obey the dictates of the will in fulfilling the will of God." DA 466. Do you see the seeming contradiction? Sin is expelled by an act of the soul [which is our work], but we have no power to free ourselves from Satan's control. To resolve this, we must also bring in the work of God, which is to imbue us with divine energy so that we will obey the dictates of our will in fulfilling the will of God.

How much does man do there? He realizes his tremendous need. How? Through the power of the Lord. He begins to love God. Why? Because God first loved him. He sees his helplessness and vileness. How? By coming to the cross, which was the greatest work of righteousness ever. He then cries out for a power out of himself. Then God works to imbue him with that power. Then he is able, by that outside power coming into him, to fulfill the will of God as he performs his own will. His will has now become God's will.

How much did we do in all this? I chose, I desired, I called, I received. I only perform by the power of God in me. But even the initial desire came from God. There would not be one human being since the earth began who would ever desire to be different except that Christ condescended to become a man and die on the cross. It is the love of God that inspires us to be humble and die to self. There is no force. It is my own choice to seek redemption. And when I cry out to God for a power outside of myself, by the power of the Holy Spirit my will is able to do what it wants to do. And in doing that, it obeys the will of God.

This is largely so far in the area of justification and conversion; and most of us think our difficulty is not there. Most think our difficulty is in sanctification. I would suggest that we have more difficulty in this area we have looked at than we realize. Too many have had a superficial, minimal surrender to Christ in our initial experience; and we have a huge anchor dragging us down because of the poor surrender.

We want to go on to look at the role of man's works in sanctification. We read in Matthew 16:24 that we must have a continual carrying of the cross—a day-by-day denying of self. Paul said, "I die daily." 1 Corinthians 15:31. He also said, "For we which live are alway delivered unto death for Jesus' sake, that the life also of Jesus might be made manifest in our mortal flesh." 2 Corinthians 4:11. In verse 10 he talks about "Always bearing about in the body the dying of the Lord Jesus, that the life also of Jesus might be made manifest in our body." There is a constant dying. It is never quite fully arrived at or achieved. "But I keep under my body, and bring it into subjection: lest that by any means, when I have preached to others, I myself should be a castaway." 1 Corinthians 9:27. I keep constant vigilance over self. This striving is less clearly understood in sanctification than it is in justification; but there in an ongoing dying to self that we understand very little.

Ellen White described this continual struggle: "It is not only at the beginning of the Christian life that this renunciation of self is to be made. At every advance step heavenward it is to be renewed. All our good works are dependent on a power outside of ourselves. Therefore there needs to be a continual reaching out of the heart after God, a continual, earnest, heartbreaking confession of sin and humbling of the soul before Him. Only by constant renunciation of self and dependence on Christ can we walk safely." COL 159,160. Often we assume we must arrive at some plateau where we level off and we can say, "Self is taken care of." There is no place you can find that in the Scripture or the Spirit of Prophecy. There are no plateaus. The quote continues: "At every advance step in Christian experience our repentance will deepen." This renunciation of self is an ongoing process, not one act at one time. It is a day-by-day thing, and there are many quotations on this.

Here is more on the constancy of the warfare: "They must maintain a constant battle with self." GW 135. "Yet self clamors constantly for the victory [it refuses to die]." 2T 537. "Sanctification is not the work of a moment, an hour, a day, but of a lifetime. It is not gained by a happy flight of feeling, but is the result of constantly dying to sin, and constantly living for Christ...So long as Satan reigns, we shall have self to subdue, besetting sins to overcome; so long as life shall last, there will be no stopping place, no point which we can reach and say, I have fully attained. Sanctification is the result of lifelong obedience." AA 560. You never reach a plateau. It is always ongoing. And when does Satan cease to reign? When he is bound for a thousand years.

Our concepts of this have caused us much difficulty, and much guile and condemnation. I am not talking about complacency with what we are, but what God expects of us. What does He do with us and for us and through us? This we must understand better than we have in the past.

"Wrongs cannot be righted, nor can reformations in conduct be made by a few feeble, intermittent efforts. Character building is the work, not of a day, nor of a year, but of a lifetime. The struggle for conquest over self, for holiness and heaven, is a lifelong struggle. Without continual effort and constant activity, there can be no advancement in the divine life, no attainment of the victor's crown." MH 452,453. Many people get paranoid about this and think that statements like this make it utterly impossible for them. Stop and back up a little ways and take a different look from a different perspective, and see what the Lord is really saying about this. We get so sensitive about sin because we do not know the way to victory; thus we misunderstand these statements. God is talking about the battles that must be waged and how He will bless us in this.

Continuing on with the quotation: "The life of the apostle Paul was a constant conflict with self. He said, 'I die daily.' 1 Corinthians 15:31. His will and his desires every day conflicted with duty and the will of God. [You get in pretty good company when you discover you are in that same condition.] Instead of following inclinations, he did God's will, however crucifying to his nature...The Christian life is a battle and a march. In this warfare there is no release; the effort must be continuous and persevering. It is by unceasing endeavor that we maintain the victory over the temptations of Satan. Christian integrity must be sought with resistless energy and maintained with a resolute fixedness of purpose. No one will be borne upward without stern, persevering effort in his own behalf. All must engage in this warfare for themselves; no one else can fight our battles."

Many people misread this. To understand the Christian life and man's efforts in that life, we must sit down and look at these things over and over again. Remember I told you we never talk about man's work without running into what God does for us. Paul was saying that every day he found his own perverse will fighting against that of God, and he had to die in order for Christ to live in Him. "For me to live is Christ." Philippians 1:21. The trouble is we assume that after conversion or a good experience, this process need not go on. We think that self is dead once and for all. That is not true. Self will try to rise up as long as we live; and we seem to be vulnerable to this. Therefore, because self is always threatening to rise up, every day it must be put down. The warfare is constant in Christ our righteousness. I must choose Christ every day, every hour, and every moment. I must never choose self. I must recognize that my difficulties are not just some remaining sins in my life. My difficulty is that self is not dead! It is not so much that I have to pray and ask God to take care of my temper, and then think when I have control over my temper, I will be in pretty good condition. It is asking the Lord to create in me a clean heart and renew a right spirit in me because I am still violently selfish—all the time!

Some people have no wars, and they assume that because they have no wars that the Prince of Peace has given them peace; and they wonder why other people have so many struggles in life. Far more people than we realize have this experience. "The reason many in this age of the world make no greater advancement in the divine life is because they interpret the will of God to be just what they will to do. While following their own desires, they flatter themselves that they are conforming to God's will. These have no conflicts with self." AA 565. They view people who have great struggles as being on the side of the devil, when the opposite is probably true. The ones with the struggles are engaged in the warfare and making advancement. The ones sitting back thinking they have it made have lowered the standards so far that they think their own desires are the will of the Lord. They have no conflicts with self.

Continuing on with the quote: "There are others who for a time are successful in the struggle against their selfish desire for pleasure and ease. They are sincere and earnest, but grow weary of protracted effort, of daily death, of ceaseless turmoil. Indolence seems inviting, death to self repulsive; and they close their drowsy eyes and fall under the power of temptation instead of resisting it." They think that the Lord does not require all of this, and they lay it all down and stop. But the Lord said, "he that endureth to the end shall be saved." Matthew 10:22. People who stop enduring want to believe there will come a time and place when they have achieved; but the Lord says the battles always go on and the achieving is fighting every day against self. That is the achieving—fighting against self, always distrusting self, always waging a war against self. Never give up. It does not matter how bad self is, you never give up fighting the war.

When you have time, go study the life of Reuben, one of the sons of Jacob, and try to figure out how he could possibly be a symbol of one of the tribes that make up the one hundred and forty-four thousand. His father said he was as unstable as water and that he would never excel. We have all seen people like him. They go to church for a few weeks, then give up and not go back for six months. Then he goes back to church for a while, and then stops again. This can continue on for thirty years. Reuben was just like that; but he never ceased coming back. I have known persons who had fallen deeply into sin and emotional problems, the most severe you can find, who tried to take their lives repeatedly; but they never ceased coming back to God for help. For years and years they had no victories, but they never ceased coming back. I could not even understand why they kept coming back, but they came back. They would sneak in and sit on the back pew and never talk to anyone, but they came back. And the Lord eventually gave them victory, because they never ceased coming back.

When you maintain the war, the Lord is always there to bless. When you give up the battle, the devil is always there to conquer. We have not understood the battle very well, and we have not put the striving and the works in the context of the battle. The Lord has not offered us some plateau of divine achievement, of great accomplishment, where we can say, "Look at me." He never offered that. He says He offers us the task of being good soldiers, of fighting and marching in a war that never ends as long as life shall last.

In all this struggle we are counseled to "be strong in the Lord, and in the power of His might. Put on the whole armour of God." Ephesians 6:10. In His strength, fight the fight and wage the war.

If you have this battle and it gets tough sometimes, memorize and use this Bible promise: "Fear thou not; for I am with thee: be not dismayed; for I am thy God: I will strengthen thee; yea, I will help thee; yea, I will uphold thee with the right hand of my righteousness...For I the Lord thy God will hold thy right hand, saying unto thee, Fear not; I will help thee." Isaiah 41:10,13. God will take His strongest hand and grasp your strongest hand, and He will never let us go! Friend, when the Lord says He will do this, where is faith? We should believe this with all our heart and say, "Praise God, this is wonderful!" No wonder we fail so constantly when we do not get excited about texts like this.

The obvious question is: If He is going to do this and never let go, how can you ever fail? How can Satan ever get at you? How can you possibly succumb to old self again when the Lord is going to do all this for you? Here is the answer, and never, never forget it: "When Christ took human nature upon Him, He bound humanity to Himself by a tie of love that can never be broken by any power save the choice of man himself." SC 72. No power can separate us from the love of Christ, or that hand that holds us except "the choice of man himself." The devil cannot do that. It is only the choice of man himself.

Continuing on with the quote on page 72: "Satan will constantly present allurements to induce us to break this tie—to choose to separate ourselves from Christ. Here is where we need to watch, to strive, to pray, that nothing may entice us to choose another master; for we are always free to do this." In the work of the Lord, there is utmost freedom. You may choose Christ with your will, and if tomorrow you are tired of it, you can choose Satan; and God will let you do that. And you will ask, "Why did He let me have so much trouble?" It is because you stopped choosing Him to rule over you. It is not the devil who forces us, for he cannot. He is not the one who crowds Christ out of our lives and takes away our hand from Christ's hand. That happens by our own choice. There is never a time when the freedom of choice is missing, or when we have arrived and no longer have to make the choice. It is every day, every moment. We must choose Him as long as life shall last. That one act of choosing Christ, inspired by the Spirit of God and His tremendous love for us, is the one single act that man can do that brings down the powers of heaven to protect us and enable us and make us righteous by His grace and His righteousness.

It is a little frightening to realize that in these vacillating decisions we make every day that we are choosing a different master; that every morning when we awaken, we can have any master we choose that day. The Lord allows this by His great love. The previous quote continues on with a little admonition and urging: "But let us keep our eyes fixed upon Christ, and He will preserve us. Looking unto Jesus, we are safe. Nothing can pluck us out of His hand. In constantly beholding Him, we 'are changed unto the same image from glory to glory, even as by the Spirit of the Lord.' 2 Corinthians 3:18."

There is something we can do. It isn't much, but it is tremendous in its consequences. The Lord never goes to sleep, and as you wake up, He is waiting to see what your choice is. Whom will you serve today? This is the question that confronts us every day. In every decision of life, in buying or selling, in planning for the future, in going this way or going that way, the question is always: Whom will you choose to be your master? There is no force used in making that choice, just perfect freedom, as long as you shall live.

At this very moment, He moves upon our hearts with tremendous love, and He asks, "Don't you love Me? Will you not by love serve Me? Will you not gladly choose Me because you want to?" There is no other Master as wonderful as He. Is this your choice? Tell Him so, even now.

13

BLESSED ASSURANCE

OUR THEME FOR THIS study begins with a short Bible text that has one term we wish to examine: "By so much was Jesus made a surety of a better testament." Hebrews 7:22. He was made a "surety" of a better testament. This word *surety* is an old fashioned term almost never used anymore in these modern days, and it describes some of the various aspects of Christ's work. Because it is so seldom used, we read it and pass over it lightly and barely comprehend what it means.

The word *surety* is frequently used in the Spirit of Prophecy, especially in conjunction with the message that started in 1888. "The Lord in His great mercy sent a most precious message to His people through Elders Waggoner and Jones. This message was to bring more prominently before the world the uplifted Saviour, the sacrifice for the sins of the whole world. It presented justification through faith in the Surety; it invited the people to receive the righteousness of Christ, which is made manifest in obedience to all the commandments of God." TM 91,92.

This word is sometimes used in the Spirit of Prophecy in conjunction with the word *substitute*. Christ is both our substitute and our surety; and this has a vital connection with Christ our righteousness. "The law has no power to pardon the transgressor, but it points him to Christ Jesus, who says to him, I will take your sin and bear it Myself, if you will accept Me as your substitute and surety. Return to your allegiance, and I will impute to you My righteousness." COR 117.

"When the sinner believes that Christ is his personal Saviour, then, according to His unfailing promises, God pardons his sin, and justifies him freely. The repentant soul realizes that his justification comes because Christ, as his substitute and surety, has died for him, is his atonement and righteousness." COR 108. These two terms are used repeatedly.

What does it mean that Christ is our surety? Who or what is a surety? First of all, as a general meaning in *Webster's New International Dictionary,* the general meaning is "state or character of being sure; sureness; certainty; security; confidence; sure knowledge." Those are nice words in these difficult, doubtful days. To be sure of something or someone is wonderful if based on fact. Other definitions of surety include: "that which confirms or makes sure; a guarantee; ground or confidence of security; security for payment or the performance of some act; one who makes a pledge on behalf of another and accepts certain occurring responsibilities, as to offer oneself as a surety for another."

There are legal definitions as well, but they are less understood because most of us do not often deal in legal matters. First, under the term law, it is defined this way: "But one bound with and for another was primarily liable, who is called the principle; one who has become legally liable for the debt, default or miscarriage of another, as for his appearance in court or payment of a debt." A surety stands good for someone who has an obligation or a debt of some kind.

Here is another way the term is defined in various codes in the United States: "one who at the request of another, and for the purpose of securing to the benefit, becomes responsible for the performance by the latter of some act in favor of a third person, or hypothecates security therefore."

These complex terms are not as difficult as they sound. In general, a surety will countersign or undersign a debt or a note. If you do not have a credit rating to get a certain loan and you must have it, you get someone to countersign for you. They make themselves liable and responsible if you do not pay. In a court of law, surety has a stronger meaning than a guarantor. A guarantor only pays in case of default, but a surety can be held liable for it even though you do not default.

The second way it is commonly used today is when you guarantee performance by another. A bondsman does this for a price. He guarantees that you will appear in court, or otherwise he loses the bond, which is the amount of money he has put down. So he is guaranteeing a certain performance. Often people are asked to countersign and they do not realize they are going surety for another person. But seldom do we hear about one who guarantees performance of another.

Quite a few years ago in my hometown, two young fellows were having a fight one Saturday morning. One ran inside, found his 22-rifle, and went out and killed the other fellow. The one with the rifle was only fifteen years old. They brought him to court, and after many weeks of trial they found him guilty of murder. He was sentenced to die in the state penitentiary. The citizens were amazed that this would happen to a boy who was only fifteen, even though in anger he murdered someone. A minister in that town who was quite well known decided to go to the judge and beg to be surety for this boy. He said he had known the boy a long time and they both lived in the same neighborhood. He said he would take him into custody and guarantee the boy's future good behavior. He did not believe he was a murderer at heart even though he committed that act. The court did not release the boy to the minister even though the minister was greatly respected. But as a result of his appeal, the public rallied around the minister and the judge changed the sentence. The boy was sent to Boys Town in Omaha, Nebraska rather than to the state penitentiary.

The concept of surety is commonly used in law, although the term itself is not always used. Whenever the president of a country, or a state governor, or a judge of some high court releases someone from prison, that official is literally guaranteeing the future performance of that person who is released. The official believes there are extenuating circumstances concerning the prisoner and believes his behavior will be good from that point on. The legal official, in becoming surety for the prisoner, guarantees the future performance of the person released.

The Bible teaches that "Jesus made a surety of a better testament." Hebrews 7: 22. Jesus was made a surety. However, the legal usage of this term today is not sufficient to describe all the roles that Christ plays as our surety. Some of them are implied and inferred. The idea of Christ being our surety is very important in the plan of salvation and in Christ our righteousness. In fact, unless we understand this term well, we will poorly understand Christ our righteousness.

We need to be educated concerning the role of Christ as our surety. In order for a person to be a surety, he must be of upright and noble reputation. Everyone must know that this person is a good, upstanding citizen, one who can be trusted, and who has a righteous character. Otherwise, the public or the courts will not trust him to be surety. So first of all he must establish his reputation. This is exactly what Christ did to qualify Himself as our surety. When He became human and walked this earth as a human being and lived a flawless life, He was establishing His position as a surety.

The Bible speaks of the flawless life of Christ: "For we have not an high priest which cannot be touched with the feeling of our infirmities; but was in all points tempted like as we are, yet without sin." Hebrews 4:15. "Though He were a Son, yet learned He obedience by the things which He suffered; And being made perfect, He became the author of eternal salvation unto all them that obey him." Hebrews 5:8,9. "For such an high priest became us, who is holy, harmless, undefiled, separate from sinners, and made higher than the heavens." Hebrews 7: 26. Is he qualified? Jesus said, "Hereafter I will not talk much with you: for the prince of this world cometh, and hath nothing in Me." John 14:30. He said Satan cannot dispute about His reputation or His qualifications to be a surety.

"All who have a sense of their deep soul poverty, who feel that they have nothing good in themselves, may find righteousness and strength by looking unto Jesus. We are not worthy of God's love, but Christ, our surety, is worthy. He presents us to the Father clothed in the white raiment of His own character. He pleads before God in our behalf, saying: I have taken the sinner's place. Look not upon this wayward child, but look on Me." MB 8,9. We are not worthy of God's love, but our Surety is worthy.

When we get this straightened out in our minds, we will stop having all those fears that beset us about how unworthy we are. It is good to know that we are unworthy, but it is better to know that we have Christ who is identified with us, and that He, as our surety, is good enough. We must identify with Him or we will never get any place trying to make ourselves look good. We will only look worse and worse as we try to do that, and everyone will know it but us.

"He will not look upon me, for I am all unworthy; but He will look upon the face of His Anointed, He will look upon my Substitute and Surety, and listen to the plea of my Advocate, who died for my sin, that I might be made the righteousness of God in Him." SD 120. He will not look upon me. He will look upon Jesus my Surety.

Sometimes when we pray, especially when we have great guilt, we get the idea God is looking down on us like a dictator just waiting to find fault, up there with His spy glasses looking at all our flaws, pointing the finger at us and saying, "Aha, you are going to burn!" We imagine He is like that; and then we feel inferior and worse than ever and wonder what to do. All of this is a lack of knowledge of Christ as our surety. God never talks about our goodness. He always talks about the goodness or our Substitute and Surety.

In order to be a surety, He must be good. This is a necessity, for no one trusts anyone who is not reputable. He must have a fine reputation to be a surety. He became a surety of noble reputation, with no sin in Him. He can be trusted, and therefore God uses Him as our surety. As our surety, He stands in our place. It is unchristian to look for goodness in self and then become discouraged when we do not find it. All true Christians look for goodness only in Jesus. The heathen are the ones who look for goodness in themselves. We must be careful not to join the wrong crowd in this area of goodness.

Jesus is worthy and sufficiently qualified to be surety for every human being. He is the good One. He lived that perfect life. Therefore, He is able to function as our surety. If you look at His goodness to determine His ability to be surety, you are indulging in a fine activity as a Christian. If you look at your own goodness, you are probably eclipsing your view of the Surety. We must find out that our hope is in the goodness of Someone else who is called our Surety. That is very important.

The second activity of a surety, after he is qualified, is that he must pay our debts if we cannot. Romans 6:23 tells us, "The wages of sin is death." According to Romans 5:12, all have sinned, all are guilty, and all have come under the condemnation of death. Since we are transgressors of the law, the law demands our lives, but this we cannot afford to pay. We need a surety. Most of us understand this concept somewhat, but we do not fully understand what it means that our Surety is paying the debt that we owe to the law.

"The human family are in trouble because of their transgression of the Father's law. But God does not leave the sinner until He shows the remedy for sin. The only-begotten Son of God has died that we might live. The Lord has accepted this sacrifice in our behalf, as our substitute and surety." 1SM 215.

"Upon Christ as our substitute and surety was laid the iniquity of us all. He was counted a transgressor, that He might redeem us from the condemnation of the law. The guilt of every descendant of Adam was pressing upon His heart." DA 753. He is our Surety, paying our debt.

Ellen White explained what Jesus meant when He said, "Therefore doth My Father love Me, because I lay down My life, that I might take it again." John 1:17. "In becoming your Substitute and Surety, by surrendering My life, by taking your liabilities, your transgressions, I am endeared to My Father; for by My sacrifice, God can be just, and yet the Justifier of him who believeth in Jesus." SC 14.

This next quote goes into more detail: "Because of transgression of the law of God, Christ became our sin-bearer. The only-begotten Son of God gave His life because of man's transgression. Christ suffered in order that through faith in Him our sins might be pardoned. He became man's substitute and surety, Himself taking the punishment, though all undeserving, that we who deserved it might be free." FE 370. Some people do not understand that Christ died in our place as our Surety, paying a debt we could not pay. As soon as you understand His role of surety, you will understand His atonement and His sacrifice much better.

The law has two requirements: death if we transgress it (Jesus paid this for us), and righteousness. In order to be saved, in order to be accepted by God, we must be righteous. The Bible tells us this is an obligation we cannot fulfill. "Can an Ethiopian change his skin, or the leopard his spots? then may ye do good, that are accustomed to do evil?" Jeremiah 13:23. Since we cannot make ourselves righteous and perform to this requirement of the law, we must have someone who is able, someone who is a surety.

"And if the righteous scarcely be saved, where shall the ungodly and the sinner appear?" 1 Peter 4:18. The law demands good performance, and in righteousness it demands obedience. How can we have that when we are so disobedient and so prone to sin? This discourages many people.

"Christ has pledged Himself to be our substitute and surety, and He neglects no one. There is an inexhaustible fund of perfect obedience accruing from His obedience." SD 22. It is like having a huge savings account of billions of dollars for us; and so huge you could never spend the interest that accumulates. Continuing on: "In heaven His merits [or obedience], His self-denial and self-sacrifice, are treasured as incense to be offered up with the prayers of His people. As the sinner's sincere, humble prayers ascend to the throne of God, Christ mingles with them the merits of His own life of perfect obedience. Our prayers are made fragrant by this incense. Christ has pledged Himself to intercede in our behalf, and the Father always hears the Son." Every time I pray, Jesus adds the fragrance of His obedience to it, and there is an inexhaustible fund there. You can pray all the time and never deplete the resources of His obedience. Every time you pray, the Son intercedes in our behalf and the Father always hears the Son.

This is why there are so few answered prayers. It is not enough to tell God we are sorry for sinning and to ask forgiveness, and then to think everything is okay. That still does not make God accessible. I must come through the obedience of the Surety and never in my own power. As I come through His righteousness, the Father always hears Him. Always! When you have so few answered prayers, you are probably leaving out the key to the Father's ear which is the righteousness, the obedience, of our Surety.

So often we look at our own unworthiness and say that God cannot hear us. We say that our prayers do not go beyond the ceiling. They don't unless those prayers ascend on the wings of Jesus' obedience, and then the Father always answers. It is not your unworthiness that disqualifies you. It is the lack of adding the obedience of Jesus. When you leave that out, your prayers do not go beyond the ceiling. When you add it, He intercedes for every sinner. He is substitute and surety for everyone. As soon as you put His obedience into it, and identify with Him and claim Him, your prayers wing their way right to the Father's ear; and answers come back every time. But it is not our goodness or lack of it. That has neither closed nor opened heaven for us. It is Christ who has opened heaven by His righteousness. He ascended to heaven, and He is there interceding for us.

We need to learn how to pray in Jesus' name and all that that means. Some today even omit it from their prayers, just assuming that everything is all right when you pray. Not at all! Just praying does not make it all right. We are qualified in the Surety, but never in ourselves. We are always unqualified in and of ourselves. A perfect person or a good person does not need a surety. It is just the sinners who need one. It is not so bad to be a sinner when you have a surety, but it is a terrible thing when you do not have one. It is a lack of our emphasis on Christ as the certainty that makes us frightened to hear about our sins. We ought to be frightened to be without Him; but as soon as we have Him as our surety, all our fears are gone. There is no reason to be afraid if He is on your team. Your unworthiness does not cast Him away; it only makes Him more necessary. Isn't that true? The more unworthy you are, and the more sinful you are, the more you need Him. The more qualified you are, the less you need Him; but none of us are that qualified. Is it any wonder that our prayers are not answered when we desperately need to have an answer? We must learn how to come to God through the Surety. This is where our help is.

Recall the two demands of the law (death to the transgressor and righteousness), and then note this final quote: "The law demands righteousness, and this the sinner owes to the law; but he is incapable of rendering it. The only way in which he can attain to righteousness is through faith. By faith he can bring to God the merits of Christ, and the Lord places the obedience of His Son to the sinner's account. Christ's righteousness is accepted in place of man's failure." 1SM 367.

I cannot pay my debt to the law of righteousness so I need a surety who is the righteous One. I claim His righteousness as my own, and I come through His qualifications and not my own; and the Lord accepts His righteousness on my behalf and takes away my sin. That is the heart and soul of Christ our righteousness. Without the concept of surety, we would never understand it. When Jesus lived that perfect life, that flawless life, He was accruing obedience as a surety for all the disobedient. He offer His righteousness on our behalf as we pray that we might be accepted through His righteous surety; and we have great certainty because we know He is so righteous. We know the Father hears Him for He is ours.

The next step in order to accomplish this work of a surety is that the one who is in debt, the one who needs the surety, must choose the surety and must believe in that person. I must accept Christ as my Surety in order to be justified as an individual. It is not just something that is done for me that I never need to know about or accept. This is part of the reason for preaching the gospel. The Bible says that this comes to us if we believe. "And therefore it was imputed to him [Abraham] for righteousness. Now it was not written for his sake alone, that it was imputed to him; But for us also, to whom it shall be imputed, if we believe on Him that raised up Jesus our Lord from the dead; Who was delivered for our offences, and was raised again for our justification." Romans 4:22-25. If we believe on Him!

Here is a similar thought: "Even the righteousness of God which is by faith of Jesus Christ unto all and upon all them that believe." Romans 3:22. To receive the benefits of the Surety on your behalf, you must choose Him and you must believe Him. Then you may come boldly unto the throne of grace and He will offer mercy to help you.

There is a proper sequence to follow. "When the sinner believes that Christ is his personal Saviour, then according to His unfailing promises God pardons his sin and justifies him fully. The repentant soul realizes that his justification comes because Christ as his substitute and surety has died for him, is his atonement and righteousness." COR 108. I believe, and then these things are true because I believe them. He operates that way for me.

"The Lord has accepted this sacrifice in our behalf, as our substitute and surety, on the condition that we receive Christ and believe on Him. The sinner must come in faith to Christ, take hold of His merits, lay his sins upon the Sin Bearer, and receive His pardon. It was for this cause that Christ came into the world. Thus the righteousness of Christ is imputed to the repenting, believing sinner. He becomes a member of the royal family, a child of the heavenly King, an heir of God, and joint heir with Christ." 1SM 215.

In this matter of righteousness by faith, you only have faith in those who are trustworthy. Correct? The courts and the judge and those who need a surety have no faith in the untrustworthy people. They must perform well. They must be dependable as well as worthy. When Christ came to establish His worthiness as a righteous person, He also came and demonstrated His trustworthiness and dependability. You may have faith in Him. In fact, there is no reason why you cannot have faith in Him. He has given every reason to show that all may have faith in Him. He is always dependable. Why not trust the Surety, why not believe in Him, and why not hang your helpless souls upon Him? How can we depend upon ourselves when there is nothing trustworthy there?

Christ is trustworthy. I trust Him, I have faith in Him, and I am justified by the activities of the Surety and my confidence in Him. And do not forget what surety means. It is a guarantee, a certainty, and a confidence. Those are nice words. You lack confidence in yourself, and that is good; but you ought to have tremendous confidence in the Surety for He is ours. God so loved the world He gave Him to us, and therefore we can do much because of Him.

The next step accomplished by the Surety is that through His righteousness and His obedience, we are restored to favor with God. He declares us righteous because of our faith in His righteousness. We have access to God and receive power from Him, and the Spirit of God comes to abide in us. In other words, divinity and humanity are combined—the unworthy is united with the Worthy, the poor performer is united with the good Performer, and the weak is united with the One who has all power. I can do all things through Christ. I can do nothing of myself.

All this gives me accessibility to God and brings me into communion and fellowship with Him. God cannot live with the sinners but He can live with the justified ones. The Spirit of God comes into my heart crying, "Abba, Father," because I am justified. Therefore, God lives with me and we are joined together. Amazing things happen when a new power comes to live with me.

We have abundant accessibility to God. Come boldly unto the throne of grace. Have no fear, not because you are worthy, but because you come to the worthy Surety. As long as you come hand in hand with Him by faith, the door is wide open. Walk right in. We do not say, "I am worthy, so open the door." We say, "He is worthy and He leads me in." What a marvelous thing it is to walk in with Jesus. Many inaccessible places are open when you are with the right friend. Heaven is like that. When you come hand in hand with Jesus, the Father says, "Come right in." All is dependent on your identifying with Jesus and your relationship to Him.

"The way of salvation is provided; for the spotless Lamb of God is revealed as the One who taketh away the sin of the world. Jesus stands in the sinner's place, and takes the guilt of the transgressor upon Himself. Looking upon the sinner's

Substitute and Surety, the Lord Jehovah can be just, and yet be the justifier of him that believeth in Jesus. To him who accepts Christ as his righteousness, as his only hope, pardon is pronounced…Jesus says, 'Him that cometh to me I will in no wise cast out.' Christ takes upon Him the sins of the transgressor, and imputes to him His righteousness, and by His transforming grace makes him capable of associating with angels and communing with God." SD 239. The surety makes us capable of associating with angels and communing with God. When you fully understand what Christ has accomplished for us, you recognize you can have fellowship with angels. When you believe in Him, God transforms the life. You are not only justified as a pronouncement but as an actuality. The angels come to protect, lead, and guide you.

When divinity and humanity live together, the weak person is empowered. The steps to this are: first, the surety qualifies Himself by His perfect life; then He pays my debt owed to the law (the debt of death and the debt of righteousness); then I am justified because I have His righteousness by faith; then as I believe in Him as my surety, I have access to the Father, and His divinity comes to live with my humanity; and when that is achieved by faith in the Surety, then amazing things begin to happen immediately because of this. "What a value this places upon man! Through transgression, the sons of man become subjects of Satan. Through faith in the atoning sacrifice of Christ, the sons of Adam may become the sons of God. By assuming human nature, Christ elevates humanity. Fallen men are placed where, through connection with Christ, they may indeed become worthy of the name 'sons of God.'" SC 15.

We become worthy of the name "sons of Adam" by our sins; but when Jesus became a human being, and by His perfect life became our Surety, as we connect with Him, He elevates us and He makes us worthy of the name "sons of God." It is not something just assumed by us without performance. He makes us worthy of that title. He guarantees performance as our surety, and good performance is the result of faith in the Surety and His goodness. This is the result of the activity of the Surety. He has two main roles: He pays our debts, and He guarantees our future performance.

"When you turn away from the broken cisterns that can hold no water, and in the name of Jesus your advocate come directly to God, asking for the things you need, the righteousness of Christ will be revealed as your righteousness, the virtue of Christ as your virtue. You will then understand that justification will come alone through faith in Christ; for in Jesus is revealed the perfection of the character of God; in His life is manifested the outworking of the principles of holiness. Through the atoning blood of Christ the sinner is set free from bondage and condemnation; through the perfection of the sinless Substitute and Surety, he may run in the race of humble obedience to all of God's commandments." 1SM 330. Through that surety and His perfection, I may humbly obey all of

God's commandments. He enables me and guarantees my future performance. You say, "He must really be gambling with me! I don't know about my future performance." Well, He does.

You ask, "Why does He do that? How can He say that?" It is quite easy. If you have ever pledged yourself as surety for another person, you know that the person will love you dearly if you bail him out. That is the way you would feel about someone who pulled you out of jail for your crimes and said, "I will guarantee the performance of this man." This is not irrational behavior on the part of the surety. He knows that any person in jail will love the one who bails him out. If he has any sense or any responsiveness at all, if he is more than a rock, he will say, "I love my surety, and I am so grateful to Him; and I believe in his goodness or he never would have bailed me out." When you understand what Jesus has done for you, you love Him and believe in His goodness (have faith in Him), and then you begin to respond to Him. Jesus said, "If ye love Me, keep My commandments." John 14:15. There is no other way we can keep His commandments.

By becoming surety for us, He brings about the love that is the fulfilling of the law; and if you do not respond to that love, you will never respond. I believe there are very few who have seen the amount of love that He has for us. As you see the magnitude of His love more and more, your heart is softened and you exclaim, "I cannot help but love Him when He first loved me!" The Surety knows that the one He blesses will always love Him; otherwise he is less than human. He knows that, and so He weighs and counts everything in relation to His working role as the surety. It is the most magnificent way that you could imagine or invent to touch someone's heart, to soften hard hearts, and to bless them.

He tells us not to worry about our bad performance, for He will take care of all the debt for that. He will even provide for future performance in my righteousness. But we must go to Him and be affiliated with Him, identify with Him, believe in Him, and trust Him as our Surety. You will be utterly amazed at what you can do when you are aligned with Jesus. It is not what I do, but what He does in me, because He has loved His way right into my heart by His role of being my substitute and surety.

Without Christ, we are always under the condemnation of the law, always a sinner. But through faith in Christ we are made just before God, not just man. And Jesus asks, "Don't you love Me? Haven't I done enough for you? Don't you comprehend all that I have done in being your surety?"

"Jesus is our Surety and Mediator, and has placed at our command every resource, that we may have a perfect character." 6BC, 1116. Our problem is that we are always trusting in what we think we can or must do. We always tell ourselves that we had better line up or burn. Everyone does this. Who are we representing with this fear? Are we *driving* people to love Him? Is that possible? It does not work that way at all. We must hold up the Surety in all His beauty and mercy and perfection, and ask people, "Is He good enough to go surety for you? Do you think the Father will listen to Him?" Jesus has an inexhaustible fund of obedience for all of us. He is able. He is good enough. He is our surety.

Concerning the message presented in 1888, Ellen White wrote this: "This message [presented through Waggoner and Jones] was to bring more prominently before the world the uplifted Saviour, the sacrifice for the sins of the whole world. It presented justification through faith in the Surety; it invited the people to receive the righteousness of Christ, which is made manifest in obedience to all the commandments of God." TM 91,92. There is no other way to obey. It is utterly impossible. Except Christ becomes our surety, we struggle alone in all of our misery and weakness; and we only discover over and over how weak we are. Some strong willed people might give a good outward appearance, but don't dig inside. We are all alike on the inside, aren't we? The Lord looks into the heart and not on the externals. He does not look at external performance of the strong willed person who thinks he is doing such a good job, but He looks on the inside and sees that the person is full of dead men's bones (as Jesus said). He always looks on the heart. He says He will give us a new heart. It is something only He can do. He will function and perform as your Surety. He is able. He is good. He will pay the debt of death, and the debt of righteousness. He will guarantee your performance as you choose and believe and identify with Him. Will you choose Him?

Friend, for years we have been choosing ourselves, believing that God demanded us to do it of ourselves. Or we have prayed, "Lord, please help me," as though with just a little boost we could do it ourselves. That is a poor prayer. The Lord wants us to focus on the Surety. He is on the job. Look upon Him and place all your confidence in Him and not in yourself. As you trust Him and His obedience, your life will change.

Imagine that you go see the state Governor. You have never met him in your whole life, but you walk in the door with the Governor's brother. The Governor hardly looks at you but he looks at his brother. He does not ask you, "How did you get in here?" for you walked in with his brother. Then his brother says, "This is my friend. I would like you to meet him." And the Governor responds, "Oh, well, I am happy to have you here." Why is he happy? Because you are friends with his brother. And suddenly he is looking right at you, for now you are acceptable because of his brother. Isn't that the way God does it? We come to Him through the obedience of Christ, the perfect Surety. The Father looks at Him. I am made fragrant by the incense of His perfect righteousness. The Father never sees me without the veil of the incense of Christ's obedience. Then He says, "I am happy to have you here as My sons and daughters, the brothers and sisters of My Son, Jesus Christ."

We must never leave out our Surety. Every moment of every day we are totally dependant upon Him. There will never be a time when you can live without Him. When you walk the streets of gold and someone asks, "How did you get here?" everyone will say, "Because of the Surety. That is why I am here." All the praise will be to Him, and we will follow the Lamb, our Surety, wherever He goes, and we will never leave Him because He is so everlastingly good and precious. We will love Him with all our hearts and never let Him out of our sight. And through the ages of eternity, we will everlastingly praise Him, the marvelous, wonderful One, who because of His goodness makes us acceptable even to God. May we walk this day and from hence forth with our eyes on Jesus our Surety.

14

HE MUST INCREASE

WE HAVE DISCOVERED SO far that there are many aspects of Christ our righteousness and justification by faith that are often misunderstood or misinterpreted. Our subject for this chapter is probably the most difficult of all to understand. It is found in Revelation 3:17-19, which is what we often call the Laodicean message. These texts are part of the message of Christ our righteousness, and in fact one of the most important aspects of it.

The text reads: "Because thou sayest, I am rich, and increased with goods, and have need of nothing; and knowest not that thou art wretched, and miserable, and poor, and blind, and naked: I counsel thee to buy of Me gold tried in the fire, that thou mayest be rich; and white raiment, that thou mayest be clothed, and that the shame of thy nakedness do not appear; and anoint thine eyes with eyesalve, that thou mayest see. As many as I love, I rebuke and chasten: be zealous therefore, and repent." This is only a portion of what we call the Laodicean message, but we will focus upon it because of the aspect that relates to Christ our righteousness.

"The Laodicean message has been sounding. Take this message in all its phases and sound it forth to the people wherever Providence opens the way. Justification by faith and the righteousness of Christ are the themes to be presented to a perishing world." 7BC 964. Notice that Laodicea says they are rich and in need of nothing. The True Witness, who is Christ according, does not agree with their self-assessment. He counsels them to buy white raiment that they might be clothed, that the shame of their nakedness does not appear.

The Scripture declares that white raiment is the cure for our nakedness, and the white raiment is symbolic of the righteousness of Christ. As soon as we talk about Laodicea, many people become negative and do not want to listen. They automatically take it as severe criticism, and they cannot bear criticism; and that makes it difficult to communicate with people about this message.

Nevertheless, in the heart of the message the Lord says, "As many as I love, I rebuke and chasten." This is not a message of criticism; it is a message of love and of great concern to those who are having difficulty with shame, which is closely connected to guilt. What is the shame of our nakedness as it is called here in these few verses?

"What is the shame of this nakedness and poverty? It is the shame of clothing ourselves with self-righteousness, and of separating ourselves from God, when He has made ample provision for all to receive His blessing." 7BC 965. This is not an easy thing for us to see concerning ourselves. We can always see it in others, but we think it does not apply to us. We are in a shameful condition, thinking we are clothed, but our clothing is made up of our own works and self-righteousness.

"Many are Laodiceans, living in a spiritual self-deception. They clothe themselves in the garments of their own righteousness, imagining themselves to be rich and increased with goods and in need of nothing, when they need daily to learn of Jesus, His meekness and lowliness, else they find themselves bankrupt, their whole life being a lie." 7BC 962.

It is one thing to lie with our lips, but it is another thing to lie with our lives. These people are in danger of being spiritually bankrupt, yet they clothe themselves in the garments of their own righteousness. To make it worse, they do not understand that they have done this. They are deceived and say they are rich, that they have beautiful garments and do not have to worry, and they seem to be quite complacent; although there is some shame attached to it.

Self-righteousness is self-deceptive. I can write the words and you can read them, but from that point on there is a problem. I go to church on the right day, pay my tithes and offerings, believe the Lord is returning soon, believe doctrinal truth, and therefore I say it cannot be speaking of me. The True Witness simply says that we are clothed in self-righteousness; and while we say we are rich, we do not seem to understand that we are spiritually poor and spiritually naked.

The Lord who commanded His disciples to clothe the naked, would surely try to take care of this problem that we have, would He not? Clothing both the spiritually and physically naked is the heart and soul of Christianity. He is concerned about this condition.

We may gain insight into this matter in the experience of Adam and Eve. "And the eyes of them both were opened, and they knew that they were naked; and they sewed fig leaves together, and made themselves aprons." Genesis 3:7. There was some kind of shame involved after they had transgressed.

"And he [Adam] said, I heard Thy voice in the garden, and I was afraid, because I was naked; and I hid myself. And He said, Who told thee that thou wast naked? Hast thou eaten of the tree whereof I commanded thee that thou shouldest not eat?" Verses 10,11. As you read on in that chapter, it tells you what God did about their nakedness. "Unto Adam also and to his wife did the Lord God make coats of skins, and clothed them." Verse 21. God offered a sacrifice. An animal died, unless you can skin an animal without killing it. God offered a sacrifice and clothed them. As soon as they transgressed they knew they were naked, and they felt embarrassed and tried to cover themselves.

"This robe of light was a symbol of their spiritual garments of heavenly innocence. Had they remained true to God it would ever have continued to enshroud them. But when sin entered, they severed their connection with God, and the light that had encircled them departed. Naked and ashamed, they tried to supply the place of the heavenly garments by sewing together fig leaves for a covering." COL 311. Do you suppose they found innocence in doing that? They were still hiding, they were still ashamed, they were no longer innocent, and they ran from the light.

Continuing with the quote: "This is what the transgressors of God's law have done ever since the day of Adam and Eve's disobedience. They have sewed together fig leaves to cover the nakedness caused by transgression. They have worn the garments of their own devising, by works of their own they have tried to cover their sins, and make themselves acceptable with God. But this they can never do. Nothing can man devise to supply the place of his lost robe of innocence. No fig-leaf garment, no worldly citizen dress, can be worn by those who sit down with Christ and angels at the marriage supper of the Lamb. Only the covering which Christ Himself has provided can make us meet to appear in God's presence. This covering, the robe of His own righteousness, Christ will put upon every repenting, believing soul." Note that it says nothing about our righteousness there. It says He will place the robe of Christ's righteousness upon every repenting, believing soul, not upon every flawlessly performing Christian, as some have believed.

As you begin to understand what took place there in the Garden of Eden and how this came about, you begin to see that man tries to provide what he cannot provide. "When they listened to the voice of the tempter, and sinned against God, the light of the garments of heavenly innocence departed from them; and in parting with the garments of innocence, they drew about them the dark robes of ignorance of God." 1BC 1084. There was light, there was knowledge in the first robes, and there was innocence. There was knowledge of God. When they parted with the garments of innocence, they drew about them the dark robes of ignorance of God.

The quote continues: "The clear and perfect light that had hitherto surrounded them had lightened everything they approached; but deprived of that heavenly light, the posterity of Adam could no longer trace the character of God in His created works." A unique darkness came when they sinned, and no longer did they have those perceptive powers. They could not see God in His created works. There came upon them a robe of ignorance concerning God, and immediately they were afraid of Him and ran to hide; and yet He was a God of love. He has always been and will always be a God of love. He never changes. But now they were suspicious and thought that God would get even. Now, in ignorance of God's true character, they ran in fear from the light and hid in darkness. They lived in fear because the light had departed.

"The fig-leaves represent the arguments used to cover disobedience." 1BC 1084. Do you ever justify your sins? Lord, I didn't mean to do that. I would not have sinned today if I had slept better last night, or if my wife had not become angry with me, or if our children had not been out of hand. We have hundreds of arguments, don't we?

The quote goes on to say, "The fig-leaves represent the arguments used to cover disobedience. When the Lord calls the attention of men and women to the truth, the making of fig-leaves into aprons will be begun, to hide the nakedness of the soul. But the nakedness of the sinner is not covered. All the arguments pieced together by all who have interested themselves in this flimsy work will come to naught."

Do you ever argue with God? Do you ever debate with Him to cover your disobedience? We pray that way all the time, even in our pulpits. When in our prayers we thank God that we are not like other people because we do this and this and this, we are arguing with God. We love to argue with Him, weaving fig leaves into aprons, trying to gain stature with God who still loves us and who has always loved us. We have not chased Him away by our sins.

This God who comes to offer us salvation in the Seed of the woman. We somehow forget and seem to misunderstand that He is a God of love; and we run in fear to hide, and say, "Don't speak to me!" That robe of light was a robe of heavenly innocence. In that innocence there was a true knowledge of God. In our nakedness, there are only garments of our own devising, our own works, and garments of ignorance of God. The garments are our arguments used to cover disobedience. Do you realize that perhaps the greatest evidence that we are still naked, that His robe of righteousness is not ours, is that we present arguments to cover our disobedience? Every time you begin to explain your sins in prayer to God, you are saying you do not have the robe of innocence, and you do not believe that Christ is your righteousness. This is hard for us to understand for we have become fearful of God as soon as we discover we are naked, as did Adam and Eve. We experience shame and guilt and we flee from God. We try to justify self and argue every invention we can think of trying to make ourselves look good, as though God has to be convinced, or as if we must twist His arm in order for Him to save us.

Is your God like that? Does Jesus love us because He died for us, but God hates us because we are sinners? Do we have a loving heavenly Father? Some people cannot even pray to the Father. They are afraid; and so they pray "Dear Jesus" as though the Father would chase them away. We must always come in Jesus name, but we must pray to the Father. But we are afraid! The greatest misunderstanding in this problem is that I can do something to cover my nakedness and guilt. If somehow the Lord by His Spirit could teach me that I can do nothing about this, what a blessing it would be. But in our fear and our desperation, in our darkness of misunderstanding God, we seek to save ourselves by our arguments and self-justification. I have nothing in me, I have no potential, I have no capability, and there is no possibility of any kind that I can cover my own nakedness. I am incapable like a little child.

The sad part about this is that we believe we can cover our nakedness, and we indulge in this. The Jews did this many years after they knew better. "For they being ignorant of God's righteousness [there is the darkness], and going about to establish their own righteousness, have not submitted themselves unto the righteousness of God." Romans 10:3. As soon as you try to establish yours, you also establish your ignorance of His. They go together. You cannot separate them. This ignorance is not caused by God, but by our own choice.

We try to cover our nakedness by our own devices and excuses. But the True Witness says we are to buy of Him so that we may be clothed, and that the shame of our nakedness does not appear. Is He in error? Is the True Witness a false witness? Is the Laodicean message a Satanic message from the deceiver? Or does God truly love us; and is this the God of love speaking? He says we are to buy of Him the clothing we need; but we say we must do something. He says that what we must do is to believe that He will provide it for us.

Adam and Eve had a difference of opinion with the Creator in Genesis chapter 3, for it says they made fig leaves and sewed them together for garments. But God provided coats of skins to clothe them. We must put off our own filthy garments and put on Christ's robe of righteousness. Adam and Eve were confronted with the very same decision as everyone of us; and for six thousand years people have been making these decisions. Some people say you must have both fig leaves and skins of animals. Can that be? The Lord did not say that in Genesis and He does not say it in Revelation. Where do you find it? He says the only thing that can cover you is His robe that He has provided. The Lord God made coats of skins and clothed them. He did not sew together fig leaves.

Jesus says we are to buy white raiment of Him. You cannot obtain it any other place in the world. There is no other place except that He provides it. You must confront yourselves with His alternatives and His ideas. It is either our raiment or His; it is never both ours and His. Either I tear mine off and throw it away and wear His, or I wear my own and have nothing to do with His.

In previous chapters we have been emphasizing the terms Christ our righteousness and justification by faith. These terms tell us that righteousness is found in someone else other than self. The term substitute and surety is talking about the righteousness of another person, and we must make His righteousness ours, and must claim it for ourselves by faith. We have been suggesting we must look elsewhere other than to self, which is exactly what both Revelation 3 and Genesis 3 say. All the teachings of righteousness say we must look some other place and that you cannot find it in a sinner. Yet this is what many refuse to do so often.

The sinner persists in arguing that he can do something. Sinners argue that we are saved by both faith and works, and they offer a gross misunderstanding of James to establish their self-deception. James merely presents a way to determine if your faith is genuine. If it is, it will produce good works. James still says you are saved by faith alone. There is no way our works can cover us. You do not find innocence in good works, no matter how perfect those works are. You do not find light in your own good works, no matter how perfect your works are. We must have these good works, but these we cannot provide. I can only receive the robe of righteousness from Christ by faith, without works. I cannot make my own and I cannot have half mine and half His. Without His, all our works will fail to cover us no matter how completely we do the job. You can work a lifetime flawlessly and still be naked. Adam and Eve provided something for themselves and assumed they were not naked. They were producing a kind of robe by their works, and they thought they were covered. The Lord asked, "Why are you hiding if you are covered?"

So you can put on something and still be naked, because it is more than a physical nakedness. There is something in the heart and the soul that troubles us. There is a shame of nakedness. There is an ignorance of God and so we flee from Him. We live in darkness and not in light, and there is not innocence, but guilt, in our souls. You can go ahead and sew fig leaves for the rest of your lives, and you can live many years, but still be naked. You can stand up and say, "I believe in Christ our righteousness, and I believe I am clothed in His righteousness." But you have made the whole thing yourself; and the Lord says you are still naked.

Adam and Eve were still naked after all their work. In no way were they innocent. They were hiding, still in darkness, still misunderstanding God, still ignorant of His character. God was not a God of anger. He might have been displeased but He was not angry with them. Does He not quickly forgive? He immediately offered a sacrifice to take away their sins. He offered them forgiveness, and yet they were afraid.

"It is the darkness of misapprehension of God that is enshrouding the world. Men are losing their knowledge of His character. It has been misunderstood and misinterpreted." COL 415. Do you know we still do not know Him very well? There is a quick way to establish how well you know Him. When you have sinned the same sin you have committed many times, how quickly do you pray? You probably say to yourself, "He will not hear me if I pray. I have sinned too many times." Do you hide and cower and believe that He is far off? Many times you have thought to yourself that your prayers do not go beyond the ceiling. So many young people think they have committed the unpardonable sin. All this is darkness concerning the knowledge of God. He is not like that! The God who sent His Son all the way from heaven to earth to live with us, to become human, does not leave because of our sins. If we were still sinners when He died for us, would He not live in us now that we are reconciled through the death and resurrection of Jesus? Somehow God is a strange, nebulous, unknown Person to us; and yet it is life eternal to know Him and His Son. We do not see God in Jesus very clearly.

This problem concerning the lack of knowledge of God is the cause of the credibility gap between those who have various theories of Christ our righteousness. Some begin to understand that their own robe of righteousness is foolishness and ridiculous, and know that they cannot provide righteousness at all. As they suddenly see the light of the character of God and His beauty, and that He provides the robe of righteousness, they become ecstatic, elated, and thrilled as if finding a first love again. But others who have never come to that realization will stand off and say they cannot understand what is so exciting about Christ our righteousness. They look upon those who have been enlightened as if they were Pentecostals. They claim to believe in Christ our righteousness, but they do not get excited about it. They do not know that they sit in darkness. Our churches are split into two groups: those who sit in darkness, and those who sit in light. A terrible credibility gap exists between the two groups. No matter how hard you try to explain the truth on this subject, people still sit in darkness.

I recall preaching in a small church on the book of Galatians for several weeks in prayer meeting. A man about forty years of age had been attending for a few evenings, suddenly one night the lights came on. He came to me after the meeting and scolded me for having withheld this light. He rebuked me strongly and said, "Why have you done this terrible thing to us? Why did you withhold this truth for so long?" So I took him back briefly to the previous studies and then I asked, "Is what I told you tonight any different than what I've been telling you all these weeks?" He would not accept the fact that during those past sermons he either would not or could not see. When he finally did begin to see, he accused me of depriving him of light. Yet the light was shining all the time. There are also many who say they see the truth on this subject, but in reality do not. They clothe themselves in their own righteousness and think they are safe; but if God would manifest Himself they would run to hide in darkness someplace to escape Him, establishing they really have not found it.

Some people find a great light, as the Bible says. "The people that walked in darkness have seen a great light: they that dwell in the land of the shadow of death, upon them hath the light shined." Isaiah 9:2. The light of the knowledge of the glory of God [His true character] beams down upon them.

Another text refers to the same thing: "Arise, shine; for thy light is come, and the glory of the Lord is risen upon thee. For, behold, the darkness shall cover the earth, and gross darkness the people: but the Lord shall arise upon thee, and His glory shall be seen upon thee. And the Gentiles shall come to thy light, and kings to the brightness of thy rising." Isaiah 60:1-3. The Gentiles—the heathen and the unbelievers—will come. Note that it did not say His people will come. They think they already have the light, so they do not come to the light when it shines forth in all its beauty.

Isaiah chapter 58 talks about the good works that we are to do, which includes loosening the bands of wickedness, undoing heavy burdens, feeding the hungry, clothing the naked, and helping the poor. When you do these things, verses 8-10 takes place. "Then shall thy light break forth as the morning, and thine health shall spring forth speedily: and thy righteousness shall go before thee; the glory of the Lord shall be thy rereward. Then shalt thou call, and the Lord shall answer; thou shalt cry, and He shall say, Here I am…And if thou draw out thy soul to the hungry, and satisfy the afflicted soul; then shall thy light rise in obscurity, and thy darkness be as the noonday." Prospering spiritually and abundantly is the promise of the Lord. Why? Because of this great light. When the sun comes up, things begin to grow and flourish.

When I lived in Canada I talked to a man who farms in Peace River, which is way up north where it never becomes dark in the months of June and July. He told me in June that he already had huge tomatoes growing. I asked him how he got such big tomatoes at that time of year; and he said it was because the sun shines all day and all night. When the light shines twenty-four hours a day, everything grows fast. Their growing season is short, but they have long days. People who have long days can grow as much or more as those who have shorter days because there is so much light. And so it is that when the light from the Lord begins to shine into our hearts, great things happen to us.

Those who think their spiritual garments must be partially woven by themselves see the illustration about the fig leaves and the animal skin to be absurd. They do not realize the infinite difference between fig leaves (symbolic of self-righteousness) and coats of skin (symbolic of Christ's righteousness). Using Bible terms, what is the difference between nakedness and white raiment? What is the difference between Christ's righteousness and my righteousness? The Bible refers to Christ's righteousness as white raiment, a wedding garment, and a pearl of great price without flaw. His righteousness is without spot or wrinkle. There is nothing more perfect than the righteousness of Christ.

What is my righteousness? It is "filthy rags, all as an unclean thing." Isaiah 64: 6. "There is none righteous, no not one." Romans 3:10. "Who can bring a clean thing out of an unclean?" Job 14:4. In other words, how can the unrighteous produce any degree of righteousness? The Bible calls our lack of righteousness "nakedness." You put something on but the nakedness is still there—still in darkness, still fig-leaves, still self-deceived, still self-effort. Which would you prefer, the Pearl of great price or your own nakedness? When I say I must have my own works to be saved, I am saying I do not like or need the Pearl of great price." Many are content with their own righteousness. It takes a unique perception to want only His righteousness. To like your own is a terrible thing. How can we like filthiness? Pride is a deceptive thing, for it brings me to the point where I do not see clearly the difference between human righteousness and Christ's righteousness. I want to keep my own, and I argue and justify my own; and the Lord asks us why we do that. He offers us something better, but we still want our filthy garments.

It is difficult for us to comprehend our own nakedness. We must realize that it is more than right actions that justify the soul. Justification is not just a legal transaction where God says you are set right. With justification there must come an innocence that all is right with God, a perfect peace where God has taken our burdens away, and where the mind is totally free. It is like being lifted up and walking on air. Is it any wonder some people get so excited? All is at peace, and Christ did promise us that peace. But we go on and on, wretched and miserable and trying to act like we have peace; and the True Witness asks, "Why are you wretched and miserable in your nakedness when I want to give you My robe of righteousness? Buy of Me white raiment. Take away the wretchedness and misery. Let Me give you something precious." And you say, "But I like my own." And He asks, "Why do you like your own when I offer you something infinitely better?"

Job, reasoning about justification, asked, "but how should man be just with God? If you will contend with Him, He cannot answer him one of a thousand [questions]." Job 9:2. In other words, I cannot answer God at all if He argues with me.

In verses 14 and 15 of that chapter, Job reasons, "How much less shall I answer Him, and choose out my words to reason with Him? Whom, though I were righteous, yet would I not answer, but I would make supplication to my Judge." I would not answer Him and retort. I wouldn't dare. I do not have the words to speak; even if I were righteous.

In verses 20 and 21 of the same chapter: "If I justify myself, mine own mouth shall condemn me: if I say, I am perfect, it shall also prove me perverse. Though I were perfect, yet would I not know my soul: I would despise my life." There is nothing good in me.

Finally in verse 28, "I am afraid of all my sorrows, I know that thou wilt not hold me innocent." I will not find innocence by trying to justify myself. He must give me that perfect peace and that innocence.

Paul reasons: "Not by works of righteousness which we have done, but according to His mercy." Titus 3:5. He also reasons: "And be found in Him, not having mine own righteousness, which is of the law." Philippians 3:9. Not having my own, but only the marvelous righteousness found in Jesus.

The bottom line is that we must experience what John the Baptist experienced when he declared, "He must increase, but I must decrease." John 3:30. We always want to reverse this. We say, "If I am righteous, I must increase and He must decrease." Some theorists of Christ our righteousness draw graphs to represent this idea. How ridiculous can we get?

He must increase and I must decrease—always! As long as I live, Christ must become all in all to me. I must always be decreasing, always going down. I can never increase myself. That would be the wrong thing to do. Yet, Laodicea tries to do that.

In addition, we need to dispel the darkness with light. I must become innocent and get rid of this darkness regarding God's character. Can I produce light? It is impossible. He is the light of the world. I am not. Unless He shines into my heart, I will never find innocence, and I will never understand Him.

In this process called justification, I must find innocence and I must find light. These I can never produce by my good works. Laodicea goes on without them, and they go on not understanding the height and depth and breadth of His great love.

Jesus commented upon this in the experience of restoring sight to the man born blind. He met with the Pharisees and had this discussion with them: "And Jesus said, For judgment I am come into this world, that they which see not might see; and that they which see might be made blind. And some of the Pharisees which were with Him heard these words, and said unto Him, Are we blind also? Jesus said unto them, If ye were blind, ye should have no sin: but now ye say, We see; therefore your sin remaineth." John 9:39-41.

We have this same problem. We continue to tell the world that we have the light. We tell them that we see, but that they are in darkness. And because we say we see, our sin remains and we are blind. Many will insist that they see because of our marvelous doctrines. Yes, but do you have the light in Jesus? Our truths can be perverted when not centered in Christ; and what terrible things we have done to what we call truth, because our truths are so often not found in Jesus. He is the truth. There is no other truth except Christ. The Jews held to a Christless law until He had to come and tell them that the law is to love God supremely and to love one another as He has loved us. And it is not the way you think you should love. The way Jesus loved is the only correct interpretation of the law.

Christ is telling all Christians that they are to keep the truths as He kept them, to believe them as He believed them, and to teach them as He taught them; not as you think they are. The Sabbath in Christ is a vastly different thing than just keeping the right day. Tithing in Jesus is most unusual. The prophecies in Christ are so different. The standards in Christ are most unusual. Few people have ever heard, or even thought about, truth as it is in Jesus. The light has not come until Jesus comes in. Many walk in darkness, but they do not believe they are in darkness.

"I have been shown the greatest reason why the people of God are now found in the state of spiritual blindness is that they will not receive correction." 3T 254. Your argument is not with me, or another church member of any church. Your problem is with Jesus, the True Witness. It is His idea that we are naked. He is the one who speaks. You can argue with Him if you want to, but I do not choose to do that myself. If I am sitting in darkness, according to His understanding of it, I cannot say I understand. If He is the light, I cannot dispute with the light when I sit in darkness. He sees because He is the light. I do not see because I am in darkness. Therefore, He understands my condition, and I do not; and I must receive correction. It is not criticism. It is correction.

Jesus says, "As many as I love, I rebuke and chasten." Revelation 3:19. The first thing we must understand about God is that when He speaks like this, He loves me. He said He came to bring sinners to repentance, not the righteous. Do I hear the call if I say I am righteous? Do I understand His love if I say I need no rebuke? Not a bit. We can lock His love out of our comprehension by some of these opinions we have that are contrary to those of the True Witness. Jesus wants us to hear His rebuke because He loves us and wants to save us from the end of the road we are traveling. He says, "Please hear My voice and repent."

At the heart of everything in Christ our righteousness is repentance. Why will I find any confidence in my miserable self-righteousness? Why? How can I love filthy garments? How can I go on not sensing my uncleanness? How can I go on in guilt and fear and misery and wretchedness and say I have peace? How can I go on in all my misunderstandings of God and His love and say I am not in darkness but in light? How can I go on in all this deception and say I am right? And yet we do. When the lights come on (and they will not come on until you open the door), He gives you the choice to live daily in light or darkness. He will not break the door down. He will knock a long time (and we should be grateful for that), but He will not break the door down.

Laodicea is inside the door, and Jesus is outside. Laodicea lives in shame on the inside, and peace and innocence are outside. He tells us to open the door, and the innocence, the light, the peace and the joy will come in; and the wretchedness and misery and nakedness will all flee away. And when that happens to you, you will, like Isaiah, say, "Woe is me!" And God will send an angel with a "live coal in his hand, which he had taken with the tongs from off the altar: And he laid it upon my mouth, and said, Lo, this hath touched thy lips; and thine iniquity is taken away, and thy sin purged." Isaiah 6:6. When the light comes on, I see how naked

I am and I repent; and I say, "Woe is me." Then God takes away all the shame, all the disgrace, all the uncleanness. Thy light has come. Come and be blessed.

Friend, the Lord has been waiting a long time. He is waiting because He loves Laodicea. He is waiting for us to discover that we are not innocent anymore. Over and over again we discuss our guilt, our misery, our lack of innocence. We ask: What do I yet lack? We have doubts and uncertainties; we argue with God; we seek to justify self. And all the time the Lord says, "You don't have to live like that. I don't want My children living in that condition. Let Me in. Let Me give you light so that you will know I am a God of love. Let Me give you innocence so that even the guilt is gone, as well as right deeds coming in. Let Me be your white raiment, and what joy you will have. Let Me take away the misery and the wretchedness, and give you happiness and peace and innocence and joy and light. What a happy life you can live then."

He is not going to continue knocking eternally. Someday we must recognize the facts that the True Witness has brought to us. We must accept what He says, and what we are, and what He is, and embrace Him with all our hearts. And then our light will break forth as the morning and we will shout songs of praise and gladness and halleluiahs, and then the Lord Jesus will come. And to us He will say after all this, "Well done good and faithful servant, enter thou into the joy of thy Lord." May you hear those sweet words soon is my prayer in Jesus name.

15

WHAT IS SANCTIFICATION?

A S WE CONTINUE THESE studies on the various aspects of Christ our righteousness and justification by faith, we realize that these are very sensitive subjects that many have strong, preconceived opinions about. This is to be expected. We want to challenge your thinking and present some things that we hope will help us to better see the picture that God has given to us.

Perhaps the most common misunderstanding among Seventh-day Adventists is the concept that justification is what Jesus does for us, and sanctification is what we do for Him as the result of our justification. We cannot justify ourselves, but we think that we can obey in order to satisfy God's requirement of righteousness. In sanctification, it seems our whole emphasis revolves around what we do.

This has become almost a galling, despairing, and hopeless subject to many people. To some it is their ticket to heaven because they are strong-willed; and because they can provide an external obedience, they feel rather comfortable in what they do. Others who might be weak feel they will never make it. We have many ideas about sanctification that are probably not true. I do not profess to understand all there is to know about it, but there are some things about it in the Bible that are quite certain.

Is sanctification what we do for Him? Or is it what He does in us? Is it what I do, or what He accomplishes in me? This statement of Paul should be familiar to us: "But of Him are ye in Christ Jesus, Who of God is made unto us wisdom, and righteousness, and sanctification, and redemption." 1 Corinthians 1:30. If Paul taught that Christ is made unto us sanctification, then it is apparently something that He performs on our behalf.

Paul also wrote this: "And be found in Him, not having mine own righteousness, which is of the law, but that which is through the faith of Christ, the righteousness which is of God by faith: That I may know Him, and the power of His resurrection, and the fellowship of His sufferings, being made conformable unto His death; If by any means I might attain unto the resurrection of the dead." Philippians 3:9-11. Paul seems to be talking about the conclusion of his experience, and he said that at some future time, he wanted to be found in Christ, not having his own righteousness but Christ's.

Many will recognize this famous quotation that has been used for years about justification and sanctification: "The righteousness by which we are justified is imputed; the righteousness by which we are sanctified is imparted. The first is our title to heaven, the second is our fitness for heaven." MYP 35. What does the word "imparted" mean? We recognize that it is not the same as "imputed," but there are similarities.

In the *Webster's Collegiate Dictionary,* imparted means "To bestow a share of; give from one's own store of abundance." Synonyms are "to transfer, dispense, grant, confer." Therefore, in imparted righteousness, something comes from one person to another; something they give from their abundance to someone who lacks. So there are similarities as well as dissimilarities in imputed and imparted righteousness. Both come from Jesus to us. It is not something that we are performing for Him, but rather something He has which He imparts to us. It does not come to us all at once, but it does come from Him.

Paul also mentions this very briefly: "Being confident of this very thing, that He which hath begun a good work in you will perform it until the day of Jesus Christ." Philippians 1:6. The One who started it will perform it to completion. The idea here is that He carries on the work of justification, which He started, to completion.

"Christ is the great depository of justifying righteousness and sanctifying grace." 1SM 398. Fort Knox is the depository of gold for the United States. Christ is the "depository of justifying righteousness and sanctifying grace." That grace which brings about sanctification is found in Him, not in me or someone else. Go to Him to find it; and by grace He gives it to you.

In all of these thoughts we discover that in sanctification, something proceeds from Him to us. We must go to Him to find it. This part of sanctification is usually omitted. We often ask God for help, or a little push or shove of some kind. That is not what we are talking about. It is more than a push or shove. It is more than assistance. There is literally something coming from Him to me, and it is more than power, or else we have misunderstood Paul's statements completely. He has something I lack, and I must go to Him to receive it. It is not something I produce in and of myself.

In no way does this eliminate obedience. This is the only way you can experience obedience. There is no other way that can be found. All other obedience is but a deception. We only call it that when it really is not.

When we are seeking sanctification, we mean we are seeking righteousness. What is righteousness? We have covered this in previous chapters, but I know how quickly we forget, especially if we do not live by this principle. Let us review it and delve into it a bit more than we have in the past.

What is righteousness in relation to sanctification? "Obedience to the law is sanctification." ST, May 19, 1890. "Sanctification is the doing of all the commandments of God." ST, March 24, 1890. Right here is where we have trouble. Many people, because of their misinterpretations of statements like this, say that righteousness and sanctification are not obedience. They say it is not right doing, but rather right relationships. It is true that right relationships produce right doing; but the relationship is not the righteousness. We must be careful about small details like this.

Some people look at the law and immediately get out a microscope and look at themselves. Most of us have done that for years, and it has caused a great deal of misunderstanding and difficulty among us. We look to see if we are doing everything correctly. Is sanctification the avoidance of every "thou shalt not" and the correct performance of every "thou shalt"? Is that sanctification? We just read that sanctification is obedience to the law. Is sanctification the perfect living of all standards of proper entertainment, and health, and dress? Many people use these to scrutinize their character and performance to see if they are being sanctified. When we have done this for years and see some flaws—some violations of the "thou shalt nots"—we begin to think that we are not going to make it. Many feel extremely guilty and give up in discouragement.

You must look at righteousness much more carefully than most of us have done in the past. Sanctification, as we read, is obedience to the law; but what is the law? Most will answer that the law is the Ten Commandments. Yes, but what is that? What are those commandments, and what are they like? You must always go back to Jesus and see the law through His eyes. "Master, which is the great commandment in the law? Jesus said unto him, Thou shalt love the Lord thy God with all thy heart, and with all thy soul, and with all thy mind. This is the first and great commandment. And the second is like unto it, Thou shalt love thy neighbour as thyself. On these two commandments hang all the law and the prophets." Matthew 22:36-40. Before you can understand anything about sanctification, you must look at the law through the eyes of Jesus. As Adventists, we have emphasized the law as written on stone tablets and left Christ out of it.

The Jews had done a terrible thing to the law. They had three hundred commandments on not bearing a load, or burden, on the Sabbath. They expanded the commandments to the place where they had figured out every possible "thou shalt not" to guarantee they were not transgressing. If they could follow every one of those "thou shalt nots," then they would be sanctified. Do you know that there are thousands of Adventists who follow the same philosophy? We have used the Spirit of Prophecy as a Talmud to find all of the "thou shalt nots" and the "thou shalts." We think that if we can get them all cataloged in a computer, we can check ourselves all the time, and thus avoid doing wrong. But as many have discovered, you can have a million laws, and never avoid doing wrong. It does not matter how many there are or how perfectly they are adapted to us, we still do wrong. Those laws do not change character. You can invent new laws to restrict your children, but they still have problems, don't they? They are not changed by laws any more than we are. Paul wrote about "what the law could not do, in that it was weak through the flesh." Romans 8:3. Remember that even though we have been justified, we still have some problems. The Lord takes care of those with His methods; but we cannot take care of them with our methods.

This fundamental interpretation of the law by Jesus is that *the law is love.* I do not mean the permissive kind of lust that people call love nowadays. I am looking through the eyes of Paul when he describes love in 1 Corinthians, and you know it very well. Since the law is love, this makes obedience to the law much different than we have seen it to be, and it makes sin much different, also. Hopefully you are becoming familiar with this quote from a previous chapter: "Righteousness is holiness, likeness to God, and 'God is love.' 1 John 4:16. It is conformity to the law of God, 'for all Thy commandments are righteousness.' Psalms 119:172; and 'love is the fulfilling of the law.' Romans 13:10. Righteousness is love; and love is the light and the life of God. The righteousness of God is embodied in Christ. We receive righteousness by receiving Him." MB 18. God is love, and the law is a transcript of His character, so the law is love. Obedience to the law is love, so righteousness is love; and sanctification, which is obedience to the law, is love, too.

All of this is different than most of us have anticipated in sanctification. We have left out love almost entirely from the sanctified life. We have tried to look in an egocentric way at ourselves to see what our hands do, what our lips speak, what we eat, what we hear, and what we see; then we ask, "I wonder if I am sanctified?" That is not sanctification. Not in the least. The whole spirit of sanctification is totally eliminated, and we are left looking at self; and the more we look at self, the more we become like self, and the less sanctified we will ever be.

Righteousness is love, and that love is expressed in action. Therefore, in sanctification there are *works,* and *doing,* and *activity.* Those who are married know this. Your spouse can say they love you all they wish, but unless they perform the acts of love, you have a difficult time accepting that they love you. Love must be expressed in action. Jesus said, "If ye love Me, keep My commandments." John 14:15. The keeping of the commandments is prompted by our love for Jesus. If we do not love Him, forget about trying. Jesus teaches that if it comes out of a heart filled with love, then keep His law of love.

His commandments are unique—supreme love for God, and to love your neighbor as yourself. It is the activity, the doing, for God and for your neighbors that fits what Jesus taught about obedience. This is described in several places in the Bible, and we want to entrench them in our minds and put them in the context of sanctification.

Our first text deals with that time in the Judgment when the sheep and the goats are divided. "Then shall the King say unto them on His right hand, Come, ye blessed of My Father, inherit the kingdom prepared for you from the foundation of the world: For I was an hungred, and ye gave Me meat: I was thirsty, and ye gave Me drink: I was a stranger, and ye took Me in: Naked, and ye clothed Me: I was sick, and ye visited Me: I was in prison, and ye came unto Me. Then shall the righteous answer Him, saying, Lord, when saw we Thee an hungred, and fed Thee? or thirsty, and gave Thee drink? When saw we Thee a stranger, and took Thee in? or naked, and clothed Thee? Or when saw we Thee sick, or in prison, and came unto Thee? And the King shall answer and say unto them, Verily I say unto you, Inasmuch as ye have done it unto one of the least of these My brethren, ye have done it unto Me." Matthew 25:34-40. According to Jesus, these are the works that are examined in the Judgment. These works were prophesied by Isaiah and describe the life of Jesus, and we are to be like Jesus in sanctification. We cannot make ourselves like Him, but He is able to make us like Him.

Here is the prophecy as described by Isaiah: "Is not this the fast that I have chosen? to loose the bands of wickedness, to undo the heavy burdens, and to let the oppressed go free, and that ye break every yoke? Is it not to deal thy bread to the hungry, and that thou bring the poor that are cast out to thy house? when thou seest the naked, that thou cover him; and that thou hide not thyself from thine own flesh?" Isaiah 58:6,7. This activity for others shows our supreme love for God and our love for our neighbor.

Job, whom I consider to be a type of Christ, wrote these words: "Because I delivered the poor that cried, and the fatherless, and him that had none to help him. The blessing of him that was ready to perish came upon me: and I caused the widow's heart to sing for joy. I put on righteousness, and it clothed me: my judgment was as a robe and a diadem. I was eyes to the blind, and feet was I to the lame. I was a father to the poor: and the cause which I knew not I searched out." Job 29:12-16.

Then Job presents similar ideas but from the negative side, or what will happen if we do not do these things: "If I did despise the cause of my manservant or of my maidservant, when they contended with me...If I have withheld the poor from their desire, or have caused the eyes of the widow to fail; Or have eaten my morsel myself alone, and the fatherless hath not eaten thereof...If I have seen any perish for want of clothing, or any poor without covering; If his loins have not blessed me, and if he were not warmed with the fleece of my sheep [if I did not give him clothing]; If I have lifted up my hand against the fatherless, when I saw my help in the gate: Then let mine arm fall from my shoulder blade, and mine arm be broken from the bone. For destruction from God was a terror to me, and by reason of His highness I could not endure." Job 31:13,16,17,19-22. If I do not use these hands and arms to bless these people in need, let my arm fall out of the shoulder blade. To just feed yourself is very selfish.

We do not understand that this is genuine Christianity. The Christianity that many of us practice is as much of a perversion of true religion as that of the Jews in Christ's day. All attempts to be righteous of ourselves, forgetting others, is pure selfishness. We are just on an ego trip, trying to enlarge our pride so that someone will pat us on the back eventually. That is not the righteousness that the law talks about, or that Jesus ever discussed. This aiming for some high position of exaltation where we will be acclaimed righteous is not righteousness by faith in Jesus. Yet the righteousness we usually want, and for which we examine ourselves, is that kind where we reach some pinnacle of success so we will be acclaimed as righteous. That is the "well done" that God's faithful servants will hear, we think. That is not what Christ or Job or Paul talked about; but it is so easy for us to see obedience to the law like that. When we realize that we must obey the law, we say, "I will try to do what it says and make myself righteous."

The type of activity described in Job and Isaiah is not an occasional once-a-week thing on Community Services day. It is not suddenly getting the idea one day to go out and help the poor, or giving away Thanksgiving baskets once a year. It is a lifestyle that goes on every day that cares for the needs of all who come within our scope of activity. It is an ongoing thing, a regular routine, yet it is far more than self-discipline. It is a heart drawn out to people in need, because they are human flesh and because we cannot bear to see them in need. Christ wept, not because Lazarus was dead, but because He identified Himself with human need, with hearts that ached. His heart ached. He was one with humanity, and His heart went out to them. Is my heart drawn out to people in need? Or do I manage to live in isolation, encapsulated in a little shell of selfishness? Normally a heart is responsive somewhat, and when the grace of Christ comes in we are even more responsive; but we can become so callous in blinding ourselves to the needs of others that we come to the place where we do not even see them.

"True sanctification is nothing more or less than to love God with all the heart." ST, May 19, 1890. "To love God supremely and our neighbor as ourselves is genuine sanctification." ST, February 24, 1890. "True sanctification comes through the working out of the principle of love. 'And we have known and believed the love that God hath to us. God is love; and he that dwelleth in love dwelleth in God, and God in him.'" AA 560. The thought that everything about God is love is seen in these quotes. As soon as I live in this heavenly love, I live in God and He lives in me. If I do not live in that love, I do not live in God and He does not live in me. I can keep ever so many right things in the word of God, but if I do not live in that love, He does not live in me nor do I live in Him. You cannot separate God from His love. If I do not live in love for you, my neighbor, I do not live in Him.

This takes us right down to the focal point of Christ our righteousness. This love, which is righteousness and only found in God, is the whole heart of our problem. Somehow in my heart there must be a love for you like Jesus has for you. I do not naturally have that. I am naturally selfish, and that wars against this love for you and tries to prevent me from loving you as Christ loves you. I can make sanctification the enhancement of self, not the death of self; and we have invented many ideas about sanctification that only enlarges self and forgets other people. We can live like that every day of our lives and say we are being sanctified, and yet forget all about our neighbor and his needs. This is warped thinking because self is so actively engaged and wants to be built up. The Jews, who looked down their noses at their neighbors, never agreed that they were not being sanctified. It was inconceivable to them.

This is our problem. John the beloved recorded these words of Jesus: "A new commandment I give unto you, That ye love one another; as I have loved you, that ye also love one another. By this shall all men know that ye are My disciples, if ye have love one to another." John 13:34,35. We have used this to argue with other Protestants, but I wish you would look at the concepts that Jesus was teaching apart from debate.

"To the disciples this commandment was new; for they had not loved one another as Christ had loved them. He saw that new ideas and impulses must control them; that new principles must be practiced by them; through His life and death they were to receive a new conception of love. The command to love one another had a new meaning in the light of His self-sacrifice. The whole work of grace is one continual service of love, of self-denying, self-sacrificing effort. During every hour of Christ's sojourn upon the earth, the love of God was flowing from Him in irrepressible streams. All who are imbued with His Spirit will love as He loved. The very principle that actuated Christ will actuate them in all their dealing one with another. This love is the evidence of their discipleship. 'By this shall all men know that ye are My disciples,' said Jesus, 'if ye have love one to another.' When men are bound together, not by force or self-interest, but by love, they show the working of an influence that is above every human influence. Where this oneness exists, it is evidence that the image of God is being restored in humanity, that a new principle of life has been implanted. It shows that there is power in the divine nature to withstand the supernatural agencies of evil, and that the grace of God subdues the selfishness inherent in the natural heart." DA 677,678.

Why are men and women bound to their spouse or children or parents or church? Is it by force of circumstances? By fear of being left alone? By self-interest? Or is it by love? When you begin to look at these motives and circumstances, it is amazing how few people are bound together by love. We can join churches out of fear of being lost or being wrong. We can work for God out of self-interest. We have schoolteachers who work at a sacrificial wage out of self-interest, thinking it is their ticket to heaven. We have foreign missionaries who become missionaries out of self-interest. I know because I have been one. I have done much in my experience about which I am embarrassed. We can hold high offices in God's church out of self-interest, and we have great ambition for those offices, thinking that it is a step towards heaven. We can give great offerings out of self-interest, and give Bible studies out of self-interest. We can send our children all through our school systems out of self-interest; and when they do not turn out just right, our self-interest gets in the way and we feel condemned at their failure.

Imagine the day when the world sees us bound together, not by force or self-interest, but by love. How wonderful it is to be married by love and not by self-interest. How marvelous. How nice it is to have parents who love us, and are not there by self-interest or force of circumstances. How wonderful it is to attend a church where we are bound together by love, and not force or self-interest. This is what the Lord was talking about to His disciples—a unique, peculiar oneness in relationship that you do not find in any other place in the world, where selfishness is pushed out and you never see it again. Imagine our people bound together with this unique tie, totally by love. That is what happened before the Spirit was poured out on the day of Pentecost.

How may I obtain this love? "Beloved, let us love one another, for love is of God; and every one that loveth is born of God, and knoweth God." 1 John 4:7. I must go to Him for this love, for "love is of God." I do not have it and cannot manufacture it. I will never develop this love out of my selfish heart. It is found only in Him.

"The first four of the Ten Commandments are summed up in the one great precept, 'Thou shalt love the Lord thy God with all thy heart.' The last six are included in the other, 'Thou shalt love thy neighbor as thyself.' Both these commandments are an expression of the principle of love. The first cannot be kept and the second broken, nor can the second be kept while the first is broken. When God has His rightful place on the throne of the heart, the right place will be given to our neighbor. We shall love him as ourselves. And only as we love God supremely is it possible to love our neighbor impartially." DA 607. If you see me misusing my neighbor, or my spouse, or any other person, you can be absolutely certain that God has been dethroned in my heart, and that I do not keep the first four commandments. When you see me loving my neighbor as myself, you will say, "He dwells in love, so the Lord must dwell in him." It is that simple. Sanctification is an unusual relationship—a dwelling together first with God, and then with one another; because He lives in us and we live in Him.

When our hearts are bound together with Him, we can be bound together with each other.

"Those who never experienced the tender, winning love of Christ cannot lead others to the fountain of life. His love in the heart [the first four commandments] is a constraining power which leads men to reveal Him in the conversation, in the tender, pitiful spirit, in the uplifting of the lives of those with whom they associate. In the heart renewed by divine grace, love is the ruling principle of action. It modifies the character, governs the impulses, controls the passions, and nobles the affections. This love cherished in the soul sweetens the life and sheds a refining influence on all around." GAG 237. Does this sound like sanctification? You can see the marvelous fragrance of Christ's love and righteousness that sweetens everybody.

"We love Him, because He first loved us." 1 John 4:19. And we love each other because we respond to His love. He is the Source. I respond. Then I love you; and I take care of the last six commandments when I do that.

Sanctification is accomplished through the right relationship with Jesus. However, it is the *result* of that relationship, and not the relationship itself. A relationship with Christ is not righteousness. The relationship is one that continues as long as life shall last, like marriage, which is a union, a coming together in love with God. We will never part so long as both shall live. The love that connects us with Christ is accomplished through a unique, and almost contradictory, bond. "Come unto Me, all ye that labour and are heavy laden, and I will give you rest. Take My yoke upon you, and learn of Me; for I am meek and lowly in heart: and ye shall find rest unto your souls. For My yoke is easy, and My burden is light." Matthew 11:28-30.

The simple language of Jesus sometimes causes us to be superficial. Whenever Jesus speaks in simple terms, then dig down deep! What is He saying here? This quote provides the answer: "'Take My yoke upon you,' Jesus says. The yoke is an instrument of service. Cattle are yoked for labor, and the yoke is essential that they may labor effectually. By this illustration Christ teaches us that we are called to service as long as life shall last. We are to take upon us His yoke, that we may be co-workers with Him. The yoke that binds to service is the law of God. The great law of love revealed in Eden, proclaimed upon Sinai, and in the new covenant written in the heart, is that which binds the human worker to the will of God." DA 329. Some say they do not feel bound by the law, but instead feel separated by it. That is because they do not understand that it is the law of love.

"The law is an expression of the thought of God; when received in Christ, it becomes our thought. It lifts us above the power of natural desires and tendencies, above the temptations that lead to sin." DA 308. As soon as you put the law in Jesus, it becomes your thought. You have a new heart and a new mind that delights to do the law of God. We are tied together by the law, but that law is love, and the doing of that law is love. Supreme love for God and loving my neighbor as myself binds us together. Obedience to the law is a binding agency.

If you still do not understand, let me go a little further. "Christ's followers have been redeemed for service. Our Lord teaches that the true object of life is ministry. Christ Himself was a worker, and to all His followers He gives the law of service—service to God and to their fellow men. Here Christ has presented to the world a higher conception of life than they had ever known. By living to minister for others, man is brought into connection with Christ. The law of service becomes the connecting link which binds us to God and to our fellow men." COL 326. As I see His great love for me in justification, and I respond, I enter into this service of love that the law is all about. By each of us responding to His love, we all draw strangely closer to each other. In blessing and serving you, I am drawn to Him. As my heart goes out to you, my heart goes out to Him. I understand Him better because I understand you better by getting close to you. And as I seek to obey God in response to His love and because of my compassion for you, I am connected closer and closer to Jesus and to the Father; and in turn, closer and closer to you.

Obedience, then, is a fantastic thing. It is not just *trying* to do something for somebody else. It is not trying to stop lying about you. How can I lie about you when I love you? It would be a terrible mistake to tell a lie. The breaking of the "thou shalt nots" become impossible when I love you so much. I cannot violate those commandments, not even to a thought. When my heart is filled with love, I am drawn out to you and am sensitive to your needs. I think more and more of you and become more forgetful of self. This is a different type of obedience. This is the obedience of love. And as I begin to serve mankind that way, from a sensitive heart filled with love for them, Jesus comes down like light from heaven.

At a church I once pastored, I decided one day to visit all the members. All day long I went from home to home, and all day long I listened to their problems. My head began to ache. I am not being critical. I am just telling you what happened that day. I discovered that people develop all kinds of problems when they continually receive love but do not dispense it. If we continually hear and receive, and never pass it on to others, we become like the Dead Sea, just bitter to the taste; and it was bitter to me to hear all those people tell me their problems. When I finished visiting in those homes, I wanted to leave the ministry. I said, "Let someone else come and take care of these sheep."

Around eight o'clock that evening, I went to visit the first non-Adventist that I had seen that day. I suppose I was not a very welcome sight to knock at her door at that time of the evening. In my depression and discouragement I was bitterly low. But she was spiritually hungry; and after she had just a little taste of the marvels of God's grace and word, she wanted more. I had forgotten that my pockets and briefcase and brain were full of good things for hungry people, because I had not met any hungry people that day; only critical, bitter ones who had been overfed and sermon-saturated. At first, I thought she was like the rest, but she began to ask me questions, and the Lord gave me answers by His grace. And every answer was like light from heaven to her. She was overjoyed and had never seen anyone like me in her life. For about an hour I dished out a banquet, and the more I dished out, the happier she became and the happier I became. And when we had prayer, I knew that heaven had come down and glory filled our souls. She was so thankful. I did not feel I had done very much, but I was literally exuberant, and she was, too. I went home from that house and slept a beautiful sleep that night. I had forgotten about all the problems of the saints, because I had fed one hungry soul.

Friend, the world is waiting to see a group of Christians who are bound together because they love God and each other. It does not matter the color or their skin or where they are from, as long as they are bound by love. In their union there is no self-interest, no pressures, no force; just the love of Christ constraining them. How wonderful is the work of the Lord when we are constrained by love. There is nothing else like it. Somehow we have gotten the idea that we must pressure people to work for God. We bring all kinds of pressures to bear, but not love. Sanctification is not like that, and I thank God it is not.

Sanctification is the marvelous love of God manifested for me until I see it in all its glory; and it softens me up on the inside. And because of this, I am a sweeter husband, a more understanding father, a more compassionate pastor, a better neighbor, a better employee or employer. And those around me begin to see that the love of God has come down and abides in my soul.

Let us lose our fears of sanctification. It is not an impossible ladder that you have to climb for a million miles. It is not that at all. It is God coming down and tying our hearts together in love for Him, until we say, "How can I help but love Him when He loves me so much." And with a heart so filled and overflowing, how can I help but love you? I will serve God and my fellow man in the same way that Jesus served mankind when He walked this earth; and for that marvelous life of service, the Lord will say, "Well done, thou good and faithful servant…enter thou into the joy of thy Lord." Matthew 25:21.

We are sanctified by His love and grace. May God help us to see this and not only to realize it, but be convicted to live the life of love and service that Christ has given to us and inspired in us by His marvelous example and love for us.

16

A VITAL DEPENDENCE

THE APOSTLE PAUL WROTE that we are to "lay aside every weight, and the sin which doth so easily beset us, and let us run with patience the race that is set before us, Looking unto Jesus the author and finisher of our faith; who for the joy that was set before Him endured the cross, despising the shame, and is set down at the right hand of the throne of God." Hebrews 12:1,2. The laying aside of sins is achieved by looking unto Jesus. He is the One who accomplishes this difficult task.

So often we read the first part of this text and then stop reading; and thus we conclude that we must expel sins by ourselves. This is not what Paul wrote. We are to look unto Jesus, the One who launches our faith and inspires us, and the One who finishes our faith, as well. He enables us to lay aside sin and run the Christian race with patience.

What is the work that we do in sanctification? What are the works that are required, if any, in this thing called sanctification? The Lord is the One who is the prime mover, and the Bible says we accomplish these things by looking unto Him. He is both the author and finisher of our faith.

Paul states this somewhat differently in another text: "Are ye so foolish? having begun in the Spirit, are ye now made perfect by the flesh?" Galatians 3:3. If God is the One who by His Spirit started us down the Christian road, do you think you can finish the work yourselves?

Ellen White discusses this problem and asks some questions about it. "Many have an idea that they must do some part of the work alone. They have trusted in Christ for the forgiveness of sin, but now they seek by their own efforts to live aright. But every such effort must fail." SC 69. So often we think that in conversion and justification, the Lord takes care of that for us; but after that, after having been launched down the Christian road, now we must grow by ourselves and be sanctified by our own efforts. Of course, this is not the way it is.

Another thought concerning this is found in this well known text: "But we all, with open face beholding as in a glass the glory of the Lord, are changed into the same image from glory to glory, even as by the Spirit of the Lord." 2

Corinthians 3:18. Hebrews 12:2 mentions looking unto Jesus, and here Paul speaks of beholding His glory. We are changed by beholding Christ. Looking and beholding are activities. They are works. They are not just mind-processes. Each is something that we do; and something happens when we do this.

Jesus said, "Abide in Me, and I in you. As the branch cannot bear fruit of itself, except it abide in the vine; no more can ye, except ye abide in Me." John 15:4. Looking, beholding, abiding. These are the three works that we accomplish in sanctification. We look unto Jesus, we behold Him in His glory, and we abide in Him. These aspects of Christianity seem so simple, and yet we do not understand them adequately. At least it is difficult for us to practice them.

This is faith in action. Faith is far more than a mental process. There is an activity that is part of faith, which functions in looking, beholding, and abiding. Jesus talked about how faith is an action, or a work: "Jesus answered and said unto them, This is the work of God, that ye believe on Him whom He hath sent." John 6:29. This is a work or activity—that we believe on Jesus whom God sent to this world. So believing is more than a mental assent to truth. It is more than believing in someone or something.

As we behold the marvelous love that God has for us as manifested in Jesus, the normal response is to love Him who first loves us. As you respond to His love by loving Him, you want to behold Him. The two demoniacs out of whom Jesus cast so many devils begged Jesus to stay with them. That is normal, for you like to be with those you love. Jesus told them to go back to their hometown and tell others what He had done for them. It was a hard thing to separate from Jesus when they loved Him so much, because He had done so much for them. Mary Magdalene, out of whom Jesus cast seven devils, always wanted to sit at the feet of Jesus. When you love someone, you want to sit and behold that person and listen to every word. It is most pleasant to do that, and it is unpleasant to be away from that person. Christ said of Mary sitting at His feet that "Mary hath chosen that good part, which shall not be taken away from her." Luke 10:42. This is a better activity, and more important than some other things we think are so necessary to do. Mary did not let her household duties crowd out her affection for Jesus. She found time to sit at His feet because she loved Him so much.

This beholding, this looking, this abiding is an activity of love. It is all based on love. It is not something I try to stir up in myself and say, "I am going to do it if it kills me." We do not love that way, do we? Love is not something we can manufacture. But if you find a lack of this love for Christ, all you have to do is take your Bible and certain Spirit of Prophecy books and start reading about how much He loves you. Sometimes He will manifest Himself to us in nature, or by other people telling you about His marvelous love for them. That makes us realize He loves us, too. Then you will want to sit at His feet and behold Him.

I recall those days when I tried to do the works of a Christian if it killed me. I determined to read my Bible through, and by sheer grit and determination I managed to read just over half way through. But nothing was accomplished. I suddenly realized that I was no better off than when I started. It was just a difficult job to force myself to read the Bible. A year or so later, I found myself, after working long hours in the field on the farm, staying up late every night reading my Bible. I could not get enough. I was the same person, but I suddenly had a different appetite.

Since Christ is no longer here personally, how do I abide in Him and look to Him and behold Him? We think the disciples had an advantage since they could see Him physically; and Mary Magdalene enjoyed His company right there in her own home many times in Bethany. But Christ said it was expedient for us if He went away. Here is a quote we need to read over and over again, for it is a subject that we barely comprehend and are seldom able to practice: "'I am the Vine, ye are the branches,' Christ said to His disciples. Though He was about to be removed from them, their spiritual union with Him was to be unchanged. The connection of the branch with the vine, He said, represents the relation you are to sustain to Me. The scion is engrafted into the living vine, and fiber by fiber, vein by vein, it grows into the vine stock. The life of the vine becomes the life of the branch. The soul dead in trespasses and sins receives life through connection with Christ. By faith in Him as a personal Saviour the union is formed. The sinner unites his weakness to Christ's strength, his emptiness to Christ's fullness, his frailty to Christ's enduring might. Then he has the mind of Christ." DA 675.

These are complex thoughts. When I discover how desperately I need Him, and what He offers me in salvation, then I begin to grasp by the faith that He has already given to me the enormity of His gift, and suddenly I love Him so much I never want to let Him go. The spiritual union is formed; and I find in me a desire to read about Him, to talk about Him, and to think about Him. We dwell together, my Lord and I. This is conversion, which is part of justification. Right now we are talking about sanctification. What is the next step beyond forming that spiritual union with Christ? What is the progression from this union to sanctification?

"This union with Christ, once formed, must be maintained [this is where sanctification comes in]. Christ said, 'Abide in Me, and I in you. As the branch cannot bear fruit of itself, except it abide in the vine; no more can ye, except ye abide in Me.' This is no casual touch, no off-and-on connection. The branch becomes a part of the living vine. The communication of life, strength, and fruitfulness from the root to the branches is unobstructed and constant. Separated from the vine, the branch cannot live. No more, said Jesus, can you live apart from Me. The life you have received from Me can be preserved only by continual communion. Without Me you cannot overcome one sin, or resist one temptation." DA 676.

This is the heart and soul of sanctification—this living in Jesus and abiding in Him. "Faith is the only condition upon which justification can be obtained, and faith includes not only belief but trust. Many have a nominal faith in Christ, but they know nothing of that vital dependence upon Him which appropriates the merits of a crucified and risen Saviour." 1SM 389. Many of us are satisfied with a belief that He is our Savior, and have a mental awareness that He died for us, and even a casual experience of some kind in acknowledgement that He is good to us. But we do not abide in Him. We do not stay there and constantly trust in Him. We go off and try to do it by ourselves. Then when we fail in that, we think that He has disowned us, which is far from the truth. He does not leave us because we fail. These are the concepts we often have as to how He works with us.

This abiding in Christ is maintaining a vital, living dependency, like children depending on a parent. We never cease to be dependents, do we? We often think that when we get older we are independent, but everyone is dependent upon someone else; and all are dependent upon God. If it ceases to rain in your state for two years, you would not be washing your car or watering your lawn. I have seen wealthy merchants suffering because it did not rain. They had to borrow money on their inventory every month in order to eat, and all because it did not rain. We are always dependent, in the physical life and in the spiritual life.

Our dependency on Christ in order to advance in the Christian life is better understood when we consider these words of Jesus: "Consider the lilies how they grow: they toil not, they spin not; and yet I say unto you, that Solomon in all his glory was not arrayed like one of these." Luke 12:27. The lilies never work, but they are growing. Sanctification has a lot to do with growing. All of us want that beautiful robe of righteousness, and some people think that the Bible teaches they have to work to have the robe; and there are many texts and quotations that seem to say that. But here we are told to consider the lilies in all their splendor and radiance. They do not work, and yet they grow. How did they get that way? Very simply because the marvelous Creator makes them that way. He not only causes them to sprout, He carries them on to all their splendor and glory. Even the richest and the wisest are not arrayed like them. We will be like Christ, the Lily of the Valley, when we are arrayed in His robe of righteousness.

There is a whole chapter on this one verse in the book *Steps to Christ*. The chapter is titled "Growing Up Into Christ." Paul prayed that we might "all come in the unity of the faith, and of the knowledge of the Son of God, unto a perfect man, unto the measure of the stature of the fulness of Christ." Ephesians 4:13. This is growing up into Christ. Those who worry about Christian perfection should spend some time reading that chapter, for it has marvelous thoughts on sanctification and Christian growth. Consider these thoughts from that chapter:

"The plants and flowers grow not by their own care or anxiety or effort, but by receiving that which God has furnished to minister to their life. The child cannot, by any anxiety or power of its own, add to its stature. No more can you, by anxiety or effort of yourself, secure spiritual growth. The plant, the child, grows by receiving from its surroundings that which ministers to its life—air, sunshine, and food. What these gifts of nature are to animal and plant, such is Christ to those who trust in Him." SC 68. It is receiving that which God supplies that causes us to grow, not our efforts at growing.

Then the quote goes on to give many Scriptures that describe Jesus as the One who produces all the elements for growth. These include "everlasting light" (Isaiah 60:19); "a sun and shield" (Psalm 84:11); "the dew unto Israel" (Hosea 14:5); and "the bread of God...which cometh down from heaven, and giveth life unto the world (John 6:33). All these are different symbols of Christ's function as a life-giving agency that produces growth as well as life itself. He is not only the Life-Giver, He is the Life-Sustainer, in spiritual as well as in physical life. As we take the simple lessons from nature, we begin to consider the lilies and how they grow and that tells us how we grow, which is by receiving the sunshine, the rain, and the nutrients that God has provided for growth, whether it be spiritual or physical.

Another illustration is given about how nature functions in this respect. "As the flower turns to the sun, that the bright beams may aid in perfecting its beauty and symmetry, so should we turn to the Sun of Righteousness [Jesus], that heaven's light may shine upon us, that our character may be developed in the likeness of Christ." SC 68. Jesus teaches the same thing when He says, "Abide in Me, and I in you." Just like the flower following the sun across the sky that it might have its beauty and symmetry, we are to abide in Christ. We do not understand this as we should.

Right in the middle of this idea of abiding in Christ are these words of Jesus: "For without Me, ye can do nothing." John 15:5. This is a text that for some is self-effacing. They think it brings us down. We always think we must do something. There is something for us to do, but He says that without Him, we can do nothing. So often we try to make a frontal attack on our deficiencies and sins and bad habits. The Lord says we can try that, but it won't help us. "Can the Ethiopian change his skin, or the leopard his spots? Then may ye also do good, that are accustomed to do evil." Jeremiah 13:23. It is not by trying to change this or that habit or external act. It is by a connection with Jesus, by looking unto Him, by beholding Him, and by abiding in Him. This changes the heart. This creates a new life. This brings a new power. We must not trust ourselves; we must trust only Jesus.

"You are just as dependent upon Christ, in order to live a holy life, as is the branch upon the parent stock for growth and fruitfulness. Apart from Him you have no life. You have no power to resist temptation, or to grow in grace and holiness. Abiding in Him, you may flourish. Drawing your life from Him, you will not wither nor be fruitless. You will be like a tree planted by the rivers of water." SC 69. Somehow there is a battle we have, insisting that we can do it, and especially after we have experienced conversion. What can I do apart from Him? It is like with small children where there is the potential for them to be an adult, but the child is not yet an adult. And we do all kinds of foolish things as little children like running out into a busy street. Maybe father and mother will let you run out there, but they have an eye like a hawk, watching you every second; and they come out to snatch you from any danger that appears. Does not God our heavenly Father stay very close to His little children? Sometimes we think He is so far away; but He said He would never leave us or forsake us. We cannot bear to have Him far away, or we will destroy ourselves. He knows this even though we may not be aware of it. "The angel of the Lord encampeth round about them that fear him, and delivereth them." Psalm 34:7. He is always there caring for the tender, little plant.

The quote continues: "Our growth in grace, our joy, our usefulness—all depend upon our union with Christ. It is by communion with Him, daily, hourly—by abiding in Him—that we are to grow in grace. He is not only the Author but the Finisher of our faith. It is Christ first and last and always. He is to be with us, not only at the beginning and the end of our course, but at every step of the way." This concept of walking with Jesus, of abiding in Him, of dwelling with Him—this is the Christian life. There is no growth without that. Somehow when we see failure in our lives, we feel that He is far away. But in reality, all we have neglected to do is to maintain the abiding. We get so busy, and by our own unbelief and our own sinful acts He seems far, far away from us. But He says He is always there. The Psalmist learned this through a difficult experience which gives us some of the reasons for his success. "I have set the Lord always before me: because He is at my right hand, I shall not be moved." Psalms 16:8. I can resolve all day long to stop sinning, but it is not the resolution, it is the presence of Jesus. He is my stability; and it is my faith in Him, not my resolution that makes the difference. If He is there, He will keep me.

Too often we think that we must perform and thus earn His presence. If we have done well, He commends us by joining with us. Then, we think, we can walk the Christian life. But we fail of ever producing the goodness that brings Him. In reality, He is a God of grace that joins Himself with us while we are unworthy. While we were yet enemies, He died for us. Otherwise we could never do a thing to be joined to Him. He comes down from heaven to meet humanity and joins with us, and says, "I am reconciled to you; be reconciled to Me." Then we walk and talk with Him because He first loved us, not because we earned that favor.

It is by faith that I recognize His presence; and He makes Himself very near to us. You can go through life and think you have forfeited His presence by some act or habits, but then suddenly, almost out of no place, He manifests Himself to you. And you say, "I thought He was gone. I thought He had forsaken me." And there He is.

I have had people who would not dare tell me about their past come to me utterly amazed and shocked that the Lord manifested Himself to them. That means that they are very precious to Him. After Jacob cheated his brother Esau and ran away, when he slept that first night he discovered that God was not far away. He called that spot Bethel—the house of God. He was literally in God's presence but all the while thinking that He was miles and miles away. But there He was. How many there are who think they have chased Him away. He does not leave quickly. It is very difficult to get rid of Him. He sticks closer than a brother, the Bible says. If the Father gave His own Son to die for you, and if Christ gave His own life, it is going to take an awful lot to get rid of Him. It is unbelief that eventually chases Him away, but not our sins and bad habits. As soon as we discover He is present, suddenly those sins and habits flee away. They do not interest us any longer when God is there. It is the abiding presence of Christ that takes care of all of our problems.

Abiding in Jesus has such a depth of meaning that we need to go back and look at the branches and the vine more carefully. We need to examine what takes place to understand what He is saying to us in this parable that is so poorly understood. "This union with Christ, once formed, must be maintained. Christ said, 'Abide in Me, and I in you. As the branch cannot bear fruit of itself, except it abide in the vine; no more can ye, except ye abide in Me.'...Abiding in Christ means a constant receiving of His Spirit, a life of unreserved surrender to His service. The channel of communication must be open continually between man and his God. As the vine branch constantly draws the sap from the living vine, so are we to cling to Jesus, and receive from Him by faith the strength and perfection of His own character." DA 676. You have seen how those little tendrils just cling to a vine; and thus we are to cling to Jesus. Remember that the plants receive the sunshine and rain and nutrients, and by receiving they grow. We are to receive from Him the things that come from His Spirit and make us grow. Even the perfection of His own character comes from Him. He is always dispensing it to those who will receive it.

In addition, there is a "life of unreserved surrender to His service." This is giving to others what we receive from Him. We know that if we only receive, we become like the Dead Sea—just poisoned springs. If we never give it away, our hunger and thirst eventually go away. We must dispense that which we receive. As soon as you begin to give to others because you love souls, then immediately you have a hunger and a thirst. And as we constantly give, we want to receive even more, and we become open channels through which God works. A vine is a channel that eventually produces fruit.

This unique process is different than many have thought it to be. "By faith you became Christ's, and by faith you are to grow up in Him—by giving and taking. You are to give all—your heart, your will, your service—give yourself to Him to obey all His requirements; and you must take all—Christ, the fullness of all blessing, to abide in your heart, to be your strength, your righteousness, your everlasting helper—to give you power to obey." SC 70. Whatever He has, we must reach out and embrace Him and take Him in, for only by Him am I able to do these things.

He is not only my help and my strength, but also my righteousness. He is my perfection. He is not only the enabling power, He is the goodness and the right-doing. He is the righteousness of God in Christ Jesus. He gives that to me, too. He is the perfection. These come to me as a gift, and I must receive them. As you partake of the very nature of the vine stock, it will produce grapes like the stock (not like the branch). The Parent Stock is the life of the person; the branch apart from Him has no life. When as branches we try to function without Him, we have problems. We receive from Him not only the power, but also the righteousness of Christ Himself.

The lesson is simple. I look to the Vine, not to the branch. I look unto Jesus, beholding His glory, abiding in Him, not in myself. So often our time is spent looking at ourselves and worrying about ourselves, and especially in the area of growth. We look to see how we are doing. That is a dangerous business. It might be occasionally necessary, but it should not become a habit of any kind. Our main occupation ought to be looking to the Source of life. We are to be good soil and not good farmers. He is the farmer. As we are good soil, He produces a good crop in us. Our hope is not in ourselves but in Him.

We have difficulty spending time looking to Jesus and abiding in Him, especially in this day and age when we are so everlastingly busy. We think that if we are busy at good things, it is alright; but it is not alright. Does anyone or anything come before Jesus? Do wives ever get upset with their husbands because they spend all their time at their jobs? After a while the wife says, "I think you love that job more than you love me." After a while, there comes to be an alienation of affections. You will never convince Jesus that He is supreme in your affections when you spend all your time doing other things. It takes time to be in love, and to maintain the love. Part of love is sharing time, is it not? If you rob your love affair of time, you have thrown away the love. Spending time with Jesus is part of our love affair with Him. Time with Him is called devotions because I am devoted to Him. Our time with Him is not something I try to manufacture so I can make Him love me. I love Him because He first loved me. He instigates the whole thing.

There is a reason why we have difficulty spending time with Jesus. Someone knows that the time you spend with Jesus will make you different. He knows it better than we do. "When the mind dwells upon self, it is turned away from Christ, the source of strength and life. Hence it is Satan's constant effort to keep the attention diverted from the Saviour, and thus prevent the union and communion of the soul with Christ. The pleasures of the world, life's cares and perplexities and sorrows, the faults of others, or your own faults and imperfections—to any or all of these he will seek to divert the mind." SC 71. I can get so wrapped up in the sins of others and all the terrible things that have happened to my church that I never see Jesus. I can get so absorbed in my imperfections that I never see Jesus. I can get wrapped up in pleasures, trying to escape my misery. I can do all of these things that break communion with Christ. There is trouble everywhere today, and the devil makes the troubles omnipresent to keep my mind off Christ.

Continuing on with the quote: "Do not be misled by his devices. Many who are really conscientious, and who desire to live for God, he too often leads to dwell upon their own faults and weaknesses, and thus by separating them from Christ, he hopes to gain the victory. We should not make self the center, and indulge anxiety and fear as to whether we shall be saved. All this turns the soul away from the Source of our strength. Commit the keeping of your soul to God, and trust in Him. Talk and think of Jesus. Let self be lost in Him. Put away all doubt; dismiss your fears. Say with the apostle Paul, 'I live; yet not I, but Christ liveth in me: and the life which I now live in the flesh I live by the faith of the Son of God, who loved me, and gave Himself for me.' Galatians 2:20. Rest in God. He is able to keep that which you have committed to Him. If you will leave yourself in His hands, He will bring you off more than conqueror through Him that has loved you."

It is easy for everyone to be self-centered. We think we must be anxious or we will not show that we value the Christian life. But our anxiety is not to be about ourselves; otherwise we will not trust Him. Is He able? Is He sufficient? Can He be trusted? Can you lean on Him? Is He a good Father? Is He a good provider? He never slumbers or sleeps. He always watches over us. When you discover the answer to all these questions, you can lean back on the everlasting arms and say, "He takes care of it." This is not a totally passive life. What about the looking, the beholding, the abiding, the seeking, the trusting? This is a day-by-day activity, making the contact like plugging the appliance into the socket. Keep it there and never let it go. Always I must abide in Him, clinging to Him like those little vine tendrils holding on to Jesus. When we have this living connection with Christ, we have spiritual growth.

This is faith. It is the whole heart of Christianity; and the Bible tells us He gives to every man a measure of faith. We are able to do this. We are not able to fight the battle of sin; but Paul tells us to "Fight the good fight of faith." 1 Timothy 6:12.

Keep trusting and keep looking up. This is the clue to all Christian living. Then, "I can do all things through Christ which strengtheneth me." Philippians 4:13. Apart from Him I have nothing.

This next quote sums up all of this: "A life in Christ is a life of restfulness. There may be no ecstasy of feeling, but there should be an abiding, peaceful trust. Your hope is not in yourself; it is in Christ. Your weakness is united to His strength, your ignorance to His wisdom, your frailty to His enduring might. You are not to look to yourself, not to let the mind dwell upon self, but look to Christ. Let the mind dwell upon His love, upon the beauty, the perfection of His character. Christ in His self-denial, Christ in His humiliation, Christ in His purity and holiness. Christ is His matchless love—this is the subject for the soul's contemplation. It is by loving Him, copying Him, depending wholly upon Him, that you are to be transformed into His likeness." SC 70,71.

This you can do. This He will inspire you to do. Day by day He will give you a loving prod to do these things. Seek Him first every morning. If you notice in the morning both the Bible and the newspaper are there, He will give you a little nudge to read the Bible first. He does not scold or rebuke or get angry or condemn. He just asks, "Won't you seek Me first? Let's talk a little while. Let's become reacquainted today. Let's walk through this day hand in hand." The Lord does this so nicely. This is my faith in action. This is expressing my love for Him in response to His love for me. And as we walk through life together, you will be amazed at the transformation. It is not by trying. It is by trusting. Just cling to Jesus, looking to Him. And that is not a distasteful task, is it? Many just revel sitting at His feet, like Mary who did not want to be taken away from His presence.

Friend, this is the Christian life. We have made it so vastly different, and it seems impossible because we keep looking to ourselves, trying to make ourselves grow; and we become so frustrated and come to think the Christian life is hopeless. And all the time the marvelous Provider of all growth and life is standing there and saying, "Let Me give you all the good things that make you grow abundantly." Aren't you amazed at how fast things grow when the sun shines, and when it rains, and fertilizer is added? It just seems to boom right out of the ground; and soon it is mature.

In these last days before Jesus returns, He will shine in all His radiance, and in all His glory and beauty. The Latter Rain will come and the Lord will literally beam down His Spirit upon the earth causing Christian plants to grow and grow, until we are like Jesus in our glorious fruitfulness. And throughout all the ages of eternity we will praise Him from whom all blessings flow.

May God bless you with much receiving, and much giving; always abiding in Him, until your heart is filled with praise for that very precious One, our Lord Jesus Christ.

17

SANCTIFIED
BY THE WORD

IT IS BECAUSE WE have such difficulty understanding certain aspects of justification by faith and Christ our righteousness that we must deal with some of the fine points. Some people ask if we have to know all the fine points. Perhaps not, but this is the way we think. We have thought ourselves into all these riddles and all these ways of looking at this subject, and somehow we must find the way out because we have so many disagreements about it.

We will continue our study of sanctification by looking first at this statement of Paul: "But the fruit of the Spirit is love, joy, peace, longsuffering, gentleness, goodness, faith, Meekness, temperance: against such there is no law." Galatians 5:22,23. Fruit is what you have when you have grown up. It is the harvest. The fruit of the Spirit is another way of describing sanctification, at least the end result. If you have all these things, would you say you are sanctified? Paul's statement does not describe our problems and some of our habits the way we usually do; but if you are meek, and gentle, and temperate, you will take care of many problems, will you not? If you have love, joy, peace, longsuffering, it takes care of so many things. This is another way of talking about sanctification.

The problem is: How do we produce this fruit? Do we work to produce the fruit of the Spirit? "Yet the Saviour does not bid the disciples labor to bear fruit. He tells them to abide in Him." DA 677. Jesus talks about being the Vine and we are the branches. He says, "He that abideth in Me, and I in you, the same bringeth forth much fruit: for without Me ye can do nothing." John 15:5. Ellen White's comment tells us that the Lord does not bid us to labor to bring forth all those fruit mentioned in Galatians 5. Rather, we are to abide in Him, and if you abide in Him and He in you, then you *will* produce fruit. This is Christian maturity—the fullness of the stature of Christ spoken about in Ephesians 4. These are various ways of looking at sanctification, both the growth and the ultimate result.

We want to add one more step; but first recall that in John 15:5, Jesus says that if we abide in Him and Him in us, we will bring forth much fruit. Then verse 7 says: "If ye abide in Me, and My words abide in you, ye shall ask what ye will, and it shall be done unto you." Instead of saying, "If I abide in you," He said, "If...My *words* abide in you."

Perhaps that causes some confusion, so let's clear it up with this quote: "It is through the word that Christ abides in His followers." DA 677. Through the word He abides in us. Jesus taught that when He abides in us, His word abides in, and we will bear much fruit. He abides in us by His word, and that means the Bible. As He abides in us by His word, marvelous things happen. In our Lord's last prayer, He prayed: "Sanctify them through Thy truth: Thy word is truth." John 17:17. Then in verse 19 He says, "And for their sakes I sanctify Myself, that they also might be sanctified through the truth." This word accomplishes something great in our hearts and our lives. This word has the ability, the effectiveness, to sanctify us—if it abides in us.

The next question is: How does the Bible sanctify us? Many people study and read the Bible, but we can easily see that they do not appear to be sanctified. How does the Bible sanctify us? What is the process that we go through?

"'Herein is My Father glorified,' said Jesus, 'that ye bear much fruit.' God desires to manifest through you the holiness, the benevolence, the compassion, of His own character. Yet the Saviour does not bid the disciples labor to bear fruit. He tells them to abide in Him. 'If ye abide in Me,' He says, 'and My words abide in you, ye shall ask what ye will, and it shall be done unto you.' It is through the word that Christ abides in His followers. This is the same vital union that is represented by eating His flesh and drinking His blood. The words of Christ are spirit and life. Receiving them, you receive the life of the Vine. You live 'by every word that proceedeth out of the mouth of God.' Matthew 4:4. The life of Christ in you produces the same fruits as in Him. Living in Christ, adhering to Christ, supported by Christ, drawing nourishment from Christ, you bear fruit after the similitude of Christ." DA 677.

We are to live by every word that proceeds out of the mouth of God. As we feast upon His word and live by it, something happens to us called "Living in Christ, adhering to Christ, supported by Christ, drawing nourishment from Christ," and then we bear fruit like Him. You can spend all day discussing this one paragraph; and we need to go back and spend much time in some of these deep thoughts. How the word sanctifies us is a unique thing. It is more than reading the Bible, it is more than studying various Bible topics; although those things are good. It is even more than understanding. It is more than a mental acceptance of the fact that the Bible is truth. Having the word abiding is us means receiving Christ in His word—just getting Him right inside of us. It is different than getting thoughts, ideas, principles, concepts, and theories into our minds. Something else takes place as we seek Christ in His word and as we abide in Him through His word. This is what He wants to happen to us. You do not have to labor to bear fruit. You have to abide in Him and have His words abide in you, to live day by day and moment by moment with Him, never getting far away.

Jesus said to Satan that "man shall not live by bread alone, but by every word of God." Luke 4:4. In that word is the way of life, the enabling power, the stimulating power, the motivating power, as well as the principles of everlasting life. This is what the Lord wants us to realize and experience.

"The life of Christ that gives life to the world is in His word. It was by His word that Jesus healed disease and cast out demons; by His word He stilled the sea, and raised the dead; and the people bore witness that His word was with power. He spoke the word of God, as He had spoken through all the prophets and teachers of the Old Testament. The whole Bible is a manifestation of Christ, and the Saviour desired to fix the faith of His followers on the word. When His visible presence should be withdrawn, the word must be their source of power." DA 390. Christ was endeavoring with all the disciples to fix their attention on the Bible when He physically was taken away. He said He wanted the word to be their source of power. There are two words in the Bible: the written word and the spoken word. Christ is called the Word, and your Bible is called the word. The above quote continues: "Like their Master, they were to live 'by every word that proceedeth out of the mouth of God.' Matthew 4:4."

This is something different. There is some unique quality in the Bible. It is a different book. These are different words. When the people said, "Never a man spake like this Man" (John 7:47), they were not only amazed, but what they said was literally true. This is the Man who spoke all things into existence by the word of His mouth. In the Bible you will find the words, "Let there be light: and there was light." Genesis 1:3. A different Being is speaking words in the Scriptures than other people who speak or write words in other books. As you by faith abide in Christ through His word, there is a different power there. Therefore, we must read and study in a vastly different way than we have in the past.

Jesus said you must "eat My flesh and drink My blood." John 6:53. In verse 63, He said, "the words that I speak unto you, they are spirit, and they are life." Eat it, absorb it, assimilate it, get it inside of you. There are more than thoughts and concepts that come inside. There is a power that comes inside. In order to be sanctified by the word of God, we must do something different with it than we do with most books. It is more than studying and reading and understanding.

Nicodemus had an unusual experience that helps us to understand this more. Christ responded to him when Nicodemus asked difficult questions, such as, "How can a man be born when he is old?" John 3:4. Nicodemus seemed to be in confusion, so "Jesus answered and said unto him, Art thou a master of Israel, and knowest not these things?" Verse 10. Are you not a scholar of the Scriptures, one of the elite in Israel and Judah, and you do not understand one of the basic elements of Christianity? How have you missed it? This man had memorized great portions of the Scripture or else he could not have belonged to the Sanhedrin. He was looked upon as a preeminent scholar of the Scriptures. He knew all these things, but somehow he missed the very heart of Christianity. Why?

"Nicodemus had read these scriptures with a clouded mind." DA 174. Something was wrong; but after this discussion where those unique ideas were proposed to him, we are told that Nicodemus "searched the Scriptures in a new way, not for the discussion of a theory, but in order to receive life for the soul. He began to see the kingdom of heaven as he submitted himself to the leading of the Holy Spirit." DA 175.

When you study your Sabbath School lessons throughout the week, do you study it so in class you can discuss a theory? Do you study it in order to be right and prove yourself right? Or do you study it for life for your soul? So seldom do we study the Scriptures for life for our souls. We study the Bible to help someone else, and preachers study it for their congregations, but how often do we study it for ourselves? We act starved, spiritually emaciated, and sometimes we are, even though physically we do not look that way. Often we just present the word in Sabbath School classes and sermons and in our Bible studies as nothing but a theory and an argument. Many are always trying to win arguments, but they are dying on the inside.

Nicodemus studied in a new way—for life for his soul; and he submitted to be led by the Spirit of God. This gives us great insight into how we are to study our Bible in a new way and how to be sanctified by the word of God. The word tells us how and what to do. We, like Nicodemus, are to study the word to receive life for the soul, and we are to submit ourselves to be led by the Spirit of God.

"The creative energy that called the worlds into existence is in the word of God. This word imparts power; it begets life. Every command is a promise; accepted by the will, received into the soul, it brings with it the life of the Infinite One." Ed 126. God's words are promises, and accepted by the will, received into the soul, it brings with it the life of the Infinite One. As I receive thoughts into my mind and understanding, I must go beyond that. Do I accept it with my will? Not my intellect but my will? Do I do more than say I think it is right? Do I get to where I want to do what the word says? These are choices my will must make. Do I receive every command into my innermost being? When that happens, it brings that creative power that makes me a different person, which I desperately want to be.

"To eat the flesh and drink the blood of Christ is to receive Him as a personal Saviour [personalizing what I read], believing that He forgives our sins, and that we are complete in Him. It is by beholding His love, by dwelling upon it, by drinking it in, that we are to become partakers of His nature. What food is to the body, Christ must be to the soul. Food cannot benefit us unless we eat it, unless it becomes a part of our being. Christ is of no value to us if we do not know Him as a personal Saviour. A theoretical knowledge will do us no good. We must feed upon Him, receive Him into the heart, so that His life becomes our life. His love, His grace, must be assimilated." DA 389.

Note these terms about eating and digesting and absorbing, assimilating His love and grace, feeding upon Him, receiving Him into my heart so His life becomes my very life. Too often we think that if we will just subject ourselves a little bit to the word and sort of bombard our brain with a few choice thoughts, then something will happen. The word has such power that something does happen, but it is minor compared to what He wants to take place in your life. He wants you to do more than just take a short look at it. He wants you to reach out and embrace the whole thing so that you do more than just think about it. The will must receive and accept it. The soul is to receive it, and there is to be an assimilation of the virtues of His life such as love and grace. He comes to live His very life in me as I study His word in a new way as Nicodemus did. Then something begins to happen.

Sanctification goes even beyond that. Sanctification is more than "eating" the Bible, or the word. Some people live to eat, but a true Christian cannot live only to eat. The eating of the word is a good thing. Eating of physical food is a good thing but it must be used properly. We must eat to live. Spiritually must eat the word in order to live; and this does not mean just to keep my heart beating and my lungs breathing air. It means I eat to work and to be active. Life produces action, and so as I eat and life comes into me by the word, I become active the way the word directs me and involves me. This *action* must take place, and this goes beyond the acceptance into the soul and into the will. Those are intermediate steps. All of that gets into me and does something in me.

That is the next step. "The truth of God is to sanctify the soul. The sanctifying power of truth is to abide in the soul and be carried with us to our business, there to apply its continual tests to every transaction of life, especially to our dealings with our fellow men. It is to abide in our households, having a subduing power upon the life and character of all its inmates. I must ever urge upon those who profess to believe the truth the necessity of practicing the truth. This means sanctification, and sanctification means the culture and training of every capability for the Lord's service." MLT 261.

Once I get the word inside of me, I must take it to my business or my job or my school, and there it must be put into effect. I must take it home and not leave it at church, or in the study or the bedroom or wherever you did your study. I must take it with me around the house and everyplace. I must take it with me in my neighborhood so that whatever has come inside of me begins to shine out of me.

What we study must be practiced. What do we call all of this? Obedience. We have trouble when we talk about obedience, and right away we arouse certain prejudiced thinking that we do not like. Sanctification is not a theory that gets in your mind and stays there and then you are sanctified because you have it in your mind. It is something that comes out of you if it is in you. It must be in you but it must come out, too. You cannot be the source of it, but He will abide in you and then reproduce His life coming out of you. There must be some activity which we call obedience; and it must be manifested in our business, our dealings with people, in our homes, and everywhere we go.

This obedience is the next step in this process. First absorbing it, receiving it, assimilating it, and then doing it. And right here is where we have problems. We do not like to think about this, and some get into deep ditches saying, "Well then, I *must* obey." The Lord did not say that.

I want to show you how obedience to the word plays a part in sanctification. "Just to the degree in which the word of God is received and obeyed will it impress with its potency and touch with its life every spring of action, every phase of character. It will purify every thought, regulate every desire." MH 136. These things will happen just to the degree that I receive and obey it.

Without the reception it does not get inside, and without the obedience it does not get outside. And without both reception and obedience, there is no sanctification. Without the obedience, and only the reception, it is only a pretense or a profession, and no one will ever see it; and we do not look much different to others, no matter how hard we try. This is a different kind of word and utilization of the word than we have in a math class or reading a book of instruction. It is a different sort of thing. There you only have to say I agree with what the book says. But now we have to do something else. We must not only agree with it, it must come into the will, into the soul, into the heart.

Even the virtues of Christ found in His book—His love and His grace—must come inside and be assimilated; and there it becomes the spring of action and the motivation of the life. Then, because my will has accepted it, I will to do His will. Once I submit my will to His will, action takes place, motivated by His presence in my life. Then comes obedience, which is that action; and that shows sanctification.

What we have said so far leaves much misunderstood, and so we have to go back and look again at this and find out just how it works. Remember, it is more than understanding. It is more than study and it is more than accepting it as truth. You must go beyond that into other dimensions, where it gets inside of you and where it produces action. This is accomplished by accepting, by receiving, by submitting, and by assimilating.

Every command of Jesus, every request, every bit of council, every example, every promise is saying literally to you and to me: "Follow Me." All through the Bible from Genesis to Revelation the Lord is saying in all these words, "Follow me." He does not demand that we follow Him, He does not exact it, He does not restrict us, He only asks if we will choose to follow Him. "If ye love Me, keep

My commandments." John 14:15. He does not say you have to love Him. He does not say you have to obey Him. He only says that if you do love Him, then respond by obedience.

We read this so differently and say, "I must do it." He does not say that. He says obey if you love Him. You can reason the other way and say that if you do not love Him, do not obey Him; and you probably will not because it is impossible to render genuine obedience to Christ if you do not love Him; although we sometimes think it is possible, but we do not do it very well. Jesus says that if we love Him, then accept His instructions because we know they are wonderful; and if we love Him because He first loved us, then we will follow Him. It is nice to follow someone you love, but it is terrible to follow someone you do not love. When His law is in my heart, I delight to do His will. When His law is not in my heart, I hate to do His will. I want to do my own will.

We do not do what is right in order to be good enough to be saved. It is not trying to climb some ladder of success into God's favor. It is not trying to earn your way to heaven. It is serving Him because you love Him supremely, with all your heart and mind and strength. All other motivations are wrong.

Here I must walk carefully; and you may be questioning everything I am saying here. When we read in the Bible and the Spirit of Prophecy about the commandments and obeying Him, we begin to look at our activities, our works, to see how we are doing or how we are not doing. The Lord says we are to behold Him and abide in Him if we love Him. Loving Him comes first, then the obeying, and not the other way around. All that works can tell you is that you do not love Him or that you do love Him. It is not how good or bad a particular work or activity is. We are always trying to find out if this or that is a good work or a bad one, or if some activity is right or wrong. This is moralizing. It is more a matter of: Do you love Him, and does He love you? Will a particular activity be nice to the One you love, or will it be bad to that One. Are you showing your love for Him or not showing your love for Him? Are you following Him, or departing and going your own way? We are talking about a love affair here. Am I alienating Jesus by my activity, or am I drawing closer to Him?

We have argued too long about what is right and wrong, and left out the love of Christ which makes it all right or all wrong in the first place. If you love Him, do the right things. We are to look at Jesus and behold Him, and not always be looking at our works no matter how good or bad we think they might be. Christ is to be my life, my inspiration, my example, my righteousness, my motivation. It is not just a matter of doing right because it is right. It is not doing what Jesus teaches and commands me because I am trying to show Him I love Him. It is doing it because I do love Him. He came and first loved me that I might love Him and show my love. He motivates me. I do not motivate Him. I do not make Him like me by doing right. He loved me so much in the first place that He brings a different life into my life. And this is all accomplished by beholding Him in the Bible, abiding in Him, feasting on Him in the word. This is a different way of looking at the Bible.

This is the way Jesus lived. He said to Philip, "Believest thou not that I am in the Father, and the Father in Me? The words that I speak unto you I speak not of Myself: but the Father that dwelleth in Me, He doeth the works." John 14: 10. He said He did not decide what words to say and what works to do, but that the Father is taking care of all that. He said the Father spoke and acted through Him, so if you have seen Him you have seen the Father. This was not slavery. This was an activity of love.

"As the Father hath loved Me, so have I loved you: continue ye in My love. If ye keep My commandments, ye shall abide in My love; even as I have kept My Father's commandments, and abide in His love." John 15:9,10. Jesus obeyed His Father because He and His Father always loved each other from past eternity. He loved His Father and was happy to obey Him. And if we keep His commandments, we abide in His love. You cannot separate love from the *activity* of love. If you give your wife a gift, what does she say? "You love me." The gift is not the love, is it? The gift is because of the love. Wives love the nice things their husbands give them. The Lord gives us nice things to show His love for us, and we respond to His love by showing our love for Him. We do the things that please Him because we love Him.

"He that hath My commandments, and keepeth them, he it is that loveth Me: and he that loveth Me shall be loved of My Father, and I will love him, and will manifest Myself to him." John 14:21. John the beloved wrote more about this than all the other apostles put together. He made this clear when he wrote: "For this is the love of God, that we keep His commandments: and His commandments are not grievous." 1 John 5:3. We have tried to segregate love and works of obedience, but John said that does not work very well. He said that it is because of our love for God that we keep them. It is all there together—the law is love, and the law is the character of God. He makes it very obvious.

"And hereby we do know that we know Him, if we keep His commandments. He that saith, I know Him, and keepeth not His commandments, is a liar, and the truth is not in him. But whoso keepeth His word, in him verily is the love of God perfected: hereby know we that we are in Him. He that saith he abideth in Him ought himself also so to walk, even as He walked." 1 John 2:3-6. If Christ has control of me and becomes the King of my life, will He not make me do what He does? Not by force, but by love. How can I say I abide in Him and He in me if I do not do what He does? As soon as He has my heart, I begin to do what He does, because He is in charge and has control of me. He has come to live inside of me.

These Scriptures are quickly and easily misunderstood and distorted. Some read this and say that loving is keeping the commandments. I love you and I love the Lord, so everything is fine. At the same time they say the law is done away with. Those who believe in the law become very critical of them, and they jump in the opposite ditch and say, "I keep the law and that proves I love Him." But it probably does not prove it. The Jews claimed they kept the law and they killed Him. We can profess to keep the law, then turn and bite and devour one another. And our enemy laughs and laughs and laughs. How can we keep four commandments and not the other six about loving our neighbor as ourselves? How can we say we do not steal from them, but eat up their reputations and characters by gossip? Have you noticed how gullible we are to gossip, especially if one of your best friends tells you? Your best friend cannot be wrong. They do not lie, do they? If they said it, it must be correct, even if it is wrong. The right person told you so it has to be true. Then you go and tell the next person, and you are believed, and then that person goes and tells someone else. We have believed hundreds of lies because the right person told us. You would be amazed at the lies we have believed about other people, and how many people have been ruined by misunderstanding and gossip. We are extremely vulnerable to this activity. Many are busy with the task of rooting out evil amongst the saints. When they see any evil thing in the saints, they root it out by gossip; and they think that is loving them and loving the church.

It is difficult for us to perceive that love is missing while we profess to keep the law. Jesus makes it a different thing by saying that when we love Him, we love one another; and the activity of the last six commandments becomes a reality. If I just receive the law without Jesus and His love, you will not find me very loving. Some people assume that the keeping of the commandments establishes the love for Christ, but that is not necessarily true. Some talk all day long about the requirements of God and almost never about their love for Him. He does not love us because we obey. He loves us in order that we might obey. We respond to His love, and then we obey Him. It is not the rules of life that He tells us to behold. He does not say, "Behold My laws and you will keep them." It is true that we may see His love and His character in the law, but He says we are to behold Him. He tells us to look unto Him, the Author and Finisher of our faith. This is the way it is accomplished. Then you will find the blessings of sanctification in the word.

This marvelous quote should be locked into the mind: "Obedience is not a mere outward compliance, but the service of love. Obedience—the service and allegiance of love—is the true sign of discipleship." SC 60. Obedience is not a mere outward compliance to the requirements of God. The Jews claimed to keep the law, but Christ found fault with them. They were most zealous for the law. They feared to be law-breakers, and yet Jesus constantly disputed with them about what constitutes true law keeping. They thought He broke the law. They accused Him of being permissive about Sabbath-keeping when He allowed His disciples to go though the fields and husk the grain in their hands and then eat it. Jesus had answers for that from the Bible. When He healed on the Sabbath, they thought He was desecrating that holy day. They had all kinds of conflicts with the Master who wrote the law because they thought they understood it correctly; and those are the ones who killed Him; and they believed themselves to be right in doing that.

We can profess to be law-keepers and do the same thing if our obedience is merely an outward compliance. Our hearts must be focused on Jesus. I must receive the law in Christ, and never apart from Him. He must come to abide in my heart with His fullness, beauty, and glory. Then He does something in me that brings about obedience. It cannot happen any other way.

This next quotation describes the steps that lead to sanctification in the study of God's word: "By His perfect obedience He has made it possible for every human being to obey God's commandments. When we submit ourselves to Christ, the heart is united with His heart, the will is merged in His will, the mind becomes one with His mind, the thoughts are brought into captivity to Him; we live His life. This is what it means to be clothed with the garment of His righteousness. Then as the Lord looks upon us He sees, not the fig-leaf garment, not the nakedness and deformity of sin, but His own robe of righteousness, which is perfect obedience to the law of Jehovah." COL 312. Do not misunderstand that.

Suppose a woman gets married to a perfect man who is tempted in all the ways she is, but never sins. Suppose that throughout his whole life he has been a flawless human being in every respect. She submits to him and gives her whole heart to that man because she loves him so much. She is devoted to him, and esteems him, and gives him her whole heart until she says, "Not my will but yours be done." She is wrapped up in him, and absorbed in him, until her heart is entwined with his and she cannot think about anyone else but him. Does being totally absorbed in someone ever happen in love affairs? Have you never been so in love to where you can think about that other person all day long? You have never been in love unless that has happened to you. You are really in love when you cannot get that person out of your mind.

When all this happens by love, what will happen to the woman? She will live his life. I illustrated this from a woman's standpoint because they are the submissive ones in love by their own natures. Men are more aggressive, so women need to explain to their husbands what it is like to submit. Submission is a quality that is difficult for men to accept. They are taught not to submit and to never give in, even if it kills them. The church is to be the *wife* of Christ, and we *all* are to submit to Him. Our wills are to be wrapped up in His will, and our hearts are to be absorbed in Him. Our whole minds are to be so absorbed in Him that we want to see Him every moment all day long. We see Him at night when we go to sleep, and we see Him the first thing in the morning when we wake up.

When, by the study of the word, you find this marvelous Christ, and He abides in you by His word; when He just leaps out at you and you begin not only to believe He is that good and loving, but your will accepts it, you will submit and receive His word into your innermost soul. When your heart is absorbed in Him, and your thoughts are consumed with Jesus in His magnificent love, then you love Him; and then you live His life. The word sanctifies in that respect.

It is because He is so ultimately perfect, the epitome of righteousness, that your union with Him brings about such perfection in you. It is His life that is in you and reproduced in you. Whatever He is, He will make you to be as you are absorbed in Him, enveloped in Him, encompassed in Him, filled with Him. The word tells about this marvelous love. It says that everything else will fail, "But love never faileth." 1 Corinthians 13:8.

The God of all might and power, the omnipotent One, the omniscient One, knows that the mightiest thing He has is love. Nothing is so great as God's love. And He said, "I will show them My love and bombard them with My love. I will surround them with My love. I will fill them with My love." God so loved the world that He gave His only begotten Son, and as they see His love, they will love Him. Then their hearts will be knit with His heart, their wills merged in His will. Then they will submit gladly. They will delight to do His will and His law, because they are just so wrapped up with Jesus. And they always look at Him and cannot take their eyes off of Him.

What a marvelous person He is. God wants us to see Jesus in the Bible, and fall so completely and absolutely in love with Him that we cannot think about another person, until those in our house will get disturbed with us and distressed because we are always sitting at the feet of Jesus looking at Him. And oh, what words you will hear Him say. As you permit yourself to believe that there is One so altogether lovely, One so loving as Jesus, and as you individualize it for yourself and accept Him as your personal Savior and your personal righteousness, as the One who wants to abide in you because He loves you individually, you can say with the apostle Paul, "For me to live is Christ." Philippians 1:21. This is not self-boasting because you will be bragging about Him. And you will ask others, "Don't you love Him, too?"

Friend, do you long for Jesus to come? We almost never talk about it. We warn people of His coming, we frighten them and we shock them, but do we teach them to long for Jesus to return and to love His appearing? You cannot wait until He comes because He is your Lover.

Before Jesus returns, all the real Adventists will be lovers of Jesus, and they will spend so much time beholding Him in His word that their very lives will be a demonstration of His presence. "Sanctify them through Thy truth; Thy word is truth." May God help us to value the precious words of everlasting life, which are the words of the Lord Jesus speaking to our souls.

18

WHERE IS YOUR CONFIDENCE?

OFTEN AS CHRISTIANS WE believe that we are helpless to do anything about justification, thinking that God does all of that for us. But after we are justified and converted, then we often assume that we are now able of ourselves to do those things the law requires of us. God does everything in justification, but we must do much of what is required in sanctification. We assume that conversion is some kind of an empowering or enabling act that puts us in the position where now we can perform, where before we could not perform. This causes many problems.

We want to find out specifically what it is that the converted, truly justified Christian can do of himself and by himself. We know the unjustified cannot keep the law because of "what the law could not do, in that it was weak through the flesh." Roman 8:3.

Apparently the justified Christian has at least the potential of doing this because "the righteousness of the law might be fulfilled in us." Verse 4. The righteousness of the law could not be fulfilled in the unjustified person, but when Christ has come to us, He makes it possible for it to be fulfilled in us.

The question before us is this: Has the flesh been made strong where before it was weak? Do we now have a capability that we lacked before? Can we now do right when before we could not?

Paul asked the question: "Are ye so foolish? having begun in the Spirit, are ye now made perfect by the flesh?" Galatians 3:3. God gives us new life in the Spirit; but do we then accomplish perfection or sanctification by the flesh, by our own works in and of ourselves? The confusion about this arises out of the strong assertions in the Bible concerning the freedom that is ours in justification and conversion.

Christ talks about this freedom in the context of sin, and because of these strong, almost violent, statements about it, we make strong assumptions, and sometimes we go too far (while some do not go far enough). "Jesus answered them, Verily, verily, I say unto you, Whosoever committeth sin is the servant of sin...If the Son therefore shall make you free, ye shall be free indeed." John 8:34,36. You are no longer a servant. You are "free indeed," and this is surely a strong statement.

Paul has much to say about this. His life was such an interesting one, so I suppose he could write about this at great length because of his experience and divine inspiration. "Know ye not, that to whom ye yield yourselves servants to obey, his servants ye are to whom ye obey; whether of sin unto death, or of obedience unto righteousness? But God be thanked, that ye were the servants of sin, but ye have obeyed from the heart that form of doctrine which was delivered you. Being then made free from sin, ye became the servants of righteousness." Romans 6:16-18. You have been made free from sin.

Continuing on is verses 20 and 22: "For when ye were the servants of sin, ye were free from righteousness...But now being made free from sin, and become servants to God, ye have your fruit unto holiness, and the end everlasting life." Paul over and over says you have been made free from sin.

As we progress through Romans, Paul comes back to the sum of these thoughts in a little different way. "But I see another law in my members, warring against the law of my mind, and bringing me into captivity to the law of sin which is in my members. O wretched man that I am! who shall deliver me from the body of this death?" Roman 7:23,24. Then he answers in verse 25, "I thank God through Jesus Christ our Lord."

He goes on with this thought in verse 2 of the next chapter: "For the law of the Spirit of life in Christ Jesus hath made me free from the law of sin and death." How free are we? I suppose many have discussed this for years and the discussion will not stop here. How free are we? What does he mean by this freedom? Why does he make these strong statements? Right here is where we get into problems after conversion and justification. What do I have in this freedom from sin?

The conclusion of some is that, since I am free from captivity, from the law of sin and death, then I can live a life without sin by my own efforts. That is the obvious conclusion that many draw from this. We ask the question: "Are we free?" Yes! As Jesus said, "free indeed." Then what do you conclude that you can and cannot do? Can we live without sin? It says free indeed—no captivity. The law has been broken in your life, but now you do not have to be subject to sin at all. Many arguments could be presented here. No captivity, no bondage, the law of death no longer controls us. Aren't you free? Jesus said so! Then why sin? Has not the weakness of the flesh now been changed? And are we not now strong where before we were weak? What can that genuinely converted person do? How strong is he, and therefore, how able is he? We arrive at many conclusions, or at least raise many questions. Our conclusions and our answers to these questions determine what we will attempt to do in the sanctified life.

This freedom from sin is good; and you must in no way diminish the freedom that the Bible talks about. We need that freedom! We must have that. But we must not make some conclusions about that freedom that are unwarranted.

Let's add another piece to the picture. It appears that the apostle Paul, after his conversion, had some problems with his body in that it did not seem to be strong. Paul said concerning himself: "But I keep under my body, and bring it into subjection: lest that by any means, when I have preached to others, I myself should be a castaway." 1 Corinthians 9:27. Another word for castaway is backslider. He found it necessary to keep under his body and to keep bringing it into subjection. Somehow my body keeps rising up to dominate, to rule, and I have to keep it down. Was Paul able to do this by himself? As we continue we will answer that in a very obvious way. What did he mean that he had to keep his body under?

Here is another statement Paul made about his body (he has several of them): "For we are the circumcision [meaning the true Christians] which worship God in the spirit, and rejoice in Christ Jesus, and have no confidence in the flesh." Philippians 3:3. We have no confidence in our bodies in its attempt to do right. He is talking here, I believe, about the Christian after conversion, after justification.

Why did Paul not have confidence in the flesh? "For the flesh lusteth against the Spirit, and the Spirit against the flesh: and these are contrary the one to the other: so that ye cannot do the things that ye would." Galatians 5:17. The flesh and the Spirit do not get along. Paul, who wished to be led by the Spirit, said he finds his flesh at war with the Spirit of God in him. He did not like that, and because he had no confidence in the flesh, he said he had to keep under his body and bring it into subjection. The flesh is an enemy that can do damage to me and keep God out of my life. He did not want that to happen to him.

The apostle John also talked about this, though far more briefly than Paul. John stated it succinctly and yet strongly when he wrote about drinking the blood and eating the flesh of Christ. "It is the spirit that quickeneth; the flesh profiteth nothing." John 6:63. These bodies of ours are of no profit, spiritually speaking. This is in total agreement with what Paul said about having no confidence in our flesh. The flesh cannot produce what God wants us to produce.

As Christians, we often believe that once we are converted and have a good experience with the Lord, then we have good bodies. There is no place in the Bible where it says that. That is merely an assumption on our part—that a good experience brings a good body. The mind can help to do some things about the body when we have a new heart in Christ, but we do not get good bodies at conversion. We get new hearts—new minds—but not new bodies. New bodies come later.

Paul wrote that "our conversation is in heaven; from whence also we look for the Saviour, the Lord Jesus Christ." Philippians 3:20. At the time of His return,

Jesus "shall change our vile body, that it may be fashioned like unto His glorious body." Verse 21. At the second coming of Jesus, the righteous will be given new bodies. But the wicked are not going to be changed, are they? All changes in the body are only for the righteous. They still have vile bodies right up to the second coming of Jesus. Some people do not like that. The Lord says that having these vile bodies is a problem.

Paul wrote: "For this corruptible must put on incorruption, and this mortal must put on immortality." 1 Corinthians 15:53. In the twinkling of an eye this will happen. Up to the time when we are either resurrected or translated, we will have vile, corrupt, bodies bringing death upon us. Paul often wrote about the difficulty of living in this kind of body that has all these problems. This he terms vileness. He recognized that he had that kind of body. He had to live in it, and so he had some problems. He said he had to keep it under subjection; and he looked with all his heart for the time when it was going to be changed. But until that change came, he knew that his vile body would cause problems.

The recognition of the sinfulness of our bodies causes us to undergo a certain transformation. This happens to all Christians. "And they that are Christ's have crucified the flesh with the affections and lusts." Galatians 5:24. If I belong to Him, I have crucified the flesh. Not only am I crucified, but I die. I have died to self with the affections and lusts of my flesh. This is what we call the death of the old man of sin that normally takes place at conversion. Now we have a crucified flesh.

Paul puts this in the context of future obedience, or future sin if you want to call it that. "Knowing this, that our old man is crucified with Him, that the body of sin might be destroyed, that henceforth we should not serve sin. For he that is dead is freed from sin." Romans 6:6,7. Back in verse 2 he reasons: "How shall we, that are dead to sin, live any longer therein?" How can a dead man sin? We look at these strong texts and say, "This freedom has come to me, and I have been liberated. I am no longer a captive. I am a new man in Jesus. I am free; therefore, I do not have to sin." Paul, in these different texts, has been speaking about his life after conversion, and not about the death in conversion.

In Romans 6, Paul is talking largely about the death of the old man and about conversion, which is the new man. But he also talks about the future life. He said that, even after he was converted, he had to keep that old man under subjection, having no confidence in him. We have some problems about this crucifixion of the old man, for Paul acts sometimes like the old man is not dead after conversion. Yet we know that Paul had a good Christian experience. He said that, after his conversion, he found the flesh still warring against the Spirit. He said he had crucified the flesh, which means it is dead, yet he found his vile flesh warring against the Spirit, and he had to keep it down. His flesh always wanted to rise up and bring his mind into captivity.

In some of Paul's writings, the flesh does not seem to be dead even after conversion. You might reason it out various ways, but can it be possible that the flesh is crucified and yet is still alive? How do you explain that strange enigma if it really is true? Can I be truly justified and converted and yet my vile flesh is not dead? This is what causes many theological arguments about this subject. To find the answer, we must put all the pieces together.

Can the flesh be crucified and yet still be alive? I want to give you a few more texts about Paul's life and the life of other Biblical characters in order to help us derive the answer. In this first text by Paul, I want you to notice the idea of dying to self. "I protest by your rejoicing which I have in Christ Jesus our Lord, I die daily." 1 Corinthians 15:31. Paul elsewhere talked about having been crucified with Christ. Here he said he dies every day. Why?

Let's put another text with it where Paul said he was "Always bearing about in the body the dying of the Lord Jesus [not the death, but the dying], that the life also of Jesus might be made manifest in our body." 2 Corinthians 4:10. It is important to note that he used the expression "the dying of the Lord Jesus." He said he was always dying with Jesus. You can find similar thoughts in verse 11. "For we which live are alway delivered unto death for Jesus' sake, that the life also of Jesus might be made manifest in our mortal flesh." I am delivered unto death all the time. I am always dying but never seeming to be dead. These are the thoughts expressed here.

Here is another similar thought: "As unknown, and yet well known; as dying, and, behold, we live; as chastened, and not killed." 2 Corinthians 6:9. "Chastened" is a system of beating a person to death; therefore, he said he has been beaten until he ought to be dead, but he is not killed, which is the same as dying and still living.

These are the peculiar contradictions we find here that make us think. People read this and say they do not understand. Crucified but not dead? How can that be? How can it be that you die every day? What is wrong here? If you are dead, are you not dead? Does the old man get resurrected every day? How does he have new life when I killed him the day before by my own choice? It seems like the cat with more than nine lives, doesn't it? How can you explain this? Crucified, yet still dying, but not dead, and having to die daily?

The answer is found in two definite facts that you must always remember in the sanctified life. If you omit these, you will never understand this idea of being crucified with Christ, and this dying daily. "Sanctification is not the work of a moment, an hour, or a day. It is a continual growth in grace. We know not one day how strong will be our conflict the next. Satan lives, and is active, and every day we need to earnestly cry to God for help and strength to resist him. As long as Satan reigns we shall have self to subdue, besetments to overcome, and there is no stopping place. There is no point to which we can come and say we have fully attained." 7BC 947. The two facts are: sanctification is not the work of a moment but of a lifetime; and there is no plateau where we can stop and say we have arrived.

The reason why sanctification must be the work of a lifetime is that, no matter how long or short your life may be, you never come to a stopping place. As long as Satan reigns, we have self to subdue and besetments to overcome. It is poorly understood amongst Christians that many of the problems we have with self are because of someone outside of self. The victories we have over self are because of a power—a Person—outside of self; and many of the problems we have with self are because of some other power outside of self. My problems are not all internal. And for this reason, one death is not sufficient. There is always someone to prod the corpse; although do not misunderstand me for I would not give the devil the power of resurrection.

How is it that the devil is still able to tempt us and bring us back to trusting in self? "When Christ took human nature upon Him, He bound Himself to humanity by a tie of love that can never be broken by any power save the choice of man himself." SC 72. Jesus bound Himself to us with a tie never to be broken by any power except the choice of man himself. That is a power you have, but not the devil. We can make the choice every day whether to stay bound to Christ, or to be free from Christ. Only the choice of man himself can sever that relationship.

Continuing on with the quote: "Satan will constantly present allurements to induce us to break this tie, to choose to separate ourselves from Christ. Here is where we need to watch, to strive, to pray, that nothing may entice us to choose another master; for we are always free to do this. But let us keep our eyes fixed upon Christ, and He will preserve us. Looking unto Jesus, we are safe. Nothing can pluck us out of His hand."

There is something in us that remains there as long as we live. Even though self is crucified, choice is not. Choice always lives as long as man lives. When I have crucified self, I have not crucified choice; and that is a good thing. We do not make a single choice once and for all. The power of choice lives on. It is a freedom given through the grace of Jesus that every one of us has. When you talk about freedom, there is nothing like the freedom of choice.

Sometimes in our Bible studies and sermons we want to deprive people of the freedom of choice. We want to drag them into church by brute force instead of by their own choice. Sometimes we try to do that to children, and we wonder why they kick and scream and holler. You just cannot coerce people into being Christians. You love them into Christ. This is a love affair, and we are always able to choose. It is never removed from us for God has granted us this blessed privilege. That is how we come to Him, and that is how we stay with Him.

Therefore, Satan is able to operate on self because of that power of choice. If that choice were gone, he could not function anymore. We still have a choice and God wants us to have it. The contact with God is made through love. We love Him because He first loved us. He so loved us He came down and became a human and wooed us to His side. You remain by His side by the power of choice. You do not have to love Him. It is just like marriage. Every day it is a willing response. When you got up this morning, you could decide to stay with your spouse or leave him or her. You do not have to stay there. You can always leave in marriage. You chose to be married to that person and you can always separate.

In this marvelous love affair with Christ, we need not stay with Him if we so choose. He does not have a yolk of bondage around us saying we must stay here. He asks us everyday if we love Him. We may have loved Him yesterday, but do we love Him today? Woman always want to ask their husbands that. If you love them, you like to answer them. The Lord wants to know that everyday. He asks, "Do you love Me today, or do you want to leave Me today?" And when particularly attractive temptations come along, He asks, "Do you still love Me, or do you love that sin more than Me?" Every day we have that marvelous privilege, that choice, of loving Him or loving something or somebody else, including self. The choice can never be forced, for love is always a willing response with no coercion of any kind. We must choose everyday to love Him in response to His love.

"In the matchless gift of His Son, God has encircled the whole world with an atmosphere of grace as real as the air which circulates around the globe. All who choose to breathe this life-giving atmosphere will live and grow up to the stature of men and women in Christ Jesus." SC 68. Not only may we live, but we may grow to maturity—if we choose to breathe His life giving atmosphere. We have studied about the vine and the branches. Paul said it is a unique thing in the relationship with Christ that at any time, we can choose to separate from Christ. We do not have to follow Him. He does not drag us along behind Him.

Because of this power of choice granted by the grace of Christ, self is potentially always alive. I am crucified with Christ, but because I have that power of choice every day of my life, self still has a potential to live again by my power of choice. It was by my choice that I died, was it not? I received Him, I chose to die with Him, and at any time I can choose not to. I can choose to serve somebody else.

It is this power of choice that makes it possible for the crucified self to live again tomorrow. I can reject Jesus. I do not have to follow Him. I can indulge self. I can turn my back on Him, and I can say I have another lover. I can harden my heart against Him. Satan knows that so he is always hanging around the edges, waiting for a chance to allure us into a new love affair. He dangles out such nice things to us, and he makes Christ look so difficult to follow by portraying Him as always exacting and demanding and oppressing.

Satan always presents Christ in a wrong light, and many believe him; but Jesus said Satan is a liar and the father of liars. Often we believe the devil more than we believe the Lord. We forget how tremendously attractive Jesus is, and how needy we are, especially when it comes to needing Him. Satan is always there presenting allurements, and we always have the power of choice. The power of choice is a part of self that lives on and on. Therefore, self must be constantly renounced, constantly crucified.

Here is perhaps the finest quotation you can find on this: "It is not only at the beginning of the Christian life that this renunciation of self is to be made. At every advance step heavenward it is to be renewed. All our good works are dependent on a power outside of ourselves; therefore there needs to be a continual reaching out of the heart after God, a constant, earnest confession of sin and humbling of the soul before Him." MH 455. This must go on and on and on.

This is a different understanding of the sanctified life than many people have. When I first read the book *The Sanctified Life* by Ellen White, I thought I was going to learn everything about sanctification. I began reading the book with great zeal, but with greater discouragement as I progressed. When I finished the book, I concluded that it did not say one thing about sanctification. Why was it titled *The Sanctified Life?* I am explaining my ignorance to you, but it did not seem to talk about sanctification at all. All I read about was Joseph and Daniel and others, and I could not see a thing in there about sanctification. After many years with the Lord working on my brain, I finally came around and realized that she was talking about their maintaining that condition of walking with God, and how everyday they had to keep their bodies under, having no confidence in the flesh, and everyday abiding in Christ and choosing Him. That seemed a very strange concept to me concerning sanctification. But this is exactly what the book teaches.

Self always has to be surrendering. "You are to maintain this connection with Christ by faith and the continual surrender of your will to Him; and so long as you do this, He will work in you to will and to do according to His good pleasure." SC 62,63. There is that constant surrender of the will, choosing Him everyday by faith and walking with Him, making Him the King of my life.

Because of this, the Bible teaches in the words of Paul that there are some things we ought to do about the flesh. "For if ye live after the flesh [if we follow its dictates] ye shall die: but if ye through the Spirit do mortify the deeds of the body, ye shall live." Romans 8:13. Mortify means to die or to kill. We must be continually putting the deeds of the body to death. Paul made that clear when he wrote: "Mortify therefore your members which are upon the earth; fornication, uncleanness, inordinate affection, evil concupiscence, and covetousness, which is idolatry." Colossians 3:5.

Go back with me now and look at this power of choice again in Paul's terminology. He does not use the term "power of choice," but in many ways he is saying this if you become aware that this is an ongoing, living power in us. Notice what he said about it, especially there in Romans 6:6-10 where he talked about this freedom from sin and the death of the old man. Then in verse 11, he wrote, "Likewise reckon ye also yourselves to be dead indeed unto sin, but alive unto God through Jesus Christ our Lord." Reckon yourself, or think about yourself this way. Count yourself as dead, and count yourself alive unto Christ. Believe it. This is a choice. You do not have to do this. You can choose to believe it by faith, or you can choose not to believe it.

In Romans 3, Paul is talking about this choice. Remember in verse 3 he talks about "what the law cannot do, in that it is weak through the flesh." Then he says that God sent His Son "in the likeness of human flesh," and a change took place, "that the righteousness of the law might be fulfilled in us." How is this fulfilled? In verse 4, the last part, "who walk not after the flesh, but after the Spirit."

When you are in a building, you can walk out through one of several doors. You can even jump out the window if that is your choice. We make a choice as to how we will walk, either following after the dictates of the flesh, or following the Holy Spirit. Thus, walking the Christian walk is a choice.

Then comes verse 5. "For they that are after the flesh do mind the things of the flesh; but they that are after the Spirit the things of the Spirit." You can choose where you will put your interest. You can choose how you will walk and where you will walk, and who or what you will or will not mind.

"For as many as are led by the Spirit of God, they are the sons of God." Romans 8:14. Whom will you choose to lead you? Whom will you follow? We must always make that choice. It is not the lack of a choice that is the problem. It is usually the wrong choice, is it not? Everyone chooses. If you neglect to choose, you have made a choice. You cannot be neutral. It is that quick and that fast.

In the Christian life we are constantly choosing, reckoning, walking, minding. "Walk in the Spirit, and ye shall not fulfill the lust of the flesh." Galatians 5:16. Paul goes on to say that if you are led by the Spirit, there is no condemnation at all. If you are lead by the Spirit, follow the Spirit. Choose that direction. The thing that does not die when the old man is crucified is our capability to choose which master we will have to rule over us.

In the sanctified life, as you begin to ask what you can and cannot do, you need to realize that it boils down to this: you can choose. You can choose one of several masters, but whomever you choose to serve, his slaves, or servants, you are; and that is the way it is. The devil would like you to serve him, or self, or sin. Christ has done everything that we might serve Him, to win our love and our esteem and our affection. All the powers are from outside, except the power of choice. But because of that power of choice, I can be crucified with Christ, or I can live apart from Him. I can follow another master and say that I will not have Jesus rule over me.

Justification and conversion bring us into contact with the power that enables us. We can abide in Him or we can separate from Him. He accomplished that for us. In sanctification, by our choice we stay or depart. The power of choice is there, but we need the power found in that other Person with whom we have made contact. I am free in Christ, but not in self; and all the freedom I have has been accomplished by Jesus and not by my choice. He makes the choice possible through what He has done for us. As I cleave to Him, as I maintain the relationship, as I love Him, as I behold Him, I make this contact by faith. And because I come into contact with power, the gospel functions in my life in a powerful way. By not maintaining the contact, I find myself floundering.

All our problems center around either making contact with Christ each day, or choosing to separate from Him. It is that simple. So often we assume that once we make contact, we just stay there without another choice. But every morning the devil knows that you might assume that, and he checks to see if you have forgotten or decided not to make contact with Christ that day. If that was your choice, he knows you will be vulnerable; and just like that, he lures our affections, our interests, our attentions, and suddenly we find ourselves walking another road. Then we wonder what happened that made us pick up that old sin again. We get depressed and begin to blame ourselves for those activities instead of our not walking closely with Jesus.

But the problem is not the wrong walk. That is the symptom, not the disease. The problem is the separation! Go back and make the contact. Find the power again. He is still waiting there. He promised He would never break the tie that binds us to Him. The tie can be broken by no power except your choice. It was not your sin that was the problem, but rather your choice to not abide in Christ.

By the way, the greatest sin of all is to perpetually choose to not walk with Christ. If supreme love for God is the greatest commandment, then not to love Him is the greatest sin. Willing separation from Christ means that I do not love Him anymore. Therefore, I must everyday look at self as potentially dangerous if I choose to follow self. I am vulnerable and weak, and I must go and look for that Power outside of self and commit my life to Him again and again, and make that marvelous choice.

"For though we walk in the flesh [we live in these human bodies], we do not war after the flesh [our weapon of warfare is not our humanity for we cannot trust it]: (For the weapons of our warfare are not carnal, but mighty through God, to the pulling down of strong holds;) Casting down imaginations, and every high thing that exalteth itself against the knowledge of God, and bringing into captivity every thought to the obedience of Christ." 2 Corinthians 10:3-5. The might of God, functioning in man, is that which comes through contact with

Him. He even brings thoughts into captivity. People say, "I don't know what to do with these thoughts I keep having." Seek that contact with Jesus. Then the Gospel, which is the power of God unto salvation, begins to function and good things happen.

"Thus saith the Lord; Cursed be the man that trusteth in man, and maketh flesh his arm, and whose heart departeth from the Lord...Blessed is the man that trusteth in the Lord, and whose hope the Lord is." Jeremiah 17:5,7. I wish we more fully realized how much those two verses say. When I make myself (what I can do) or other people my trust, it is like being cursed. But when my hope is in the Lord, when I trust in Him, I am blessed; and it is obvious to me and to you and to everyone else that I am blessed.

It is all found in making the choice of whom you put your confidence in. Paul wrapped the whole thing up in this classical statement: "I am crucified with Christ [but I am still alive and free to choose]: nevertheless I live; yet not I, but Christ liveth in me: and the life which I now live in the flesh I live by the faith of the Son of God, who loved me, and gave Himself for me." Galatians 2:20. Paul had been crucified, but he is not dead; but the life he is living is not of himself. It is Christ living in him, which he lives by the faith in the Son of God, who loved him and gave Himself for him.

The sanctified life is a most unusual one, and it is not nearly as confusing as we and the devil have made it. We continue with our love affair with Jesus, not because we must, not because of duty, not because of fear, and not because of coercion or force, but because it is so delightful to love Him who first loved me. It is just wonderful. The big question everyday is: Do you love Jesus?

We are told that when James White was dying and Ellen was at his bedside, over and over she asked him the question as he lingered there, "James, do you love Jesus? James, do you love Jesus?" Let me tell you, she knew what it was all about. And we need to learn what it is all about, and fast. Everyday the question is: Do I love Jesus? Do I choose Him? Do I fall in love with Him all over again? Is it sweet to walk with Jesus? Is it precious? Is it wonderful to sit at the feet of Jesus? Is it hopeful? Is it blessed to trust in Him? Have I found Him, the One who is all together lovely, the lily of the valley, the bright and morning star? Is He good to me? Am I delighted to know Him, to be close to Him? Is there anything in this life more alluring, more precious, than being with Christ?

Friend, God has done marvelous things for us. What a privilege to choose. Wouldn't you hate it if you had to be forced? Let's make sure that we do not force our children and church members, pressuring them to do what we think they should do. That is not Christianity. No wonder we have such trouble with sanctification, because it depends so much on the power of choice. Liberty of conscience should be foremost within our ranks like no other people on the face of the earth. We should demonstrate to the world that tremendous security in Jesus, that wonderful hope, that glorious freedom; and it all comes by choice.

As for me and my house, we will serve the Lord. Choose this day whom you will serve. May you see the allurements of Jesus in all their splendor, looming above all the other attractions of this world, until every day and every moment He is so precious you would never choose anyone else. This is my prayer for you in Jesus' name.

19

BETTER, BETTER, BETTER

OUR TITLE FOR THIS chapter poses a misunderstanding that many Christians have regarding Christ our righteousness and justification by faith. Many think that sanctification is becoming good enough so that we are finally accepted into heaven. We might refer to this as the pursuit of excellence, which would be a more sophisticated term. The idea is that I can arrive some day to a certain level of performance, and when that happens, the Lord will accept me into the kingdom. This concept involves and demands a great deal of striving so that I might achieve some kind of flawless performance, or at least to become as flawless as I am able. This concept of getting better and better makes it almost impossible to accept Christ as our righteousness.

I would like to state this concept of getting good enough in a way that we can all understand, which is by putting it into an educational, or academic, perspective. Will only the A students get into heaven? They are honored in our society, and especially in the academic community; and many look upon heaven as an achievement like that. I am not saying that those who do well in school will get into heaven. I am talking about those who receive an A in righteousness. Will they be accepted into heaven? Or might the Lord accept those with a high B? Or possibly all who are above average? Would God say that all who are average or below average would be left out? Is it possible that anyone else might get in besides the A students? The Bible talks about how only the righteous will be saved, but how righteous do you need to be?

We have already asked the question: What is righteousness? We have many problems with this. Has God drawn some arbitrary line where if you attain above that level you are good enough, and if you are below it you are not good enough? Some say they do not believe in Christian perfection at all. Others believe in Universalism and say that all will get in. If they all cannot get in, who is left out? And why are they left out? Who will make it? Why do they make it? If you believe in absolute Christian perfection, perhaps you think only the A students will get in. Or maybe only the top A student—the valedictorian—will make it.

We have so many concepts about what it requires, or what is demanded of us, to be accepted into the kingdom; and because of our misunderstandings, we have many fears and problems. We become frustrated and anxious, and feel inferior as non-achievers. When you use the criteria of pursuit of excellence for acceptance into heaven, you run into a multitude of problems that no one seems to have answers for.

For instance, Jesus said, "But many that are first shall be last; and the last shall be first." Matthew 19:30. He put it more dogmatically when He said, "So the last shall be first, and the first last: for many be called, but few chosen." Matthew 20:16. Some think that the word "first" means first in time. The word "first" is translated from the Greek word *protose,* which according to *Young's Analytical Concordance to the Bible* means "foremost," or "preeminent." This same word is found in Mark 9:35. "If any man desire to be first, the same shall be last of all, and servant of all." Jesus was saying that the foremost, or preeminent ones, shall be last; and the last (the least of these) shall be first.

Perhaps you think that text does not fit, so let me give you another one. "Verily I say unto you, That the publicans and the harlots go into the kingdom of God before you [before the Pharisees]." Matthew 21:31. The publicans and the harlots are certainly not very good performers, are they? You cannot exactly say that they have been pursuing excellence. How do they have an entrance before others who thought they were doing very well? How do they accomplish this foremost position of going in first? How do you harmonize that with being good enough, or getting better, better, better?

One of our problems with this subject is that we use worldly standards of achievement to measure our qualifications or our excellence in Christianity. Jesus reminded us that His kingdom was not of this world. The value system in His kingdom is not like the value system of this world. In fact, there is no similarity. Unfortunately, most of us use the value system we understand in this world to measure our qualifications for the kingdom of God. We look at ourselves according to worldly ideas and say, "Well, it doesn't look like I am making it."

Christ said, "for that which is highly esteemed among men [here in this world] is abomination in the sight of God." Luke 16:15, last part. But we do not think so.

There are a few texts that illustrate some of the things that are an abomination in His sight. "But all their works they do for to be seen of men." Matthew 23:5. They like to be on display. Then there are those who "love the uppermost rooms at feasts, and the chief seats in the synagogues, And greetings in the markets, and to be called of men, Rabbi, Rabbi." Verse 6. Today, it is highly esteemed among men to be called "doctor," or "Reverend," and many other titles that men seek after. Jesus' point is that we should not desire to be called by those titles because we have only one Master.

Here is one more illustration: "But he that is greatest among you shall be your servant. And whosoever shall exalt himself shall be abased; and he that shall humble himself shall be exalted." Verse 11. This is the complete opposite of worldly criteria of success. We like to do our works to be seen of men, don't we? Yes, we love it. It is delightful, it is honorable, and we love it. We like titles, and we like to hear titles concerning ourselves. We love high positions. In fact, we even worship high positions, and have adulation for those in high positions. Many a conference President has been idolized; and we love to invite the people in prestigious positions to our homes. Everyone thinks it is good to gain high status in our educational system, or to climb the ladder of success in our denomination, or to get voted into some high office. We honor valedictorians, but who has ever honored F students, or D students? Who has ever given them any award at graduation time? We never think of it. We single out certain people. They are special. And Dad nudges you when the valedictorian walks to the podium and says, "Why aren't you up there?"

We have a variety of methods in the church of showing that we like worldly standards for esteeming people. Look at all of our promotional systems where we honor the ones that brings in the most money. If you do not bring in a certain amount, you do not get a ribbon at the big Sabbath day victory dinner. The colporteur with the highest amount in sales is honored with what they call the Million-Dollar Club. He gets the trip to Hawaii with all expenses paid. The fellow that worked as hard and slaved away as many hours was not in the Million-Dollar Club, and he stayed home where it is cold in the wintertime. Sorry, fellow.

When we want to raise money, we honor people who give large amounts of money. Those evangelists and pastors who win the most souls are honored by getting their names printed in Ministry Magazine. Those who win one hundred souls in one year become members of the Century Club, although fifty Bible workers did most of the work, and never a mention of the Bible workers' names.

We do the same thing with musicians. The perfect musicians who perform flawlessly are esteemed among men. If you make one mistake out of a thousand notes, nobody applauds you. You did not practice enough. You are not sufficiently perfect, so you will not make it. We do all sorts of things like this for athletes and the finest artists and craftsmen. All through life the emphasis and praise centers on the pursuit of excellence. Almost every human believes in this. We cannot blame the students and the schools and the faculty because father and mother believe it at home. The preachers believe in it. It is that way with everyone, in the world and in the church. We have been brainwashed into believing that this is a good system that is acceptable and is to be pursued, and almost everyone follows it.

It is not easy to convince people that this is contrary to the kingdom of heaven, because we like this system. We hate it, but we like it. Some people keep dangling before their eyes the day when they will be acclaimed. They dream about that wonderful day when all men will applaud them. They do not want to lose that day, and so they long for it and do not want this system destroyed, even though they have been failures so far. Some preachers and teachers would not like this system taken away because they would lose all their pressures on people to pursue excellence. They would not know what to do if this methodology was taken away.

Jesus taught something different, and I wish to spend as much time on His concepts as possible. He spoke about righteousness in terms of the law. "Jesus said unto him, Thou shalt love the Lord thy God with all thy heart, and with all thy soul, and with all thy mind. This is the first and great commandment. And the second is like unto it, Thou shalt love thy neighbour as thyself." Matthew 22:37-39. He said that the law is supreme love for God and to love your neighbor as yourself. Jesus taught this, and He was the Author of the law if I understand the Old Testament well.

Does the system of rewarding a few, but not others, truly demonstrate loving your neighbor as yourself? Most people like to be rewarded. But suppose someone else gets rewarded but you do not. What happens in your thinking process? You feel like you are a failure because you were not rewarded. You are not a failure because I say so, but because you feel that way. I am talking about what you think, and not what other people think about you. You feel like a failure because you did not make it.

As you reward a certain few, you are saying to the ones not rewarded that you love them less. You are saying that you love the ones who achieve excellence. You esteem and praise them. If you are only a C student, then too bad. The teacher may try to tell you that a C is not such a bad grade. Then why do you honor only the A students?

Some people will say that the C students did not deserve a reward. Does anyone deserve heaven? Is there anyone so good that he or she will deserve heaven? I have not read about that in the Bible, have you? If you say that the A students deserve the reward, then you are saying that there are some who will deserve heaven, and they must struggle to deserve it. Do those who receive the better grades deserve acclaim and rewards? Do they? Well, they worked harder. Do you mean the others were more lazy or neglectful or disinterested? What do you mean by that? You are talking to more than one person when you say, "He worked harder." You are talking to the whole class, or the whole school. At least they are all listening. Are you implying that everyone else but the one who got the reward is lazy? Are you saying that only those who work harder get into heaven?

Consider what Jesus meant by the parable of the laborers where those who worked one hour received the same wages (or reward) as those who worked twelve hours. The ones who worked all day long "murmured against the goodman of the house." Matthew 20:11. They did not think he was fair. The owner of the vineyard said, "Friend, I do thee no wrong: didst not thou agree with me for a penny?" Verse 13. They had agreed to that, but now they had many arguments and good logic to try and get more than those whohad only worked for one hour. The owner replied by saying he had treated them nicely. He gave them all the same reward, no matter how long they had   worked or how hard they had worked.

This challenges our theology, and we have not faced the hard facts. Christ our righteousness is confusing to most people because they use worldly ideas of success to determine if they are becoming righteous enough for heaven. The Lord does not judge as man judges, and thank God for that, or most of us would be left out. Very few would make it if God used worldly criteria for success. The Lord does not judge that way.

Why is it that people work hard to be a top student? First of all, they like to be applauded. Few people are immune to that selfish desire. We like to be praised and we like to be honored. Some like it so much that they will sweat and labor for years to make it. And you will praise them because they worked so hard. The A on the report card is given to reward the effort people make. It is not that way in the kingdom of heaven. There is effort, but it is quite different. Some slave for high grades because they are frightened of what their dad will say when they get home if they do not have it. Some parents can get hyper over a C on a report card. We often try to drive our kids to get better grades.

Maybe we strive for high grades because we want the acceptance of our peers or teachers. If we do not achieve, we do not feel accepted. There are others who, because of an honorable birth, have great intellect, and they hardly work hard at all to get high grades. Should they be honored? Should others not be honored who did not have the good fortune to be born of better parents with more intellect? Would you reward people for their good birth and deprive them because of poor birth? Where would you place the credit?

I am trying to help you see how God thinks about all this in comparison to what our ideas are. The ways of the world create a terrible problem for everyone, and people suffer more than we realize with this worldly system of rewards. Whenever you reward winners you create losers. When you reward success you create failures who are not as successful. When you acclaim the few, you discredit the many; and we are communicating a message to everyone when we reward only a few. They believe what we have to say. The adverse affects of this system do not end right there. Even many A students feel like failures. They have told me so. Why? They did not receive the top grade. Only the top one is really acclaimed, they say. It is amazing how people can strive for success but feel slighted because only the one with the top A is acclaimed.

This worldly system of rewards is hurting our denomination and all other denominations. Those in high positions whom you would esteem as having great prestige have told me that they feel inferior and unsuccessful. They feel like failures while sitting in those high positions. They have told me why they feel that way. Unless everything goes their way, unless everyone bows down and acclaims them, they are not successful. As soon as someone starts to snipe at them and criticize them a little bit, they feel like failures. They begin to scrutinize all their actions and all their votes to see how much of a failure they are, even though, by worldly standards, they are in high positions. So even successful people can feel inferior.

This worldly system has become a disease that adversely affects both young and old. It is difficult to give people hope who have been brainwashed into believing this system. It is difficult to give them sufficient success so that they feel they are somebody. The system says that only the top one is really worthy of honor. People have come to believe this after years and years of this system being demonstrated in the church, the home, the school, and the community. Making people feel that they are successful is most difficult, if not nearly impossible. And I believe the devil sits back and laughs and laughs and laughs.

Success, prestige, and esteem are like money. When you get your first million you need five or ten; and when you get ten you need twenty. You become addicted and can never get enough. It is like Hollywood actors who once were on the throne with everybody acclaiming them, and now they are forgotten; and they do everything to make themselves look as beautiful as they once did so they can appear on the screen once more and rescue their image. We do some foolish things to rescue our image, and it is a pathetic thing to see people lured on by a philosophy that we have accepted as being so valuable.

Jesus did not believe in a system like that. We like it because it motivates people and drives them to achieve, beyond their limits sometimes. It does not matter to us if they end up in the hospital with ulcers or in a psycho ward. When that happens we say, "Oh, that poor person. They just didn't know how to handle it." But we continue to increase the pressures to drive more people to more excellence, and we trust in this system. We think that putting more pressure on people is a way to show them we love them. Is there anyone who does not hate pressure? We take vacations to escape pressures; and we cannot invent enough entertainment these days to get rid of the pressures.

Jesus condemned this system when He said, "For they bind heavy burdens and grievous to be borne, and lay them on men's shoulders; but they themselves will not move them with one of their fingers." Matthew 23:4. The pressures are heavy burdens and are breaking our backs. We are overloaded with pressures, and yet people say, "Try more pressure and you will get more A students." And you will get more physically, mentally, and spiritually sick students, too. Parents use this system with their children, our churches use it in promotions, we think it works well in politics, and teachers would not know what to do without this system when it comes to the grading system.

People argue with me and say, "But Elder Lehman, in heaven they have systems of awards and rewards. In heaven they have position and status. Will not some be nearer the throne than others? Will not some have more stars in their crowns than others? Will there not be certain prestigious groups like the one hundred and forty-four thousand with special privileges? Heaven has a system like that." No, they do not have a system like that. They have rewards and awards and different positions, but they are vastly different than in the kingdoms of this world. There is no similarity whatsoever. It is true that some will stand near the throne, and some will have more stars and all these things, but those awards and rewards are vastly different than you think.

In heaven, the work that is rewarded is not that work done for ourselves. Christ described the work that is rewarded: "And the King shall answer and say unto them, Verily I say unto you, Inasmuch as ye have done it unto one of the least of these My brethren, ye have done it unto Me." "Then shall the King say unto them on His right hand, Come, ye blessed of My Father, inherit the kingdom prepared for you from the foundation of the world." Matthew 25:40,34. You are blessed and you are praised, but only because you are a blessing to other people and not to self. It is not enhancing and developing self, but rather building up others that Christ honors. To those who work for others, He says, "Come inherit the kingdom." But those who forget about others and only think about self are left out.

Prestige and honor in heaven is different from that here on earth. These people have been bought with a price—the dear Son of God, and He claims them as His own. Whatever you do to them you do to Jesus because they are His property. Jesus will say, "Come ye blessed because you have been working for Me and for souls, and not for self."

There is another aspect to heaven's reward system that is different, and this refers to our talents, skills, intellect, and abilities. "For who maketh thee to differ from another? [Why are you brighter than others?] And what hast thou that thou didst not receive? Now if thou didst receive it, why dost thou glory, as if thou hadst not received it?" 1 Corinthians 4:7. Why do you brag about your skills as if they were yours, and as if you originated them? God has given them to you, and if you are the steward of them and not the originator, why do you boast of them and accept awards for them?

Peter and John at the beautiful gate of the temple raised up a crippled man, and people began to worship them. They told the people they did not heal the man through their own power, but through the name of Jesus. They said they were only trustees of the healing gift. This is true of all gifts, and of their developments. You would never be able to develop talents and skills if God did not give you a clear memory and good mind, and hands with good coordination. He puts you in good stead with your teachers and employers. He gives you good schools and good parents and the right environment. God is not only the Giver and the Originator of our talents, but He fosters their development, for without Him we can do nothing. All the praise for every talent should be to Him and never to ourselves. We act as though we originated these talents and skills that we demonstrate so capably. We do not think He is around to hear and receive the praise so we take it all ourselves. And we are advertising that God is dead every time we take the credit for what He does with us and for us and through us.

There are two quotations about physicians and their skills that I want us to see. "He would have the members of the medical profession expel from their practice everything which has been brought in by selfishness, avariciousness, injustice. He has given wisdom and skill to physicians, and He designs that nothing savoring of robbery and injustice shall be practiced by those who make the law of Jehovah the rule of their life." MM 121. In other words, all the skill they have is from God. The next quote is even clearer. "The exorbitant price charged by physicians in this country [Australia], when called upon to attend suffering humanity is robbery, fraud. God gave physicians their wisdom and skill. It is not man who saves life; it is the GREAT RESTORER." And Ellen White put in the bold words.

All the skill that a doctor has is not his. He did not achieve it and he did not originate it. God gave him that skill. God receives the price for the utilization of it, the blessing of it, and the praise—if we believe in God. The same is true of pastors. They are not the originators of inspiration or knowledge or anything else. None of us have that ability. The same is true of good teachers, good farmers, good mechanics, and good students. Whatever skill you look at or whatever ability, we are neither the responsible agents for that, nor the originators. It is all of Him. Those who are in the kingdom of heaven know that, and all praise resounds to Him.

Read in the book of Revelation about how the inhabitants of heaven constantly praise Him day and night—praising Him from Whom all blessings flow. He is the giver of every good and precious gift according to James 1:17. We are not the giver of those gifts and we do not deserve them. God gives them to us because of His goodness, mercy, and love for us. This is how it comes about, and not because we work so hard for them as many would like to think. Therefore, the status and honor that heaven bestows, is on those who praise God for the blessings received and used, and they are used for the benefit of other people.

Jesus spoke the following parable about debtors when He was visiting the home of Simon the leper: "There was a certain creditor which had two debtors: the one owed five hundred pence, and the other fifty. And when they had nothing to pay, he frankly forgave them both. Tell me therefore, which of them will love him most? Simon answered and said, I suppose that he, to whom he forgave most. And He said unto him, Thou hast rightly judged…Wherefore I say unto thee [Simon], Her [Mary's] sins, which are many, are forgiven; for she loved much: but to whom little is forgiven, the same loveth little." Luke 7:41-43,47. Mary looked upon herself as a terrible sinner who had been forgiven for an enormous debt. But Simon thought he was a good fellow and needed forgiveness for little.

The following quote is in reference to what Jesus said to Simon: "Those whom Christ has forgiven most will love Him most. These are they who in the final day will stand nearest to His throne." MH 182. The greatest lovers are the ones who have been forgiven most, and they will be the closest to Jesus. This is the excellence that heaven values—those who love Him most. Why do they love Him so much? Because they have been forgiven for so much. In order to be forgiven for much, you must have looked upon yourself as a vile sinner. We love Him in proportion to our awareness of our sinfulness, and we thank Him, and we praise Him for amazing grace. Those are the ones who will stand nearest to His throne. They look upon themselves as the worst failures, but saved by grace. They love Him most and thank Him most and praise Him most. The greatest praisers of God are the closest to the throne; and they praise Him because they love Him so much, and that is because He loved them so much.

This is a different kind of excellence than the world rewards or esteems, and the pursuit of this excellence is vastly different than many people have supposed. Our praise is in proportion to how much He has done for us. What has He done for you? It is not how right you are in all of your theology, even though that is important. It is not how much men praise you. It is how much you love Jesus, and why you love Him, and what you do to and for others because you love Jesus so much.

Remember that love is righteousness. God is love, and the law is a transcript of His character; so righteousness is love, and love is righteousness. And Christ our righteousness is Christ our love. The better, better, better concept in the kingdom of heaven is more and more and more love for Jesus and for others.

Love is a strange thing when it comes to excellence. In that classic chapter in 1 Corinthians 13, it says in verse 5 that love "seeketh not her own." The excellence that we try to develop in our skills and talents is always seeking our own eminence, our own achievement. It is always looking at self and striving for perfection in self. But love does not seek its own. Love esteems every man better than himself. Love seeks another's welfare. Love is not mindful of self but always mindful of others, and doing for others. Therefore, excellence in love is the very opposite of excellence in some skill or ability.

Jesus described this love: "If any man will come after Me, let him take up his cross and deny himself." Luke 9:23,24. In the next verse He talked about how, if you seek to save your life, you will lose it; but if you lose your life for His sake, you will save it. If you try to make yourself somebody in this world, you will lose everlasting life; but if you lose your life, buried in the wants of others and trying to help them to achieve and succeed, then you gain everlasting life. Therefore, self-denial is the way of eminence and excellence in God's kingdom of grace. Self-achievement is the way of excellence and ability in this world. We confuse the two in Christ our righteousness, but there is no similarity. One is total forgetfulness of self. The other one is total absorption with self.

The worldly concept of how to gain the kingdom of heaven is vastly different than what men suppose. In self-development, I look at those things inherent in me—my abilities, my talents, my intellect—and I try to cause them to grow and to progress. But love is a different thing. In fact, it is not even in me, for "love is of God." 1 John 4:7. Love is of God, not of men. You cannot manufacture it. You can strive to be loving but that will not cause you to be loving. You must receive all love from Him. It is the development of characteristics found in someone else, not those things found in yourself. You can only receive them by coming to Him. There is no other way. We love Him because He first loved us. He instigates, He motivates. I do not. He also says, "If God so loved us, we ought also to love one another." 1 John 4:11. All the love that comes from me out to you is the result of His love to me. I am always receiving from Him. Pursuit of excellence in love is to come into contact with the One who is love. I do not develop what is inherently in me. I receive it from Him. I must establish communication channels, relationships, and connections so that I can receive; otherwise I will not have it. I must be tied to Jesus and identified with Him.

Those connections, those relationships, are faith and love. We are bound to Him by love and faith, and they really work. We are tied to Him by faith and love, but even they come from Jesus. Love is of God and to every man is given a measure of faith. I must receive even those from Him, and He is waiting to bestow them upon me. While I try to go about developing love and faith in me, God tells me that He has them and wants to give them to me. As we give ourselves to Him, He gives Himself to us with faith and love and righteousness. But I must give myself fully to Him. He will not accept a divided heart.

The striving that must take place is in maintaining the clear channels of communication, of relationships, of connections, so that I know every day that I am His and He is mine. And then every day there is a divine bestowal of love, faith, and righteousness; and through His strength I can do all things, because He has the power and the authority and the ability. I do not.

The abilities, the talents, the skills, the heavenly rewards are all found in Jesus. And Christ our righteousness is laying hold on Jesus and never letting Him go until He blesses us every day. It is coming into that marvelous relationship of love, that divine connection of the vine and the branches, until, as Paul said, "For me to live is Christ." Philippians 1:21. Then love grows because there is more love flowing out from Him. As I come closer and closer to Him, I see my own sinfulness more and more, and I have more reason for forgiveness. And as He forgives me more, I love Him more. Those who have been forgiven most will love Him most and will stand nearest to His throne. We have been fighting against learning about our sins. We do not want to be forgiven for more, and so we do not want to love Him more. We hate to hear about our sins because we do not think He forgives; yet He can hardly wait to forgive us.

"If we confess our sins, He is faithful and just to forgive us our sins, and to cleanse us from all unrighteousness." 1 John 1:9. When He forgives you much, you love Him much. When you love Him much, you love others; and you tell them that if they only knew the love of the Father and of Jesus, they would love Him, too.

Do you see that achievement in the Christian life is so vastly different from worldly achievement? It is forgetfulness of self, not development of self; and it is the development every day of a bond with Jesus, looking unto Him, the Author and Finisher of our faith. Everyday we embrace Him. Everyday we receive from Him abundant grace; for where sin did abound, grace did much more abound. I bring His love and grace into my very soul until it is like a living fountain, bubbling over and refreshing to me and to others. To those who have this experience, the Lord will say, "Come, ye blessed of My Father, inherit the kingdom prepared for you from the foundation of the world." Matthew 25:34.

Why are we so anxious? Why are we striving and struggling to perfect self when Christ waits to bestow all that we need to enter into the kingdom of heaven? We must feel our need, for only those who hunger and thirst after righteousness will be filled. The self-sufficient who believe they are doing a pretty good job are not hungry. It is the needy souls, those who feel sinful, lost, such failures, and inferior that He tells to come to Him and be filled with acceptance and love. He wants to embrace us and make us members of the greatest family in all the universe. He wants to extend the invitation to "Come ye blessed of My Father."

There is no other pressure in God's kingdom but the pressure of love. Nothing else but the love of Christ constrains me. How wonderful it is to live under that one pressure. How abominable it is to live under the other pressures. The Lord is waiting for His church, His people, His families, and His institutions to demonstrate just one pressure—the excellence of love, the love of Christ constraining us. And people will marvel and take note that we have been with Jesus because the transformation is so great, and the excellence of character and morality so mighty. They will ask, "How did those people become like this?" And we will answer, "The love of Jesus constrains me. How can I help but love

Him when He loves me so much? How can I possibly thank Him when He is so good to me? All praise to Him from Whom all blessings flow!"

Friend, the world is waiting, our children are waiting, our spouses, our parents, our neighbors are waiting for the pressures to be taken away, and to know that one prodding—the gentle prodding of sweet, sweet love that is so great it freely forgives and embraces us as God's very own possession. Jesus wants to come soon because He loves us so much. We are keeping Him away because we keep using all the systems of the world, and the kingdom of God is not being established in our heart as we respond to the pressures of life. The kingdom of God is the kingdom of love. How wonderful that kingdom is; and what a joyful, peaceful, happy, fulfilling life it is to serve Him in that kingdom. May God grant you relief from all pressures except the sweetness of His love, is my prayer in Jesus' name.

20

RAGS, RIGHTEOUSNESS, REPENTANCE

MANY TODAY ASSUME THAT since they keep the Sabbath and do not commit adultery, or kill, or steal, or lie, then they must be righteous. And since they are righteous they believe they are assured of an entrance into God's kingdom. Many have believed and taught this for a long time. Others who have problems keeping the commandments do not view themselves as commandment keepers. Because of their habitual sins, they do not claim to be righteous, and therefore they feel that they cannot get into the kingdom.

Could both groups be wrong about their assumptions? When you keep the law, you assume that your law keeping is righteousness; therefore this qualifies you to stand in God's presence. The message that came to this denomination in 1888 found fault with the concepts of righteousness of most Seventh-day Adventists. Do you know that? That message says that our righteousness is not good enough, no matter how good it appears to you or to me. You must have the righteousness of Jesus or you are unqualified for heaven. Some have still not understood that this message of Christ our righteousness says that our righteousness is not good enough. No matter how good you might think your righteousness is, the message of 1888 says loudly and clearly that it is not good enough. It finds fault with all our righteousness, and that is the heart and soul of it. But we argue with this because we think that since we are commandment keepers, we must be righteous, and therefore qualified to enter heaven.

This problem of righteousness involves much more than we usually assume. It is more than making the hands do the right things, and the lips say the right words, and so forth. It is more than attempting to be good.

Righteousness is symbolized in the Bible, and we can understand much more about it when we understand this symbol. "And to her was granted that she should be arrayed in fine linen, clean and white: for the fine linen is the righteousness of saints." Revelation 19:8. In this verse, righteousness is symbolized by clothing, and when you study righteousness as clothing it means much more. It covers some of those areas that we often omit from the understanding of the word. Righteousness is spiritual clothing. Why does the Bible call it clothing? Does

God hide our sins behind clothing? We must understand what He means by the symbol of clothing.

Sin produces a strange kind of undressed condition, and because of that undressed condition, a certain kind of clothing is required. This is introduced in the book of Genesis, but it is not easily understood. Talking about Adam and Eve, it says, "And they were both naked, the man and his wife, and were not ashamed." Genesis 2:25. They had no problem with their nakedness whatsoever. They were totally unashamed. But then they were tempted, and as we know, Eve partook of the forbidden fruit and tempted her husband, and he partook. "And the eyes of them both were opened, and they knew that they were naked; and they sewed fig leaves together, and made themselves aprons. And they heard the voice of the Lord God walking in the garden in the cool of the day: and Adam and his wife hid themselves from the presence of the Lord God amongst the trees of the garden. And the Lord God called unto Adam, and said unto him, Where art thou? And he said, I heard Thy voice in the garden, and I was afraid, because I was naked; and I hid myself." Genesis 3:7-10. Was Adam still naked when God came to the garden? No, he was not; yet some will say he was; and they are right, too. He already had some form of clothing on to cover his physical nakedness. It might not have been the most fashionable covering, but Adam and Eve were wearing fig leaves. They were not totally naked by any means.

The Lord asked Adam where he was and why he was hiding, and Adam answered, "I was afraid, because I was naked; and I hid myself." He said he was naked, but he really was not. He had at least some type of clothing on, but he said he was naked.

We must understand this and what he meant by this undressed condition, or we will have difficulty understanding what the right spiritual clothing is and make assumptions that are not necessarily true. He was not afraid when he was with Eve, and she was not afraid. They did not hide from each other and they were not ashamed to be together, even though they were unclothed. There was no hiding and no fear until the Lord God came. It was the presence of the Lord that caused the problem.

"Naked and ashamed, they tried to supply the place of the heavenly garments by sewing together fig leaves for a covering. This is what the transgressors of God's law have done ever since the day of Adam and Eve's disobedience. They have sewed together fig leaves to cover the nakedness caused by transgression. They have worn the garments of their own devising, by works of their own they have tried to cover their sins, and make themselves acceptable with God." COL 311.

The problem is more than covering my body or Adam's body or Eve's body. It is more than embarrassment over physical nakedness. They were concerned about covering their sins and about appearing in God's presence. There did not seem to be much of a problem until God came to visit them. As long as the Lord seemed to be away, it was not too difficult. How do you cover sins? With good works? We think we can. They might have been good at sewing fig leaves, but it did not seem to help.

The following quote says that no amount of our good works can accomplish this: "But this they can never do. Nothing can man devise to supply the place of his lost robe of innocence. No fig-leaf garment, no worldly citizen dress, can be worn by those who sit down with Christ and angels at the marriage supper of the Lamb. Only the covering which Christ Himself has provided can make us meet to appear in God's presence. This covering, the robe of His own righteousness, Christ will put upon every repenting, believing soul." COL 311.

Many have the idea that if they try hard enough, they will be good enough. Others say that if they have done the best they can, they will be good enough to appear in His presence. But that is not the problem. The problem is that we have to cover far more than we realize. There are many other issues to take care of than our goodness. Goodness is not the only problem. Our goodness does not counteract what we have been in the past. It does not matter how beautifully you sew or design your own fig leaves. Fig leaves are always unacceptable. Always! You can never do well enough with man's devising to accomplish acceptance. God insists on something different, and He offers to give that to us.

This thought was expressed by Jesus in a parable where a man entered a wedding feast clothed in his common dress. He had refused to wear the robe provided by the king. "And when the king came in to see the guests, he saw there a man which had not on a wedding garment. And he saith unto him, Friend, how camest thou in hither not having a wedding garment? And he was speechless. Then said the king to the servants, Bind him hand and foot, and take him away, and cast him into outer darkness; there shall be weeping and gnashing of teeth." Matthew 22:11-13. No problem seemed to exist as they waited for the bridegroom who tarried, but when the king came in, then the problem arose, so much so that he was speechless. He seemed to be in good standing prior to that time, but now he was not. This clothing is a most unique problem, and, of course, the clothing in Christ's parable is righteousness.

Referring to Adam and Eve, Ellen White wrote: "The love and peace which had been theirs was gone, and in its place they felt a sense of sin, a dread of the future, a nakedness of soul." PP 57. Not of body but of soul. We try to make ourselves acceptable to people, and try to cover what we think is our nakedness. We try to do our best, but this is not the problem. I might look very good to you, but God does not look on the outside. He looks on the heart or the soul. He sees things you never see in me and in you. Sometimes He sees things in me that I am unwilling to see. What can I do about those things that are deep down in my soul? I can make my lips say right things and my eyes see right things and my hands do right things, but what about my soul? Does it like to cooperate with behavior changes? Or does it grudgingly say it will do only what is necessary to look good to my peers?

The Lord looks on the heart. It was contaminated by my first sin and by all my sins since then, and no matter how many good things my hands do, my soul still has some problems. When Jesus comes around, my soul seems to be naked. Jesus is capable of looking right into my soul. He does not seem to miss a thing.

We know about the time when Christ drove the money changers out of the temple, and how He looked into the hearts of those Pharisees and Priests. They ran for fear even though they were leaders. Was it because of the whip in His hand? It was the look in His eye. They felt undressed before Him. Everything was laid bare before His vision. Nothing was hidden from His sight. This is the problem. It is not a question of how much good or bad you see in me, or that I see in you. The question is: What will the King see in me when He comes in? What will I look like when exposed to His view? It is like He has x-ray vision, and my garments do not hide a thing from Him. That is the way Adam and Eve felt, standing there with nothing concealed. My righteousness might look good to me, and even to you, but He looks beyond the external right into the depths of my heart; and He finds things there I do not like. I hardly ever look at them, so I don't feel well when I see them.

"One ray of the glory of God, one gleam of the purity of Christ, penetrating the soul, makes every spot of defilement painfully distinct, and lays bare the deformity and defects of the human character. It makes apparent the unhallowed desires, the infidelity of the heart, the impurity of the lips. The sinner's acts of disloyalty in making void the law of God, are exposed to his sight, and his spirit is stricken and afflicted under the searching influence of the Spirit of God. He loathes himself as he views the pure, spotless character of Christ." SC 29.

Somehow we think that when we feel that way, the preacher did it, or our parents did it, or the teacher. I become sensitive and say, "Get off my back and stop criticizing me!" We become afraid and we want to run and hide; and we say, "I don't ever want to go back there again. I don't want to hear that person again. They criticize me too much!" Did God criticize Adam and Eve? Not a word. Somehow they came to the conclusion that God was their enemy, but He had come every day in the cool of the day, because He was their friend and they were His friends. It was a pleasant occasion to meet together, and there they would sit during that heavenly visit in paradise. But with just one act of sin they supposed that a God of love was a God of hate who only criticized.

Our paranoid condition and our sensitivity about our sins is not necessarily caused by the law or the standards of the school or church. Our sensitivity is innate. It is inherent in transgression. Adam and Eve had no one else to blame for being so sensitive, did they? They tried to blame it on each other and on the serpent, but there was none to blame but themselves. God had not criticized them or harassed them. But they were very sensitive, so much so that they were afraid and tried to defend themselves, which is exactly what we do. We say it must have been the harsh standards of my home or my church or my teachers or my school, and we leave out the very nature of sin itself. We wrongly understand God. He suddenly becomes someone after us, against us; yet He only desires to come for a very friendly visit. In Eden, there was no change in God. All the change was in two people who used to fondly welcome His visits, but now feared them. We wonder why we sometimes fear going to church, or to Prayer Meeting, or Bible classes.

I wish you would think about this. We have so many misconceptions of God, and yet He is so different than what most of us think because we all have problems with our sins. Thus, we become afraid and run when we think He might be around. He is not what we often imagine or portray Him to be. We must not only learn to live with God in the hereafter but today. He wants to walk and talk with us today. He wants us to abide with Him. He desires a close intimacy with us because He is our friend; and in many ways the Bible tells us that. Because of our problems and our sins, we think that He is no longer our friend and that He is against us. This is something He has never said.

I wish you would go back and think of how in 1888, the righteousness of Jesus was preached. In reality they were preaching the Laodicean message; and that was an unpopular message then as well as today. The Laodicean message does not pat us on the back and make us feel good.

Laodiceans have a clothing problem. I hope you know who Laodicea is. The True Witness says, "I counsel thee to buy of Me gold tried in the fire, that thou mayest be rich; and white raiment, that thou mayest be clothed, and that the shame of thy nakedness do not appear." Revelation 3:18. Then He goes on to talk about the eye salve that we all need in order to rightly see our condition.

The counsel is to buy white raiment so you can be clothed and cover the shame of your nakedness. This is the Lord's wish. He offers that white raiment to us. It is not something I do so that I am able to stand in His presence. It is something He gives to me. I keep trying to produce the righteousness that will qualify me, but He says, "Let me give it to you. I have it already. I would like to make it yours. Will you allow Me to do this?"

The nakedness of Laodicea makes them similar to Adam and Eve, but there is another problem here that makes it dissimilar. The Lord did not come into the presence of Adam and Eve, if you will check very carefully in Genesis 3:8. They only heard His voice, and when they heard the voice of God speaking to them, they were afraid and ran to hide.

The Laodicean message is the voice from the True and Faithful Witness. And according to Revelation 1:5 and 3:14, Jesus is the Faithful Witness. He says He is speaking to us, and wants to know if we can hear Him. Adam and Eve ran to hide, afraid when they heard God's voice; but Laodiceans have the voice of God speaking to them, but they do not run and hide. In fact, they do not even think they are naked according to verse 17. "Because thou sayest, I am rich, and increased with goods, and have need of nothing; and knowest not that thou art...naked." We do not know it. God speaks, but somehow I am not afraid, and somehow I do not want to run and hide. I do not even sense that I need clothing. Instead, I say I am dressed like a wealthy person with the finest clothing, and I am very well satisfied. How is it that the people in Laodicea can have the voice of God speaking to them, and still be so satisfied, believing that they are clothed? How can it be that they do not feel naked and afraid?

Here is the answer: "Behold, I stand at the door, and knock: if any man hear My voice, and open the door, I will come in to him and will sup with him, and he with Me." Revelation 3:20. Laodicea has trouble listening. Their ears somehow do not function well. He knocks, and the knocking is His voice. If we would only hear, He would speak to us and tell us many wonderful things. If we could only hear Him knocking and then respond by opening the door, He would come in and we could be together with Him. Then something would happen. When I come into the presence of the Lord, He sees me and I see Him. As long as I can keep Him outside of the door, apart from me, I can be very comfortable. As long as I can keep my ears from hearing, I can be quite satisfied. Therefore, I work hard at not hearing, and especially at not meeting Him. I avoid all occasions where I might meet Him. If only I could go to church every Sabbath and not meet Him, and never hear the still, small voice, I would go home feeling wonderful and certain that I am on the road to heaven. I would be content and smug and complacent. But I must not hear His voice. If I can sit in your Sabbath school class, or even teach your class, so that no one ever meets or hears Jesus, that is a very satisfying class. In fact, I can sleep nicely during class, and afterward and at night.

We can have our daily devotions without ever meeting Jesus or hearing Him. We may study our Sabbath school lesson, and visit our friends, and discuss theology, and even preach, yet never meet Jesus, and never hear His voice, continuing on as if we are extremely satisfied, never afraid and never wanting to run and hide. We have become experts at avoiding Jesus. In fact, we can talk about Christianity and theology and never mention His name. Preachers can preach for a whole hour and never mention His name. We can even mention His name, but neither hear Him nor meet Him.

Two young people once came to me who at that time were attending a college of another denomination, and they asked me a puzzling question. "Elder Lehman, we are not opposed to the Sabbath nor the law. In fact, we rather like it and have even attended church here on the Sabbath. But why can we not talk to the people on this campus about Jesus? All they want to do is talk about the Sabbath and other subjects. Why will they not talk about Jesus?" It was just a question, not a criticism. Are you comfortable talking about Jesus, as comfortable as you are about talking about the Sabbath? Or are you uncomfortable? Do you get uneasy when someone asks, "Do you love Jesus?" Do you want to run and hide? Do the wheels in your mind begin to spin and you just want to get away?

It is not until I see Jesus, until I hear His voice, that I can ever discover what I am like in my soul. You do not make me feel undressed, so far as clothing the soul. Even when you get critical of me, I can excuse and justify everything I do. I have invented many good arguments. I can just push you away and you cannot make me cringe or afraid. I can always defend myself. But Jesus does not quibble, does He? He just looks and does not say anything. He just comes knocking on the door wanting a friendly visit. I feel like He hates me because I misunderstand Him so much. I become afraid because I misunderstand why He comes. He does not come to make us afraid. He comes because He loves to be with us. He comes to supply the great deficiency that makes us feel so naked. He comes to protect us, to clothe us. He comes to bless us so that we can stand in His presence with no fear. He says He has all that is required to enable you to stand. We don't believe Him. We have been afraid of Him for so many years. We have been taught that God is against us unless we are totally right in commandment keeping; and therefore we must qualify ourselves for His first visit. But that is impossible for us to do—to qualify ourselves, or make ourselves worthy to meet with Him. We are all unqualified for the first visit.

How do you hear His voice? "You who in heart long for something better than this world can give, recognize this longing as the voice of God to your soul." SC 28. I hear many people expressing a dissatisfaction with their experience. That is the voice of God. Recognize this longing as the voice of God to your soul. Ask Him to give you repentance, to reveal Christ to you in His infinite love, and He will do that. Do not run away and be afraid of the One who loved you so much that He died for you. We all need that visit and every succeeding visit. He is reconciled to us, but we think we are still alienated. Paul said, "be ye reconciled to God." 2 Corinthians 5:20. He can even reach the hearts of the hard-hearted, and even the hearts of Laodiceans. He knows exactly what they need and what to do for them.

There are those who think they are righteous enough. "We may have flattered ourselves, as did Nicodemus, that our life has been upright, that our moral character is correct, and think that we need not humble the heart before God, like the common sinner: but when the light from Christ shines into our souls, we shall see how impure we are; we shall discern the selfishness of motive, the enmity against God, that has defiled every act of life. Then we shall know that our own righteousness is indeed as filthy rags, and that the blood of Christ alone can cleanse us from the defilement of sin, and renew our hearts in His own likeness." SC 29,29.

We either fear to visit with Jesus, or we say we are good enough and do not need to spend time with Him. We isolate, or insulate ourselves from Him, even from His voice. We say we have no need, so why, then, should I open the door? He has nothing I need. I have it all. For one reason or another we keep Him away, and we go on in life saying that we will be able to stand when every eye shall see Him. Christ knows He is coming back soon, more than we accept that fact. He knows every eye will see Him, and He wants all to meet Him in peace, and not cry for the rocks and mountains to fall on them and hide them from the face of Him that sits on the throne. He does not want that or He would not have died for us. He wants to enable us to stand now and forever. Let Him make you acceptable, let Him hide that nakedness and cover it so that you never need to be afraid again.

God was pleased to say to Israel, "put on thy beautiful garments, O Jerusalem," Isaiah 52:1. Joshua the high priest was clothed in filthy garments and standing before the angel of the Lord; and the Lord said, "Take away the filthy garments from him. And unto him He said, Behold, I have caused thine iniquity to pass from thee, and I will clothe thee with change of raiment." Zechariah 3:4.

Luke tells the story of how the prodigal son went back to the father, totally unfit, and how he said, "Father, I have sinned against heaven, and in thy sight, and am no more worthy to be called thy son." Luke 15:21. And the Father said, "Bring forth the best robe, and put it on him." Not just any robe, but the best he had. Put it on him, the unfit one. Then he made a great feast for the one who was dead and is now alive. This is what our God says and what our Lord teaches. The prodigal son came home very hesitant because he knew all he lacked, and wondered how his father could accept him. What did the father do? He fell on his neck and kissed him.

Some people do so such damage to Christianity that it is unbelievable. We wonder why so many of our children stay away. They are wise, because we make it difficult for anyone to come the way we exact things from them. It is the father who made that son fit, and no one else. The young man probably did not even have a bath, but the father said to bring forth the best robe and put it on him. Not until we come to Jesus in all our great need can the nakedness of our souls be covered. The Lord says he is knocking at your door and wants you to hear His voice and let Him in. He also says, "As many as I love, I rebuke and chasten." Revelation 3:19. If He did not love us, He would stop knocking on the door. He is persistent because He loves us so much.

Peter taught that the Lord "is longsuffering to us-ward, not willing that any should perish, but that all should come to repentance." 2 Peter 3:9. He knocks, and knocks, and knocks, and He continues knocking. He has been knocking at the door of Laodiceans since 1883. And everyday that He keeps knocking He is saying, "Do not fear Me. Do not run and hide. Do not chase me away. Do not be afraid to open the door. I have stayed here so long because I want you and want to be with you. Let Me in." But how often we think it is different. Some say they have everything and are already qualified for heaven. But He knocks at their hearts, too, and says He has something they do not have but greatly need.

The apostle Paul asks if we know that "the goodness of God leadeth thee to repentance?" Romans 2:4. He is trying to teach us that the goodness of God's forbearance and His longsuffering should lead us to repentance. Why do you think that God is delaying the return of Christ? Do you think He is waiting on the world? He loves those in the world, but He is especially waiting on the Laodiceans who are afraid to let Him in, and those who think that they are good enough without Him.

In the message of Christ our righteousness, the Lord is knocking everyday. It is a tragedy that we misunderstand His knocking. It must break His heart to realize that we hear Him but are afraid to let Him in. He does not want to criticize us. "For God sent not His Son into the world to condemn the world; but that the world through Him might be saved." John 3:17. He is not out to find fault with us or to spy on us. He is not an enemy. He is our Lover, and we should know that.

It must break His heart that with all His expressions of love, and all the demonstrations of His goodness, that we still think He is against us. With all the beauty of holiness that the Lord possesses, it is a wonder that we would think that our righteousness might be good enough by comparison. Our own righteousness will continue looking good as long as He is outside the door.

No matter what your thoughts are about this, the Lord is patient, longsuffering, longing for you as though you were the only soul in the universe. He wants to take care of that emptiness in your heart; and right now any emptiness you feel is the Lord's voice asking, "Why do you keep Me so far away? Why do you refuse to hear? Why do you listen to everyone else?"

He does not want us to be too emotional lest we fail to use our good judgment; but He certainly wants us to sense our great need, to hear His voice, and sense His strong desire to live with us so that we might never, never part. He wants to live with us now, and He wants us to meet Him in peace when every eye shall see Him, and with longing in our hearts say, "Lo, this is our God; we have waited for Him and He will save us." And thus we can live together forever with this precious One, because you are so precious to Him.

May God help us to realize this day that "If God be for us, who can be against us?" Romans 8:41. May we correctly understand the knocking and hear the sweet voice; and may we put away all our fears, and the temptation to run. May we let the Savior in.

21

RIGHTEOUSNESS BY UNFAITHFULNESS?

I WILL BEGIN THIS chapter by reviewing an Ellen White quote you should now be familiar with: "Several have written to me, inquiring if the message of justification by faith is the third angel's message, and I have answered, 'It is the third angel's message in verity.'" COR 64.

Some have thought that Christ our righteousness would be a fad, but the Bible and the Spirit of Prophecy teach that justification by faith is the third angel's message in verity. If we are ever to preach the last message of God, we must do much better in understanding and experiencing this message of Christ our righteousness, or we shall never rightly preach the third angel's message.

Often we have thought that denouncing other denominations is the third angel's message; or that we are better than they because we do certain things; and in this legalistic context we have tried to preach the three angels messages. But Christ our righteousness—justification by faith—is that message. This is a message of love. As we study the third angel's message, I hope you begin to see how much of God's love is involved in this most interesting theme.

Our problem in this study involves the difference between faithfulness and unfaithfulness, for we often put it into a context that omits the real meaning of the term faithfulness. John the Revelator wrote these words about Babylon: "And he cried mightily with a strong voice, saying, Babylon the great is fallen, is fallen....And I heard another voice from heaven, saying, Come out of her, My people, that ye be not partakers of her sins, and that ye receive not of her plagues." Revelation 18:2,4.

How did God's people happen to be in a place called Babylon, or in a condition called Babylon? We all know the story of how the ancient Jews ended up in Babylon, and we know that their experience is a parallel of modern Babylon. Let us review how the Jews found themselves in Babylon in the days of Jeremiah, Ezekiel, and Isaiah. Often we say they were captured and taken over there. While that is true in one sense, it only tells part of the story. In the third chapter of Jeremiah, you can read his introduction to the reason for their captivity, and it is an interesting story. I hope that you will find it a good explanation to what happens to us as we sometimes find ourselves away from God.

"The Lord said also unto me in the days of Josiah the king, Hast thou seen that which backsliding Israel hath done? she is gone up upon every high mountain and under every green tree, and there hath played the harlot [talking about the places where they worshipped idols]. And I said after she had done all these things, Turn thou unto Me. But she returned not. And her treacherous sister Judah saw it. And I saw, when for all the causes whereby backsliding Israel committed adultery I had put her away, and given her a bill of divorce; yet her treacherous sister Judah feared not, but went and played the harlot also. And it came to pass through the lightness of her whoredom, that she defiled the land, and committed adultery with stones and with stocks." "Go and proclaim these words toward the north, and say, Return, thou backsliding Israel, saith the Lord; and I will not cause Mine anger to fall upon you: for I am merciful, saith the Lord, and I will not keep anger for ever. Only acknowledge thine iniquity, that thou hast transgressed against the Lord thy God, and hast scattered thy ways to the strangers under every green tree, and ye have not obeyed My voice, saith the Lord. Turn, O backsliding children, saith the Lord; for I am married unto you: and I will take you one of a city, and two of a family, and I will bring you to Zion." Jeremiah 3:6-9;12-14.

Return "for I am married unto you" is the language of Jeremiah. So often we forget that God took Israel as His bride when He brought her out of Egypt, and the new covenant promise makes that very clear. "Not according to the covenant that I made with their fathers in the day that I took them by the hand to bring them out of the land of Egypt; which My covenant they brake, although I was an husband unto them, saith the Lord." Jeremiah 31:32.

When the Lord chose them to be a peculiar people, uniquely His own, He entered into a covenant with them becoming their God and they becoming His people. He said He was a husband to them. Righteousness by faith is in the context of a love relationship. It is faithfulness to a lover that is described in righteousness by faith. The unfaithfulness of Babylon in God's people is unfaithful to marriage vows, not just to some doctrines, not just to a church, or some ideas that people propound. It is faithfulness to a Person to whom we profess to be joined in marriage, as the Bible describes it in many places. God was Israel's Husband, and the Old Testament makes it plain how precious she was to Him.

But Israel chose other lovers. For some reason she did not always respond to the love of her Husband; and, of course, this has reference to the idols that she worshipped. She worshipped stones and stocks, and idolatry is adultery in the spiritual realm. "That they have committed adultery, and blood is in their hands, and with their idols have they committed adultery." Ezekiel 23:37.

This is the unfaithfulness that the Lord is talking about. In spite of her adultery, He loved her very much and for a long time. He appealed to her over and over again through the prophets Isaiah and Jeremiah; but she would not come back to Him. She persisted in her other love affairs. Before she went as a captive to Babylon, she was first captivated by the gods of Babylon. When she was captivated by their gods, she forsook her Husband and gave her affections to many others. She was found spending all of her time with them, and she had no time for her Husband. God had placed His house there with His bride. He had them build a sanctuary so He could dwell among them. This was His abiding place with His wife. He wanted to be close to her; and while He was there manifesting Himself in the Shekinah Glory, physically present in that glory, she still went off to inanimate idols and loved them more than the precious Lord Jehovah. It seems impossible, but that is what the Bible describes. They thought the gods of the heathen were more effective, more productive, and they thought they received more blessings from those gods. They envied the people outside the church.

When she withdrew her affections from her husband, He continued to appeal to her for many years. When she persisted in her love affairs with others, He finally permitted her to have her choice. Love must permit choice. Love cannot be commanded or forced. Israel was taken captive after she was captivated. She went to find out what is was to live with those lovers twenty-four hours a day, all year long. The Bible tells the story of life in Babylon and the things that went on with the idol worship. You remember how they were commanded to bow down or they would be killed. They had gone to live in a kingdom of force. Is that what they preferred to the kingdom of love back in Jerusalem where they had a choice?

She insisted on going to Babylon by constantly giving her affections and devotions to another lover. God allowed her to do what she wanted to do. Love is like that. But He still wanted her back, and He even prophesied that He would take her back. Seventy years later, all who chose to do so went back to be with Him and rebuild His house of worship. They returned only by choice, and it seems not too many wanted to go back as compared to the large number who went over to Babylon.

Unfortunately, she was more than an adulteress. The prophet said that she "hast played the harlot with many lovers." Jeremiah 3:1. One lover was not sufficient. She sold her body for a price; and she sold her purity, her innocence, her holiness, her respect, and her affections for gain. I hope you understand we are talking about the church in all this. You must apply the literal meanings to the symbolic meanings that are found here. She sold out, turning away her affections from the One who loved her so much, to Whom she was so very precious. Yet the Lord said He loved her and wanted her. What kind of love is this that desires her after all these activities? What is the law or the love that justifies? We speak of justification by faith, but how little we really understand about it. To many it has become a trite phrase that is spoken unthinkingly.

"They say, if a man put away his wife, and she go from him, and become another man's, shall he return unto her again? shall not that land be greatly polluted? but thou hast played the harlot with many lovers; yet return again to Me, saith the Lord." Jeremiah 3:1. This is a very complex text and you must understand all that the Bible says about it. The law that God gave to Moses said that if you were married to another you could not go back to your first husband or wife. The Lord said that doing so would pollute the land greatly. His people had left Him, but He wanted them to return to Him. It would seem that this makes God a violator of the law that He gave. How could He take her back when she is married to another, which is something He forbade to take place? If you understand justification by faith in its true meaning, this becomes a precious thought.

Paul sheds light on this with these words: "Know ye not, brethren, (for I speak to them that know the law,) how that the law hath dominion over a man as long as he liveth? For the woman which hath an husband is bound by the law to her husband so long as he liveth; but if the husband be dead, she is loosed from the law of her husband. So then if, while her husband liveth, she be married to another man, she shall be called an adulteress: but if her husband be dead, she is free from that law; so that she is no adulteress, though she be married to another man. Wherefore, my brethren, ye also are become dead to the law by the body of Christ; that ye should be married to another, even to Him who is raised from the dead, that we should bring forth fruit unto God." Romans 7:1-4.

The only way that Christ could take her back was to die. Otherwise He would be a violator of His own rule. When He died, her first husband was gone, and now she was free to be married to another, even to Him who rose from the dead. Theoretically and legally, He was a new husband, for by law when you are dead, you are dead. When He rose from the grave He was a new man; and I am not saying that in a theological way at all, so do not misunderstand me. Legally she can now be married to Him and not be called an adulteress, for she was never married to the resurrected Jesus. Therefore, to justify a wife who left Him and joined herself to another, He died for all her sins, and then He arose from the grave so that she might be married to Him, a new lover, perfectly joined to Him.

My mind staggers at the concept and the depth of love presented here, and I hardly grasp the meaning. Do you? "Oh love that will not let me go," the hymn writer wrote; and how little we understand what that really means and implies. He cannot let me go. All of these things in the plan of salvation have been done to express His great love for us, even though we have wandered so far away and given ourselves wholly to idols. Still He says He wants us back. He cannot let us go. He makes that possible by justifying love.

Paul wrote that Christ was "raised again for our justification." Romans 4:25. Much is said in so few words. This is the love that justifies. The New Testament church had a similar experience to the Jews of the Old Testament, for the Bible teaches that Christ is married to the New Testament church. "For I am jealous over you with godly jealousy: for I have espoused you to one husband, that I may present you as a chaste virgin to Christ." 2 Corinthians 11:2.

But the New Testament church left her lover, too, just as the Old Testament church did; and it is stated so briefly that we often pass by it. "Nevertheless I have somewhat against thee, because thou hast left thy first love." Revelation 2:4. This is the first of the seven churches that we understand to be the New Testament church. Some say she lost her first love because she could not avoid doing it, that it was a mistake; but the Bible says she left it. That's a little different, isn't it? She neglected, she forgot, she failed to respond to the love of her husband, and she left her first love.

This experience is described by Ellen White, and she gives both the Old Testament and New Testament concepts: "The unfaithfulness of the church to Christ in permitting her confidence and affection to be turned from Him, and allowing the love of worldly things to occupy the soul, is likened to the violation of the marriage vow. The sin of Israel in departing from the Lord is presented under this figure; and the wonderful love of God which they thus despised is touchingly portrayed: 'I sware unto thee, and entered into a covenant with thee, saith the Lord God, and thou becamest Mine.' 'And thou wast exceeding beautiful and thou didst prosper into a kingdom. And thy renown went forth among the heathen for thy beauty: for it was perfect through My comeliness [this is Christ our righteousness], which I had put upon thee. . . . But thou didst trust in thine own beauty, and playedst the harlot because of thy renown.' 'As a wife treacherously departeth from her husband, so have ye dealt treacherously with Me, O house of Israel, saith the Lord;' 'as a wife that committeth adultery, which taketh strangers instead of her husband!'" GC 381,382.

This unfaithfulness, this turning away from the love of her Husband, is described in the Bible in many ways. This happened to both the Old and New Testament churches, and how little we realize what we are doing when we neglect the Lord's cause.

One more statement from page 382: "It was by departure from the Lord, and alliance with the heathen, that the Jewish church became a harlot." We must apply all of this to our times and begin to understand it well, or we will have difficulty with some of the things that happen to us.

James applied this to the spiritual aspects that involve us today. "Ye adulterers and adulteresses, know ye not that the friendship of the world is enmity with

God? whosoever therefore will be a friend of the world is the enemy of God." James 4:4. Many times we tell our children they cannot do this or that, they cannot associate with the world or get involved with them. Over and over again they ask, "But why can't we?" The church says the same thing to adults, and they ask, "But why can't we?" All sorts of logical reasons are offered as to why it is okay to associate with the world, but little do we realize that it involves giving our affections to another lover. When we associate with the world, we are saying that we do not like the Husband of the church. We love something else more than Him. Of course, if you have never fallen in love with Him, affection for the world is almost meaningless. It is not until we have tasted the love of Christ for us as individuals and begin to love Him in response to His first loving us, that we begin to see the difference between Him and other lovers. Often our hearts have not been removed from the world in what we call conversion. We are still in love with everything else but Him. Too often we only love right doctrines, or we only love the church, but we do not love Him even though the church is His body. We do not make that very fine distinction; and we do not really come to love Him.

The New Testament church, just like the Jews, loved the world and the things of the world far too much, and turned her back on the greatest Lover in the universe. God called His people again out of Babylon in the Protestant Reformation, and there the preaching was justification by faith as they came out of Babylon. He still is calling His people to come out of Babylon in this day and age. Babylon today is wide spread and the book *The Great Controversy* makes this very plain. We understand from Revelation 17:5 that Babylon is the mother of harlots. Apparently her offspring indulge in the same practice as she does, and how true today that there are many denominations and churches guilty of adultery as described by James when he wrote: "Ye adulterers and adulteresses, know ye not that the friendship of the world is enmity with God? whosoever therefore will be a friend of the world is the enemy of God." James 4:4.

It is difficult for us to understand why someone who is friends with the world is the enemy of God, for we live in this world and like the things of this world. Apart from a love affair with Jesus, there is no way you can really understand this.

The Lord tries to make it plain in the following Bible texts: "If the world hate you, ye know that it hated Me before it hated you. If ye were of the world, the world would love his own: but because ye are not of the world, but I have chosen you out of the world, therefore the world hateth you." John 15:18,19. "I have given them Thy word; and the world hath hated them, because they are not of the world, even as I am not of the world." John 17:14. "And be not conformed to this world: but be ye transformed by the renewing of your mind, that ye may prove what is that good, and acceptable, and perfect, will of God." Romans 12:2. "Love not the world, neither the things that are in the world. If any man love the world, the love of the Father is not in him. For all that is in the world, the lust of the flesh, and the lust of the eyes, and the pride of life, is not of the Father, but is of the world. And the world passeth away, and the lust thereof: but he that doeth the will of God abideth for ever." 1 John 2:15-17.

Love not the world. This is not a command, for love is by choice. It is not a restriction or forbidding us to do this. It is a plea. If you love God you will not love those things. True Christians are not like those in the world. But today the Christian churches, who profess to love their Master and Lord supremely, seem to have much love for the world. We love the world's approval. In fact, we are desperate for the world's approval. We love the world's entertainment, the world's food, the world's materialism, its wealth, its styles, its fads. We love the world's customs, its luxuries, its interests. We like its recreation, its education, its degrees, its prestige, its achievements, its attainments. In fact, we advocate them strongly in our homes first of all, then in our schools, and even in our churches. Most Christian churches do; therefore, it seems that it is acceptable if the majority is right. We forget that this is unfaithfulness to our Lover and that His mortal enemy is the world.

He says the world will hate you if you are really His. Give Him your heart for He is not willing to share you with another. He wants all your affections. Is not love like that? The Husband of the church is very different from the world, and how little we understand the difference. He is the meek and lowly one. What a clash that is with the world. He is the humble and self-denying one. The world is the complete antithesis of self-denial and humility. He said that the foxes have holes, the birds of the air have nests, but the Son of man had no place to lay His head. Such was His poverty.

Do you love Him more than what this world has to offer? Do you love His kind of lifestyle better than the lifestyle of the world? He was born in a barn of peasant parents. He had no high office, no degree, no position. Twelve common men were His followers. He was despised and ridiculed. He was treated unjustly and unfairly, and finally crucified like the worst of all criminals. This individual says, "Follow Me, for I am the Husband of the church." And we have problems with that, don't we? When you read that Christ our righteousness is laying the glory of man in the dust, it is very meaningful when you compare your love for the world and your love for Christ.

It is no wonder that there are very few who experience Christ as their righteousness, when the clash between the world and its styles is so different from that of Jesus. We have come today to the place where we want to make Jesus like the world; therefore we make the church like the world. We try to make the two compatible, but they are incompatible. You cannot serve God and mammon, but we indulge in that type of activity. If you love the world and its ways, you love that which is the opposite of Christ's way, of His lifestyle. If you love Christ, you love a life that is the opposite of the world's. There is no similarity. If you love the world you hate Christ, and if you love Christ you dislike the ways of the world. All who profess to love Him supremely turn their back on the world and do not look back. Looking back is called backsliding, which is giving your affections to someone else. It is not just leaving the church, or violating some regulations of the church. Backsliding is falling away from your love affair with Christ.

Those churches that turn to the world are fallen. "But they fell by the same desire which was the curse and ruin of Israel—the desire of imitating the practices and courting the friendship of the ungodly." GC 383. This is the great apostasy.

The New Testament church appeared quite pure under the apostles. "What was the origin of the great apostasy? How did the church first depart from the simplicity of the gospel? By conforming to the practices of paganism, to facilitate the acceptance of Christianity by the heathen. The apostle Paul declared, even in his day, 'The mystery of iniquity doth already work.' 2 Thessalonians 2:7. During the lives of the apostles the church remained comparatively pure. But 'toward the latter end of the second century most of the churches assumed a new form; the first simplicity disappeared, and insensibly, as the old disciples retired to their graves, their children, along with new converts, . . . came forward and new-modeled the cause.'. . . To secure converts, the exalted standard of the Christian faith was lowered, and as the result 'a pagan flood, flowing into the church, carried with it its customs, practices, and idols'. . .As the Christian religion secured the favor and support of secular rulers, it was nominally accepted by multitudes; but while in appearance Christians, many 'remained in substance pagans, especially worshiping in secret their idols.'" GC 384,385.

The church throughout the ages has formed love associations with the kings of the earth, as in Revelation 18:3 and Revelation 17:2, where we are told that she commits fornication with them. She seems to have some kind of an affinity for rulers. The Christian church is supposed to be in the kingdom of grace, which is a kingdom that has been in existence for two thousand years. In that kingdom of grace, nothing but love is used. Force is never used. And the King of that kingdom is the Lord Jesus, and we are citizens of that kingdom first and foremost above all of the nations. We have a dual citizenship, but primarily we are to be citizens of the kingdom of grace; and then secondarily citizens of the nation wherein you dwell. Yet, while professing to belong to the kingdom of grace and to serve the King of grace, it seems we have some kind of relationship with the kings of the earth. The Bible calls it an illegitimate relationship, or fornication, and the Lord does not seem to be happy about it.

"Many of the Protestant churches are following Rome's example of iniquitous connection with 'the kings of the earth'—the state churches, by their relation to secular governments; and other denominations, by seeking the favor of the world." GC 383. Being in Babylon is not only loving the things and activities of the world, it is also loving the rulership and the kings and what they can provide for the church.

There are quite a few state churches. The Lutheran church in some Scandinavian countries is a state church. The Church of England is a state church. The Presbyterian Church has been a state church in Scotland. Protestants have had these affiliations, or intimacies, with kings and governments other than the kingdom of grace. Even in America today, supposedly the land of religious freedom where the conscience is supreme, it seems that many denominations are clamoring for the government to provide them with funds. Not only do we accept gifts from her, we even seek her support. Supposedly we have a Husband who supports us; but somehow we think He does not take good enough care of us because we need money from other husbands. Apparently our King is not providing for us, so we go to other kings to become intimate with them that we might receive more loans, more grants, more funds for hospitals, for students, for schools, and so on.

Churches are seeking federal and state aid. The Lord, in my understanding, is strongly opposed to this for a very unique reason. It is not a "thou shalt not" for He calls it going to another lover, and you cannot command love. Love is won, love is wooed, love is a choice. It is a response, not a demand or exaction, so He does not command it. He is amazed that after loving us so much, we would give our affections to somebody else and seek the support of somebody else. All government funds are the result of taxation. Governments do not have businesses producing a lot of money. Their business is extracting it from our pockets; and in the kingdom of men they force you to give. If you do not pay your taxes you end up in prison. And the churches that believe in love gifts, or voluntary gifts of tithes and offerings, say they would like to have some forced gifts, too.

Supposedly the kingdom of grace is not identified with the kingdoms of force, but we decided we want to be identified with them, and we ask for tax money. Every dime that any church receives from the government is tax money. Someone was forced to give that money who in good conscience may not want to give to any church. But he does not have that freedom of conscience any more when we want their money. He loses that freedom of conscience. Supposedly we want freedom of conscience for ourselves, but we do not want the other man to have that when we seek his tax money to support us. He is *forced* to support us when we go to the government for money. Some think that loans for hospital and students are legitimate because they pay it all back; but you need to think about that and ask the ones who paid out the money if it is all paid back. Those privileged loans have a lower interest than what Uncle Sam has to pay for the money he borrows, and he borrows billions and billions. Someone pays the difference between Uncle Sam's interest rate and the rate you pay. The difference is paid by taxpayers. Low interest rates are available because taxpayers make up the difference between low and high interest. Taxpayers have to pay for churches or go to jail. This is true of all loans that are low interest, privileged loans.

I have difficulty with all this. I hope you understand that the Lord does, too. Some people cannot see anything wrong with this. The problem is that the church has a Husband already, and He is King. He has a government, a kingdom called the kingdom of grace, which is a kingdom of love that does not include forced taxation.

Somehow we have difficulty seeing the difference between His kingdom and the kingdoms of this world. Suppose a wife comes home to her husband with a very expensive mink coat that cost far beyond what he can afford, and he asks, "Where did you get that?" She answers, "A very nice man bought it for me." He says, "That is interesting. I am happy for you." Does he say that? And for some reason, the next time she kisses him, he does not seem as responsive as the time before. Later she comes home with an expensive car, and then jewelry. All the time the husband asks, "Where did you get that?" And she always answers, "From a very nice man who likes me and gives me what I want."

Some people try to sell that kind of love these days as good or proper love, but I do not believe a word of it because as soon as you find your lover loving those things and appreciating the giver of those things, you will have to conclude that she loves those things and not you. If it does not bother you, you are saying that you do not care if you lose her affections. You do not care if she stops loving you. And you are also saying that you do not love her, either. If the husband loves his wife, he must care about her affections and where she places them. He does not want her to love other things and other lovers because he loves her too much; but he cannot force her to stay with him, and he certainly cannot force her to give her love to him, for then it would not be a choice. He is concerned about losing her love.

The Husband of the church sees us giving our affections to other things, to another lover or a benefactor, and He is afraid that soon our love for Him will be all gone. And somehow we spend less and less time with Him, and our overwhelming, consuming interest seems to be with these other things. The Husband is able to provide for the church any luxury she can possibly desire. He is able to give her everything she needs. He is the Creator of all things. Why does He not give her more? Because He knows that if He gives her all she wants, she will love things more than Him. He wants her to love Him.

The Spirit of Prophecy tells us that "the law of self-renouncing love is the law of life for earth and heaven." DA 20. The law of giving is the law of life, and He must lead His bride into a special kind of love which is self-forgetful, self-renouncing, self-denying. He must lead His bride into that unique quality of love, or He will lose her; and since He does not want to lose her, He does not give her everything she wants now. He gives her everything she needs and He promises that, does He not? He gives Himself to her and says He is with her always. But He asks her to deny herself of some of these things that might lure her away from Him. He asks for a self-renouncing love, for a love that forgets self and gives to others, a love that is a benefit to others, which is the law of life for earth and heaven. Strange as it might seem, the world and those in the church who go to the world, can justify their activities by saying that getting funds from the government is good for the church. Just look at how we are growing. Look at the multitudes that come in. Look at how our institutions are prospering. We are finishing God's work, they say. The world will understand us if we get closer to them. We will understand them and win them for the Lord.

The New Testament church brought in multitudes, but what they brought into the church was paganism, that confusing amalgamation of Christianity and paganism, and they were no longer wholly Christ's. They tried to have two lovers, but the Bible calls that unfaithfulness. Love is righteousness, according to page 18 of *Thoughts From the Mount of Blessing*. It is self-renouncing love, self-denying love. It is supreme love for one Person—the Lord Jesus. All of our affections, all of our esteem, all of our devotions are for Him. The center of all our life is the Lord Jesus, and we love Him with all our hearts and our neighbors as ourselves; and someday He will say, "Enter thou into the joy of thy Lord."

But if you divide your affections, no matter for what reason, He will ask the question, "Are you really Mine? Why do you spend so much time with other things? Why do you have so little time for Me?" And He will come to us as He did to the apostle Peter there in John 21, and He will ask, "Do you love Me more than the others?" And He will ask us the second time, "Lovest thou Me?" And the third time, "Lovest thou Me?"

Jesus today is asking for faithfulness, not because you must or have to, not because He demands it or exacts it, but because He has loved you so much that He thinks it is natural for you to love Him. And He simply asks the question, "Lovest thou Me? Will you give Me all your heart, all your affections, all your interests, all your attentions? Will you make Me the center of your whole life? Lovest thou Me?"

I believe with all my heart that the Lord has been waiting a long time for the church to respond. Don't you? He has not been finding fault with all our activities as many say. He has been simply asking, "How can you love those things and still claim to love Me? How can you call it righteousness when it is unfaithfulness? Don't you know that if you love Me with all your heart you will depend upon Me alone, and be faithful to Me, for you know I am faithful to you? Don't you know you can trust Me? I will give you everything that you will ever possibly need; and in the kingdom to come I will give you things you never dreamed about."

Let Him know today that you love Him.

22

A MATTER
OF AUTHORITY

WE LEARNED PREVIOUSLY THAT justification by faith "is the third angel's message in verity." COR 64. We want to continue the study of the relationship of Christ our righteousness to the message of the third angel. One of the confusing aspects of Christ our righteousness concerns obedience. Some think that righteousness is *relationship*, but not obedience or performance. But there are strong statements in both the Bible and Spirit of Prophecy concerning performance that we must take into account in order to understand Christ our righteousness. There is much discussion about what degree of obedience the Christian is expected to reach. Many even talk about perfection or perfectionism. So it is the topic of obedience that we want to examine in more detail.

One of the main problems in the third angel's message concerns obedience. "And the third angel followed them, saying with a loud voice, If any man worship the beast and his image, and receive his mark in his forehead, or in his hand." "Here is the patience of the saints: here are they that keep the commandments of God, and the faith of Jesus." Revelation 14:9,12. There are two kinds of performance or obedience being contrasted here: obedience to the beast by worshipping him, or obedience to God's commandments.

The same was true in old Babylon, and we are studying Babylon because it is an integral part of the loud cry of the third angel. We all know the story about the three Hebrews in the fiery furnace. You may recall what the people were told they had to do when the music sounded. "That at what time ye hear the…music, ye fall down and worship the golden image that Nebuchadnezzar the king hath set up. And whoso falleth not down and worshippeth shall the same hour be cast into the midst of a burning fiery furnace." Daniel 3:5,6. They had to worship the image or else suffer dreadful consequences. Obedience in this case was demanded. It was required and legislated.

The same is true in Revelation 13:12, where it speaks about the first beast power causing the world to worship the beast whose wound has been healed. In verse 15, it says that they will be killed if they would not worship the beast and his image. There is an activity or performance required here that many will submit to. In contrast to worshiping the beast are those who keep God's commandments as described in Revelation 14:12.

What I want you to see is that obedience is at the heart of the controversy concerning the third angel's message. There are two kinds of obedience found here: obedience to the beast and his image, and obedience to God. Both are obeying, are they not? But they are obeying vastly different authorities. The Bible says that this power would think to change times and laws and to present those laws as God's laws, so that obedience to them would be serving God.

I would like to suggest that every human being is obedient, but not necessarily to God. Sinners do obey some authority; but God is the authority that Christians obey. Disobedience to God is, in reality, obedience to an authority other than God. Every human being obeys. But to be obedient is not enough. We must be obedient to the right authority, or we do not understand what this subject is all about.

Obedience is an unusual thing. Some people obey governments, but not everyone does. Some obey bosses or their employer, some obey parents, some obey their friends or their peers, some obey their desires and self, some obey success, some obey intellect and logic (not their conscience), some obey philosophies (and there are a great variety of philosophies), some obey thought leaders. The primary difference is whom we obey and why we obey. Obedience in and of itself is not enough.

We usually think that we as a people understand obedience because of our emphasis on the law and obedience. But I think that our emphasis has been on the right and wrong of obedience rather than on a correct understanding of what obedience really is. If you are primarily concerned with what is right and wrong, you might totally miss the meaning of obedience. It is not enough to know what constitutes right obedience. We must also know what obedience is. Understanding obedience is a difficult thing sometimes. It seems obvious, but it is vastly different than the way we often think about it.

Webster's Collegiate Dictionary says the word "obey" means "to be ruled or controlled." Some people do not like the idea of being controlled. For the word "obedient," the dictionary says it means "submission to control, to restraint, or to command." We do not like restraints, either. By the way, all authorities have restraints, not just God and the church. Your friends have restraints, such as never telling their secrets (that would make you a traitor to them). There are certain things that you must do or you are not a friend. You must identify yourself with that group by what you do or do not do. With all bosses there are certain restraints—both things that you cannot do and things you must do. The government has many restraints such as traffic regulations and paying taxes. Every authority has restraints. And obedience is submission to authority, to their restraints, commands, and controls. Other definitions included in the dictionary for the word "obedience" include ' due and willing submission to authority or control." Since it is *willing,* you make the choice to obey or not to obey.

In essence, obedience means unconditional surrender. That may sound confusing at first, but ultimately, obedience does mean unconditional surrender to some authority. When captured by a superior force in war, the vanquished become obedient as part of the terms of unconditional surrender. They lay down their weapons and the fight is over; and they obey. This is a difficult thing for us to accept. We might have a mental comprehension of surrender, but that is not enough. It must go way inside us until we act properly because of our firm grasp on this concept of obedience.

Since every one is obedient to some authority (or authorities), and since everyone is in willing submission to a chosen authority, then a certain unique relationship is established between you and any authority you choose to serve. That relationship is described by Paul; and I wish you would at least memorize this text and think about it for a while. "Know ye not, that to whom ye yield yourselves servants to obey, his servants ye are to whom ye obey; whether of sin unto death, or of obedience unto righteousness?" Romans 6:16.

As soon as you obey someone, you make yourself a servant of that person, or that authority. In several Bible translations, it does not say *servant.* It says *slave.* To whomever you yield yourselves slaves to obey, his slaves (or bondsmen) you are. This is the correct interpretation of the Greek word *doulos.* As soon as I yield myself to obey some authority. I become his slave. To any who say they do not believe that, I answer that it was God who inspired this to be written, not I. I hope you recognize that none of us are superior to Him. He said it that way. As soon as I yield my life to obey an authority, I become his slave. He has domination over me. The Bible teaches this clearly, and you need to understand it.

All of life is submission to some authority. Since everyone is yielded to some authority, this then makes one thing extremely necessary, which the Lord took into consideration. "Know ye not that to whom ye yield yourselves servants to obey, his servants ye are." Romans 6:16. If I yield to an authority, it means I do so of my own choice. It means that to some extent, I have deliberated about this submission, and I willingly choose to serve that authority. I am not talking about which authority; just that we willingly choose to obey an authority. The Lord decreed that we would yield, that we would choose, that we would submit willingly, not forcefully.

There is a difference between the slavery in Romans 6:16 and the slavery seen in the United States over a century ago. Those were unwilling slaves. They never chose slavery. They did not want it. They despised it and wanted to get away. The slavery mentioned here is a free choice. We willing yield ourselves as servants to obey. This involves a choice to go into that type of submission to that particular authority. That is different. It is not a forced submission but a willful submission. The Bible says that all of us are in willful slavery by our own selection and choice with premeditation and forethought.

I am sure that many would like to disagree here, but I wish you would take the time and ask the question: Is God right? Try to understand what He is telling us, which is that everyone lives in submission to some authority of their own personal choice.

The slavery that Paul wrote about—the slavery of the Christian life, or slavery to sin or Satan—is vastly different than forced slavery. Inherent in this type of slavery is a freedom to choose. If we lack this freedom of choice, then once we find ourselves subject to an authority, we can never escape. You might discover you have chosen the wrong authority, but if there is no freedom of choice after you have made the wrong choice, you can never choose another master. Salvation would be meaningless, and Christianity would be a mockery. There is no salvation without freedom of choice as to whom you will serve. Salvation is based on freedom of choice. If I make one misstep and choose the wrong master, I am dominated as long as I live and I cannot get out, unless there is freedom of choice.

God has decreed and has guaranteed freedom of choice for you and for me and for everyone. We ask people in the gospel message to choose. They cannot choose to stop sinning, but they can choose to serve a new Master. He becomes the power in their life that enables them to cease from sin. He gives me the opportunity to change masters.

This is made clear in the following quote: "Many are inquiring, 'How am I to make the surrender of myself to God?' You desire to give yourself to Him, but you are weak in moral power, in slavery to doubt, and controlled by the habits of your life of sin. Your promises and resolutions are like ropes of sand. You cannot control your thoughts, your impulses, your affections….What you need to understand is the true force of the will. This is the governing power in the nature of man, the power of decision, or of choice. Everything depends on the right action of the will. The power of choice God has given to men; it is theirs to exercise. You cannot change your heart, you cannot of yourself give to God its affections; but you can choose to serve Him. You can give Him your will; He will then work in you to will and to do according to His good pleasure. Thus your whole nature will be brought under the control of the Spirit of Christ; your affections will be centered upon Him, your thoughts will be in harmony with Him." SC 47.

God knew that this freedom of choice was basic and the most vital point of all Christianity, because everyone at some point finds themselves serving the wrong master. How do I escape from servitude to the wrong master? Not by trying to stop sinning. The will does not function there. It is incapable. But I may choose Someone who has the power to lead me in a different life. I may choose a new

Master, and the Bible guarantees that freedom of choice. All willing slavery comes because of choice; but after slavery to the wrong master, I still may choose to escape by choosing a new master. This ought to make us extremely happy. If you do not recognize that you are a slave, I am sure you will not be happy about this. Or if you are blissfully happy in slavery to the wrong master, you will not recognize any value to the freedom of choice. But if you are miserable and wondering how on earth you can escape from the terrible rut you are in, the discovery that God guarantees the power of choice is a joyful thing. When Christ came down to this planet, He was guaranteeing the power of choice. A new Master came to be our Brother and our King to rule in our lives. What a marvelous thing!

The Bible assures us of the privilege of repentance. Repentance in the Bible means a turning around; and the Bible says you can always turn around and go in the other direction. I can turn around and make a new choice by His grace, and start all over again with a new master.

Keep some of these thoughts in mind as we go back and look again at what happened in Babylon. Notice this power of choice now that you understand how basic it is in Christianity. "And whoso falleth not down and worshippeth shall the same hour be cast into the midst of a burning fiery furnace." Daniel 3:6. What were their choices? If they would not worship and obey as the king said, they would die. Christians will choose death over obedience to the wrong master. But those are not equal options or choices because the result of making one particular choice would lead to their death. When man was deprived of his privilege of choosing his master, what did God do in Daniel 3? He countermanded the king's decree, which was supposed to be impossible with the unchangeable law of the Babylonians.

Daniel chapter 6 tells how the leaders in Media Persia (the daughter of Babylon, as she is called by the prophets) deprived man of the privilege of prayer. "All the presidents of the kingdom, the governors, and the princes, the counsellers, and the captains, have consulted together to establish a royal statute, and to make a firm decree, that whosoever shall ask a petition of any God or man for thirty days, save of thee, O king, he shall be cast into the den of lions. Now, O king, establish the decree, and sign the writing, that it be not changed, according to the law of the Medes and Persians, which altereth not." Daniel 6:7,8. It was decreed that for thirty days the people could only ask petitions of the king and of no other authority. They knew Daniel would pray during that time, so they intentionally deprived him of choice because the only other option was to be cast into the lion's den. What did God do? He changed the king's commandment. And those who came down to rob men of freedom of choice ended up where they wished their enemies to be. They ended up in the lion's den because they deprived men of freedom of choice.

There are many things we can do wrong in this life and be forgiven, but when we begin to deprive people of their freedom of choice, we are treading on dangerous ground. Sometimes we think that as Christians we can do this legitimately because the end justifies the means, but it does not. The means must always be freedom to choose, even though the loss of salvation is the result. We can never deprive people of that personal choice. God does not want to force choice. He always wants a willing, conscientious decision. It must be that way. In all our Bible studies and in our dealings with our children and everyone else, they must have the utmost freedom. No coercion ever. Soul winning is not forcing people into the baptistery. We have much rebellion in our ranks because we sometimes try to force people. We cannot choose for them. When they become old enough, they choose for themselves, and it must always be their choice.

We are all willingly in subjection to that great Master. Too often we make attendance to church a legislated activity, a decree by parents or the church. This is legislated worship. We are depriving people of freedom of choice. They will serve by fear or by force, but not by willing choice. We are breaking their will when we dominate them that way. God does not break the will. He seeks the cooperation of the will. We must allow people to exercise their will or we will not have Christians. We will have fearful slaves, not willing servants of the Lord.

God has always intervened at some point whenever man's will was taken away. When in the last days the ruling authority shall decree "that as many as would not worship the image of the beast should be killed" (Revelation 13:15), God will intervene. People must be allowed the freedom to choose whom they will serve. The only true freedom is the freedom of the conscience—the freedom to choose and make choices of our own volition. Some people define freedom in a way that is pure license and permissiveness; but doing your own thing is not freedom for it deprives another person of his thing. Whenever I want to do my own thing, I am not considering you or anybody else; just self, and that is not love for others.

Both the Bill of Rights within the American Constitution and God Himself guarantees freedom to all peoples, not just to one person. Therefore, my freedom is in the context of your freedom, and yours is in the context of my freedom; and therefore we have a joint freedom. It is individualized and personal when it comes to choosing a master. We must be careful about our definitions of freedom and thank the Lord for countries in which the citizens have been permitted the guarantee of freedom of choice in the matters of conscience, and especially in matters of religion. It is a glorious privilege that has been a blessing to our church and to many others.

God will allow me to choose self or Satan. He wishes I will choose Him and He will seek to woo me to Himself. But He will permit me to go into slavery to self. If He forced me elsewhere, He would not be granting freedom of choice. When we make the choice for self to be our master, many will ask God why He did not stop them. He did not because He would deprive them of freedom. You must be able to choose at all times. He dare not stop you or He would not be a God of love. He would be just like the authorities of this world and like the beast that would legislate your activity. He will not stop you from making your own choice. Many have discovered that they can do anything they please; and they also discover that they are in slavery to all kinds of sins. God lets you do that, not because He wants you to fall into sin, but because He desires you to have the choice that you wish. You have that kind of freedom; and once you start obeying, you are in submission to that authority. Our freedom is not in the authority, but in the choice of authority. After we make our choice, the obedience to that authority puts us into subjection. But we have the freedom before we get to that point.

Man is always free to turn around and leave one master and choose another. The Old Testament's symbolism was beautiful about this in the book of Exodus. It is found in many places, but we seldom think about it this way. "If thou buy an Hebrew servant, six years he shall serve: and in the seventh he shall go out free for nothing." "And if the servant shall plainly say, I love my master [notice the word love], my wife, and my children; I will not go out free: Then his master shall bring him unto the judges; he shall also bring him to the door, or unto the door post; and his master shall bore his ear through with an awl; and he shall serve him for ever." Exodus 21: 2,5,6.

How did He get into servitude forever? He loved his master and chose to stay there. The master did not choose for the servant to stay. The servant chose to stay because he loved his master. They could change their master every seven years under the old Hebrew economy. In the year of Jubilee, all were free and the land was free, and all land reverted back to its original owner; and there were no debts for they were all paid up every fifty years. We think we are modern, but we are behind many thousands of years. Imagine all debts being wiped out every fifty years. No debts!

This also means that I can escape from the mastery of sin, this terrible thing that drags us down and oppresses us. I can choose God as my new Master and He delivers me. I serve Him by choice, and not by fear. At this point, some will say, "But if I do not serve God, I am going to die." Therefore, we might think that He is just like all the rest—like Nebuchadnezzar, Belshazzar, the beast and the image. People mistakenly think that God forces them, too. They say it is not a free choice because the options are unbalanced, for I will die if I do not obey God. I do not think the Bible teaches that. It is in fact a perversion of the Scriptures.

As Jesus left the temple for the last time (which was His house among men and God's presence with man), He gave these thoughts about Jerusalem and the Jews: "O Jerusalem, Jerusalem, thou that killest the prophets, and stonest them which are sent unto thee, how often would I have gathered thy children together, even as a hen gathereth her chickens under her wings, and ye would not!" Matthew 23:37. Note that He did not say they *could* not submit to Him, but that they *would* not. The word *would* has to do with the will. You will not. A mother hen gathers her chickens for protection from a hawk or an eagle. She gathers them under her wings so they will be safe. The Lord tells His people that He has often wanted to protect them, and has sent messages of love to them through the prophets, and invited all that labor and are heavy laden to go to Him for rest. But many will not go to Him. They will not choose Him to rule over them.

God's plea to mankind has always been: "Say unto them, As I live, saith the Lord God, I have no pleasure in the death of the wicked; but that the wicked turn from his way and live: turn ye, turn ye from your evil ways; for why will ye die, O house of Israel?" Ezekiel 33:11. God is saying He cannot understand why you want to die. He came to give you life that you might have it abundantly. He has no pleasure in your death. Turn from your sins unto Him. Choose a different master. Choose Christ. The Bible holds before us the privilege of another choice. Choose Him, for He has chosen you.

Wherever you go, the Lord will seek to remind you that He has chosen you. You will experience little pangs of conscience when you seek to do the things of another authority. There is no pressure or force, just the still, small voice of the Holy Spirit. The voice of condemnation and the guilt is usually from the devil. There is no wooing or enticing in condemnation or guilt. God sent not His Son to condemn us but to save us. Never accuse Him of being the accuser. The word Satan means accuser, but God is not the accuser. He is the Savior. He is the comforter and He seeks to woo us back to a joyful, willing, chosen service to Him. He does not enslave us against our will. Choose you this day, is what the Bible says. He wants to allure me and win me, not force me. And I gladly make that choice, and I am delighted when I have done it.

Remember that we are studying Christ our righteousness and how it relates to the third angel's message. You may not yet have seen the connection between what you have been reading and the subject of the third angel's message. If you go back to Romans 6:16, the connection is found there. "Know ye not, that to whom ye yield yourselves servants to obey, his servants ye are to whom ye obey; whether of sin unto death, or of obedience unto righteousness?" By yielding myself to the right Master, I find myself in righteousness. I must choose the Master of righteousness. This is the way to find salvation.

"Knowing this, that our old man is crucified with Him, that the body of sin might be destroyed, that henceforth we should not serve sin." "Neither yield ye your members as instruments of unrighteousness unto sin: but yield yourselves unto God." Romans 6:6,13. Yield to His mastery. It is your choice.

"Being then made free from sin, ye became the servants [or slaves] of righteousness." Romans 6:18. When you are a slave, someone tells you everything to do. They command and order your life. Christian slavery is like that. We willingly choose the Master to be over us. We willingly choose to obey Him at all times. We are always free to stay with Him or leave Him. We can always escape; and the choices we make are not whether we are going to sin or not, but to whom we are going to listen, and who we will choose to be our master. Those are the choices. Whenever I come to a crossroad in my life, I must make a choice of which master I will allow to guide me.

Some people say that our choice is to either sin or to do what is right. I do not think so. I think we can only choose which master we will have to rule over us. Will I let Christ dominate in my life? Or will it be self, or a friend, or somebody else? Which will it be? I become righteous by serving the right Master. I do not become righteous by trying to be good or by choosing not to commit this or that sin. There is only One who can make us righteous. We cannot make ourselves righteous. A slave cannot make himself anything, not even free. Only someone else can do that for us, and so we must come to Him.

Most have seen this text: "This is His name whereby He shall be called, THE LORD OUR RIGHTEOUSNESS." Jeremiah 23:6. The Bible supplies the bold text. What does the word "Lord" mean? It means *Master*. When I make Him my Lord and my God, He masters me, He dominates me, He controls me, He restrains me, He commands me; and it is my willing submission that permits Him to do that. He is the Master of righteousness and He rules me in righteousness. He is Christ our righteousness.

How little we understand about obedience. When it comes to obedience, some will say, "Okay, He wants me to obey, so I will try my best to obey." That is not it at all. You cannot serve God and mammon, you cannot be enslaved to two opposites. Therefore, it is not trying to obey Him, but rather surrendering and submitting to Him, and making the choice for Him to dominate you.

It is somewhat like getting married. There is a certain domination and restraint in marriage. When I was young fellow, I had a ball-and-chain concept of marriage. I wasn't sure if I wanted that kind of slavery. Some tolerate that kind of slavery. Others find fault with it. But many find it enjoyable or they would get a divorce. Some people can hardly wait to get into slavery when it comes to marriage. And some young ladies are actively campaigning to put the fellows into slavery, and the ladies can hardly wait; and some fellows are just like that, too. They are waiting for the right person to capture them. Getting married brings about certain restraints. I have had young people come to me after they have been married for a few months and say they never dreamed they would not be free when they got married. It is a revelation to them. When two people get together, sometimes they do not agree on the things they want to do. But in the marriage relationship, there are certain restrictions on what a spouse can and cannot do. But if you love the other person, those restrictions are not so bad, are they? Many people have enjoyed fifty years in slavery, and their fiftieth wedding anniversary is like a big blowout. They gather their families and friends to help commemorate this great event with them—celebrating fifty years of slavery! It all has to do with the choice they each made and continue to make.

The Lord desires freedom for you and for me. When we choose the right Master, He becomes the Lord our Righteousness. As He commands us, we obey Him because we love Him, and we find ourselves doing what He wants, and His will is righteousness. It is and always will be.

Some will get the wrong idea about this slavery, so I must explain more about it. We know that "Righteousness is love." MB 18. We also know that "Obedience is a surrender of the heart to the sovereignty of love." MB 46. A sovereign is a king. He rules. Obedience to God is a willing obedience, a willing submission, to the sovereignty of His love.

Christ is described in the New Testament under the symbolism of Melchisedec. Christ is called the "King of righteousness." Hebrews 7:2. He is the King, or Ruler of righteousness, the One who dominates people in righteousness. As we give our hearts to Him, He rules us in righteousness.

The Spirit of Prophecy wants us to understand that "obedience is not a mere outward compliance, but the service of love….It is a service and allegiance of love." SC 60. This is not something that is exacted of us. It is not something demanded any more than you can demand someone to marry you. If you demand someone to marry you they will say, "Forget it!" You cannot exact love. Therefore, when the Lord wants obedience or He wants righteousness, He has to win it, He has to woo us, He has to allure us and entice us. He loves us first so that we might love Him in response. This is freedom; and all submission, in this context, is always and ultimately our free choice. I am motivated by love to make the choice to submit and to tell God I want Him to rule me. When I am happy with Him telling me what to do, I have found true Christianity.

Do you understand obedience? I said at the beginning that this is difficult for us. Most of us have had our minds trained to think of obedience in ways that prove we really do not understand obedience. We can intellectualize on the subject and theorize about it, but that does not mean we know it. Even after we hear the truth about obedience, we have a tendency to go right away and say, "I *have* to obey." I have to keep the Sabbath. I have to do this or that. No, you do not have to keep the Sabbath. You do not have to go to church, you do not have to pay tithes and offerings, you do not have to give Bible studies, you do not have to be a vegetarian. You are free to obey any master you decide to serve. But the Lord is always seeking to draw us unto Himself by His great love. Always.

He wants to be the Master of my life, providing that it is my willful, free choice. Many think they have to go to church school, or to church, or to Sabbath school. That is not it, friend. We are training our children to believe that our God is a

God of force. He is not. He is a God who wins us by His tremendous love and goodness to us. There is no forced submission. He is always seeking to win us.

When we submit willfully, tremendous things happen. "Through the right exercise of the will [that is the choice], an entire change may be made in your life. By yielding up your will to Christ [a free choice we all have], you ally yourself with the power that is above all principalities and powers. You will have strength from above to hold you steadfast, and thus through constant surrender to God you will be enabled to live the new life, even the life of faith." SC 48. As I choose the highest of all authorities, the One above heaven and earth itself, I have allied myself to might and to power, to love, and to righteousness; and as He manipulates me by my choice, He leads me in paths of righteousness for His name's sake. And righteousness is always love. Always! And love is righteousness for "love is the fulfilling of the law." Romans 13:10.

What a perversion we have made of obedience. Obedience is one of the most blessed things you can find. Obedience is not trying to be good. It is not trying to do the right thing. Obedience is an absolute surrender to His sovereign love. I yield everything to God, and ask Him to take over and rule me.

In Ephesians 5, Paul puts all this in the context of Christ and the church by talking about wives submitting themselves to their husbands, and husbands loving their wives. The reason why a wife should submit to her husband is because of his love. If a wife submits, but is not convinced of her husband's love, she is submitting by force. A good husband will love his wife so much that she cannot keep from loving him and submitting to him. Submission is a natural response to love. The church is the bride of Christ, and He asks us to submit ourselves to Him, and in so doing, He will make us happy. Righteousness is a result of that submission, and that submission is evidenced by obedience. But it is not the obedience that saves us. It is the surrender, the submission to Him, and He saves us. When we know He loves us and wants to save us, we submit to Him and gladly obey. We allow Him to save us by our choice.

It is that freedom of choice that the devil does not like. He knows that freedom of choice will lead to obedience to the right Master, and therefore to righteousness; and the fact that people willingly submit to the sovereignty of God's love proves that the devil is a liar. It makes him appear so vilely wrong that the whole universe will know it; therefore, he seeks to attack the very foundation of freedom of choice. He seeks to prevent us from exercising our freedom of choice. He tries to get us involved with a different master and convince us that we cannot have the freedom of choosing another master; and thus he makes us feel that we will be eternally lost. That is exactly what the beast does. He attacks freedom of choice. He will set up circumstances where we must either obey him, or die.

Many people will believe that it is God who gives us that choice because the beast power professes to speak for God. He sits in the place of God, and claims to represent God. Many, even within our own ranks, believe that God is like that—that we must obey Him. And the devil has convinced many that, once we are enslaved, we cannot get out, and that we can never choose another authority. And too often we use the devil's tactics in coercing our children, our converts, our neighbors, our friends, our acquaintances. We do not woo them by love. We restrict them. We exact of them, we demand from them, we threaten, we oppress, we do all kinds of things and think that we are doing God's work. That is not God's work.

The Lord said, "And I, if I be lifted up from the earth, will draw all men unto Me." John 12:32. Once you see His great love, your heart will be softened. In these last days, when the devil seeks to misrepresent God, He wants a people to demonstrate a love that is courteous and kind and tenderhearted. He wants a people that will love others so much that they will grant them ultimate freedom of choice. And as they walk by your house they say, "You are a different kind of Christian. Everybody else twists my arm, but you make me feel free to choose. You use only love to win me over. I like your God."

It is a marvelous privilege that we have to choose whom we will serve. And the Authority of all authorities, the King of all kings says, "I want you to choose Me. Will you choose Me because you love Me? Don't serve Me by fear or by force. Choose Me because you see My great love for you. I love you with an everlasting love. I cannot let you go. Why will you die? Turn and go the other way. Choose Me."

Whom will you serve? As for me and my house, we will serve the Lord. May God bless you as you make your choice, today and every day.

23

THE KING'S WORDS

OBEDIENCE IS AN IMPORTANT topic concerning righteousness. "Know ye not, that to whom ye yield yourselves servants to obey, his servants ye are to whom ye obey; whether of sin unto death, or of obedience unto righteousness?" Romans 6:16. Our destiny is determined by whom we become servants to obey. Everyone obeys someone. Not all obey God, but all obey some authority. Sin is obedience to someone else other than God. Righteousness is the result of serving the right Master. Often we have a different concept of righteousness than that.

This is not a forced or legislated obedience because "Righteousness is love." MB 18; and obedience is "a surrender of the heart to the sovereignty of love." MB 46. Also, obedience is "the service and allegiance of love." SC 60.

Therefore, the motivation for serving God is vastly different than in all other kingdoms, or all other realms of life. It is not something exacted or demanded of us. The Lord woos us by His love and wins us to His side, so that by love we are motivated to serve Him. This is a different kind of obedience and a very delightful activity. Too often we have made it an irksome thing, but that is not the way it is in the kingdom of Christ. Righteousness is the result of serving the King of righteousness.

Jesus is called "The Lord our Righteousness" in Jeremiah 23:6. He is the Master our righteousness, the Ruler our righteousness, Christ our righteousness. He rules us in righteousness, and by serving Him in love we become righteous. Righteousness is serving the right Leader, the right King; but too often we think it is struggling to do something that is right.

This makes the proper choice of kings vital to the Christian life; but unfortunately we have not thought that we had a choice or have not realized that we can serve different kings. When discussing righteousness, we have mainly been concerned about the things that the law says we must do or must not do. Ellen White wrote that "Righteousness is right doing, and it is by their deeds that all will be judged." COL 312. But is that the only definition of righteousness? We must be careful not to make this our only definition. We usually leave out the definition that "Righteousness is love" MB 18. There is more to righteousness than merely the *what* of Christian living—what we must do, what we must eat, what we must say. We must also be concerned about the *whom* in righteousness—whom will you serve? Righteousness is also determined by whom we serve and not merely by what we do. Otherwise heaven will be filled with Pharisees. Jesus taught that our righteousness must exceed that of the Pharisees. It is true that the *what* is important, and I am not leaving that out at all; but the primary importance is the *whom*. Some people have trouble understanding that.

In Acts chapter 17, when Paul went to Athens and preached, he told the people that they served an unknown god. He went on to make the true God known to them, for Jesus taught that "this is life eternal, that they might know Thee the only true God, and Jesus Christ, Whom Thou hast sent." John 17:3. It is life eternal to know Him. We must know Him to serve Him right. Therefore, acquaintanceship with God is most important.

John wrote that "every one that loveth is born of God, and knoweth God. He that loveth not knoweth not God; for God is love." 1 John 4:7,8. If you know Him, you will love Him because God is love. And "love is the fulfilling of the law" according to Romans 13:10. To know Him is to serve Him aright. Then you will love Him, and love is the keeping, or fulfilling of the law. Knowing and serving God produces righteousness, which is a vastly different thing than we often think about. In righteousness, it is the *Whom* that we serve that makes all the difference.

When Jesus came to this earth, born in Bethlehem, He came as a King to rule over the kingdom of grace. Some think that He will only take up rulership when someday He returns to this earth. He has already come to rule according to that marvelous verse in Isaiah 9:6, where we are told that "the government shall be upon His shoulder." He came to rule over the kingdom of grace. He does not rule in glory at this time, but He rules in grace. The wise men from the east asked, "Where is He that is born King of the Jews?" Matthew 2:2. They knew He had come to rule, and after they saw His humble birth they were tempted to doubt, but they knew He was the King; and they bowed before Him and gave gifts fit for a King. Jesus preached that "the kingdom of heaven is at hand." Matthew 4:17. It is here right now, and He invites people to come and be subjects of His kingdom.

He did not establish a kingdom of glory because that is future at His second coming; but He did establish a kingdom of grace at His first advent, and He has been ruling ever since. Therefore, the important questions are: Are you a subject of His kingdom? Do you serve Him in love? Every member of the church professes to be His subjects, but we do not refer to it that way. We call it membership in a church and we talk about what our church does and does not allow us to do. It is not a matter of what our church requires, but what our King asks us to do. Are we subjects of the King? The King is in command, so we do what the King says. Not because we have to, but because we have chosen to serve Him. It is not what you think but what He says. We do not have to be ruled by Him for it is our free choice. This is different than other kinds of servants in other kingdoms where there is a forced submission. There you either obey or are put into jail or killed if you do not serve and obey. By understanding His love, we love Him in return; and therefore, because we love Him, we keep His commandments and serve Him.

Some people ask, "How can He rule when He is not here anymore?" Most kings rule like that. Kings do not go all over their countries to visit all the people everyday to rule. Very few people in a kingdom ever saw a king before television came along, but they were still ruled by the king. How did he do it? He had helpers and administrators, and he ruled through his laws, decrees, and commands. In other words, he ruled through his words; and wherever his word was, the king was ruling. There were people there to administer his laws. The king always ruled by his word or his decree, and the king's words were most important.

Christ has left us His word. The King still rules by His word. We have it, and most people on earth today have it in their own language. The King still rules, and through His words, we know exactly what He wants, what His desires are, what His plans are, His wishes, and what He is like. We can know Him through His word and through His representatives. Therefore, we have adequate opportunity to serve Him knowledgeably and intelligently. Our King has been ruling through His word and through His administrators for a long time.

As soon as this King was born, His rulership was contested. The wise men asked Herod, "Where is He that is born King of the Jews?" Matthew 2:2. Herod then went to inquire about this King and found out where He would be born. When the wise men did not come back, he issued a decree to kill all children less than two years of age. He did not want any competitors. The ultimate antagonist of Christ was a more terrible enemy than Herod. "And she being with child cried, travailing in birth, and pained to be delivered...And his [the dragon's] tail drew the third part of the stars of heaven, and did cast them to the earth: and the dragon stood before the woman which was ready to be delivered, for to devour her child as soon as it was born." Revelation 12:2,4. And verse 9 tells us that the dragon was "that old serpent, called the Devil, and Satan." He is the one who did not want Christ to rule. He has a lot of friends today, does he not? Even in the church there are many who do not want Christ to rule. Satan never wanted Christ to rule. If you are against the authority and rulership of Christ, you have joined forces with Satan.

This was made plain in the third temptation of Jesus in the wilderness. "Again, the devil taketh Him up into an exceeding high mountain, and sheweth Him all the kingdoms of the world, and the glory of them; And saith unto Him, All these things will I give Thee, if Thou wilt fall down and worship me. Then saith Jesus unto him, Get thee hence, Satan: for it is written, Thou shalt worship the Lord thy God, and Him only shalt thou serve." Matthew 4:8-10. Jesus was saying to Satan that God is in charge, not him.

Since the fall of Adam and Eve, Satan has claimed ownership of all the kingdoms of this world, and he still claims ownership. He says the inhabitants of this world belong to him because he conquered all human beings, and that since they have all sinned, they are all his. Unfortunately, too many people believe him. He claims to dominate us because he has overcome us.

Satan does not mention that his rulership has some strings attached. "When Satan declared to Christ, The kingdom and glory of the world are delivered unto me, and to whomsoever I will I give it, he stated what was true only in part [he always tells half truths], and he declared it to serve his own purpose of deception. Satan's dominion was that wrested from Adam, but Adam was the vicegerent of the Creator. His was not an independent rule. The earth is God's, and He has committed all things to His Son. Adam was to reign subject to Christ. When Adam betrayed his sovereignty into Satan's hands, Christ still remained the rightful King. Thus the Lord had said to King Nebuchadnezzar, 'The Most High ruleth in the kingdom of men, and giveth it to whomsoever He will.' Daniel 4:17. Satan can exercise his usurped authority only as God permits. When the tempter offered to Christ the kingdom and glory of the world, he was proposing that Christ should yield up the real kingship of the world, and hold dominion subject to Satan." DA 129,130.

You must remember that in the very beginning, back in the garden, as soon as Satan saw that Adam had rulership, he wanted to usurp that rulership so he could dominate all of Adam's successors and lead them all to sin. What he did not acknowledge, of course, was that this was all subject to Christ. This was not an independent rule that Adam had, and so Satan does not have it, either. Satan sought immediately to take control as soon as Christ was born. He has always contested about the kingdom and the rulership of mankind.

This contest, or this great controversy between Christ and Satan as we often call it, is more clearly seen under the symbol of the king of Babylon. Remember that we are studying justification by faith, and especially how it relates to the third angel's message where it discusses Babylon. You must discuss the king of Babylon when you discuss Babylon. Otherwise you cannot possibly understand what this is all about.

The king of Babylon is discussed in Isaiah, and notice that he is the same individual that tried to devour the Christ child as soon as He was born. "That thou shalt take up this proverb against the king of Babylon, and say, How hath the oppressor ceased! the golden city ceased!" Isaiah 14:4. How has Babylon come to its end or fallen? Isaiah discusses more about Babylon in succeeding verses;

and finally in verse 12 are the familiar words: "How art thou fallen from heaven, O Lucifer, son of the morning!" If you read the context, he is talking about the king of Babylon. Lucifer is termed and symbolized by the king of Babylon. Why was he cast down to the ground? "For thou hast said in thine heart, I will ascend into heaven, I will exalt my throne above the stars of God: I will sit also upon the mount of the congregation, in the sides of the north: I will ascend above the heights of the clouds; I will be like the most High." Verses 13,14. Satan aspires to the pinnacle of authority and rulership of this earth.

Isaiah goes on to describe the results of Babylon's (and Lucifer's) aspirations: "For I will rise up against them, saith the Lord of hosts, and cut off from Babylon the name, and remnant, and son, and nephew, saith the Lord. I will also make it a possession for the bittern, and pools of water: and I will sweep it with the besom of destruction, saith the Lord of hosts." Isaiah 14:22,23. In other words, He will destroy this place.

Lucifer wants to rule and dominate just like God. He aspires to everything that God has. Therefore, when the Christ child was born he was suspicious and knew that somehow he must get rid of Him for He would compete with him. Satan did not succeed when Christ was born, so he tried to do it through the temptations in the wilderness. He was always trying to get rid of Christ's Kingship. Satan came to dominate men for he knows he must dominate us in order to prevent us from being saved. He knows that if we are ever won to Christ, his cause is lost, and we will become righteous because we serve a righteous King. More than we realize, Satan understands this.

We have come to the day and age when many despise authority. The devil wants to imbue us with feelings of anarchy and rebellion to the point where we would never submit or subject ourselves to any authority. Today we see the results of this emphasis in the attitude of children toward parents, of parents toward grandparents, the young toward the aged, employees toward employers, citizens toward government, students toward teachers, members toward pastors and conferences. Everywhere this spirit of rebellion, this anti-authority, is rampant. In some cases it might be justified, but such a widespread, anti-authoritarian attitude pleases the devil to no end, because it makes us rebellious and anti-submissive. The spirit of not wanting to be subject to anyone is destroying marriages because there is no subjection in marriage anymore; but the Bible teaches there must be. Not forced subjection, but a willing, loving subjection. We see thousands of divorces because no one likes authority. Everyone wants to do his own thing. No one wants anyone to tell him what to do. This anarchy is sweeping all over the land and throughout the world as nation rises against nation.

Nebuchadnezzar, the king of Babylon, was an unusual person, and you begin to understand some of his activities as you study about him in the book of

259

Daniel. Remember, we are still talking about Lucifer and how he is depicted and symbolized in the activities of the king of Babylon, for he is termed that by Isaiah, the gospel prophet. We are all familiar with the dream of Nebuchadnezzar and the image he saw. Notice also what is said about the king himself. "Thou, O king, art a king of kings: for the God of heaven hath given thee a kingdom, power, and strength, and glory. And wheresoever the children of men dwell, the beasts of the field and the fowls of the heaven hath He given into thine hand, and hath made thee ruler over them all." Daniel 2:37,38. Nebuchadnezzar came to realize that God had given him his kingdom. He said, "Of a truth it is, that your God is a God of gods, and a Lord of kings." Verse 47. He knew that he might be a ruler over other kings, but Jehovah is Lord, a Master of kings.

This is the heart of the book of Daniel, and it has much to do with the book of Revelation. Nebuchadnezzar liked everything about the dream except the fact that the God who could raise up kings could also take them down. He found out that another kingdom would come after his, and he did not like that. So he had an image built entirely of gold, not merely with a head of gold like in his dream. This was to show that his kingdom would be everlasting, and that God would never raise up another kingdom after his. Now he was in a contest with God who had given him the kingdom and who said there was someone coming after him. To guarantee no one would come after him, he had all those he ruled gather together and bow down and worship this image, showing there would be no rebellion in his kingdom. Everyone bowed down except three; and you know the story as described in Daniel chapter 3. When they refused to heed the decree of the king to worship the image, the king said he would destroy them. The king was in contest, not with three men, but with a God whose decree he was trying to countermand by the image of gold. God said that Nebuchadnezzar was only a head of gold in the image in the dream, but Nebuchadnezzar said he was to be all of gold, and not just the head.

When Nebuchadnezzar saw that there was One like the Son of man in the fiery furnace with the three Hebrews, he discovered that there was Someone greater than he. This is evident in these words he spoke. "Then Nebuchadnezzar spake, and said, Blessed be the God of Shadrach, Meshach, and Abednego, who hath sent His angel, and delivered His servants that trusted in Him, and have changed the king's word." Daniel 3:28. The law of the Medes and Persian and of the Babylonians was unchangeable. But God changed the king's word. This meant that there was some authority much greater than the king of Babylon who was able to countermand his word. At first the king had difficulty with a superior force, but he acknowledges it here.

Then after a while Nebuchadnezzar changed his mind, and he said, "Is not this great Babylon, that I have built for the house of the kingdom by the might of my power, and for the honour of my majesty?" Daniel 4:30. He no longer acknowledged that the King of kings had given him his kingdom. The result was a terrible humiliation where he became like a beast. Why did he become like a beast? You must read it carefully or you will miss it. "That they shall drive thee from men, and thy dwelling shall be with the beasts of the field, and they shall make thee to eat grass as oxen, and they shall wet thee with the dew of heaven, and seven times shall pass over thee, till thou know that the most High ruleth in the kingdom of men, and giveth it to whomsoever He will." Daniel 4:25. Not just understand, not just realize, not just acknowledge, but do you know that the Most High rules in the kingdoms of men?

It is God's choice, and not popular demand. God raises up leaders and God takes them down. You do not vote them into power; you just think you do. God is in charge, not you or me or a political party. This king thought he was in charge. God does not operate a democracy, which is a little shocking to those in countries like the United States. He operates a kingdom and He is a selector of those kings. The kings of the world belong to Him, not to Satan. Satan claims them, but God says they are His. When Satan tried to dominate this world through the king of Babylon, God told him that all kings are His. If they honored God, they could stay king. If not, He can get someone else. The experiences of Nebuchadnezzar and Cyrus make it plain that God is the one who raises up kings and takes them down. He is in charge.

Whether it is in Babylon or in the church, Satan has always tried to get God off the throne by one method or another, and too often we cooperate with him. Originally God was the King of Israel, a symbol of the church as a nation. Recall the experience of how the Israelites desired a king. We have some problems with this today that we have not studied quite carefully enough. "And when ye saw that Nahash the king of the children of Ammon came against you, ye said unto Me, Nay; but a king shall reign over us: when the Lord your God was your King." 1 Samuel 12:12. This same idea is brought out in the book of Judges. "And Gideon said unto them, I will not rule over you, neither shall my son rule over you: the Lord shall rule over you." Judges 8:23. They wanted to make him king after a successful battle, but he said neither he nor his son would rule over the nation. He said the Lord would rule over them. We have difficulty in understanding this. The Lord had ruled His people through prophets down through the centuries. As He gave His commands and His words, the prophets spoke for God. The prophets went to the people with His messages. If they refused the prophet, they refused God.

The people desired to be like other nations. They desired to be like the world, just as we do today. The other nations had kings and they were successful sometimes, and the Jews said they wanted a king just like the other nations. Samuel told the people what would happen when men rule over them, and how they would be oppressed and enslaved and pay heavy taxes. When He finished his talk, they still said they wanted a king. So God gave them what they wanted. But He gave them a king under certain conditions. Many think that God no longer was ruler after a man became king, but the Bible does not teach that.

The Spirit of Prophecy elaborates on this. "Samuel then set before the people 'the manner of the kingdom,' stating the principles upon which the monarchial government was based, and by which it should be controlled. The king was not to be an absolute monarch, but was to hold his power in subjection to the will of the Most High." PP 611. There was a higher power over the king, and to make that clear, God Himself chose the king. In fact, He always chose the king. When they tried to choose their own king, He would overrule. He has always remained in charge of raising up kings and taking them down.

"The government of Israel was administered in the name and by the authority of God. The work of Moses, of the seventy elders, of the rulers and judges, was simply to enforce the laws that God had given. They had no authority to legislate for the nation. This was, and continued to be, the condition of Israel's existence as a nation. From age to age men inspired by God were sent to instruct the people and to direct in the enforcement of the laws. The Lord foresaw that Israel would desire a king, but He did not consent to a change in the principles upon which the state was founded. The king was to be the vicegerent of the Most High. God was to be recognized as the Head of the nation, and His law was to be enforced as the supreme law of the land." PP 603. Therefore, even after they had a king, God was still in charge.

Why did He not want a man to rule? Why did He want to be over the king? "God desired His people to look to Him alone as their Law-giver and their Source of strength. Feeling their dependence upon God, they would be constantly drawn nearer to Him. They would become elevated and ennobled, fitted for the high destiny to which He had called them as His chosen people. But when a man was placed upon the throne, it would tend to turn the minds of the people from God. They would trust more to human strength, and less to divine power, and the errors of their king would lead them into sin and separate the nation from God." PP 606.

The Lord knew what He was doing. Let us suppose that all Israel had followed king Saul. That would have been a tragedy. There would have been no survival of anyone. The whole kingdom would have been destroyed unless God had been over king Saul when he began his downward spiral into perdition. At some point God had to put another king in his place.

The unique thing about this kingdom is that, during the reign of all the kings of Israel and Judah, God was in charge and He manifested His authority by speaking to the king through a prophet. God always directed the king, and therefore the nation, through prophets. Some of the kings listened to the prophets, but some of them despised the prophets. But this is how God took charge of His kingdom when He had a human king over them. You can imagine what happened when king Saul went down to the witch of Endor and listened to a prophet of the devil. In doing so he was saying that he did not want the Lord to tell him what to do. He would rather let the devil tell him what to do.

All this gives us a better understanding of Revelation 12:17, where it says that Satan is angry with the remnant, and he goes to make war against those who keep the commandments of God and have the testimony of Jesus. And Revelation 19:10 tells us that the testimony of Jesus is the Spirit of Prophecy. Why does that make the devil furious? Because they are listening to the voice of God through the prophet, which means that God is ruling them. They not only keep His commandments but they listen to His directions through His prophet. Satan is furious and he wars against them. He does not want anyone to be subject unto God for he wants to rule in the place of God. He does everything he can to prevent people from listening to the King. This is why we have so much trouble about the gift of prophecy. It is not your logic that gives you so much trouble; and I know you use it all the time. Our problem with the Spirit of Prophecy is our selfishness and the devil deceiving us and tempting us. He does not want anyone to listen to the King of kings and Lord of lords. He wants everyone to listen to him. This is why there is so much controversy about the law and obedience, even in the Adventist church. The subjects of obedience and the Spirit of Prophecy are two of the most controversial subjects we have in the whole denomination. Why? The devil is angry and he does not want anyone to listen to the voice of God. That would deprive him of subjects, and of victory, and it would be certain death for him. He still has hopes of conquering everyone, and so he goes on and on in his campaign.

You can also see why in the last days he will have many who falsely claim to be Christ, and why he raises up so many false prophets and teachers claiming to speak for God. This is needed to keep people from serving the right Christ. Satan knows that when you serve the right Christ, you will have life, the devil will be whipped, and you will be successful. All these things are the devil's inventions to keep us from serving King Jesus. When he finds you obeying the commandments of God, truly obeying them and not just professing, and listening to the directions of His prophet, it frightens him and wars take place in a hurry.

In modern Babylon we still have the same issues, for modern Babylon "reigneth over the kings of the earth." Revelation 17:18. She claims to be a king of kings and ruler of rulers. For centuries she has claimed to set up kings and to tear them down. This is demonstrated by many stories in history. It is still true, and it will become more so as we near the end of time. Satan has always had a beast, or a kingdom, for he always wants to rule over the people of this world through that kingdom. And the beast is so successful that the people ask: "Who is able to make war with him?" Revelation 13:4. The Bible provides the answer: "And

I saw heaven opened, and behold a white horse; and He that sat upon him was called Faithful and True, and in righteousness He doth judge and make war." Revelation 19:11. Christ conquers Babylon, establishing Himself as King of kings and Lord of lords.

Prior to that time, the devil wants to make sure you are not saved. "Satan will not only appear as a human being, but he will impersonate Jesus; and the world that has rejected the truth will receive him as the lord of lords and king of kings." 5BC 1106. The world that has rejected the truth will receive Satan as their lord. He will actually come with the same profession as Nebuchadnezzar, claiming to rule over all the earth. The devil, when he comes impersonating Jesus, will claim to have arrived at the point where he rules the earth.

Friend, this idea of ruling and being ruled is not a game. We look at it often as something we can play with. We think we always have tomorrow to make up our minds as to whom we will have rule over us. We have very peculiar ideas about this kingship and being in submission to a ruler. The devil knows it is a game of life and death, and the Lord knows it, too; but unfortunately the church has not discovered it yet. In this day and age when the devil aspires to establish that he is king over all the earth, there are many who cannot even tell when they serve him and when they serve Christ. Many argue that they are serving Christ when they are really serving Satan.

Are you beginning to understand these concepts of obedience and authority and rulership? We have envisioned it as someone telling us what to do, and we do not like that. We think that someone is always picking on us and we say, "Get off of my back and leave me alone." That is not the problem at all. People do invent rules and all sorts of things that give an appearance of righteousness, like the Pharisees, but that is not what the problem is. There are two kings contesting for your allegiance, your loyalty, and your service. It is a fight unto death for us and for them. We may choose whom we serve, but we must also *know* whom we serve. We do not serve an unknown god as the heathen do. If we do not know Christ, we can never know Satan. If you cannot tell the difference, it simply means you do not know Jesus. But His word makes it clear who God is. He is planning before He returns that His saints will make it obvious who the righteous are, so that every human being will know what it is to be like Jesus. Christ is counting on you and me to demonstrate to the world what it is like to be like Jesus. This is a most important thing.

We can never be like Jesus while we try to be righteous by ourselves. We can never be like Jesus while we do not know Him. We can never be like Jesus by trying to do what is right. We can only be like Jesus by submitting to the sovereignty of His love and obeying Him as our loving King. It is more than just going through the external motions of doing what is right.

Jesus is humble, self-denying, and self-sacrificing. He is meek and lowly. Our King wants us to be like Him. His invitation to all is: "Come unto Me all ye that labor and are heavy laden and I will give you rest." Matthew 11: 28.

Jesus was different from the proud, ambitious, prestigious, world-seeking sophisticates. He was totally self-forgetful and mindful only of others and their needs, and He came to serve and to bless others and to demonstrate God's love. The world will never know God until Christians obey the King of righteousness because they love Him; and they love Him because He first loved them. In their loving actions, they will demonstrate to the world what God is like. Genuine Christians will demonstrate the loving, forgiving, merciful, sacrificial acts of Christ to the world. Jesus is waiting for this, but the devil says it will never happen. He claims that humans are as selfish and greedy as he is, and he says he can have them all. The devil still claims that we are all his because we have all sinned.

The Bible teaches that "of whom a man is overcome, of the same is he brought in bondage." 2 Peter 2:19. Since Satan has overcome us, he says we are his. But Christ said that Satan is the originator of all lies. The truth is that Christ has conquered Satan. Satan was the master of human beings, but Christ came to do battle with our master. He has defeated the king who claimed to own us, and now all that belonged to Satan now belongs to Jesus, for Satan is a defeated foe. Everything that was Satan's property is now Christ's property, but many will not believe that yet. Not even those who attend church will believe that Satan is defeated, for they let him go on claiming victories in their lives when Christ has already conquered. The Lord says to us in Christianity, "I have already won you in battle, and you belong to Me! I claim you as My spoils, My prize, in warfare. Will you acknowledge that you belong to Me?" There is still a choice we must make even though He has won. In addition, He says, "I have redeemed you with My precious blood as though you were the property of Satan, and I bought you from him to be Mine." By creation (original ownership), by redemption (buying us with His blood), and by conquering (winning us in a battle), He says we are His; and He asks if we will love and serve Him because we are His.

That is a decision that the Christian church offers everyone today. And the King of kings today asks the question, "Have I won you yet?" Every day as we awaken we must decide if He has won our heart, our affections, our time, our interest, our money, our plans. Has He won me? He says He has. What do you say?

We must acknowledge the truth that Christ is King of kings. He has won everything and soon He is coming to claim all who acknowledge that He has won them. He wants you to be in that precious group. This is our God and there is no other. He is the God of gods. He is our King. "Lo, we have waited for Him, and He will save us." Isaiah 25:9.

May the Lord help you today to realize that Christ has conquered you, that He has conquered Satan and every enemy; and that you are His precious prize and He wants you desperately. Give Him your heart today and every day.

24

THE PATH
TO THE HEART

THE SUBJECT OF MEDICAL ministry is intimately related to the subject of Christ our righteousness. You cannot understand Christ our righteousness apart from medical ministry. Unfortunately, we try to do that sometimes.

You may recall the experience of John the Baptist while languishing in prison. He began to have some doubts, this mighty man of faith, and he sent his disciples to ask some questions of Jesus. I especially want you to notice the answer that Christ sent back. "And John calling unto him two of his disciples sent them to Jesus, saying, Art Thou He that should come? or look we for another? When the men were come unto Him, they said, John Baptist hath sent us unto Thee, saying, Art Thou He that should come? or look we for another? And in that same hour He cured many of their infirmities and plagues, and of evil spirits; and unto many that were blind He gave sight. Then Jesus answering said unto them, Go your way, and tell John what things ye have seen and heard; how that the blind see, the lame walk, the lepers are cleansed, the deaf hear, the dead are raised, to the poor the gospel is preached. And blessed is he, whosoever shall not be offended in Me." Luke 7:19-23.

They took this marvelous news back to John. The servant of the Lord commented on this and helps us to see the scope of the work that was conducted that day by Jesus. "The Saviour did not at once answer the disciples' question. As they stood wondering at His silence, the sick and afflicted were coming to Him to be healed. The blind were groping their way through the crowd; diseased ones of all classes, some urging their own way, some borne by their friends, were eagerly pressing into the presence of Jesus. The voice of the mighty Healer penetrated the deaf ear. A word, a touch of His hand, opened the blind eyes to behold the light of day, the scenes of nature, the faces of friends, and the face of the Deliverer. Jesus rebuked disease and banished fever. His voice reached the ears of the dying, and they arose in health and vigor. Paralyzed demoniacs obeyed His word, their madness left them, and they worshiped Him. While He healed their diseases, He taught the people. The poor peasants and laborers, who were shunned by the rabbis as unclean, gathered close about Him, and He spoke to them the words of eternal life. Thus the day wore away, the disciples of John seeing and hearing all. At last Jesus called them to Him, and bade them go and tell John what they had witnessed, adding, 'Blessed is he, whosoever shall find none occasion of stumbling in Me.' Luke 7:23, R.V. The evidence of His divinity was seen in its adaptation to the needs of suffering humanity. His glory was shown in His condescension to our low estate." DA 216,217.

What a testimony John's disciples took back! John had read Isaiah 61 concerning the Messiah, so after hearing his disciples' report, he knew this was the Christ. This was Immanuel—God with us. He was verily God who had taken human flesh. Jesus said to Phillip, "Have I been so long time with you, and yet hast thou not known Me, Philip? he that hath seen Me hath seen the Father; and how sayest thou then, Shew us the Father?" John 14:9. If the Father Himself had walked this earth, He would have done the same as Jesus. We have strange mental pictures of our God, but Jesus worked like this many days during His ministry. Healing and teaching the people was the common routine of His ministry. He left some villages where there was not one sick person left. All day long, people came to Him for healing. This was the evidence of His divinity and that He was the Messiah. Surely, righteousness is like this.

We have had many concepts of righteousness that are not much related to this. Many of our ideas revolve around ourselves and our own improvement; but His whole life revolved around doing for others and thinking about others. This was the Christ, the righteousness of God manifested to men.

By now we should all know that "righteousness is love" (MB 18) and that obedience is the "service and allegiance of love" (SC 60). Righteousness and obedience are not self-serving. They both involve being a blessing to others.

We usually think about so many other things when we think about righteousness, and view it as some kind of flawless performance in our own behavior and habits. I would not diminish the importance of our behavior, but the life of righteousness that was manifested to us was a life of service to mankind. It was a life of self-forgetfulness and of total interest in other people. That is the way He lived. And I think this is the concept He had in mind for the Seventh-day Adventist Church and its institutions.

In Matthew 25, there is a scene of the righteous and their reward in the Judgment. Notice that they did the same activities as Christ did. They gave food to the hungry, clothing to the naked, visited the fatherless and widows in their affliction; and as He speaks about this, they ask Him when they saw Him hungry, and naked, etc. Christ responds in verse 40: "Verily I say unto you, Inasmuch as ye have done it unto one of the least of these My brethren, ye have done it unto Me." The neglect of these things—the lack of concern for other human beings—was met with punishment. This idea that sin is the neglect and abuse of people is a different concept of sin than we have often had. Sin is not just a mistake I make, or some slip in my life. Sin is hurting others. It is destructive of humanity and of life. The wicked are punished because they just do not care about people; and the righteous ones are rewarded because they do care about people. The Lord loved people. Every human was precious to Him. None were slighted; all were valuable. Those who really love Jesus love His people; and all are His. As they love people, they cannot bear to see them hurt. This is the idea we find in true medical ministry.

This has a unique application to our role and our calling, especially in our medical institutions. For many years we have said that the verses in Isaiah 58 (12-14) that deal with building the old waste places has a direct application to the work of the Seventh-day Adventist Church. This is true. But notice there is something that precedes the repairing of the breach and the restoring of the paths to dwell in. It is a work very much like that of Christ's. "Is not this the fast that I have chosen? to loose the bands of wickedness, to undo the heavy burdens, and to let the oppressed go free, and that ye break every yoke? Is it not to deal thy bread to the hungry, and that thou bring the poor that are cast out to thy house? when thou seest the naked, that thou cover him; and that thou hide not thyself from thine own flesh?" Isaiah 58:5,7. John asked, "he that loveth not his brother whom he hath seen, how can he love God whom he hath not seen?" 1 John 4:20.

Isaiah continues on in verse 10: "And if thou draw out thy soul to the hungry, and satisfy the afflicted soul; then shall thy light rise in obscurity, and thy darkness be as the noonday." What is this light that "shall rise in obscurity" when this practical work of caring for the physical and spiritual needs of humanity is conducted? What is this light? "The Lord is my light." Psalms 27:27. When Jesus came, He was called "the true Light." 1 John 1:9. He wants us to reflect the light of His glory to others.

What is this light that the Lord is? "So the followers of Christ are to shed light into the darkness of the world. Through the Holy Spirit, God's word is a light as it becomes a transforming power in the life of the receiver. By implanting in their hearts the principles of His word, the Holy Spirit develops in men the attributes of God. The light of His glory—His character—is to shine forth in His followers. Thus they are to glorify God, to lighten the path to the Bridegroom's home, to the city of God, to the marriage supper of the Lamb." COL 414. So the glory is His character, and it is to shine out to a dark world through us, His followers.

"It is the darkness of misapprehension of God that is enshrouding the world. Men are losing their knowledge of His character. It has been misunderstood and misinterpreted. At this time a message from God is to be proclaimed, a message illuminating in its influence and saving in its power. His character is to be made known. Into the darkness of the world is to be shed the light of His glory, the light of His goodness, mercy, and truth." COL 415.

I wish all the darkness was outside of the church, but our children have a misapprehension or misunderstanding of God. Often we do. Much of our work as pastors and leaders and members of the church could be quickly dispelled if we knew that God is love. But so often we fear Him, and believe that He is against us and not for us. Some think that He sent His Son to condemn rather than to save us, and that the Comforter does not comfort but criticizes and finds fault. We have so many wrong concepts of God. I do not believe in a permissive God, but I do believe in a gracious and merciful God. The first attribute of His character revealed to Moses was "the Lord merciful." Exodus 34:6. People need to know that these days. It is no wonder that so many young people do not like to attend churches where they must meet a God who will condemn them. The light of His glory, and His glory is His character and His character is love, must beam out in human beings. They must see Him in us. This is the light that He wants to go to the whole world. This is the light we have the privilege of sharing and shedding to those in our own communities.

We are told that this is the very last work. I would also suggest that this work has much to do with the Loud Cry of the third angel. "Those who wait for the Bridegroom's coming are to say to the people, 'Behold your God.' The last rays of merciful light, the last message of mercy to be given to the world, is a revelation of His character of love. The children of God are to manifest His glory. In their own life and character they are to reveal what the grace of God has done for them. The light of the Sun of Righteousness is to shine forth in good works—in words of truth and deeds of holiness." COL 415. This is the message of God's character—that God is love; and His love is to be seen in good works to mankind.

Sometimes we have had the notion that preaching the truth was just going out and verbalizing; and we have said many good things. But these days the Lord must be seen through His messengers, and not just heard. The world must know and see that God in near, and that He loves them as He ministers to them through us. This is the last message. Therefore, we must conclude that this is part of Christ our righteousness and justification by faith, which is the third angel's message in verity.

The quote in *Christ's Object Lessons* goes on to remind us of the great commission of Christ found in Luke 4; then it references Isaiah 58, verses 7 and 8 about how when we do this work, our light "will break forth as the morning." And finally it speaks of how we should let our light shine before men "that they may see your works, and glorify your Father which is in heaven." Matthew 5:16. Following those words are these thoughts: "Thus in the night of spiritual darkness God's glory is to shine forth through His church lifting up the bowed down and comforting those that mourn. All around us are heard the wails of a world's sorrow. On every hand are the needy and distressed. It is ours to aid in relieving and softening life's hardships and misery. Practical work will have far more effect than mere sermonizing. We are to give food to the hungry, clothing to the naked, and shelter to the homeless. And we are called to do more than this. The wants of the soul, only the love of Christ can satisfy. If Christ is abiding in us, our hearts will be full of divine sympathy. The sealed fountains of earnest, Christlike love will be unsealed." COL 417.

I don't know what you think about these words, but they impress me as encompassing our entire message. The activity that Jesus was doing when the disciples of John went to ask Him if He was the One sent of God is the very work we are to engage in. The world today is asking the question: "Where are the people of God?" They want to see Jesus. They want to know where He is and what He is like. Too often He has been misrepresented. Too often we have acted as if He is a selfish God, or a demanding and exacting God, when in reality He is an unselfish and loving Person.

Medical ministry is at the very heart of this work. It is not just welfare ministry, and gospel ministry, but it is also medical ministry. They are all closely interrelated and cannot be separated. And the spiritual needs must be put together with the physical needs. We must minister to the soul as well as to the body. Therefore, we do not believe alone in medical work, or welfare work. We believe in medical ministry in addition to welfare ministry. This is not just work. It is service where we serve the needs of mankind. It is not a profession or working for a livelihood or for wages or fees. It is working for God and for man. The money does not satisfy. We all have troubles with materialism. Many of us think that money will satisfy us. But go see those who do have money and ask if they are satisfied. The more we get, the more we want. It can be a form of addiction, and it does not satisfy.

The wants of our souls and the wants of other souls are only satisfied in working for others, motivated by love for God and for people. There is nothing else that satisfies. Yet everywhere I go, I find dissatisfied workers—dissatisfied ministers, medical workers, and people in all phases of the work. They have material blessings, but they have told me they want to do something for people. I would ask them, "But don't you work for people every day?" And they answer, "Yes, but we want to do something for people, and not for a living." They want to do something that will feed their own hearts. There is a craving these days in people to do this kind of work. But somehow the devil has hindered it, or we just do not see it as clearly as we should.

The reason why I bring up the subject of medical ministry is to impress on you why this work is so vitally important. Of all the work our Lord could have done in this earth, why did He choose this activity? Why is it so special? Why should we invest so much money and time into this work of medical ministry? Why did

God work many miracles to found institutions in places like Loma Linda and other localities? There is something most unique about this ministry.

The first reason is that Jesus said, "Inasmuch as ye have done it unto one of the least of these My brethren, ye have done it unto Me." Matthew 25:40. When we feed and clothe those who need our help, it is the same as doing it unto Jesus. He has a strong identity with all humanity. He claims them as His own. "For whosoever shall give you a cup of water to drink in My name, because ye belong to Christ, verily I say unto you, he shall not lose his reward." Mark 9:41. Humanity belongs to Christ.

Another reason for taking up this work is found in the words of Solomon the wise man. "He that hath pity upon the poor lendeth unto the Lord; and that which he hath given will He pay him again." Did you ever think the Lord would want to borrow something? Lending to Him is a most unique thought. When I take pity on the poor and give to them whatever it is that they need, I am not just giving to them. The wise man teaches I am lending to God, and He will repay me again.

In these verses and others, the Lord is teaching us that all humanity belongs to Him. All of us "are bought with a price." 1 Corinthians 6:20. "Behold, all souls are Mine." Ezekiel 18:4. "The earth is the Lord's, and the fulness thereof; the world, and they that dwell therein." Psalms 24:1. Humanity is His property. He simply asks us what we think about His property. What is your concern about mankind? What is your interest in people and how do you feel about them? They are God's property.

May I suggest that we live in a time of great mistreatment of people, from the wars that rage throughout the world to strife in our own families. Our children feel greatly neglected, not for lack of things, but for lack of dad and mother. The parents are so busy obtaining the things they think their children need and want that the children do not have the benefit of time with them. Dad and mother are so worn out trying to get those things that they do not have time for their children. We are rushing through life in our mad pursuit of things, and people have become unimportant. We do not intend to be that way, but we act like it. Do not visit the old people in your community if you do not want to be told that they are not important. There are many singles in our communities, both young and old, who can tell you how unimportant they are. And even students far from home can tell you how unimportant they are. We do not have small schools anymore. Students are just a number in a computer. The computer knows who you are but the teacher does not. It is not the teacher's fault in all cases, for some have classes with hundreds of students. It is difficult to find somebody who cares. Never in the history of this world have people needed other people so much as today. We need friends, but how little time we have for each other. In our hearts we think more of each other than we take time to prove. We just do not seem to find time. We seek education and all sorts of good things, but people seem to be left out.

This is the society we have, friend. But the Lord said that the last work is to understand people's needs and to minister to those needs. Doesn't your heart go out to people in need? Don't you want to do something about it? I suggest that taking time, and having genuine concern for people within your sphere of influence, is the reason why the Lord speaks so much about satisfying the needs of humanity. If Jesus came all the way from heaven to spend all day long doing things like this, then who and what is more important than this type of activity? Almost everything we are doing could be left undone if we only took time for people. When you have gone through your day on the treadmill of life but have left out precious humanity, it is a dissatisfying day, and the stress gets to you, and you do not look forward to the next day and its treadmill. But helping just one human being that day brightens the whole day, does it not? And that night when you kneel down to pray, you thank the Lord and say it was a good day.

Some people believe all this, but ask, "What can I do?" It seems a mystery and we make it so difficult. Jesus only said to give them what you have. It can be kind words, or a firm handshake. We need to get close to people. We need each other. What you have may not be food. It may be a room for a while in your home or kind words. It does not matter how much you have; just give what you have. And everyday the Lord will send the right people to you. He does not send a person who needs millions of dollars to a poverty-stricken person. He sends the people we can help.

"In the gift of His Son for our redemption, God has shown how high a value He places upon every human soul, and He gives to no man liberty to speak contemptuously of another. We shall see faults and weaknesses in those about us, but God claims every soul as His property—His by creation, and doubly His as purchased by the precious blood of Christ." MB 56,57.

We are always judging people by appearances, and some people just do not look like His property. But they are. God does not judge us by our appearance or by what we are now. He judges us by our potential. "I will make a man more precious than fine gold." Isaiah 13:12. It is not what a person is; it is what the Master Craftsman can do with human clay. Let us not minimize the Potter, for we can do all things through Christ who strengthens us. When the Lord goes to work on us, we are like jewels in His crown, precisely cut. We all know people who we never dreamed would become such agents for the Lord. It is difficult to imagine that some of our high school students, those wiggle worms and rascals, could ever do anything for the Lord. But they often turn out to be missionaries and outstanding leaders, very dedicated to the Lord and His work. It is not the outward appearance, but rather the potential. The Lord looks down into the future, but we cannot; and He sees what He can make of men and women.

These are the marvelous things about humanity. God can do such great things with so little. Therefore, I must treat with great respect every human being. It will come back to haunt us when we abuse human beings. We must learn the difficult lesson of how priceless is every human being for whom Christ has given His life.

There is another aspect to this problem, and that concerns life itself. Right here is where medical ministry comes into its own, for sickness has much to do with life or the lack of life. Helping people in their affliction when they are sick is caring for life. This is the path to the heart. "The medical missionary work is growing in importance and claims the attention of the churches. It is part of the gospel message and must receive recognition. It is the heaven-ordained means of finding entrance to the hearts of people." MM 241.

We have invented many gimmicks, and many promotional devices—all well-meaning things—but nothing will ever take the place of blessing people with life. Just wait until your spouse is ill, or your children; and I mean deathly ill. A very fine physician and his best nurse spend three days and three nights with your loved one to keep them alive. Let me assure you that they occupy a tremendous place in your heart immediately. When they hover over your loved one, and never leave until the person is well and safe, something happens to that loved one and all the other loved ones in that family. And you wonder, why such dedication? Why do they forget their families? Why do they forget sleep itself and even food? Why do they do this when neither my family nor I are important? These people are on a fixed salary and it does not increase one dime when they stay there three nights and three days. And you want to know what they have found that you have not discovered. What makes people like that? And never has there been such a big opening for medical workers to teach the marvelous love of Christ as there is today.

Medical ministry is unique because it has to do with life, and nothing is closer to our hearts than life—our own and that of our loved ones and friends. There is nothing like this work; and you cannot separate it from eternal life. Life winning is soul winning. In its true understanding, it always has been and it always will be, for as soon as you touch the life, you touch the soul, and the heart is as receptive as it can ever be. The hardest hearts, the most difficult to reach, will be reached by those in this ministry. Therefore, God says that not only the physicians and nurses and paramedics must get involved, but the ministers and lay members must get involved in meeting the physical needs of people, because this is the path to the heart. God will find an abundant entrance into the hearts of people when we become intensely interested in their lives.

Life is of God. He is the Life Giver. He is the Life Provider every day. Jesus said "I am come that they might have life, and that they might have it more abundantly." John 10:10. As His followers, we must say that we have come that they might have life and have it more abundantly. We establish that by bringing them the physical life first. Then the heart is open to receive the spiritual life. "For in Him we live, and move, and have our being." Acts 17:28. If I am interested in life, I am interested in you.

When you see a hungry person, you find someone on the road to death. If their needs are not soon satisfied, they will die. When you meet a person not adequately clothed in cold weather, they can die of exposure; and they are on the road to death. The homeless, orphans, and widows can become so discouraged and lonesome that in one way or another they are on the road to death. Diseases that kill can follow depression and discouragement. All of these things are an attack on life in mankind. The destroyer has come to bring death; and all of those on the Lord's side are fighting the enemy of mankind and fostering life, whether it be providing food or clothing or a home or friendship or in attacking and fighting sickness. We are fighting the enemy of all mankind—the destroyer and death-giver. All of those on the Lord's side have come that mankind might have life and more abundantly.

I would like to suggest that this activity is true righteousness, because righteousness is loving, and living, and giving. As I forget myself and minister to you and are mindful of you, the Lord begins to live in my heart and occupy a larger place than ever before. This, I believe, was God's plan for our medical institutions and our churches, and for all our missionary work. If I understand Isaiah 58 correctly, when we do this work, motivated by love for man and for God, concerned about life and God's property, then it will be that verse 10 of Isaiah 58 is fulfilled. "And if thou draw out thy soul to the hungry, and satisfy the afflicted soul; then shall thy light rise in obscurity, and thy darkness be as the noonday." God's character will be truly seen, revealed in the activity of men.

Other things will also take place as seen in verse 9: "Then shalt thou call, and the Lord shall answer; thou shalt cry, and He shall say, Here I am." We will see answers to prayer, almost immediately. We are always in close contact with Him because we so intimately identify with Him and represent Him. He can bless our true representation of Him.

Verse 11 also takes place: "And the Lord shall guide thee continually, and satisfy thy soul in drought, and make fat thy bones: and thou shalt be like a watered garden, and like a spring of water, whose waters fail not." We should be amazed at the constant guidance in founding our medical institutions. Every day the right answers came at the right time and with the right amount of money. "And the Lord shall guide thee continually."

Then verse 12 can take place: "And they that shall be of thee shall build the old waste places: thou shalt raise up the foundations of many generations; and thou shalt be called, The repairer of the breach, The restorer of paths to dwell in." Verses 12 and 13 talk about a Law Giver whose law is love—love for God supremely and love for our neighbor as ourselves. It is not just talking about a day of the week that we keep—the Sabbath. It is talking about the God of the Sabbath, the Creator and Father of all mankind. We are the apple of His eye. He is the One who has given life to all of us. What does the Father think about His children? Do Sabbath-keepers think the same thing about humanity as He does? What do our medical workers think about those precious lives they can care for in the medical work? Do we see and know the Creator of man, the Father of man, in the Sabbath and in the law? He said to show and reveal Him and manifest Him in His creatorship as we deal with human beings. Then light will come in answers to prayers. You will be like a refreshing stream that gives life to all around.

The Lord planned the most marvelous work that we can possibly imagine in our fondest dreams for this people who have such great light. Our institutions are to be centers that train workers for this kind of activity, and it is to encircle the globe. We are to manifest to the world what it is like to love life, and to bring life to those who are dying. This is a precious work the world is crying for.

This is a nice work, and even an easy work. It is not a struggle to love people. It is a struggle to forget self. It is wonderful to love people; and the next time we meet someone with the love of Christ in our hearts, they can feel it all the way down to their toes. That love warms you on the inside.

The Lord still has this plan for us, doesn't He? He said He never changes. He is the same yesterday, today, and forever. He believes in great kindness, and tremendous compassion. He patiently waits that we might see Him, that we might know Him, and that we might walk with Him, abiding in Him and He in us. Then we may manifest this tremendous love that the world might know that God is love. And we will receive credit (not praise) for doing the work He accomplishes through us. He will say to us along with millions of other people as we get to that heavenly home, "Well done, thou good and faithful servant. Enter thou into the joy of thy Lord." Matthew 25:21. People will be waiting in long lines to thank you for representing Him. Can anything else be so wonderful?

May God help us to sense in our hearts and inmost souls the great need of the world today, and the tremendous opportunity and calling that is ours. It is our gracious privilege to establish and manifest that God is love, and that our Creator and our Father is greatly concerned about every need of every human being.

25

OWNED AND OPERATED BY?

WHO CONTROLS YOU? WHO tells you what to do? People these days like to say they do their own thing. In a previous chapter we investigated the principle of obedience to the right authority, and we discovered that obedience to that authority brings righteousness. "Know ye not that to whom ye yield yourselves servants to obey, his servants ye are to whom ye obey, whether of sin unto death, or obedience unto righteousness." Romans 6:16. The context in this next verse makes it clear that we are servants of God. "Neither yield ye your members as instruments of unrighteousness unto sin; but yield yourselves unto God as those that are alive from the dead, and your members as instruments of righteousness unto God." Verse 13.

Obedience and authority are not very tasteful words to many people these days. How easily we misunderstand God's authority and the idea of yielding to authority. We have been told so many times that we must or must not do this and that, and when we discover we are unable to do some of those things we are required to do, we experience great guilt; and we seek to avoid that by avoiding authority. This is a different kind of obedience than most of us think about.

We studied previously that "Obedience is the surrender of the heart to the sovereignty of love." MB 46. This obedience is not legislated or forced. It is not demanded or exacted. Obedience is the willing surrender of the heart to love.

God asks for our obedience, but He wins our obedience. It is difficult for us to understand that. Most parents and leaders do not win obedience, and we assume that God is like most of us. But He is not. He has a marvelous way of winning our hearts. If Jesus is our Lord, if He reigns through the sovereignty of His love, then He can lead and direct us by His love, and He becomes the Lord our righteousness—the Master and the King of righteousness. True righteousness comes by yielding to the right authority so that He reigns over us. He is the Lord of righteousness in our lives.

Satan knows this better than any of us, and since he is aware that this produces righteousness, he seeks to hinder or impair such a procedure in our lives; and he does this in a most unique way. "For there shall arise false christs, and false prophets, and shall shew great signs and wonders; insomuch that, if it were possible, they shall deceive the very elect." Matthew 24:24. There will be false christs and false authorities who have false laws and directions. A false christ does not come only to the heathen but to the Christian world who anticipate the return of Christ, and he will come as a false authority. People will follow and serve the false authority and therefore be led to unrighteousness, or to a false concept of serving God. The Seventh-day Adventist Church is not immune to a false christ. In the early days of my experience, I thought I would be immune, but I no longer believe such a thing. In fact, I think we are very vulnerable to false christs, so much so that it frightens me. Satan is a wise person, and we assume that we cannot be deceived by a false christ. But within the church there exists varying concepts of Jesus, of His life, His law, and His work. Sometimes we make ourselves uniquely vulnerable to the concept of a false christ.

Satan seeks to confuse us as to who the right authority is. Who is the right authority? Whom can we believe? Whom shall we serve? In seeking to counteract obedience to the right authority which leads to righteousness, he will bring many authorities, many voices claiming to speak for God, and many misrepresentations of God.

"And he opened his mouth in blasphemy against God, to blaspheme His name, and His tabernacle, and them that dwell in heaven." Revelation 13:6. Here we find that someone who claims to speak for God will blaspheme God. Paul described the same power this way: "Who opposeth and exalteth himself above all that is called God, or that is worshipped; so that he as God sitteth in the temple of God, shewing himself that he is God." 2 Thessalonians 2:4. All of these ideas suggest how Satan has set up other authorities who demand obedience; and they will demand obedience instead of winning it. Around us will be a multitude of authorities presenting a confusing picture as to whom we should serve. All will say, "I serve the Christ," as though there were no other; when in reality, Jesus predicted there will be many. All claiming to be Christ will say they are the right one, and everyone will obey some Christ or some god, but not necessarily the true God. All will say they are obedient, all will say they are righteous, and all will be content that others are not obedient because they serve a different god. This presents a very confusing picture.

The Bible says that the false christ will blaspheme God. When Jesus forgave the man let down through the roof by his friends, the Jews said he blasphemed God, for He, being a man, made Himself to be God, claiming the rights and prerogatives of God. The Bible teaches that Satan will do this through certain agents and powers in the earth today.

Authority asserts itself through laws and decrees. If you obey those laws and decrees, you become the subject of that authority. We know that Satan has set up a power that will "seek to change times and laws." Daniel 7:25. He attacks the authority of the Lawgiver and attempts to make the law of no effect. It is prophesied that a decree will go forth where people must worship the image to the beast. "And deceiveth them that dwell on the earth by the means of those miracles which he had power to do in the sight of the beast; saying to them that dwell on the earth, that they should make an image to the beast, which had the wound by a sword, and did live. And he had power to give life unto the image of the beast, that the image of the beast should both speak, and cause that as many as would not worship the image of the beast should be killed." Revelation 13: 14,15. In all these ways, Satan is manifesting his authority by laws and decrees; and He is most interested in attacking the one commandment that points out the authority of the Lawgiver.

"The Lord commands by the same prophet: 'Bind up the testimony, seal the law among my disciples.' Isaiah 8:16. The seal of God's law is found in the fourth commandment. This only, of all the ten, brings to view both the name and the title of the Lawgiver. It declares Him to be the Creator of the heavens and the earth, and thus shows His claim to reverence and worship above all others. Aside from this precept, there is nothing in the Decalogue to show by whose authority the law is given." GC 452. The fourth commandment is the object of Satan's wrath and attacks, because he wants to be the authority. He wants to be like God.

The Bible points out in the fourth commandment that the Creator is the Law Giver. The Creator is a unique person, and He gives the Sabbath a unique quality that we as Sabbath-keepers fail to understand very well. "The duty to worship God is based upon the fact that He is the Creator and that to Him all other beings owe their existence. And wherever, in the Bible, His claim to reverence and worship, above the gods of the heathen, is presented, there is sighted the evidence of His creative power." GC 436,437. Then she lists several texts about why we should worship Him, such as: "O come let us worship and bow down: let us kneel before the Lord our Maker." Psalms 95:6. Another text is given that explains why the holy beings in heaven who worship God owe their homage to Him: "Thou art worthy, O Lord, to receive glory and honor and power: for Thou hast created all things." Revelation 4:11. God is before all creatures, and thus He is due the honor of our worship.

Then (at the bottom of page 437), Ellen White quotes from a book titled *History of the Sabbath* written by J. N. Andrew, where he wrote: "The importance of the Sabbath as a memorial of creation is that it keeps ever present the true reason why worship is due to God...The Sabbath therefore lies at the very foundation of divine worship, for it teaches us great truth in a most impressive manner, and no other institution does this. The true ground of divine worship, not that of the seventh day merely, but of all worship, is found the distinction between the Creator and His creatures."

This has many perspectives as you begin to look at it. Have you spent much time thinking about the fact that you are a creature? Someone before and above all things has created you. This, like the fifth commandment about honoring our parents, is a unique commandment. Because of our parents, we have been born and were sustained in our weakness as little children. Because of them we have had health, food, clothing, protection, and all sorts of things that parents provide for their children. If you like the good life, if you love life, then you will honor your parents. We often think of the present and forget the past, but there could be no present without the past. As I look back as to why I have life and clothing and a home and the blessings of life, I must look back to my parents. Honor and respect them. Why? Because you like your life and health and the other blessings. I know all the problems some have these days with poor parents, but it is still true that life itself has come through them. In a unique way, the Bible points out that God is our Father. He is the source of all life, and He is the provider and sustainer of all that live. All are His. Therefore, in a very unusual way, the Bible says for us to remember this.

There is a comparison found in Isaiah that some may not like, but God found it necessary to be strong and firm in dealing with His people. They had difficulty listening to and heeding His word. "Hear, O heavens, and give ear, O earth: for the Lord hath spoken, I have nourished and brought up children, and they have rebelled against Me. The ox knoweth his owner, and the ass his master's crib: but Israel doth not know, My people doth not consider." Isaiah 1:1,2. The ones God nourished and kept had rebelled against Him. Animals, as far as they are able to manifest it, have affection for their owners and their providers. When the farmer walks in the barn, the cattle react in a certain way, like a dog that wags his tail. The good master, the one who cares for them, has come. And they obey. He just touches them and they move right over. But they will not obey a stranger.

The Lord wonders how His people, whom He constantly provides for, can constantly rebel. How can they be so unfeeling and insensitive? By creation and redemption, God owns us. He feeds and nourishes us. We think that the supermarket provides us with food, or perhaps the farms. But farmers know that it is not the farm that provides the food. The farmer cannot make it rain or make the sun shine. He cannot keep the all the pests and diseases away. He knows there is One that oversees everything in life, and who keeps the sun rising and the rain coming in due season. Someone who never slumbers or sleeps always provides. As we sense His protection and provision, our hearts respond. He says that if we love Him, then obey like the animals. If you love your Master, obey.

There is another aspect of this creatorship of God. We will give just a brief thought here, and later bring in more to add to it. "Every child lives by the life of his father." MB 78. We are indebted to our earthly father for his energy. He expends his energy in work, whether it be physical or mental. He gives his talents, his wisdom, his skill and perseverance, that we might have food, a home, clothing, medicine, protection, and all the good things in life. He provides the necessities. By his life, all the children exist. The children live by the life of the father. This is a Biblical concept, and God wants to bless the fathers. We owe much to our mothers for bearing us, but without the father that would not happen.

The quote goes on and branches off into the spiritual: "If you are God's children, begotten by His Spirit, you live by the life of God. In Christ dwells 'all the fullness of the Godhead bodily.' (Colossians 2:9); and the life of Jesus is made manifest 'in our mortal flesh' (2 Corinthians 4:11). That life in you will produce the same character and manifest the same works as it did in Him." The author of the book of Acts wrote that the Lord "giveth to all life, and breath, and all things." Acts 17:25. We His children live by Him and are indebted to Him. He originates and sustains our life.

This spiritual quality is speaking of the new birth, and Paul described it this way: "That ye put off concerning the former conversation the old man, which is corrupt according to the deceitful lusts; And be renewed in the spirit of your mind; And that ye put on the new man, which after God is created in righteousness and true holiness." Ephesians 4:22-24. That new life and new birth is a creation process. The Creator creates in the new birth. It is not evolutionary, or something man inspires or instigates. It is all of God the Creator. "Therefore if any man be in Christ, he is a new creature: old things are passed away; behold, all things are become new." 2 Corinthians 5:17. A Creator is conducting His business as we become the children of God through the new birth. Only He can do this.

This new creation, or conversion, is the object of Satan's attack, for it is the heart and soul of righteousness by faith in Christ. Without it we have no righteousness. Satan knows the centrality of conversion and the new life, and he seeks to attack this in a most unusual way. He claims that man cannot keep God's law (see *The Desire of Ages,* page 761). When Satan tempted man to sin and Adam fell, he declared that it is impossible to obey God. Far too many today believe that Satan is right—that we cannot keep the law. There are texts and quotes that tell us of our inability, but in Christ we can do all things. Satan leaves Christ out of the picture.

Our heavenly Father intervenes when man has fallen, and by demonstrating His law (or His character), which is love, He comes and loves man. As He loves the fallen man, who is still in the image of God and rightfully the property of our heavenly Father who still claims all mankind as His children, man responds. This is what God is talking about in Isaiah in regard to animals that know and obey their owners. Will the animals respond and obey better than we?

Here is a nice description of the new heart: "The light shining from the cross reveals the love of God. His love is drawing us to Himself [not demanding, not exacting]. If we do not resist this drawing, we shall be led to the foot of the cross in repentance for the sins that have crucified the Saviour. Then the Spirit of God through faith produces a new life in the soul. The thoughts and desires are brought into obedience to the will of Christ. The heart, the mind, are created anew in the image of Him who works in us to subdue all things to Himself. Then the law of God is written in the mind and heart, and we can say with Christ, 'I delight to do Thy will, O my God.' Psalm 40:8." DA 176.

The devil does not want anyone to hear these words, because if God can make a new life in you, you will be brought into harmony with God, and into harmony with His law and character of love. If we respond by loving Him who first loved us, our love is the fulfilling of the law. As you start loving Him, you begin to be righteous—you begin to obey the right authority.

This harmony with God is described by Ellen White. "In the new birth the heart is brought into harmony with God, as it is brought into accord with His law. When this mighty change has taken place in the sinner, he has passed from death unto life, from sin unto holiness, from transgression and rebellion to obedience and loyalty. The old life of alienation from God has ended; the new life of reconciliation, of faith and love, has begun." GC 468. The devil says we cannot keep the law, but Jesus says that He will love His people, and they will love Him. And when they love Him with all their heart and mind, then they will keep the law, for love is the fulfilling of the law. God seeks to break down the enmity by loving us. The devil seeks to prevent this.

Only the Creator can recreate, and there is only one Creator. The false christ cannot. He can give you a marvelous experience. In fact, you might jump up and down and holler. You might speak in gibberish and get goose bumps all over. You might even do miracles. But that is not conversion. Those things might be related to conversion, or they might not be, but the experience is not conversion. The Bible teaches that conversion is a new heart and a new mind that is brought into harmony with God and His law. It is an experience where we love His law and His way, loving Him supremely and our neighbor as ourselves. There is a vast difference in the two experiences, if you wish to confine it to experiences. One is what the Creator does in us, but the other is vastly different.

Our Father claims us as His, and as we respond to His love, He comes to fashion us like unto Himself. He remakes us and recreates us. The devil does not like us to think about the Creator. In order to prevent that, he gets people to forget the Sabbath, because the Sabbath is a constant reminder of a marvelous Creator who made man in the beginning and makes all good things for man's blessing. Will He not bless me now? Certainly He will! The devil wants us to forget that. He does not want us to keep the Sabbath holy for that would lead to a new birth, which will lead to obedience and righteousness. The devil in a variety of ways seeks to hinder the remembrance of the Creator who can make all things new in the life as well as in the earth. Satan uniquely attacks this one commandment and puts himself before God. He must attack the law in order to eliminate the Sabbath, and this he does in many ways. For years I thought the devil could not attack the law of Seventh-day Adventists, but a long time ago I discovered he attacked my concepts of God's law. He perverted the law in my mind. I made the law all "thou shalt nots" and "thou shalts." I must do or not do something, or else. I made the law a list of demands, and I made the Judgment, where we are judged by the law, a God looking down on me with a microscope looking for every flaw and deviation to see how bad I was, so He can make me burn. Far too many of us have taught that concept of the law and the Judgment. Jesus never understood or taught the law that way.

I would like to suggest that the Judgment is looking to see if we respond to His love. Do we respond to His love or do we rebel against His love? When I see His magnificent love for me, do I in turn love Him supremely and my neighbor as myself? Do I adore Him as a Father and a provider? Or am I rather calloused? The Bible teaches that He will give me a heart of flesh, and how meaningful that symbol is. He will take away the heart of stone—the unfeeling, insensitive, lukewarm, and careless heart. Half of the commandments deal with our feelings for people. It is not trying to avoid telling lies. It is having feelings for people so that I do not want to hurt them. It is not avoiding adultery or coveting. Is my heart concerned for you? Is there any sensitivity there? Do you mean anything to me? Is your life precious to me, as well as to our loving Father? I cannot bear to see your life hurt or see you suffer, whether it is emotional, physical, or spiritual agony. Life is too precious. Our God has such a tender regard for all life, even for the sparrow, as Jesus taught. God has a tender regard for us. The Bible teaches that God's people will be like Him when He comes—feeling for people, understanding, compassionate, perceptive, and sensitive. I cannot bear to see you suffer. God wants His work conducted like that. And He wants us to let this light of love shine all over the earth, to every human being that they might know the Fatherhood of our God; that they might know our Creator who made all good things for man, and who still wants to make things good for fallen man and restore in him the image of God. He wants the world to see that God is love. This is not a permissive God, but a God of grace who understands.

I discovered years ago that I had a heart of stone when it comes to people. I could say I loved people, but I could think evil thoughts about them. Can you? I could misinterpret their actions. I could have vengeful thoughts, and even hateful thoughts. I could lose my temper with people. I could even figure out ways to get even. The Bible says that this is an unfeeling heart—a heart of stone. The Lords wants to take it away. That is why the nation of Israel could rebel when

God brought them up as children and blessed them. It was the heart of stone. He wants to take it away and give us a heart of flesh, a tender and compassionate one. But Satan says he wants us to have a heart of stone that is demanding and exacting, the legislated and forced heart. Do what I say, or else. Satan's followers will be manifested especially in the death decree when they legislate to take life, and all because others do not think as they think do. It worries me when I find in my own heart, and in my church, people who like to legislate such things. I am afraid we have an organizational heart of stone sometimes, and not a heart of flesh. Our Lord is understanding and gracious and long suffering, though not permissive.

In the last days, there will be two kinds of people: those with hearts of stone, and those with hearts of flesh. There will be those who love life and those who destroy life. There will be those who love and adore the Life Giver, and those who have allegiance to the destroyer. And the contrast will be great. Like Jesus, the righteous will pray for those who seek to take their lives, for we cannot bear the thought of them being lost for all eternity. It will break our hearts because they are precious to Him. Jesus will look at those who follow the destroyer and say as He said to the rebellious Jews, "How often would I have gathered thy children together, even as a hen gathereth her chickens under her wings, and ye would not!" Matthew 23:37.

Those with hearts of flesh, the feeling and loving people, will manifest the marvelous attributes of the Life Giver, who every day fosters and gives life and cares for it. He has been caring for us a long time. We have been special to Him. Will you respond to all His love and affection? Will you say, "I am wholly Thine, O Lord. Control me with the sovereignty of love. Take over my thoughts and use me according to Thy will. Own me and operate me. Not my will but Thine be done. And all because You are so loving, so understanding, so patient; and because by a miracle of creation, You have given me a new heart that feels—a heart of flesh."

The Sabbath is at the heart of this controversy because it points out a loving Creator and a loving Father, who claims you, and says to everyone, "Son, give Me your heart. Let Me use you to shed My love to others. I don't want to dictate. I just love you. Will you submit to My love?"

May God help us to understand in these very confusing times what He is really like and what He is trying to do for everyone of us. And may we have those beautiful, tender hearts that say, "My Jesus, I love Thee. I know Thou art mine. And I am wholly Thine."

26

THE GOD MAN

ONE OF THE MOST controversial aspects of Christ our righteousness is the humanity of Jesus. In 1888, Elder A. T. Jones strongly emphasized the humanity of Christ as it relates to Christ our righteousness. He also spoke about the humanity of Jesus as it relates to the problem of the Trinity, for there was that conflict in his day, also. All he said about the humanity of Christ does not necessarily relate to Christ our righteousness. It is very important how you understand the humanity of Christ, because whatever your concept of it is determines your understanding of righteousness by faith in Christ. What Jesus became, what He did, and how He did it tells us about righteousness by faith in Him. Whatever opinion you have about His humanity will determine your theology of righteousness by faith and the plan of salvation.

There are essentially two main divisions of thought. One is that Christ took the nature of Adam prior to his fall. There is a large number of prominent people and theologians who believe that. Another group believe that He took the fallen nature of man after the four thousand years of sin. That is, He took man's sinful nature. I would like to suggest that there could be other opinions. Too often, those who discuss this merely classify you in the opposite opinion if you disagree with them; which is highly unfair. Depending upon which opinion you hold, there are Bible texts and quotations to support you in that opinion. And, of course, we interpret that text or quotation to fit our preconceived meaning, and so the opposite view disagrees with your interpretation.

I would like to give you some of the evidence each group uses to support their view. "And so it is written, The first man Adam was made a living soul; the last Adam was made a quickening spirit. Howbeit that was not first which is spiritual, but that which is natural; and afterward that which is spiritual. The first man is of the earth, earthy: the second man is the Lord from heaven." 1 Corinthians 15: 45-47. These verses establish that Jesus was the second Adam. He was "the Lord from heaven" according to verse 47, and some people that say since He was the second Adam, then He must have been like Adam before he sinned.

Here is a quote often used to support this view: "Be careful, exceedingly careful as to how you dwell upon the human nature of Christ. Do not set Him before the people as a man with the propensities of sin. He is the second Adam. But not for one moment was there in Him an evil propensity. He was assailed with temptations in the wilderness, as Adam was assailed with temptations in Eden…Never, in any way, leave the slightest impression upon human minds that a taint of, or inclination to, corruption rested upon Christ, or that He in any way yielded to corruption." 5BC 1128.

Here is another quote used to support the idea that Christ took the nature of Adam prior to his fall: "The incarnation of Christ has ever been, and will ever remain a mystery. That which is revealed, is for us and for our children, but let every human being be warned from the ground of making Christ altogether human, such an one as ourselves; for it cannot be." 5BC 1129.

In a popular worship book, these two sentences are found: "Christ is called the second Adam. In purity and holiness, connected with God and beloved by God, He began where the first Adam began." MLT 323.

"He [Christ] vanquished Satan in the same nature over which in Eden Satan obtained the victory." 5BC 1108.

In a book titled *Questions on Doctrine,* there are many quotations used by both sides of this issue. For example, on page 657, we see that "He was *born without a taint of sin* [Ellen White's emphasis], but came into the world in like manner as the human family." Then on page 651 of the same book: *"We should have no misgivings* in regard to the *perfect sinlessness of the human nature of Christ* [original emphasis]." All of these and more support the idea that Christ took the nature of Adam prior to his fall

There are also many examples of texts and quotes that seem to support the idea that Christ took man's nature after four thousand years of sin. Here are two prominent texts that A. T. Jones used: "Forasmuch then as the children are partakers of flesh and blood, He also Himself likewise took part of the same; that through death He might destroy him that had the power of death, that is, the devil." "Wherefore in all things it behoved Him to be made like unto His brethren, that He might be a merciful and faithful high priest in things pertaining to God, to make reconciliation for the sins of the people." Hebrews 2:14,17.

This next quote is perhaps the strongest quotation concerning Christ taking our nature after four thousand years: "It would have been an almost infinite humiliation for the Son of God to take man's nature, even when Adam stood in his innocence in Eden. But Jesus accepted humanity when the race had been weakened by four thousand years of sin. Like every child of Adam He accepted the results of the working of the great law of heredity. What these results were is shown in the history of His earthly ancestors. He came with such a heredity to share our sorrows and temptations, and to give us the example of a sinless life." DA 49. This quote is quite specific that Christ took man's nature after four thousand years of sin, and not prior to Adam's sin.

Here are a few more examples used to support this view: "He assumed the liabilities of human nature, to be proved and tried." 1SM 226. "He became flesh even as we are." MH 422. "For four thousand years the race had been decreasing in physical strength, in mental power, and in moral worth; and Christ took upon Him the infirmities of degenerate humanity." DA 117. "He bore the sins and infirmities of the race as they existed when He came to earth to help man." 5BC 1081. "Taking upon Himself our fallen nature." QD 657. "He took upon His sinless nature our sinful nature, that He might know how to succor those that are tempted." MM 181. "He took man's degraded nature and defiled by sin." 4BC 1147.

These are just some of the many supporting quotations and Scriptures that are used for the two opinions. Several have told me they wrestle and wrestle with this trying to figure out what to believe about it. There just seems to be so much evidence on each side of the question.

I would like to suggest that you do not have to go to either view. When fine scholars and Christians disagree, it often (but not always) means that the right opinion is somewhere between the two of them. It is difficult for any of us to be always right and totally right, even though we think we are. Often the Lord tries to lead us into all truth and guide us, but unfortunately we have preconceived opinions, and we are usually proud of our opinions. This makes it difficult for Him to teach us all things. Perhaps He teaches some people some things and other people other things, and maybe as we put the pieces together we may arrive at the truth.

There is one thing we must make certain of about Christ as we study, and the following quote makes that clear: "But the first Adam was in every way more favorably situated than was Christ. Christ was tempted by Satan in a hundredfold severer manner than was Adam." MLT 323. Did you get that? The first Adam was more favorably situated than Jesus. So He certainly did not have as many advantages as Adam had. It goes on and tells how in human nature He conquered where Adam failed. That is important to remember.

He also did not have advantages over mankind in general. "If Christ had a special power which it is not the privilege of man to have, Satan would have made capital of this matter. The work of Christ was to take from the claims of Satan his control of man, and He could do this only in the way that He came—a man, tempted as a man, rendering the obedience of a man." 7BC 930.

In no way did Jesus have any privileges or opportunities or rights that we do not have, and certainly far less than Adam had. I would like to suggest that He had far greater temptations than any human being will ever have, and therefore far fewer privileges and advantages.

Stop to consider what it means to be tempted in all ways like as we are yet without sin. When all the forces of evil assailed Him, everything depended on His resistance to temptation. We do not quite grasp the enormity of the tests on Jesus. In no way would I ever suggest that He had advantages. Rather, He must have had great disadvantages compared to us and to Adam.

In order to discover the humanity of Jesus, we must agree on the humanity of man, but we cannot. There are many opinions about our own humanity. What are we like as we are born of our parents? For instance, some people believe, and will argue loud and long, that we are born guilty because of our parents' sin and because of Adam's sin. Many have been taught that as long as they have been Seventh-day Adventists. Others say it cannot be, and they will show you some quotations to prove their point. But please read all the contexts about the quotations, will you? I would suggest that we become guilty by our own acts and not by our parents' acts.

Here are some texts and quotations that deal with our own humanity. "As related to the first Adam, men receive from him nothing but guilt and the sentence of death." 7BC 9. "Because the carnal mind is enmity against God: for it is not subject to the law of God, neither indeed can be." Romans 8:7. "Can the Ethiopian change his skin, or the leopard his spots? then may ye also do good, that are accustomed to do evil." Jeremiah 13:23. "…in his sinful nature he [man] could not keep the law of God." PP 373. "[man] has no power and no disposition to resist Satan." PP 53. "Our hearts are evil and we can not change them." SC 18. "In our own strength it is impossible for us to deny the clamors of our fallen nature." DA 122. "The image of Satan was upon men and Christ came that He might bring to them more power and efficiency." 7BC 925.

Man's fall was radical and severe. Our evangelists in days gone by used many texts to describe our condition as sinners, texts we seldom hear anymore. Here is the most popular one: "Behold, I was shapen in iniquity; and in sin did my mother conceive me." Psalms 51:5. When we are embryos, we are being formed or shaped in iniquity, and in sin did my mother conceive me. We assume the psalmist is speaking for the entire human family.

Job asked, "how can he be clean that is born of a woman?" Job 25:4. He also asked, "Who can bring a clean thing out of an unclean? not one." Job 14:4. The Bible teaches that "we are all as an unclean thing." Isaiah 64:6. It is impossible for sinful humanity to reproduce righteous, sinless humanity. It is impossible for weak and helpless humans to reproduce strong humans when it comes to the problem of sin and righteousness. In our pride we try to say that this is not true, but we will learn our lessons if we live long enough.

One of the huge questions on the humanity of Christ is: Do these texts that describe our human condition refer also to Him? Was Jesus born contaminated, or unclean? Could it be said of Him as it is said of us, that we are all as an unclean thing? Did He need to be cleansed? Did He need to be purified after His birth? Was that a necessity? Did He become like us in our uncleanness and contamination? Some would say He must be identical to us or He cannot be our righteousness and our example and our Savior; and therefore, if He is identical, He must be unclean. This is a key point. Was Jesus born contaminated? I am not talking about His activities after He was born. I am talking about His human inheritance. How was He born, and what was He like? Was He shapen in iniquity, and was He conceived in sin as the Bible says about you and me?

If He was conceived in sin and shapen in iniquity, if He was unclean and contaminated, then we are left to explain what the Bible means when it says, "And the angel answered and said unto her, The Holy Ghost shall come upon thee [Mary], and the power of the Highest shall overshadow thee: therefore also that holy thing which shall be born of thee shall be called the Son of God." Luke 1:35. There are many translations and commentaries to confirm this translation. There are some others that seem to imply that He becomes holy after His birth. So it does not settle it entirely to look at all the translations, but there are many that support the King James Version, and a few good commentaries as well.

Was He a holy thing when He was born, or was He an unclean, contaminated person? We are only talking about His birth and not His activity, for it is His birth that gives us trouble. This we must understand. You might disagree, for some people think that when we call Him a holy thing we are saying He had an immaculate conception, and then we get into all the entanglements of that doctrine and the problems concerning it.

If we can settle one question about this, we will clarify many issues concerning the humanity of Jesus. Just one question is necessary in my estimation: Was it necessary for Jesus to be converted, or born again? Was Jesus ever converted? Was it necessary to convert Him? I know He was baptized, but "Jesus did not receive baptism as a confession of guilt on His own account." DA 111. Therefore, I assume that He had no guilt when He was baptized. He was not baptized to change from the old to the new. He was not converted at His baptism. It was not a new birth for Jesus. He was fulfilling all righteousness, and setting a right example. But He was not baptized with confession of His own sin, neither by birth nor performance.

Again, the question is: Did He need to be born again, or converted? If He did need to be born again, then you must conclude that He was in some way contaminated and guilty as a sinner. If He was never a sinner and did not need to be born again or converted, then He was not contaminated and need not be purified. This to me is a key issue in this problem; and it does not take a tremendous amount of wisdom to settle it if we just stop to think about it. It is not as big a problem as we have made of it. One of the difficulties we all have is our need to realize that arguments seem to confine us and restrict us into very narrow issues until we are in a deep ditch and cannot see out. We have to gain perspective by backing off and looking at this issue a little differently than we have in the past.

It is certain that I need to be born again and I need to be cleansed. Being born of my mother is not sufficient. I must have a new birth, the Bible teaches. If the humanity of Jesus were exactly like ours, He would have to be converted, too, and be born again. But since I can find no evidence of this in the Scriptures or the Spirit of Prophecy, I conclude that He did not need it. Then there must have been a great difference between Jesus, when He was born of His mother, and me, when I was born of my mother. If I need to be converted and have my old nature taken away, and He does not, there must be a great difference.

Don't get too frightened or upset. Let me explain further. I would like to suggest that the humanity of Jesus was not like us in our first birth, but like us in our second birth. I think that will satisfy all the requirements of those who want Him to be like us after four thousand years of sin. There are three births we must deal with rather than two, and these are: the birth of Jesus, the birth we have of our mothers, and the birth we have called the new birth. If we confine ourselves to only two of these births, we can get into distortions and misunderstanding. I believe that Jesus is like us in the new birth, but not like us entirely in the first birth, but He is still much like us. Now let me show you why I believe this.

Jesus taught: "Verily, verily, I say unto thee, Except a man be born of water and of the Spirit, he cannot enter into the kingdom of God. That which is born of the flesh is flesh; and that which is born of the Spirit is spirit." John 3:5,6. When I have been born of my mother, I am only flesh. When we are born again by the Holy Spirit, then we are spirit, too. We must be born again of Him to be different people, to be converted.

This happened to Jesus, I believe, at His first birth. "Now the birth of Jesus Christ was on this wise: When as his mother Mary was espoused to Joseph, before they came together, she was found with child of the Holy Ghost. Then Joseph her husband, being a just man, and not willing to make her a public example, was minded to put her away privily. But while he thought on these things, behold, the angel of the Lord appeared unto him in a dream, saying, Joseph, thou son of David, fear not to take unto thee Mary thy wife: for that which is conceived in her is of the Holy Ghost. And she shall bring forth a son, and thou shalt call His name Jesus: for He shall save his people from their sins." Matthew 1:18-21.

Jesus was conceived by the Holy Ghost at His birth, but we are not conceived by the Holy Ghost until we are born of the Spirit. "That which is born of the flesh is flesh; and that which is born of the Spirit is spirit." John 3:6. We are born of the spirit in our second birth. If you were conceived by the Holy Ghost, could you not then be called that holy thing? The Lord calls us that after the new birth. "And that ye put on the new man [the new birth], which after God is created in righteousness and true holiness." Ephesians 4:24. Man is recreated, born again, converted in righteousness and true holiness. Why? Because he is born of the Holy Spirit, and that makes a difference. And so they can call you holy if you are born of the Holy Spirit. The Bible does. And they can call Jesus that holy thing because He was conceived by the Holy Spirit. Go back and study what influence the father and mother have when it comes to nature and to character and to legal involvements and responsibilities. Apparently, since He was conceived by the Holy Ghost, He was holy because of His Father, the Holy Spirit; yet He was human because of His mother. This to me solves many problems.

This next statement relates to the idea of being conceived by the Holy Spirit: "The Spirit works upon man's heart...implanting in him a new nature as we are born again." COL 411. This word "implanting" has something to do with conception in my understanding of the word. I do not think you would object to Jesus being called the holy thing in this context, would you? It is an entirely different perspective of looking at Him as the holy thing, and it shows how much we can be like Him, for we are made in His likeness as we are born of His Spirit. We are not like Him because of our fallen nature. We are naturally more like Satan.

This brings about a little confusion because when you look at man in his converted condition, he becomes much more like Adam in his perfection before he sinned. Not physically so much because man still has a degenerate, fallen body. We look forward to the day when we will have new bodies, when we will grow up like calves in the stalls, as the Old Testament prophet said. Even though I am encumbered with this degenerate body, I may have a new heart, a whole new nature, and become a new creature in Christ. In our born-again condition, we are much more like Adam than when we were born of our parents. This is speaking mainly of our spiritual likeness to Adam before he fell into sin. Physically we are not very much like him at all. Look at how tall and majestic he was. Once we grasp the fact that Christ was born like man in the second birth, then we understand much more of the argument and the diversions of opinions than if we leave this out.

I think that we are talking about the second birth condition as it relates to the nature of man, because by then man has partaken of divinity as Christ did at His first birth. And once converted and born again by the Spirit, man is able to do some things Christ was doing because Christ enabled man by bringing divinity to us. Therefore, to me it helps greatly to look at this as being like the second birth condition rather than the first birth. I do not believe that Christ ever had to be converted the first time.

Another reason for so many disagreements about the humanity of Christ is His duality of nature. We are told that the disciples "had not understood the mystery of His incarnation, the dual character of His nature." DA 507. "But although Christ's divine glory was for a time veiled and eclipsed by His assuming humanity, yet He did not cease to be God when He became man. The human did not take the place of the divine, nor the divine of the human. This is the mystery of godliness. The two expressions 'human' and 'divine' were, in Christ, closely and inseparably one, and yet they had a distinct individuality." 5BC 1129. These are contradictions to the human mind. They were closely and inseparably one, and yet they had a distinct individuality. Continuing with the quote: "Though Christ humbled Himself to become man, the Godhead was still His own. His deity could not be lost while He stood faithful and true to His loyalty." While He was one He was two, which is exactly what it says. Two distinct natures in Christ while intimately one, closely united, yet they had their distinct individuality. These are marvelous words for us to grapple with. He was like that, but we cannot understand it all that well, which is why it is called a mystery.

In addition to His duality of nature, He had some other positions to fill. He not only represented me and was an example for me and gave me hope as an average man, He also was the second Adam (and all that implied) regarding His position and not His nature. He was the second Adam in position. Adam was the father of all humanity. No matter what person you talk about, if you go back far enough, Adam is their ultimate grandfather. We all came from him. Christ literally becomes the father of all living as the second Adam for He recovers us all from death. "For as in Adam all die, even so in Christ shall all be made alive." 1 Corinthians 15:22. These are marvelous thoughts.

Adam was the king of all this earth and everything in it. His kingship had an influence on all of his kingdom. After his sin, leaves fell from trees for the first time, the weather changed, and one son killed another. I am talking about his influence and his position as the father, as the king, as the head of humanity. These are concepts we do not understand well. We say like father like son, like teacher like student, like king like subjects. It seems to be the function of natural law that we are that way. Christ had many positions to fill, and not just to be like one of us and to help us. He did that, but He did much more, and this we must understand.

Jesus came to be the second Adam in terms of position, and this is confirmed many places in the Spirit of Prophecy. For example, we are told that Jesus "stands at the head of humanity." MH 399. At one time Adam stood at the head of humanity, but now Christ does. Christ takes Adam's place, and in this position as the second Adam, He must conquer where Adam failed; otherwise we are all lost. He must redeem what Adam lost. He must be righteous where Adam was sinful, and He must be righteous for the whole human family. I cannot even be righteous for myself, much less be righteous for you. He must be righteous for all or He is not the Lord our righteousness. He made provision to save the whole human family. There is only one Savior. Adam lost the whole human family, and Jesus, the second Adam, came to save the whole human family. He is a very unusual individual.

"Wherefore, as by one man sin entered into the world, and death by sin; and so death passed upon all men, for that all have sinned…death reigned from Adam to Moses, even over them that had not sinned after the similitude of Adam's transgression, who is the figure of Him that was to come…For if through the offence of one many be dead, much more the grace of God, and the gift by grace, which is by one man, Jesus Christ, hath abounded unto many…For if by one man's offence death reigned by one; much more they which receive abundance of grace and of the gift of righteousness shall reign in life by one, Jesus Christ. Therefore as by the offence of one judgment came upon all men to condemnation; even so by the righteousness of one the free gift came upon all men unto justification of life. For as by one man's disobedience many were made sinners, so by the obedience of one shall many be made righteous." Romans 5:12-19.

The influence of one Person at the head of the human family is vastly different. None of us have been asked to be the head or the father of the human family. We have not been asked to be the Savior, the Redeemer, or the righteousness of the human family. He is all of these. Much has been required of Him, and He fully succeeded in all these roles. This requires unique capabilities, and I am afraid that sometimes we do damage to Jesus in His positions and His many offices when we talk about His humanity. We must be careful about this.

Let us look at just one of His positions to see how it required a unique capability. Look at His position of Savior. Did He save us in His humanity alone? Was the humanity of Christ capable of saving all human beings who ever lived? We read in the Spirit of Prophecy that humanity died, but divinity did not die. Therefore, since that happened, how then did He save us? Was a human being sufficient to save all mankind?

The answer is an important one for us. "No sorrow, no agony, can measure with that which was endured by the Son of God. Man has not been made a sin-bearer, and he will never know the horror of the curse of sin which the Saviour bore. No sorrow can bear any comparison with the sorrow of Him upon whom the wrath of God fell with overwhelming force. Human nature can endure but a limited amount of test and trial. The finite can only endure the finite measure, but the nature of Christ had a greater capacity for suffering; for the human existed in the divine nature, and created a capacity for suffering to endure that which resulted from the sins of a lost world." 5BC 1103.

In other words, something was required for our sins that required a different capacity for suffering than man alone would have. That result required a greater capacity than man alone had. Jesus had it because He had both divinity and humanity, and therefore a greater capacity. The quote continues by saying, "The agony which Christ endured, broadens, deepens, and gives a more extended conception of the character of sin, and the character of the retribution which God will bring upon those who continue in sin. The wages of sin is death, but the gift of God is eternal life through Jesus Christ to the repenting, believing sinner. Justice demanded the sufferings of man; but Christ rendered the sufferings of a God. He needed no atonement of suffering for Himself; all His sufferings were for us." FLB 102.

Jesus provided the sufferings of a God. How much can God suffer? Had only man had to suffer, we would minimize the atonement. And while He suffered in His humanity, divinity also suffered for us. This totality of Jesus produced a capability that pays all my debt and all my punishment; and how happy and grateful we should be. There is no other one like Jesus. He is the one Savior. I am not and you are not. All our hope is found in Him; and He performed all those roles, all those offices and positions for this whole human family.

What an unusual individual Jesus is. By that salvation provided by both His divinity and humanity, I am justified by faith in Him and His righteousness, for He takes away my condemnation, all my sin and guilt, and makes me just. This is all closely related to salvation by grace.

As a result of all these various aspects, it appears to me that Christ did take man's simple nature after four thousand years of sin. But He does not become like man in his natural birth, but rather like man in his rebirth. This does not give Him any advantage that I cannot have. I am still human. I still have to walk this earth faced with all manner of temptations; but now I have an enabling power brought to me by Jesus. This does not give me any advantage, and therefore He can be a perfect example, perfect righteousness, and perfect hope for me.

While He did not take Adam's nature before sin, He performed the requirements of the second Adam. He performed flawlessly and perfectly, yet in the fallen nature of man. It is easy to see why people might think He looks so much like Adam because He is performing all those positions and doing it much better than Adam did. And yet He was tempted much greater than Adam was and thus was at a great disadvantage. It is something that no one else could do. Only that one, unique Person could do that. He is distinctive, He is unique, and we must remember that. There is only one second Adam. No other human being is required to do that. There is only one Savior, there is only one Redeemer, there is only one King of all mankind, and there is only one Lord our righteousness.

All of this centers in Jesus, this most unusual individual. Because of this, I make certain conclusions that you might disagree with. "Wherefore when He cometh into the world, He saith, Sacrifice and offering Thou wouldest not, but a body hast Thou prepared Me." Hebrews 10:5. I believe that this text applies to His birth because of this uniqueness of Christ. I conclude that He was made like us in some ways, but not in all ways; and I also believe He was made like Adam in some ways, but not in all ways. God prepared Him a body, not His mother. There was something different about His body, yet it was very much like ours.

I believe that it was the sacrifice of that body that saves us. "By the which will we are sanctified through the offering of the body of Jesus Christ once for all." Hebrews 10:10. His body was offered because justice required the sufferings of a God as well as the death of a human. The offering of that body saves and justifies. No other one could do that. God in His marvelous plan and design to save you and me made Jesus like that. Every eye and every hope is to center on Him for there is no other one. We must never diminish what He is able to do, for He brought to mankind power from heaven. He is *the* Lamb of God. There is no other. He is not the Lamb of man. He is a Lamb for man, but He is God's Lamb. He belongs to Him. And in order to save us, God offered Him for us.

"For God so loved the world that He gave His only begotten Son...." John 3:16. The Greek term for "only begotten" indicates He was the only one of His kind, a very unique individual. Other translations say "His only son" rather than only begotten son. There is no other one like Him, even though there are many sons of God, such as in Job where it describes how the "sons of God came to present themselves before the Lord." Job 1:6. Jesus is unique, and He became one of us after four thousand years of sin, and identified with us completely by taking our frail human nature and our degeneracy; yet He was still verily God, and in Him was the fullness of the Godhead bodily. He was *unique,* and I think this describes His nature better than any other term.

We have no connection with God except through Jesus. "No man cometh unto the Father, but by Me." John 14:6. That also makes Him unique. All our hope, all our help, all our power, all the enabling is in the divinity of Christ. He trusted in the divinity of His Father, and we trust in His divinity. If He had not come, how utterly helpless we would be, for without Him we can do nothing, according to John 15:5. Therefore everything is in Jesus. All this power that you and I need—the power to recreate fallen man—is in Jesus. That power bridged the gulf of the separation that sin brought, and God came over to our side of the gap in the person of Christ. In no one else is that true; only in Christ. God was coming to man, and He came all the way from divinity, not just from heaven; and He came all the way past the angels, a little lower than them. And still lower because man was fallen, to take our fallen nature that He might bring us power, and salvation, and redemption, and hope, and righteousness.

This is my Jesus, and yours. I may not understand all about Him, but I know He loves me and He loves you. And He did this because you are so extremely precious. Somehow may God help us to grasp in all these discussions the beauty of Jesus, the fullness of what He has done for us, and the enormity of the atonement. How marvelous is the Lord Jesus Christ, our Savior. May God help us to respond in our innermost souls by acknowledging our love for Jesus. There is no one like Him. He is all the world to me. May we accept Him as God gave Him, is my prayer in Jesus' name.

THE LAW IN CHRIST
OUR RIGHTEOUSNESS

THE LAW IS AN important part of the topic of Christ our righteousness, and there is a large controversy concerning it. Many of the advocates of Christ our righteousness are accused of diminishing the importance of the law, and even bypassing it. Those on the other side of the question are accused by many of the advocates of Christ our righteousness as being legalists and of attempting to keep the law in their own strength. Then there is another group of people who emphasize only the spirit of the law and are not so concerned with the letter of the law. They are often termed as permissive or liberal concerning Christian behavior. Each group believes it is right and they are convinced the other is wrong. We have strong differences of opinions, and too often we do not try to sit down and settle these issues in our own hearts. I have learned that when we have such strong differences of opinion, the Lord is trying to teach everyone something, that there is no single group that is totally right or totally wrong, and that somehow we are all missing something. Whenever good people argue, there is correctness on both sides, and we must make the effort to learn where we are wrong.

Seventh-day Adventists have been proud of their teaching of the law, but somehow we have not preached the law correctly or we would not find such statements as this one: "You will meet with those who will say, 'You are too much excited over the matter. You are too much in earnest. You should not be reaching for the righteousness of Christ, and making so much of that. You should preach the law.' As a people we have preached the law until we are as dry as the hills of Gilboa, that had neither dew nor rain. We must preach Christ in the law, and there will be sap and nourishment in the preaching that will be as food to the famishing flock of God." COR 48.

According to the Spirit of Prophecy, we have not preached the law correctly. We sometimes do not like to admit how wrong we can be. If you leave Christ out of the law, as she suggested we have been doing (and I think we still do), you are preaching old covenant law; and supposedly we believe that was gone a long time ago. The law is an integral part of both the Old and the New

297

Testament covenants, but the law is not the same in both places. The Bible finds something wrong with the old covenant of which the largest part was the Ten Commandment law.

Here is what the apostle Paul wrote about the old and new covenants: "For if that first covenant [the old one] had been faultless, then should no place have been sought for the second [the new one]. For finding fault with them, he saith, Behold, the days come, saith the Lord, when I will make a new covenant with the house of Israel and with the house of Judah: Not according to the covenant that I made with their fathers in the day when I took them by the hand to lead them out of the land of Egypt; because they continued not in My covenant, and I regarded them not, saith the Lord." Hebrews 8:7-9. He found fault with the old covenant, of which the Ten Commandments were the largest part.

Does God change His law in the new covenant? Some people say no. Paul provides the answer. "For this is the covenant that I will make with the house of Israel after those days, saith the Lord; I will put My laws into their mind, and write them in their hearts: and I will be to them a God, and they shall be to Me a people." Hebrews 8:10. There is something different about this. Where is the law in the old covenant? It is on stone, and that is the only place it is. Where is the law in the new covenant? The heart. Is there a difference between our hearts and stone tablets? Our hearts are not to be like stone. They are to be soft. There is a difference in the place where you find the law and the two covenants. If you preach the law on stone only, that is entirely old covenant preaching, and we have done very much of that, haven't we? Preaching only the law in stone helps no one. You must also put the law some other place. I find no fault with it being on stone; so do not misunderstand me. There are certain things symbolized by that. But the new covenant promises something better than that. It must be in another place. Therefore, the difference between the law in stone and the law in the heart is primarily a change in location.

Here is a text that we sometimes like to avoid in our discussion with those who disagree with us about the law. "Forasmuch as ye are manifestly declared to be the epistle of Christ ministered by us, written not with ink, but with the Spirit of the living God; not in tables of stone, but in fleshy tables of the heart." 2 Corinthians 3:3. This is speaking specifically about the Ten Commandment law, for not other law was written on "tables of stone." Do not try to evade the fact that this is speaking of the Ten Commandment law or you will make the Scriptures a deception. Under the new covenant, God said He would write the law on the fleshy tables of the heart. The law written on stone is critical and condemning, while that same law written in the heart is made powerful and effective in my life. One is transforming, and one is unchanging. The law does not change, but when it is in my heart it changes me.

There is a vast difference between the two. Suppose you have some medication the doctor prescribed for you, and you keep it in the bottle all the time. How much good does it do for you? But when you open the bottle and take the medication, providing it is the proper medication, and you ingest it, then something happens. Keeping the law outside the heart is like medication in a bottle—it does no one any good. It just looks like beautiful pills. When we take the law inside, then it can go to work on our hearts and change us.

Therefore, the new covenant provides something that the old covenant did not provide. We must be cautious about preaching only the law on stone. We must be certain we preach the law in the heart, also.

What was wrong or faulty about the old covenant? Paul talks about "a better covenant, which was established upon better promises." Hebrews 8:6. There is something better than the old covenant. Ellen White made clear what the problem with the old covenant was. "'For what the law could not do, in that it was weak through the flesh'—it could not justify man, because in his sinful nature he could not keep the law—'God sending His own Son in the likeness of sinful flesh, and for sin, condemned sin in the flesh: that the righteousness of the law might be fulfilled in us, who walk not after the flesh, but after the Spirit.'" PP 373. The law could not change me because in my sinful nature I could not keep it. The law could only condemn me.

"The terms of the 'old covenant' were. Obey and live: 'If a man do, he shall even live in them' (Ezekiel 20:11; Leviticus 18:5); but 'cursed be he that confirmeth not all the words of this law to do them.' Deuteronomy 27:26." PP 372. The terms of the old covenant were that we must obey the Ten Commandment law and live; but if you do not obey them, you will die. And if you do not keep all of them all of the time, you will die. It is not enough to believe that the law is right. Under the law in stone you must keep them all the time and never transgress. Some of us have attempted to live under the old covenant not realizing its requirements. No one has ever succeeded living the old covenant, have they? Therefore, if you teach *only* about the law in stone, you are condemning everyone to eternal death. The law cannot save and we are incapable of keeping it. "Can the Ethiopian change his skin, or the leopard his spots? then may ye also do good, that are accustomed to do evil." Jeremiah 13:23.

You must accept the Bible teachings about man's incapability in righteousness. When you arrive there, then you are ready for God to do something for you that you cannot do. This is the reason for the new covenant. Too many of us are preaching only the law on stone, and it only condemns and frustrates people; and we often act like a condemned people. We have so many guilt feelings, so many problems, we struggle and strive and agonize and do not seem to do any better than we did the day before. This is advertising that we are still trying to live under the old covenant. There the law is only on the stone and not in my heart. We need to change our view on this.

The Scriptures teach that the new covenant is based on better promises. Christ is the Mediator of a better covenant that was established upon better promises. What are the better promises? It is here that we begin to distinguish between the old and the new covenants.

"The 'new covenant' was established upon 'better promises'—the promise of forgiveness of sins and of the grace of God to renew the heart and bring it into harmony with the principles of God's law." PP 372. There was no forgiveness in the old covenant at all. You had to perfectly obey all the time, and that was impossible; and you are never forgiven in the old covenant once you break the law, even once. We can see that one better promise the new covenant is established on is the forgiveness of sins.

Another better promise is the grace of God to renew the heart, which brings it into harmony with the principles of God's law. "This shall be the covenant that I will make with the house of Israel; After those days, saith the Lord, I will put my law in their inward parts, and write it in their hearts. . . . I will forgive their iniquity, and will remember their sin no more." Jeremiah 31:33, 34. God is going to forgive our sins by His grace, and by His grace He is going to renew our hearts and bring them into harmony with the principles of His law. That is different than just leaving it on stone.

Notice that it is not something that I do. I do not bring my life into harmony with His laws. I cannot! By His grace, my life is brought into harmony with His laws, and not by a life long struggle to conform to His laws. He brings me into harmony. It is His activity. It is His work, not my work. He performs a good work in me and in you. This is how it is accomplished. For a long time we have thought that sanctification is a life long struggle to bring our lives into harmony with God's law; but that is not sanctification at all. That is what He accomplishes as He renews my heart by divine grace. By His grace He brings me into harmony with these principles. It is vastly different than we have often taught.

Notice the Bible says, "I will put My laws into their mind, and write them in their hearts." Hebrews 8:10. It also teaches that the law is written "with the Spirit of the living God; not in tables of stone, but in fleshy tables of the heart." 2 Corinthians 3:3. Something is done by a divine agency on my heart, and the heart is the mind. It is not what I do to change the mind, but what He does. Often in Christian living we are trying to change our minds, but we are incapable. He must do this, and He promises to do it, and He wants to do it, and He is able to do it. Thousands have testified that He has done it. Therefore He will do it for you and for me.

The preaching of the law in stone alone will never make us righteous. We need better promises than to obey and live, because none of us have obeyed. We try to obey, but that is not obedience. We must have better promises that come only when God writes the law in our hearts, and only God can accomplish that. We must preach the law in our hearts in addition to the law on tables of stone.

The same is true of Christ our righteousness. You can preach a wonderful message about Christ our righteousness, but it will accomplish little unless Christ has written His law in your heart. We have much fine talk about this subject, but the crux of the whole problem concerns whether the law is written in my heart. Have I experienced this transformation wrought by God? There can be no righteousness in any of us without this transformation.

The law and Christ our righteousness correctly understood are so intertwined and interrelated that you cannot separate them. They are almost like being one and the same thing; but you can talk about them distinctly and separately as different messages and different experiences. But they are so closely related you must always keep them together. We often attempt to preach Christ our righteousness without the law, and we also have tried to preach the law without Christ our righteousness. Therefore, we talk about writing the law in our hearts without even understanding what the law is all about or what Christ our righteousness is all about. They go together.

This quote puts them together: "The same law that was engraved upon the tables of stone is written by the Holy Spirit upon the tables of the heart. Instead of going about to establish our own righteousness we accept the righteousness of Christ [the same context as writing it in our hearts]. His blood atones for our sins. His obedience is accepted for us. Then the heart renewed by the Holy Spirit will bring forth 'the fruits of the Spirit.' Through the grace of Christ we shall live in obedience to the law of God written upon our hearts. Having the Spirit of Christ, we shall walk even as He walked." PP 372. She talks about writing the law in my heart and Christ our righteousness, just back and forth in the very same paragraph. Why? It is all the same, and it is a perversion of Christ our righteousness to teach it without teaching the law in the heart. And it is a perversion of the law to teach it without teaching Christ our righteousness. You are leaving out big portions of either one if you preach one without the other. We have preached the law without Christ our righteousness, and we have succeeded in preaching Christ our righteousness without the law. But this is not the way the Bible or the Spirit of Prophecy presents it. We must put the two together.

"The law requires righteousness,—a righteous life, a perfect character; and this man has not to give. He cannot meet the claims of God's holy law. But Christ, coming to the earth as man, lived a holy life, and developed a perfect character. These He offers as a free gift to all who will receive them. His life stands for the life of men. Thus they have remission of sins that are past, through the forbearance of God. More than this, Christ imbues men with the attributes of God." DA 762. This is that writing in our hearts where He imbues men with the attributes of God. This is something He takes from outside and puts into us. The quote continues: "He builds up the human character after the similitude of the divine character, a goodly fabric of spiritual strength and beauty. Thus the very righteousness of the law is fulfilled in the believer in Christ."

Notice that He imbues men with the attributes of God. He builds up the human character after the similitude of the divine character. I do not build it up. He is the builder. We are the clay, and He is the potter. We are the good ground, and He is the farmer, the husbandman. In Christ our righteousness, He comes and imbues me with the attributes of God, and all this co-mingles back and forth, writing the law in my heart and also Christ as my righteousness in my heart. They are all the same.

You might have difficulty with this, so you need to understand how the law in the heart and Christ our righteousness are the same. How can that be? And secondly, how do you write the law in someone's heart? How do you get it inside? These two things must be made very simple or we will have difficulty in Christianity.

Let us review how Jesus taught the law. "Master, which is the great commandment in the law? Jesus said unto him, Thou shalt love the Lord thy God with all thy heart, and with all thy soul, and with all thy mind. This is the first and great commandment. And the second is like unto it, Thou shalt love thy neighbour as thyself." Matthew 22:36-39. Jesus taught us that the law is supreme love for God and to love our neighbors as ourselves. The Bible teaches that "God is love." 1 John 4:16. And since the law is a transcript of God's character and God is love, the law has to be love. When God writes His law in our hearts, He writes His divine love in our hearts. He does not put the law in stone in the heart (not even for rock hounds). It has to be that way or I am misrepresenting God. I am not sure our law preaching has always accurately represented God.

It appears to me we can make the law very condemning and extremely critical, and I wonder what kind of a God people see when I finish preaching like that? Have I then correctly presented the law that is a transcript of His character? Have I rightly presented the God who sent not His son to condemn the world but through Him the world might be saved? God is love, and the law is love because it is a transcript of His character.

Again, to get the law written in my heart, the love of God must be written there. It is impossible to get the law in stone in the heart; but you can get love into your heart, can you not? People can entice you and woo you until you love them. Love is an activity of the heart in which we are capable; so God can woo us that we might love Him. He wins our love through His goodness. And when His love is in my heart, His law is there, because the law is love and God is love.

We have used this quote several times: "Righteousness is holiness, likeness to God, and 'God is love.' It is conformity to the law of God, for 'all Thy commandments are righteousness,' and 'love is the fulfilling of the law.' Righteousness is love, and love is the light and the life of God. The righteousness of God is embodied in Christ. We receive righteousness by receiving Him." MB 18. So whether it is the law written in my heart, whether it be His righteousness imputed and imparted to me—put into my life—or whether it be His love, it is all the same thing. For the law is love, God is love, righteousness is obedience to the law, and obedience to the law is love. The whole thing is love. The Lord specifically taught that. When I receive Him for righteousness, the law is in Him, and love is in Him. When I receive Him I receive righteousness, I receive the law, and I receive the love of God for me. Therefore, the whole secret of getting the law in the heart is when I love God with all my heart, when I reach out and embrace Jesus and make Him the King of my life, until all my affections and my whole world revolve around Him. Then His love is there, and then His law is there.

Is it clear how you get the law into the heart? You fall in love with Jesus. But how do you fall in love with Jesus? Everything is wrapped up in that question. You can teach doctrine, you can teach truth, you can teach salvation, you can teach Christ our righteousness, you can teach the law, you can teach repentance and confession and conversion and everything else, but you come right down to the most basic essential which is: How do I love Jesus? The greatest thing in Christianity is to love God with all my heart. Then I will love you as myself. All this writing of the law in the heart is encompassed when God puts His love inside of you. It is an activity of God. But in love there is no force. There are pressures but they are different kinds of pressures. The love of God constrains us. It is a gentle, drawing type of pressure, a wooing, an enticing, an alluring thing, not sticking you with a pin and condemning or accusing. It is something that wins us rather than pushes us. The Bible says, "We love Him, because He first loved us." 1 John 4:19. If I find a lack of love in my heart for Him or for you, I somehow have not seen His love for me or for you.

The sequence involved in falling in love with Jesus is described in the Spirit of Prophecy. "The light shining from the cross reveals the love of God. His love is drawing us to Himself. If we do not resist this drawing, we shall be led to the foot of the cross in repentance for the sins that have crucified the Saviour." DA 176. There is only one way you can avoid coming to the cross, and that is to dig your heels in and put on the brakes and say, "I will not come." When you resist it long enough, you hardly sense you are putting on the brakes. When you live like that so long it becomes automatic. How do you like riding opposite the driver when they come so close to a big truck up in front or they take the corners very rapidly. Why do you straighten up with your feet hard against the floor? Some people live like that incessantly. The cross is drawing them but they are always putting on the brakes. You can come to church all the time with the brakes on. You can almost see the smoke and smell it in church. They say, "I will not be drawn no matter what He says." We are not fighting with human beings. As the Lord said to Saul, "It is hard for you to kick against the pricks." And Paul asked, "Who are you?" "I am the Lord Jesus. You are not fighting with anybody else, you are fighting with Me."

All the time you keep the brakes on you are fighting the love of Christ that constrains us. We look at our watches because we do not want to hear. We look at the hymnbook trying not to hear. We do all sorts of things trying not to hear; and we become well established in the habit of smoking brakes. The idea of being drawn to the cross causes some kind of fear inside. Do you have to be afraid with Jesus? If you have to fear anyone, fear other people for they are all sinners who might do wrong things to you; but do not be afraid of Him. We need to learn to discern that Jesus is wooing us, enticing us, and speaking kind words to draw us to Him.

He draws us by the love of the cross, and if we do not resist, He will lead us to the foot of the cross in repentance. "Then the Spirit of God through faith produces a new life in the soul. The thoughts and desires are brought into obedience to the will of Christ. The heart, the mind, are created anew in the image of Him who works in us to subdue all things to Himself. Then the law of God is written in the mind and heart, and we can say with Christ, 'I delight to do Thy will, O my God.' Ps. 40:8." DA 176.

There is something very joyful and pleasant about having the law in my heart. It is exciting, good, and peaceful. I delight to do the law when it is in my heart. But it is a different kind of delight, a different kind of joy than just having fun. The law in the heart does something wonderful for us for it brings that peace that we all need.

Nicodemus, who was a scholarly and spiritual man, asked Jesus, "How can these things be?" John 3:9. He was an educated man and thought he understood everything; yet he had to ask Jesus to explain how a person can be born again. It seems that the Lord did not answer him. Try to find the specific answer to Nicodemus' question. It's as if the Lord was being a little evasive. Christ finally explained to him what He was trying to say about the new life, and He referred to the experience of the brazen serpent where the children of Israel were bitten by poisonous serpents and were dying. A serpent made of brass was put up on a pole, and all who looked at it would live.

The following quotation discusses the thinking of those people and of Nicodemus, and I think it applies to us as the Lord tries to draw us to the cross and to His love: "Whether for the healing of their wounds or the pardon of their sins, they could do nothing for themselves but show their faith in the Gift of God. They were to look and live. Those who had been bitten by the serpents might have delayed to look. They might have questioned how there could be efficacy in that brazen symbol. They might have demanded a scientific explanation. But no explanation was given. They must accept the word of God to them through Moses. To refuse to look was to perish." DA 175.

How does that settle into your heart? Imagine yourself in that situation, bitten by serpents and with only a short time to live. A doctor comes along and says he has no medicine for you. Moses is busy praying only for those people who had not been bitten. Then you hear the Lord tell Moses to make an inanimate object of brass and raise it up before the people, and the word goes out that everybody who looks at it will live. Moses, who had a university education in Egypt, forgot all that his teachers had taught him, because there was no science in this that he could see. He told the people to look at the brass serpent and live. Would you like to explain that to a science class somewhere? They would laugh at you. And we laugh at it, or at least are skeptics, and we ask, "How can these things be?" The Lord says that just how His remedy worked is not important, but only that you do what is required. If you do not look you die. If you look you live. Some people don't like that, and God knows it. It requires faith, and some do not like faith. We are to walk by faith, not by sight. So He says, "Look and live."

"There are thousands today who need to learn the same truth that was taught to Nicodemus by the uplifted serpent. They depend on their obedience to the law of God to commend them to His favor. When they are bidden to look to Jesus, and believe that He saves them solely through His grace, they exclaim, 'How can these things be?'" DA 175. This is our big problem today. We are so scientific, so well educated, and so logical. We have figured out every little detail of our doctrine a thousand times to prove we are right. But how can you prove what happened there in the wilderness? Only by testimonies, only by witnesses, and there is no other way. The only evidence came from those who tried it and did not die.

Those who in faith look unto Jesus are new creatures in Christ; and those who are not looking are dying. We have the word of God and we have the testimony of those who have experienced it. That leaves some of us uncomfortable, and we ask for proof. Those who have experienced it say, "Look and live." But many do not listen and go away dissatisfied.

The quote continues on to talk about what Nicodemus learned from this. "Not through controversy and discussion is the soul enlightened. We must look and live. Nicodemus received the lesson, and carried it with him. He searched the Scriptures in a new way, not for the discussion of a theory, but in order to receive life for the soul. He began to see the kingdom of heaven as he submitted himself to the leading of the Holy Spirit."

There are some things we will never understand well, but if the right Person is leading me, and I know He loves me, and I follow Him, He will lead me rightly even though I do not understand why. My God has given me thousands of reasons to prove that He is a God of love, and that He does not mislead, and that He will not hurt or harm me. His question to me is: Can you trust Me? He does not ask if we understand, just whether we trust Him. If we trust Him, look and you will live. If you have never been in a place where you had to trust your life to another person, you probably do not understand all this, and you may be fearful. When you have been in that position a few times, you begin to find out that there are many things in life to which you have to entrust everything to one person. Is there anyone as trustworthy as Jesus? Yet how often we mistrust Him and trust ourselves.

The Bible talks about sin being blindness and darkness, and it truly is. It isn't a matter of not having the capacity to understand how, but an incapability of believing and an unwillingness to look without answers to every question, until there is no faith. The Bible says we walk by faith and not by sight. Believe that He is a God of love, believe that He wants to bless you, believe that He can do this for you, and look because He commands it, and you will live. What a terrible time we have these days just simply believing.

The matter of believing and looking and acting on the commands of Jesus is described in an experience of a man who had been crippled for thirty-eight years, and who came every day to the pool of Bethesda hoping to be healed. "The poor sufferer was helpless; he had not used his limbs for thirty-eight years. Yet Jesus bade him, 'Rise, take up thy bed, and walk.' The sick man might have said, 'Lord, if Thou wilt make me whole, I will obey Thy word.' But, no, he believed Christ's word, believed that he was made whole, and he made the effort at once; he willed to walk, and he did walk. He acted on the word of Christ, and God gave the power. He was made whole." SC 50. He believed the impossible, and he was healed.

Notice the sequence. First was the command, then the belief, and then acting on the belief and the command. We usually say we will act first. I will do good and then He will love me and accept me. Then I can follow Him. Jesus did not put it that way. He bids us first to rise up, to walk. We believe Him because He is so good and so trustworthy, and then we act on the command. And that is the obedience of righteousness. It comes in that order.

"In like manner you are a sinner [just like the helpless paralytic]. You cannot atone for your past sins; you cannot change your heart and make yourself holy. But God promises to do all this for you through Christ. You believe that promise. You confess your sins and give yourself to God. You will to serve Him. Just as surely as you do this, God will fulfill His word to you. If you believe the promise—believe that you are forgiven and cleansed—God supplies the fact; you are made whole, just as Christ gave the paralytic power to walk when the man believed that he was healed. It is so if you believe it. Do not wait to feel that you are made whole, but say, 'I believe it; it is so, not because I feel it, but because God has promised.'" SC 51.

It all depends on the trustworthiness of Jesus, the centrality of Christ my Savior and Christ my righteousness. Jesus is all the world to me. When you look to Him in faith, you live. Our problem is our unwillingness to look in faith and to realize that looking to Jesus makes us whole. Everything is accomplished by looking unto Jesus, the Author and the Finisher of our faith. Everything! He is righteousness, He is love, He is law, He is obedience, He is salvation. We put so many things in His place or in the way. Allow the beauty of Christ to attract you with the magnetism of the cross. "And I, if I be lifted up from the earth, will draw all men unto me." John 12:32.

The cross has a kind of magnetism, and if you do not resist, if you allow yourself to submit to be drawn to Him, He will bring you right to the foot of the cross. And there your heart will be melted. Being at the foot of the cross is a humbling experience, but it is miserable to be away from Him. But the humility lasts only for a short time. There my heart is broken by love, not by ridicule or condemnation or criticism. As He breaks my heart, as I recognize what I have been doing to Him, then by His Spirit He writes His law in my heart. My sins are taken away at the cross. He imputes His righteousness to me, and we can live together because sins no longer separate. And we walk together, my Lord and I. I delight to do His will for His law is in my heart. It is a thrilling, joyful, ecstatic experience. There is nothing like it.

I beg you to look into your heart for this experience. He has not stopped drawing people. The cross still allures and appeals. He still draws everyone who looks as He is lifted up. If you find emptiness in your heart, and hardness like the stone tablets of the law instead of tenderness and a love for souls, let the cross draw you. Take off the brakes and He will draw you faster and faster as you approach the cross. Then linger there. Just stay there. Don't run away so quickly. Let your heart bask in His love and sacrifice and the manifestation of it. Realize that the cross is for you, and that Jesus would have died for only one soul. It was all for me that He did that. Let your heart be filled with that scene until you cannot take your eyes off of Him. You will ask, "How can this be?" You will begin to realize it is not because we are good, but because of His marvelous grace. Look full into His wonderful face until His radiance of love fills your own heart. Fight against the doubt, not against the drawing, until Christ becomes the hub of everything in your life.

I believe we have been pretending to be Christians for years, ministers and lay members going through the motions without the law in our heart. Trying and striving and frustrated and condemned and guilty until church can become miserable. We feel criticized when the Lord really wants to say, "You are forgiven, and you are Mine." He wants to make it possible and probable for people to be law keepers. By His marvelous presence in our lives we are able to do things we never thought possible.

The Lord wants the world to see Jesus in you and me. All the impossible things of the work will be accomplished when that greatest miracle of all, the law in my heart and in your heart, is accomplished. The work will become easy in the Middle East and in China and Russia. How can they resist such love? They would all have to be rocks, just unfeeling and hard. People are not like that. The Lord is waiting for His love to melt the hard hearts of people all around the earth, but He wants to start in your heart today.

Before you close this book, open your heart. Believe Him when He says He will write His law, His love, in your heart. There is nothing like that. It is so unbelievable. All that you hope for in Christianity is found in those few words, "I will put My laws into their mind, and write them in their hearts: and I will be to them a God, and they shall be to Me a people." May God so fill your heart with His love and His law and His righteousness that you will shout for joy and praise His holy name.

THE ILLNESS
AND THE MEDICINE

AS YOU HAVE PROGRESSED through these studies, you have noticed how there are various aspects of Christ our righteousness that are often misinterpreted and cause misunderstanding. This chapter will deal with a conflict, or disagreement, that arises between our public relations efforts as an organized denomination and the truths of Christ our righteousness. Most probably do not realize that there is a disagreement between the two.

Let me first explain how our public relations operate. In our publications, in interviews and speeches, and in other ways, we advertise how successful we are as a people and as a denomination. We tell about how we are building more schools, hospitals, and churches, and how we are growing with more member and students. We advertise our success in the mission field and with health programs and community service work. We love to read good reports about all these things; and in fact many swell with pride when they see those reports that advertise what a wonderful work we are doing. We feel good that we belong to such a movement as this. We like to revel in the fact that Seventh-day Adventists live longer due to a better lifestyle. We like it when the world is told that we have better health, less cancer, and more endurance than the rest of the population. We announce to the world that we give more offerings, have more schools and more missions in foreign countries than any other protestant denomination.

Don't you like hearing about all these things? Your mind is probably quite suspicious about where I am going with this; but is it not true that we say and write these things? Yes we do, and when they appear in newspapers, magazines, and on television, we say, "Yes, that is us. It is wonderful and you ought to try it. There is no one like us." And we swell with pride.

This emphasis on the good work we are doing draws certain conclusions, one of which is that God must be abundantly blessing us or we could not do all those things. Since God is blessing us and we are doing so many right things, we conclude that we must be right with God. In order to finish God's work, all we have to do is get more people doing the same thing we are already doing. Do not change anything because we are too successful. Just keep sending out more glowing reports. Since this is the attitude that many have, it leads to a certain conclusion in the minds of many that all is well with us and that God is prospering us. We need nothing, except more people. And that worries me because that is the condition that the True Witness (Jesus) speaks about in Revelation 3:17. We think we are blessed and rich and have no needs, but the True Witness does not think this is a good attitude. In fact, it is a detrimental attitude.

This attitude is the mortal enemy of Christ our righteousness. We think that those who criticize us and undermine our public relations efforts are against us. We think that those who advertise how good we are must be on our team and doing us a favor. But good public relations that lead us to say we are doing very well when Jesus thinks otherwise is the enemy of Christ our righteousness. Not only are they mortal enemies, but complete opposites. What we have called a blessing is really a curse in many ways.

I know you might not agree with me, and that is your privilege. I only hope you will examine some of these thoughts. The condition of being in need of nothing keeps Christ outside, according to Revelation 3:20. The absence of Christ or the presence of Christ makes an enormous difference.

It is a fact that we have grown in numbers quite rapidly, and also have increased our number of schools, churches, hospitals, projects, and missions. There has been tremendous growth and we do have great successes in many ways. Therefore, we are doing great things for Him and He is doing great things for us. Why then does the Spirit of Prophecy seem to criticize us so strongly when according to our estimation we are so successful? Those who like our public relations efforts do not like the criticism. Those who focus on the criticism do not like the public relations. We have some major differences of opinion concerning our church.

Don't get too upset with me as I present here some Spirit of Prophecy quotations that cover a broad area of so-called criticism. I am only trying to help us see a problem that exists which creates confusion. "It is a solemn statement that I make to the church, that not one in twenty whose names are registered upon the church books are prepared to close their earthly history, and would be as verily without God and without hope in the world as the common sinner." CS 41. In other words, they go to church and do lots of good things, but they are as hopeless of entering heaven as the common sinner.

"Not one in a hundred among us is doing anything beyond engaging in common, worldly enterprises." 8T 148. That means only about one percent are doing anything for the Lord. The rest are mostly engaged in worldly enterprises.

"The new birth is a rare experience in this age of the world. This is the reason why there are so many perplexities in the churches. Many, so many, who assume the name of Christ are unsanctified and unholy. They have been baptized, but they were buried alive. Self did not die, and therefore they did not rise to newness of life in Christ." 6BC 1075. There are many unconverted people who profess conversion.

"And what has caused this alarming condition [where those who profess to look for the return of Jesus engage in worldly pleasures]? Many have accepted the theory of the truth who have had no true conversion." 5T 218.

"I am filled with sadness when I think of our condition as a people. The Lord has not closed heaven to us, but our own course of continual backsliding has separated us from God. Pride, covetousness, and love of the world have lived in the heart without fear of banishment or condemnation. Grievous and presumptuous sins have dwelt among us. And yet the general opinion is that the church is flourishing and that peace and spiritual prosperity are in all her borders. The church has turned back from following Christ her Leader and is steadily retreating toward Egypt. Yet few are alarmed or astonished at their want of spiritual power." 5T 217. It does not seem to bother us that we lack in spiritual power. We are complacent and happy, and that is why we are lukewarm.

Here is a classic statement that many have read: "There is not one in one hundred who understands for himself the Bible truth on this subject [justification by faith] that is so necessary to our present and eternal welfare." COR 87.

Do all of these statements apply only to the time in which they were written? In your estimation, are we much better than they were? About the same? Worse? What do these things mean today, if anything? If you believe that these statements apply to our day, you probably are not promoting good public relations for the church. If you do not believe these things apply to our day, you probably like to hear glowing reports of our success. Some think that those who do not give a glowing report are against the church, and that those who do are on our team. Again, I want to let you know that this public relations concept is totally contrary to Christ our righteousness, because Christ our righteousness assumes we have a tremendous need that is not being taken care of.

Does the Laodicean message, which is identified with these criticisms, have any application today? Or has it been terminated? Has it carried out its task and completed its work so you do not have to worry about it? "I asked the meaning of the shaking I had seen and was shown that it would be caused by the straight testimony called forth by the council of the true witness of the Laodiceans." 2SG 270. In other words, that Laodicean message will cause a shaking among us. Have you seen the shaking? Is it completed? If not, then the Laodicean message has not completed its work and still must be in effect today. Therefore, what it has to say about the church must still apply.

"It [meaning the Laodicean message] was designed to arouse the people of God to discover to them their backslidings, and lead to zealous repentance, that they might be favored for the presence of Jesus, and be fitted for the loud cry of the third angel." 2SG 224. Have you seen the loud cry yet? Is the third angel's message going everywhere? Then we still need the Laodicean message.

These quotations say that the criticisms of the Laodicean message are still in effect today. Why does Ellen White make such strong statements concerning the church? Why does God say those things about us when we seem to be enjoying such success? How can we have such conflicts or contradictions concerning the same movement? The problem is with what you term success and how you judge success. If success is numbers, if success is more schools and hospitals, if success is bigness, if success is materialism and wealth, if success is acclaim and prestige, then we are very successful. Our articles and statements from the pulpit quote bigness, and growth, and numbers, and acclaim, and prestige; and we say that all of this establishes that God is blessing us, that we are successful in doing a great work for Him. If that is success, then we are successful; but there are other denominations that are more successful than we are. Some churches make us look like tiny ants by their hundreds of millions of dollars in wealth and by their bigness. We do not look so successful by comparison. Yet many believe that things like growth rate are the criterion for success.

There are evidences of success other than these. The criteria we have used are the standards of the world regarding success. Apparently the True Witness, who is Jesus, has a different yardstick when it comes to measuring success. In Revelation 3:17, He points out five defects, or deficiencies, in this church. The defects are described by these words: wretched, miserable, poor, blind, and naked. Those terms cover a wide territory. In verse 18 there are three remedies for those defects, which are gold, white raiment, and eye salve. The deficiencies and remedies are all found there in just two verses. I want you to notice that the source of all the remedies is found in one statement of the True Witness: "Buy of Me." Everything we need, everything we must have, every deficiency will be supplied in Christ. He has it all; just buy of Him. Somehow we are not responding to His knock on the door; therefore, we lack those riches that He is there to offer to us.

Laodicea's lack of success and her deficiencies are due to the lack of Christ. He is outside attempting to obtain entrance. This is a different measure of success than we usually think about. Do you measure the success of your home by the presence of Jesus? Do you measure the success of a hospital, or a school, or a church by the presence of Christ in its members or the institution? We never talk about that. We talk about the other standards and criteria (bigness, wealth, growth) in all our articles and speeches, but Christ in us is hardly ever mentioned. We assume He must be there or we would not have the bigness and the growth, but Jesus does not equate the two. Bigness and the presence of Christ are not synonymous, for His church was exceedingly small and poor when He left this earth; yet it was successful. Look at the power of its members and their total dedication to Him.

Laodicea believes she is rich and successful and does not need anything, including Jesus; but she does not have Jesus according to the True Witness. He is on the outside trying to get in. But she says she is comfortable and satisfied and successful. This is a deception. Christians can be Christless and not know that Christ is not in them, or in their church, or movement, or hospital. Their main deficiency is the absence of Jesus.

In Christianity, there is no success without Jesus. If He is absent, there is no Christianity. We might call it that, we might try to prove it from the Bible, we might argue for it, we might show many good works, but without Jesus there is no Christianity. And it is not just thinking about Him. True Christianity and its success are measured by its likeness to Christ, and there is no other yardstick. We cannot compare ourselves with ourselves, or our denomination with another denomination. The only comparison, the only yard stick, the only standard, is Jesus. This is much different than the world's concepts of success. The world is unlike Christ and Christ is unlike the world; therefore their standards are very different.

The True Witness says in Revelation 3:20: "I will come in to him [the one who opens the door]." Jesus is knocking, and if you hear His voice and open the door, He will come in. He is outside but He wants inside. The presence of Christ determines success.

Note these words of Paul: "To whom God would make known what is the riches of the glory of this mystery among the Gentiles; which is Christ in you, the hope of glory: Whom we preach, warning every man, and teaching every man in all wisdom; that we may present every man perfect in Christ Jesus." Colossians 1: 27,28. These riches that we should consider as the criteria of success are contained in the expression: "Christ in you, the hope of Glory." We do not preach *about* Christ. We preach Christ. That is a different idea than most of us think about.

Having Christ is having true riches. Laodicea says they are rich, but He says they have the wrong riches. All those riches we have focused on will be destroyed. Every Seventh-day Adventist hospital, every school, every church, will come crumbling down. All these things shall pass away permanently. They are not eternal success. But Christ shall never cease, and those who possess Him have more than things. He is from everlasting to everlasting. Without Him we are poor, no matter how much wealth, or education, or knowledge we have. In that sense, all who are without Christ are poor; but He has promised that He will be with us if we open the door. Nothing can take the place of His presence.

There are many texts regarding the presence of Christ. "Lo, I am with you alway." Matthew 28:20. "I will not leave you comfortless: I will come to you."

John 14:18. "At that day ye shall know that I am in My Father, and ye in Me, and I in you." John 14:20. "I in them, and Thou in Me." John 17:23.

Jesus, in His sermon on the mount, said, "Ask, and it shall be given you; seek, and ye shall find; knock, and it shall be opened unto you." Matthew 7:7. Ellen White discussed the word "seek" in this verse: "Desire not merely His blessing, but Himself. 'Acquaint now thyself with Him, and be at peace.' Job 22:21. Seek, and you shall find. God is seeking you, and the very desire you feel to come to Him is but the drawing of His Spirit. Yield to that drawing. Christ is pleading the cause of the tempted, the erring, and the faithless. He is seeking to lift them into companionship with Himself. 'If thou seek Him, He will be found of thee.' 1 Chronicles 28:9." MB 131. Do not just ask Him to help you or bless you. Ask for *Him*. That is different from the way we usually pray.

We should desire and seek not only for His blessing, but Himself. What He gives is not as important as what He is. If you go to a wealthy man and ask him for money, and he gives you a few dollars, that is a blessing to you if you are poor. Now you have the money. But is there something better? How would you like to have *him,* the person who has all the money, and not just the amount you asked for? Don't just ask for Christ's blessing; ask for Him. Are you content with things when you may have the God of heaven as yours?

Christianity is not just receiving blessings from God. Christianity is having God all the time. He promised to be with us always, and never to forsake us because we are so precious to Him. It is not enough to know about Him; you must know Him. "And this is life eternal, that they might know Thee the only true God, and Jesus Christ, Whom Thou hast sent." John 17:3. It is not just receiving the truth about Jesus, it is receiving Jesus as the truth, in His very person. It is more than receiving the law on stone tablets as the standard of righteousness. It is receiving Jesus into my heart who is the very personification of the law. He is the standard of righteousness and obedience. He is the law perfectly lived out. Receive Him and you receive the law and the character of the Father. It is not receiving a principle of love alone. It is receiving Christ who is love by His very nature. It is not receiving Christ as a sacrifice who died two thousand years ago for us. It is receiving Christ in person who sacrificed for me. Receive Him as your sacrifice, as your hope, as your righteousness. We must embrace Him, and not simply accept information about Him. As we have already pointed out, it is not so much the *what* and the *how* of Christianity, but the *Who*. Christianity is Christ. Success in Christianity is Jesus. It is not just doing everything right. It is possessing Him in all His rightness, and goodness, and love. Laodicea has an absence of Jesus and they do not even know that they can be richer than they are. When Christ is outside trying to get in, we have no love, no hope, no truth, no righteousness. He is the only source of those things.

As long as we persist in using the world's criteria, we will look quite successful; but when you begin to judge Christianity by the presence or absence of Jesus, then what about our public relations? We must learn that Christ is everything. The Greeks went down to Jerusalem and said, "Sir, we would see Jesus." John:12:21. They did not say they wanted to see the temple. But "His disciples came to Him for to shew Him the buildings of the temple." Matthew 24:1. They were proud of that physical structure. But Jesus answered them by saying, "See ye not all these things? verily I say unto you, There shall not be left here one stone upon another, that shall not be thrown down." Verse 2.

In the days of Hezekiah, the people were shown all the wealth, all the things that God had given them when they came over from Babylon; and when they came back to get those things they ended up being slaves. Hezekiah never did show them his God. Instead, he showed them the things that God had blessed them with; and they became envious and came back from Babylon to obtain those things, even the vessels of the temple.

When people come to our churches, they are not impressed with our carpet, or chandeliers, or pews, or even us. Many come seeking only Jesus. But we take them on a tour of our edifices and all our modern facilities. Those things do not help the people who are hurting and depressed. They do not help the guilty. They do not help those who are ready to give up hope when they feel lost. They need Jesus, not a church building with fancy carpet. They want to see Jesus in us, and not just hear lectures about Him. Many thousands have come to our churches looking for Jesus. Do they find Him? Are you sure? It seems that today the world is crying out, "We want to see Jesus. Where is He?"

Apart from Him, Laodicea looks pretty good, but not so good when He comes in. Recall our previous quote that "The church has turned back from following Christ her Leader and is steadily retreating toward Egypt." 5T 217. Then at the bottom of the page and on over to page 218: "Have we not been seeking the friendship and applause of the world rather than the presence of Christ?" We get very satisfied when the world says nice things about us; but this, too, shall pass away. Do they find Jesus in our churches? Do we seek His presence more than acclaim and prestige and bigness? Without Jesus in my heart, there is no conversion, and I have no new covenant experience where the law is written in my heart.

This brings up another problem. The Spirit of Prophecy has much to say about our lack of conversion. Do you realize that most of us interpret and understand Christ our righteousness by our experience? We try to see how it fits into our experience, and we sometimes assume we have been converted when we might not have been; and we are told that few have been. Then our understanding of Christ our righteousness is also perverted, judging by our experience. We begin to say that Christ our righteousness must be like this because nothing else will fit our experience. Try to discuss the last dozen or so verses of Romans 7 with someone without putting it in the context of your own experience. We almost entirely interpret those texts by our experience, not by the truthfulness of it.

Christ our righteousness is determined by the presence of Jesus, not your experience. If Christ is in you, you have His righteousness; if He is not in you, you do not. I will not go into all the ramifications of that. He is the only standard of success that exists in the Christian church, and there is no other standard. The Bible promises that we may literally have Christ in us, yet how seldom we think that we may have Him. We think about so many other things. It is the presence of Jesus that determines whether or not Laodicea sees her poverty. She looks good without Him, but she looks bad when He comes in.

"The closer you come to Jesus, the more faulty you will appear in your own eyes; for your vision will be clearer, and your imperfections will be seen in broad and distinct contrast to His perfect nature. This is evidence that Satan's delusions have lost their power; that the vivifying influence of the Spirit of God is arousing you. No deep-seated love for Jesus can dwell in the heart that does not realize its own sinfulness. The soul that is transformed by the grace of Christ will admire His divine character; but if we do not see our own moral deformity, it is unmistakable evidence that we have not had a view of the beauty and excellence of Christ." SC 64.

When I am without Jesus, I look good to myself. As long as I can keep Him far enough away, so I never see Him, I think I look wonderful; but as soon as I am brought into His presence, I will be like Isaiah when he exclaimed, "Woe is me! for I am undone; because I am a man of unclean lips, and I dwell in the midst of a people of unclean lips: for mine eyes have seen the King, the Lord of hosts." Isaiah 6:5. When we have seen the King, we feel vile in His presence. Does that mean I am lost? Not a bit. The fact that He permits you into His presence means that you are not lost. He just wants you to discover some things you did not know. When He comes in, we look bad to ourselves; but we are blessed because Christ is there. When we look good to ourselves, we are failures because Christ is not there.

It bothers me when I hear us singing such beautiful music about how good we are. It makes many of us feel elated, and we think that God must be for us or we couldn't be so thrillingly successful. Nothing, no matter how beautiful, no matter how magnificent, no matter how much sacrifice required to do it, no building, no institution, no organization, no group, nothing can take the place of Jesus. Nothing! There is no one like Christ, and we can never find satisfaction in institutions and things, unless we have Jesus, and know that we have Him. Then Christianity is Christianity because Jesus is there. Then the hovel or tent or cottage becomes a temple as long as Jesus is there. Poverty becomes riches because I have Jesus. Nothing can offend, nothing can upset because Jesus is there. This is the only standard of true Christianity that ever existed. You cannot find the success of the original New Testament church in things, for they hardly had a church, and they surely did not have a temple; and yet the Lord commended them.

Friend, I do not know whether you are able to think about this well. Our prejudices become strong and obliterate clear thinking about true Christian success. We feel picked on and criticized when we look at success as the Bible and the Spirit of Prophecy teach it. We object, and the truth is that the critics are sometimes our best friends, and those who tell us about our good public relations are our worst enemies, even though they mean well. They are lulling us to sleep and into complacency so we will not understand we are Christless until it is too late. We wish those who sound negative and pessimistic would be quiet and let us slumber on, but that is a dangerous condition.

Jesus is so wonderful, He is so precious, He is everything, and we must go back and make sure He dwells in our hearts and that we have not walked off and left Him. The illness of the church is the absence of Jesus. But we may literally possess Him, for God so loved the world He gave Him to us. "But as many as received Him, to them gave He power to become the sons of God, even to them that believe on His name." John 1:12. "He that hath the Son hath life." 1 John 5: 11,12. You may have Him. God so loved the world that He did not just give us power and health and blessings of all types. He gave us of Himself in the person of Jesus. You may have Him, for God has given Him to you. If you merely accept the material things He has, He will say as a wealthy man once said to me, "You love my money but you do not love me." Many love Jesus' power but they do not love Jesus. They want His power to heal them or to give them all manner of things, but they do not love Him. They want Him to bring peace into the home and help them, and they love His help, but they do not want Him to stay. They want His help for more money and more education and more this and more that, but they do not want Jesus.

Jesus says we may have Him. Will you receive Him? Will you embrace Him and fall in love with Him so that you will never let Him go? Do you want Him, or do you want what He has and what He is able to do for you?

It is like a man whose plumbing gets stopped up in the middle of the night, so he calls a good friend and asks for his help. His friend goes over and fixes the plumbing, and the next day the man sees the plumber on the street and does not even say hello to him or thank him. We do that to Jesus. In my desperations and emergencies, I cry out for God to help me. Fix my emotions, fix my heart, fix my family, fix my job. And He asks, "When are we going to be friends so that we will never part? When will you want Me and not just My help?"

The Bible says, "Seek ye the Lord while He may be found, call ye upon Him while He is near." Isaiah 55:6. He has been knocking a long time, and Laodicea has said, "Don't bother us, we are doing fine." God wants us to see that this is a strange kind of deception, this idea that Christians do not need Christ. Has a person truly discovered what Christianity is all about if they think they can get along without Jesus? Jesus has watched us going along with all our worldly ideas of success, but knowing that we have not seen Him. And all the time He is knocking because He wants to come in and be with us. What a different church, a different home, a different school or hospital we will see when Jesus comes in and abides in the hearts of our people.

Some will take all this as violent criticism and go away with a dismal, hopeless attitude. The Lord does not want that. He is asking, "How can you get along without Me? How can you leave Me outside your heart and then sing, 'Jesus is all the world to me'? How can you call this Christianity when you do not possess Me? How can you talk about Me and not know Me?" He wants to gather us unto Himself and give us life eternal. The most pathetic person I can think of is a Christian who is without Jesus.

Many Adventists who are awaiting His return have not found Him. The Lord is not pointing the finger and finding fault and condemning. He is hurt that we could substitute all these things for the beauties of Jesus. He cannot imagine how you could love a building or an institution more than Him. He cannot imagine how you can love money or blessings more than Him. It is unbelievable to Him. He cannot imagine how you keep asking Him for help but do not want Him. Today He is knocking and asking, "When will you let Me inside and keep Me there and never let go? Christ is the medicine for all our spiritual illness.

Seek not just for His blessings, but for Jesus Himself. This is Christ our righteousness, for He is righteous. This is Christ our Savior, for He is salvation. This is Christ our love, and this is Christ our success. This is everything, for Christ is everything. And when you let Him inside, then the Christian is successful because Jesus is there.

There is nothing so precious as Jesus. May we this day choose Christ above every other thing and every other person until He is truly all the world to you and to me.

29

OUR BLIND
SPOT

WHAT IS RIGHTEOUSNESS? WE discussed this in a previous chapter, but here we will examine this subject from a different viewpoint. There are many views as to what righteousness is. Jesus indicated that when He said, "For I say unto you, That except your righteousness shall exceed the righteousness of the scribes and Pharisees, ye shall in no case enter into the kingdom of heaven." Matthew 5:20. Apparently, the Pharisees assumed they were righteous, but the Lord said that except our righteousness exceeds theirs, there is no way we can enter into the kingdom of heaven.

The Pharisees had their own unique idea of righteousness, which was described by Ellen White. "The greatest deception of the human mind in Christ's day was that a mere assent to the truth constitutes righteousness. In all human experience a theoretical knowledge of the truth has been proved to be insufficient for the saving of the soul. It does not bring forth the fruits of righteousness. A jealous regard for what is termed theological truth often accompanies a hatred of genuine truth as made manifest in life." DA 309.

She goes on to describe how those who professed to be righteous killed Christ because of His righteous life. Then she makes this statement: "The same danger still exists. Many take it for granted that they are Christians, simply because they subscribe to certain theological tenets. But they have not brought the truth into practical life. They have not believed and loved it, therefore they have not received the power and grace that come through sanctification of the truth. Men may profess faith in the truth; but if it does not make them sincere, kind, patient, forbearing, heavenly-minded, it is a curse to its possessors, and through their influence it is a curse to the world." You can have the truth and be a curse to yourself and to mankind. We can call it finishing the Lord's work by going to far off fields with our theological truth, but if it does not make us kind, patient, forbearing, heavenly-minded, then our truth is not blessing us. Truth must be brought into the heart and into the life in order to be a blessing. For a long time we have thought that, as long as we have the truth, that would be sufficient; but it is far from sufficient.

"A profession of faith and the possession of truth in the soul are two different things. The mere knowledge of truth is not enough. We may possess this, but the tenor of our thoughts may not be changed. The heart must be converted and sanctified." COL 97. This strikes too close to home to be comfortable for any of us. The fact that we say we have the truth and are theologically correct creates a great problem for us. The Jews professed the same philosophy. Since we have ascribed to and received certain truths, we feel quite safe in concluding that we must be righteous, or at least on the road to righteousness. We have been baptized into the right church, we believe and teach right doctrines, we practice many right doctrines such as Sabbath keeping, tithing, and observing high standards; and so we logically ask how we can be unrighteous under such circumstances. Others do not have all these things, and therefore they are unrighteous; and since we have them and practice them, we must be righteous.

I would like to suggest that you examine that part of the Sermon on the Mount where Jesus brought up the issue concerning the Jews and how their righteousness must exceed the righteousness of the Pharisees. In His sermon, Jesus brought out a different tenor, or spirit, of righteousness that we seldom think about. He said, "Blessed are the poor in spirit." Matthew 5:3. The poor in spirit are those who do not think highly of their righteousness, and who recognize their spiritual poverty. " Blessed are they that mourn." Verse 4. This mourning is related to repentance, and to those who mourn because of their sinfulness that crucifies the Son of God afresh. "Blessed are the meek." Verse 5. This meekness is a lack of self-justification and self-righteousness. "Blessed are they which do hunger and thirst after righteousness." Verse 6. This is because they realize that they do not have it. "Blessed are the merciful." Verse 7. Do we treat other people as Christ treats us?

Here are some additional characteristics of those who are blessed: "Blessed are ye, when men shall hate you, and when they shall separate you from their company, and shall reproach you, and cast out your name as evil, for the Son of man's sake. Rejoice ye in that day, and leap for joy: for, behold, your reward is great in heaven...woe unto you that are rich!...Woe unto you that are full! for ye shall hunger." Luke 6:22-25. This recalls how Laodiceans are described as being rich and increased with goods and have need of nothing. Woe unto them.

Somehow these things have not been fitted into our Christianity and our concept of righteousness. The best evidence that we are not righteous (and I am speaking in general terms) is that we seem to be so absorbed in establishing our own righteousness. There is a high degree of self-justification, of self-protection, and a craving to establish ourselves as righteous. Paul wrote about people with that attitude. "For they being ignorant of God's righteousness, and going about to establish their own righteousness, have not submitted themselves unto the righteousness of God." Romans 10:3. People like this are not righteous.

If we try to establish our own, or produce it, or build it up, it verifies that we are ignorant of His, and that we have not submitted ourselves unto His. This is difficult for us to see because we believe that we *must* be performers of the law; therefore, we set out to do what the law requires. But this is not the way to righteousness. When we go out to establish our own, we are not finding His. This creates a problem that we frequently overlook, for we think we must establish our righteousness or we will be lost in the Judgment.

Righteousness is a vastly different thing than we sometimes think. It all refers back to the question: What is righteousness? If you are successful in establishing what you consider to be at least some level of righteousness in your life, then you are prone to make the mistake of believing that you can continue on and fully establish your own righteousness. Almost everything in Christianity is dependent upon your concept of what righteousness is.

An illustration of this is found in the experience of the Jews. They were told to "love thy neighbour as thyself" Leviticus 19:18. When Jesus came, He seemed to change that law, or at least He called it a new commandment. He evidently was not changing it according the way it was written, but according to the way it was understood. "A new commandment I give unto you, That ye love one another; as I have loved you, that ye also love one another." John 13:34. He was giving us His understanding of the command in Leviticus. In doing so, He adds, "that you love one another as I have loved you." This was new. The Jews had a certain interpretation of loving their neighbor, and as they reasoned and studied about it, all the Jews had come to accept the idea that their neighbor did not include everyone. After Jesus told the Jews that they were to "love thy neighbour as thyself," a lawyer asked, "And who is my neighbour?" Luke 10:27,29. He had a certain idea as to what it meant to love his neighbor, but he did not consider everyone, especially Samaritans, to be his neighbor. Jesus then gave the parable of the Good Samaritan; and when He finished He asked, "Which now of these three [the priest, the Levite, or the Samaritan] thinkest thou, was neighbour unto him that fell among the thieves?" Verse 36. The Jews would not even answer the question lest they defile their lips by saying the word "Samaritan."

Those Jews had some unusual ideas about what constitutes righteousness, and these ideas are not all gone. Many today have the same attitude towards people and towards loving our neighbor. Jesus taught that the only right standard of loving your neighbor is to love your neighbor as He loves us. There is no other standard; and you do not understand righteousness if you do not love your neighbor as Jesus has loved you. This is as hard for us to understand as it was for the Jews. They read about love in the Scripture, they professed to have it, but they did not understand the kind of love that Jesus came to establish for us. Jesus is the only true standard of loving your neighbor. When we go about attempting to keep the law, we usually try to keep the law according to our concepts of the law, and we have many concepts of law keeping.

Some Protestants say that the law has been nailed to the cross and thus done away with. What, then, is their standard of righteousness? Well, it surely is not the law, because they say that is done away with; so they have to discover a new standard. I have asked several people who believe that the law was done away what they think righteousness is and what must a person do to be saved. I asked these questions in order to discover what they believe is the standard of righteousness. I am amazed at the answers I have heard, for most professed Christians have invented their own standard of righteousness. If you accept man's wrong interpretations of righteousness, you will not be very happy because you will often place the standard so low that God is not giving you all He desires you to have.

Those who believe that being righteousness is simply being a good citizen or church member will not be very thankful, either, because many out there who do not profess to be Christians are also good, upstanding citizens. They also try hard to be good. They do not get thrown into jail or get into trouble with their neighbors; but they do not go to church, either. Nor do they read their Bibles. If they are righteous because they try to be good, then you do not need Christianity to be righteous. Therefore, God has nothing special for those in the church who think righteousness comes by trying to be good.

There is still a problem even among those who believe in the law, because they do not always understand righteousness, even though they believe in the law. In fact, they easily misunderstand righteousness as much as those who do not believe that the law exists. We tend to think that the law is merely a checklist of rules where, if we just discipline ourselves to avoid the "thou shalt nots" and force ourselves to do the "thou shalts," then we are righteous. If this is your concept of righteousness, then you do not have very much, for the law is not in the heart. It is only manifested in the external behavior. People who think this way usually end up saying, "I thank God I am not like other men," and they praise themselves and establish their own righteousness, and all because of their misconception of righteousness.

There are too many of us who think that if we avoid the "thou shalt nots" and do the "thou shalts," then we are righteous. That is not true at all. It is not just a matter of rigidly conforming to a list of rules. It never has been and never will be, but that is what many people have thought it to be. Strong-willed people like this idea, but weak-willed people usually end up hating this idea. Many who hold this concept of righteousness stand up and say they are going to be righteous no matter what, but only they will think so. Their spouse and children and fellow church members will not think so because they know how such people can act when their will is crossed or when someone steps on their toes.

Some people understand that the law is love. This is what Jesus taught when He said, "Thou shalt love the Lord thy God with all thy heart, and with all thy soul, and with all thy mind. This is the first and great commandment. And the second is like unto it, Thou shalt love thy neighbour as thyself. On these two commandments hang all the law and the prophets." Matthew 22:37-40. When we discover that the law is love, we have a tendency to think that we have arrived, that now we understand righteousness. But how many concepts of love exist in the world today? Therefore, as soon as you arrive at the conclusion that the law is love, you have still not arrived, for you must then discover what genuine love is. Righteousness will be no higher than your concept of love. To some, love is merely doing your own thing and satisfying self. We can understand that the law is love, and that righteousness is love, yet neither understand nor possess righteousness because of our false understanding of love.

The sad thing about this is that whatever we think about righteousness, and whatever we understand to be the standard of righteousness, determines what we think about conversion, Christian growth, sanctification, the gift of righteousness, our behavior, and our relationship with others. Everything involved in practical Christian living depends on our true understanding or our misconception of righteousness. And today we have many arguments and disagreements because we cannot agree on what righteousness is. It has been like this in the Christian community for many centuries now.

Jesus said, "A new commandment I give unto you that you love one another as I have loved you." John 13:34. He is really saying that the only standard of law keeping, the only standard of righteousness, the only standard of love which God honors, is that which meets the life of Christ. The life of Jesus is love, and therefore the life that Jesus lived is righteousness. His life was the law lived out, and there is no other standard. God has not left it for man to define righteousness or law keeping. He has not given us that privilege. He knows that if we are left to ourselves to define what both law keeping and righteousness are, we will misunderstand as did the Jews. During the fifteen hundred years from the time of Moses until the time of Jesus, the Jews had developed some very distorted ideas as to what law keeping was all about.

Jesus came to demonstrate to us what love is, what righteousness is, and what law keeping is. "The Lord Jesus came to our world to represent the character of His Father. He came to live out the law, and His words and character were daily a correct exposition of the law of God....Jesus was a living manifestation of what the law was,..." ST March 14, 1895. You can see what true law keeping is by looking at His life and His words. He has made these things manifest to us. Christ is the only true interpretation of righteousness. He is the correct interpretation of love and of the law. All others are a sham, a misrepresentation, and are man's fabrication out of a sinful heart, trying to reduce righteousness down to their own abilities. Trying to be righteous in and of ourselves only leads to frustrations.

Here is where so many of our problems hinge. The devil realizes that the sinful heart is selfish and proud, so he dangles before us what we can do; and then he says, "If you will only do a little bit better." And we struggle and strive and labor trying to be good enough for God to love us, and to save us, and to call us righteous. We get ulcers in the process, and we lose our tempers when someone finds fault with us. We quibble, we quarrel, we compete in all this process simply because we think we must struggle to attain to a righteousness that the Lord will approve. Love never comes into the picture, and the devil knows that. I recognize that the devil does not truly understand the spirit of righteousness, but he seems to understand enough about it to be able to destroy the true concepts of righteousness in the minds of many. How he can be so close and yet so far is beyond my understanding, but he has certainly disrupted our thinking concerning this subject.

The only standard that God will ever look at, the only interpretation of love and righteousness and law keeping, is the life of Jesus. There is no other. I know you might not like that, but if you have read the chapters previous to this one, it should not discourage you, for we have been talking about righteousness by faith in Jesus and not by faith in self. If you have sufficient faith in Him, it should not be discouraging to discover that your standard of righteousness has been pretty low.

The Bible teaches that God is love. This love is the kind that Jesus manifested, which has a unique quality and is quite different from what men teach to be love. Jesus was the outshining of the Father's glory, and we are told that His glory is His character, and that the law is His character written down; so Jesus is God's character lived out, and God's character is love. He said, "If you have seen Me you have seen the Father." John 14:9. Therefore, He is the manifestation, the demonstration that people can see and hear of true righteousness, of true love, and of true law keeping.

We must never trust in our own concepts of this. Like the Jews, we discuss and argue about what righteousness is. There are many theories, such as in a book published in bygone years written by four authors who apparently had divergent views about perfection. Jesus is perfection. There is no other definition but Jesus. (We will talk about perfection in the last chapter of this book.) You can try to pick perfection apart in all its minute pieces, but Jesus is perfection. There will never be a better definition than that by anyone. He is God's definition of righteousness. God is love, and Jesus is love because He came to show us the Father.

The Bible says, "There is none righteous, no, not one." Romans 3:10. You cannot look around and trust somebody else's interpretation, or their definition, or their description. You cannot do that or you will misunderstand, misinterpret, and wrongly define. Jesus is the only righteous Person, and He alone has the correct interpretation and the accurate description of love and righteousness and perfection. He is God's interpretation of these things. There are few people who truly accept the concept that the life of Jesus is the righteousness that God prescribes.

If you have a standard other than the life of Jesus, then you either destroy, or at least minimize, your experience in righteousness; and that covers everything in righteousness. If your standard is not the same as that of Christ's, then you destroy righteousness by faith in Christ, because righteousness by faith is based on what righteousness is.

I would like you to see how we can literally disrupt and misunderstand and minimize righteousness by our wrong concepts. Let's look at justification by faith, which is conversion or the new birth, and see what it is like when you begin to see the standard of righteousness is Christ, and not self. What happens to you in the new birth? "Whosoever is born of God doth not commit sin; for His seed remaineth in him: and he cannot sin, because he is born of God." 1 John 3: 9. You have no doubt seen someone's daughter and said, "She looks just like her mother." How did she get that way? She was born that way. What happens to a born-again Christian when they are born of God? Not of their mother or their father but of God? What are they like? Do the laws of heredity cease to function in the spiritual life? Are we not like Him when we are born of Him? What happens when we are made a new creation in Christ? What happens to a human being no matter what his past life has been like? What are people like when they are "created in righteousness and true holiness"? Ephesians 4:24. In all this I am talking about conversion, or justification by faith, and I would like to know what happens when God goes to work in the heart of a person so that we are born of Him, and recreated by Him in Christ.

If we expect little in justification because our concept of righteousness is so meager, then not very much happens. If it is just a human invention as to what righteousness is, then being born again, justified by faith in His righteousness, accomplishes almost nothing, because my standard is so low. Literally, our poor understanding of righteousness has caused many people to have a miserable experience in conversion. They did not expect much because in their way of thinking, righteousness is not very much; and so they are not converted very much, and yet they say they are converted. The question is: To what were they converted? Were they converted to the standard of righteousness that is found in Christ, or just to a church, or a mental assent to truth, or to their parent's religion? There are all sorts of things we are converted to.

I would like to read a few descriptions of genuine conversions found in the Spirit of Prophecy. Especially notice the use of the word love or those actions related to love, and there are many of them found here. "The grace of Christ received into the heart [speaking about that new experience in Jesus] subdues enmity; it allays strife and fills the soul with love. He who is at peace with God and his fellow men cannot be made miserable [not should not be, but cannot be]. Envy will not be in his heart; evil surmisings will find no room there; hatred cannot exist. The heart that is in harmony with God is a partaker of the peace of heaven and will diffuse its blessed influence on all around. The spirit of peace will rest like dew upon hearts weary and troubled with worldly strife." MB 27,28. Do these words jolt you like they do me? God makes it impossible for envy and evil to exist in the new heart.

"In the heart renewed by divine grace, love is the principle of action. It modifies the character, governs the impulses, controls the passions, subdues enmity, and ennobles the affections. This love, cherished in the soul, sweetens the life and sheds a refining influence on all around." SC 59. Wouldn't you like to have that happen in your house, in your school, in your church, where love is the governing principle all the time?

There is more on this. "Those who become new creatures in Christ Jesus will bring forth the fruits of the Spirit, 'love, joy, peace, long-suffering, gentleness, goodness, faith, meekness, temperance.' Galatians 5:22,23. They will no longer fashion themselves according to the former lusts, but by the faith of the Son of God they will follow in His steps, reflect His character, and purify themselves even as He is pure. The things they once hated, they now love; and the things they once loved, they hate. The proud and self-assertive become meek and lowly in heart. The vain and supercilious become serious and unobtrusive. The drunken become sober, and the profligate pure. The vain customs and fashions of the world are laid aside. Christians will seek not the 'outward adorning,' but 'the hidden man of the heart, in that which is not corruptible, even the ornament of a meek and quiet spirit.' 1 Peter 3:3,4." SC 58. Who is that "hidden Man of the heart"? That Man is Jesus. The Bible says that God is love, and Christ is like Him, therefore He is love. For Christ to be in your heart is to love Him.

"Received into the heart, the leaven of truth will regulate the desires, purify the thoughts, and sweeten the disposition. It quickens the faculties of the mind and the energies of the soul. It enlarges the capacity for feeling, for loving. The love of Christ with its redeeming power has come into the heart. This love masters every other motive, and raises its possessor above the corrupting influence of the world. The word of God is to have a sanctifying effect on our association with every member of the human family. The leaven of truth will not produce the spirit of rivalry, the love of ambition, the desire to be first. True, heaven-born love is not selfish and changeable. It is not dependent on human praise. The heart of him who receives the grace of God overflows with love for God and for those for whom Christ died. Self is not struggling for recognition. He does not love others because they love and please him, because they appreciate his merits, but because they are Christ's purchased possession. If his motives, words, or actions are misunderstood or misrepresented, he takes no offense, but pursues the even tenor of his way. He is kind and thoughtful, humble in his opinion of himself, yet full of hope, always trusting in the mercy and love of God. The grace of Christ is to control the temper and the voice. Its working will be seen in politeness and tender regard shown by brother for brother, in kind, encouraging words. An angel presence is in the home. The life breathes a sweet perfume, which ascends to God as holy incense. Love is manifested in kindness, gentleness, forbearance, and long-suffering. The countenance is changed. Christ abiding in the heart shines out in the faces of those who love Him and keep His commandments. Truth is written there. The sweet peace of heaven is revealed. There is expressed a habitual gentleness, a more than human love. The leaven of truth works a change in the whole man, making the coarse refined, the rough gentle, the selfish generous. By it the impure are cleansed, washed in the blood of the Lamb." COL 101,102.

Then it goes on and tells how it strengthens and changes the whole life by partaking of divinity. And finally one little sentence, perhaps the most important of all: "A new standard of character is set up—the life of Christ." COL 99. The standard of character is the life of Christ. All other standards are thrown out the window, for they are useless. This is conversion, and we cannot be converted until we accept that the life of Jesus is the only standard of love, of righteousness, and of law keeping. Everything else is far less than this kind of experience. The Lord has blessed us and helped us. He understands our ignorance and our weakness. He does not condemn or criticize; but I really believe He wants us to see more of the fullness of the life of Jesus.

The big question is: How do you obtain such righteousness? How do you become like Jesus? The process is simple. Bring your righteousness to Christ, yours that you have right now, every shred of it, bring it to Jesus. Just hang it up where you can see the whole thing; and then see what happens. I would like to dare you to do it. No matter how exalted you think your righteousness is, bring it all to Jesus, and on your knees, hold it up and say, "This is righteousness." Then see what happens. You, like Isaiah, will say, "Woe is me! for I am undone; because I am a man of unclean lips." "All our righteousnesses are as filthy rags." Isaiah 64:6; 6:5. And like Ezekiel, you will loathe yourself when you see Jesus.

This is a difficult experience. In the past, we have compared our righteousness to everybody else's, which is what I call comparative religion—better than, holier than. That is the very opposite of Christianity. There is only one comparison we can make and that is with Jesus, because the Bible says that "when He shall appear, we shall be like Him." 1 John 3:2. It is not enough to be better than the conference president or the pastor or the elder. You are going to have to do much better than that. You are going to have to be much better than the General

Conference President or you will never make it. You will have to do much better than Ellen White, a lot better, or you are not going to get there, because they are not going to get there because of their goodness, not one of them. They are going to be there because of Jesus and no other reason.

We must be like Jesus, and not until you bring your righteousness to Him can you ever find out what a sham your righteousness really is. We can look good compared to other people, but we do not look very good compared to Jesus. He is so different, and His righteousness is so different from what people teach to be righteousness. His love is so different.

The correct understanding of the Judgment in the first angel's message is something we have left out of our teaching on the Judgment. We have made people cringe in fear from a God spying on us. But the real heart of it, if we understand that justification by faith in Christ is part of all three messages and not just the third, is that we are going to be judged by the Man Christ Jesus. This is confirmed by several texts such as: "Because He hath appointed a day, in the which He will judge the world in righteousness by that Man whom Me hath ordained." Acts 17:31. "In the day when God shall judge the secrets of men by Jesus Christ." Romans 2:16. I would like to suggest that in addition to being judged by a decision of Jesus, we are judged by comparison to Jesus because we have had offered to us the righteousness of Christ. God will simply look at us to see if we have received it. Jesus stands there beside the record of my life, and God asks, "Is he like Jesus?" Being judged by Jesus is a comparison as much as a decision on His part, for we are to be like Him.

"We must renounce our own righteousness and plead for the righteousness of Christ to be imputed to us." 5T 219. Renounce our own and plead for His, not going about to establish our own. One of the finest Scriptures concerning this is where Paul said that he wants to be rid of his own righteousness. He said he counts as dung all his own righteousness. Instead, he said he wished to be "found in Him, not having mine own righteousness, which is of the law, but that which is through the faith of Christ, the righteousness which is of God by faith." Philippians 3:9.

If Jesus is righteous, and we know that He is, and if God so loved the world He gave Him to us, when we have received Him as our salvation and our righteousness, then we have His righteousness as a free gift from heaven. And as righteous as He is, He gives to you all of that. This is why the Lord can expect us to be like Him. He gives it to you, and by faith you receive it, this gift of love. As I respond by loving Him, I embrace the gift and say it is mine, not because I feel it, not because I am worthy, but because God is so good and because I desperately need it. I do not have any other righteousness but His. Everything else is as filthy rags. Therefore, I must have His.

Righteousness is Christ in you the hope of glory (Colossians 1:27). Righteousness is Christ in me and I in Him (John 17:23). Jesus gets inside of us by revealing His love over and over again to our hearts, manifesting this tremendous love for you and for me until we love Him because He first loved us.

John the beloved, who received that name rightfully, wrote, "Behold, what manner of love the Father hath bestowed upon us, that we should be called the sons of God." 1 John 3:1. Remember that love is righteousness, and love is keeping the law. We must see this love, which is so different from the love we find elsewhere in the world. His love has that quality of God which, when we were yet rebels and enemies, sinning against Him, He so loved us that His Son came all the way from heaven to be one of us, to buy us back with His precious blood, to make us clean, forgiven, pardoned, and to take away our penalty. "There is therefore now no condemnation to them which are in Christ Jesus." Romans 8:1. His love is such that He will not let us go, and all of this while we were His enemies. This is righteousness. This is self-renouncing, self-sacrificing love.

It is this kind of love that Christ demonstrated throughout His whole life. It is this kind of love that is true law keeping, and true righteousness. It is this kind of love that breaks my heart and melts your heart. It is this kind of love that He wants to manifest to the world in you and me, a self-sacrificing and self-renouncing love in my thoughts and deeds towards others, in my attitudes, in my feelings, in my words, in my gestures, in my touch, in my gentleness, in my compassion, in my understanding, in my sensitivity to you, in my realization and awareness of you.

This self-renouncing love is righteousness. This is the righteousness of God in Christ Jesus, for God is love. This is the righteousness He wants to give you at this very instant. This is the righteousness that exceeds that of the Pharisees. He wants to push away all the other concepts and standards of righteousness by the supreme definition of righteousness—that we love one another as He has loved us.

There is only one perfect example of righteousness. In the marvelous experience of righteousness by faith in Christ, He will make you like Jesus. What a tremendous opportunity is ours when we understand true righteousness by faith.

30

I CAN DO IT!

IN A PREVIOUS CHAPTER we dealt with what man is able and unable to do in terms of obedience and obtaining righteousness. Since this issue is so important, and because there are so many misunderstandings regarding it, we will take a closer look at the knowledge God wishes us to have in order to experience Christ our righteousness.

What is man able to do, and what is he unable to do after sin entered the human family? Most of us do not know what it was like before sin, except for what we read in the Scriptures. It is easy to make certain assumptions about this topic that can be dangerous to our spiritual welfare. For years we have believed that if we could only convince people that the law of God is still to be kept, that the standards are still to be observed, then they will do it; and if they fail to do it we think they need more convincing, or perhaps they should pray more or try harder. This concept of righteousness has been held for many years...

Is man able to obey after conviction? Some think so. If it is possible, how does man obey? "It was possible for Adam, before the fall, to form a righteous character by obedience to God's law. But he failed to do this, and because of his sin our natures are fallen and we cannot make ourselves righteous. Since we are sinful, unholy, we cannot perfectly obey the holy law. We have no righteousness of our own with which to meet the claims of the law of God." SC 62. Since Adam and Eve sinned, mankind has lacked the ability to obey the law, and often we do not recognize this.

"It is impossible for us, of ourselves, to escape from the pit of sin in which we are sunken. Our hearts are evil, and we cannot change them. Education, culture, the exercise of the will, human effort, all have their proper sphere, but here they are powerless." SC 18,19. The idea that it is necessary only to develop the good that exists in man by nature is a fatal deception.

We have problems here that some people do not like. This makes it almost impossible to understand Christ our righteousness, for if we do not understand what man is and is not able to do after sin, it is certain we cannot figure out how to be changed or how to improve. We must accept where we are and what we are, and the truth on this is not agreeable with some people. It is true that we must be educated about what is right, but that does not accomplish all we hope it will. We can produce an outward correctness of behavior, but Jesus taught that at the same time we can be filled with dead men's bones, still vile on the inside.

Others say: Just do your best and Christ will make up for the rest. What can a sinner do that is his best? This is not exactly truth, for how much good is in us that we can develop? As soon as you mention this, it causes a violent reaction in some who think this is criticizing them. They become spiritually paranoid. Legalists have always found fault with our poor performance, and we think this is doing the same thing. We begin to squirm and demand for everyone to get off our back. But if you are lost and do not know it, you will never be found. If you are in a weakened condition and assume you are strong, you will never get strong. Somehow you must understand what you are and where you are or you can never find the way out.

Because some people are so sensitive about this subject of discovering our inability, there are those who say we must help people find self-worth, self-esteem, prestige, self-love. If we can help them to do that, then they will achieve. Is that true? It might make you feel good but does it make the life different? Does it really help you to achieve? And people call this Christ our righteousness, just as they do about doing your best and having Christ make up the difference. There are many things termed Christ our righteousness that operate on assumptions that might be less than certain.

What is man's condition after sin came into the human family? This is the most basic point in any development of the human being, because he must discover what he can do and what he cannot do. What has sin done to man? When Eve had eaten the forbidden fruit, she went to tempt Adam. He loved her so much and was so afraid of losing her that he also partook; thus they would not be separated. But after his sin—only that one sin—he told the Lord that Eve was to blame. Just one sin changed love to accusation.

"He who, from love to Eve, had deliberately chosen to forfeit the approval of God, his home in Paradise, and an eternal life of joy, could now, after his fall, endeavor to make his companion, and even the Creator Himself, responsible for the transgression. So terrible is the power of sin." PP 57.

One sin accomplished all of that. What has happened after nearly six thousand years of sin? In the second generation after creation, love had so diminished and hatred so increased that Cain killed his brother without a cause. In the short span of time from father and mother to children, that is all it took. We are discovering what sin does to human beings.

In the account of early man, we find that after only ten generations, the Lord said, speaking about the human family, "that every imagination of the thoughts of his heart was only evil continually." Genesis 6:5. God repented that He had made man and sent a flood to destroy all but eight people. He started over again with Noah and his family who were spared in the ark, and you know the story well. After the flood, Noah became intoxicated, and his son Ham committed some kind of moral sin. Then Nimrod, the great grandson of Noah, began to build a nation called Babel. The outcome of that rebellion against God is described in Genesis 11 where they attempted to build a tower to reach the heavens. They wanted to keep from being destroyed again by a flood, even though God had promised He would not do that again. They were trying to secure their own salvation, not trusting God to save them. That happened in the fourth generation after Noah.

Finally, because of these problems, God chose another person and began again with Abram. When he arrived down in Egypt he seemed to have trouble telling the whole truth. Then difficulties arose between him and his relative Lot, and between Lot's herdsmen and those of Abram; and the troubles were so extreme and violent that they had to divide. Lot decided in his materialistic viewpoint to go down to Sodom to make a good living, and you know the results of that venture.

The Bible is the history of the intrusion of sin. We sometimes think that those who lived back then were ignorant and that we are wiser than they. Since we are wiser, we think that none of those things can happen to us. This is a gross assumption. The Bible talks about sin as being in darkness, a sort of blindness and deception, which means we have an incapability of understanding how it functions in our lives and what it does to us. When we begin to examine issues like what we can and cannot do, we must have a certain amount of distrust of our judgment, for it is been clouded and obscured and confused by past sin.

There are many Bible texts that specifically reveal what has happened to man as the result of sin. The gospel prophet wrote that "we are all as an unclean thing, and all our righteousnesses are as filthy rags." Isaiah 64:6. Job asked, "Who can bring a clean thing out of an unclean? not one." Job 14:4. Another prophet said, "The heart is deceitful above all things, and desperately wicked: who can know it?" Jeremiah 17:9. The psalmist wrote that "man at his best state is altogether vanity...Surely every man is vanity." Psalms 39:5,11. "I was shapen in iniquity; and in sin did my mother conceive me." Psalms 51:5.

The most extreme viewpoint on this was penned by the apostle Paul. "What then? Are we better than they [meaning the Jews]? No, in no wise: for we have before proved both Jews and Gentiles, that they are all under sin; As it is written, There is none righteous, no, not one: There is none that understandeth, there is none that seeketh after God. They are all gone out of the way, they are together become unprofitable; there is none that doeth good, no, not one. Their throat is an open sepulchre; with their tongues they have used deceit; the poison of asps is under their lips: Whose mouth is full of cursing and bitterness: Their feet are swift to shed blood: Destruction and misery are in their ways: And the way of peace have they not known: There is no fear of God before their eyes." Romans 3:9-18.

This is not only talking about people two thousand years ago, it is talking about us today. It is not only talking about the heathen, it is talking about Jews and gentiles, believers and unbelievers, and it says we are like this. Some will say, "I do not believe I am like that." Perhaps we cannot see ourselves as we really are. Some do not like to read these things, for it frightens them, and makes them appear as wretched individuals.

If the doctor tells you that an x-ray reveals you have some pretty bad things down in your colon, you would not think the doctor is a horrible person. We are not sensitive when a physician tells us bad news about our bodies, but when God tells us about our inabilities and our defective characters, we just scream. If you do not know your physical defects, if you refuse to accept what the doctor has found, you may very well die from those defects. However, if you acknowledge them and seek correction, you might live a long time. The same is true with the Great Physician and our souls. He knows us better than we do, and you have just read His diagnosis. You can accept it or reject it. He will not try to thrust it upon you. If you reject it, the Great Physician cannot work for you; but if you accept it, He can. It is that simple.

Here are a few statements from the Spirit of Prophecy that are very specific about our condition after Adam sinned: "Nature had become depraved by sin; they [Adam and Eve] had lessened their strength to resist evil and had opened the way for Satan to gain more ready access to them." PP 61. "Sin not only shuts us away from God, but destroys in the human soul both the desire and the capacity for knowing Him...The faculties of the soul, paralyzed by sin, the darkened mind, the perverted will, He has power to invigorate and to restore...There is in his nature a bent to evil, a force which, unaided, he cannot resist." Ed 28,29. "In our own strength it is impossible for us to deny the clamors of our fallen nature." DA 122. "But should they [Adam and Eve] once yield to temptation, their nature would become so depraved that in themselves they would have no power and no disposition to resist Satan." PP 53. "There is in the nature of man, when not under the direct influence of the Spirit of God, a disposition to envy, jealousy, and cruel distrust, which, if not subdued, will lead to a desire to undermine and tear down others, while selfish spirits will seek to build themselves up upon their ruins." 3T 53. "The fallen nature of Adam always strives for the mastery." PP 80. "Through sin the whole human organism is deranged, the mind is perverted, the imagination corrupted. Sin has degraded the faculties of the soul. Temptations from without find an answering chord within the heart, and the feet turn imperceptibly toward evil." MH 451.

If this is our condition, will convincing us that we are wrong and telling us what is right accomplish anything for us? We may agree that our natures are fallen, but we say we cannot do anything about it. The nature is still depraved after conviction, and it is still helpless. Will education accomplish anything? The nature is still as bad as it was before. Education does not change the nature of man. Doing your best does not help, either. Developing what is good in us accomplishes nothing because we are depraved, so we only develop more depravity.

Many give up in discouragement when they sense these restrictions, these inabilities. But the Lord does not want us to do that. He wants us to seek for help, and that help is available, but it is not in self. That help has always been outside of self since man sinned. There is One who can do this who comes to bless us. There must come a change in the old nature, but only Jesus can accomplish that change, for He said that without Him we can do nothing, but with Him we can do all things.

Let's read again the quote about our helplessness: "It is impossible for us, of ourselves, to escape from the pit of sin in which we are sunken. Our hearts are evil, and we cannot change them. Education, culture, the exercise of the will, human effort, all have their proper sphere, but here they are powerless." SC 18. The answer to our dilemma is found as the quote continues. "There must be a power working from within, a new life from above, before men can be changed from sin to holiness. That power is Christ. His grace alone can quicken the lifeless faculties of the soul, and attract it to God, to holiness."

For years we have not acknowledged that the nature of man has to be changed. We discuss it once in a while; we have some realization of it. But it is not something we commonly teach. We teach obedience and then we leap over the change that is necessary before obedience. And we assume we have been changed too often when we have not been; and without that change we are helpless. The quote continues: "The Saviour said, 'Except a man be born from above,' unless he shall receive a new heart, new desires, purposes, and motives, leading to a new life, 'he cannot see the kingdom of God.' John 3:3, margin." These things must come to us and we must receive them or we are utterly helpless in conducting our lives according to the will of God.

Another difficulty we have is not realizing how complete the change must be. Many assume that the change of one or two habits is a change of nature, but that is not quite true. Strong willed people can give the appearance of an outward correctness of behavior by changing one or two habits, but no human being can change the heart. You often find in those who try to perform outwardly a bitterness coming out of the inside, and you detect that there is something inside that should not be there. It could be that the outward performance is nothing but a way to gain heaven. The person may not be different at all. All you have to do is cross that person's will and vile things come out of the inside.

This complete change required by the Lord is described in several quotations. "The Spirit works upon man's heart, implanting in him a new nature." COL 411. "Jesus made the infinite sacrifice, not only that sin might be removed, but that human nature might be restored, rebeautified, reconstructed from its ruins, and made fit for the presence of God." 5T 537. "The word destroys the natural, earthly nature, and imparts a new life in Christ Jesus." DA 391. The next quote confirms the totality of the transformation that is to take place. "The whole heart must be yielded to God, or the change can never be wrought in us by which we are to be restored to His likeness. By nature we are alienated from God. The Holy Spirit describes our condition in such words as these: 'Dead in trespasses and sins;' 'the whole head is sick, and the whole heart faint;' 'no soundness in it.' We are held fast in the snare of Satan; 'taken captive by him at his will.' God desires to heal us, to set us free. But since this requires an entire transformation, a renewing of our whole nature, we must yield ourselves wholly to Him." SC 43.

This is where we have problems. Again, it is not true that dropping off a few bad habits means we have a new nature. We assume that because we might go to church on the right day and pay our tithe that our natures have been changed. That is not proof that the heart is changed, because you might go to church unwillingly or forcibly (because someone is pressuring you), or because it might not look well if you did not attend, or it might keep you employed in the denomination. None of these are proof of a transformation of the heart. The Lord is interested in the heart; then the outside takes care of itself. God is interested in an entire transformation. Often we have problems in what we call sanctification because we assume we have had the entire transformation.

After we have been justified, there is another problem that confronts us. When I have been changed by His grace and by His power, do I then have two natures, or one nature? This is a real riddle, and many is the argument that rages over Romans chapter 7, contending we have two natures after conversion, or the new birth. But the Bible talks about the death of one nature and the life of another. Some would have the growth in Christian life to be a gradual dying and a gradual living. In other words, I am not yet quite born again. Or I am just a babe and not grown up; and I am not quite dead, I am just dying. This is sort of an evolutionary death and evolutionary life, but not a creative life, which the Bible teaches very strongly. Do we gain victory by evolution? Then how do you explain that some seem to gain victory immediately, overnight, to which many thousands can testify. Some say that because I still have the old body, even though the heart has been changed, the body is the old nature and the new heart is the new nature; and therefore, sometimes I serve the old, and sometimes the new.

If you go back and study this well, you will find out that only one thing is changed in the new birth, and that is the heart. The body will not be changed until resurrection or translation. And the reason why the heart is changed is that it is the ruling agency in the human being. It is the authoritative organ in the body. It can command the body and can rule. All stimulation in the body must be funneled through the mind, or the heart as the Bible calls it. Everything is centered in that heart, with new purposes and new interests and a new nature. That new heart, then, can keep the body under, as Paul calls it. The problem is not with the old nature of the body. It functions through the mind and does not have a separate mind of its own. If it functions through the mind, so the new heart controls it.

Why does there seem to be this dual activity in the life? How is that sometimes I serve the Lord and sometimes I serve self, after I have a new nature? The problem is always with the heart. "For with the heart man believeth unto righteousness." Romans 10:10. "For out of the heart proceed evil thoughts, murders, adulteries, fornications, thefts, false witness, blasphemies: These are the things which defile a man. But to eat with unwashen hands defileth not a man." Matthew 15:19,20. Out of the mind, or the heart, proceed the things that corrupt us. The reasons and motivations we have, and not what we take inside our bodies, are what defile us. There is a cycle, where what is in our minds causes us to eat as we do, and what we eat can in turn have a negative influence on the mind. But the sins we commit come from the heart, according to Jesus.

The Lord knows this, so He deals with the heart in conversion, or this transformation that takes place. He says He will give us a new heart, or a new nature, that will function differently. All the problems we have are with the mind, or heart; and I am not eliminating the influence of the body on the mind at all.

The one key issue of the heart is that it always has the power of choice by God's grace. Before conversion, and after conversion, and all during your Christian life, you can always choose. The reason for this is that Christianity is a love affair. The conscience cannot be forced. It is always free to choose, every moment, every hour, every day. All of your life you can choose. And it is not one choice for life. The Lord always asks you, "Do you still want to be Mine?" This morning when you woke up, He asked, "Are you still Mine?" Sometimes we go through the whole day and do not acknowledge the fact that we belong to Him, but He would like to know. In all our decisions that day, He asks us one thing: "Are you still Mine? Or have you given your affections to another lover? You have the choice. I will not force you. I only have one pressure which is the pressure of love." The love of Christ constrains us. We may do what we please, but God would have us to be His. And He shows this in thousands of ways.

Because of this option, this power of choice, we sometimes choose Him today and choose the world tomorrow. James called that spiritual adultery, for if you love the world, you are at enmity with God. God tells us that there is no harmony between Him and the world, and we cannot get along very well with God as long as we try to have two lovers. But the Lord is longsuffering, and He will take us back, and take us back, and take us back, even from prostitution if I read Hosea correctly. Because of His longsuffering and patience, and because He is constantly wooing us and trying to win us back to Him, even though we have left Him by choice, we are permitted to vacillate in our choices and our love affairs, and we can go on and on with two lovers. But we are always troubled and dissatisfied by this. Something seems not quite right in our inmost souls. When you come back to the Lord you sense a strange distance or coldness, and you say, "It used to be so warm and satisfying here." He is still begging us to come back, but the problem is with our memories. Where was I the night before? If I could just forget that other lover, then there would be no distance between me and God. But I do not forget that other lover. And Jesus senses a strange lack of warmth, too, and almost no communication. But He waits, and He woos, and He continues to love in spite of our waywardness and unfaithfulness. He does this for years because He loves us so much He cannot let us go.

The Christian life is like the national life of Judah and Israel. He continued to want her, but she chose to go to Babylon. He did not choose to send her there. Read how she worshipped their gods and brought them to Jerusalem. She insisted on loving the heathen's customs and practices, not just the people. They insisted on being like the world in thousands of ways. God could not take away the power of choice from them and still have them love Him. He had to permit them to choose. If they wanted another lover, then He allowed them to go to Babylon to be with their lover. He was not punishing her. He was allowing her freedom of choice. That is exactly what He does to me. He cannot force me to love Him. He will allow me to love whatever I choose.

But strange things happen to our spouses in love affairs where we go off and share that love with someone else. Over the months and the years, the coldness gets colder and the gap gets wider. We cannot see how He can still love us when we have chased around so much. He still does, but we cannot see how He can. We cannot imagine a love that is so boundless that it continues loving the one who is always going away to another lover. Eventually we become unbelievers in His love for us. It is dangerous to share your love with someone else. In no way are we being forced to stay with Him except for that marvelous love that constrains us.

I do not think that there are two natures living in me that back and forth are dominating me. I think there is the power of choice, and I can either choose Him or choose another lover. And I can do it all day long every day. But I will have trouble with my soul and my relationship with God if I do that. Christianity is a loving submission to a Husband who has earned the right to rule us in love. It is a loving submission on our part, a delightful submitting to the Husband who has earned the right to our submission. He does not dominate us by force. It is a delight to have Him dominate us because He is so kind, so understanding, and so good to us. So everyday I must choose the same Master, for there are two masters in the great controversy. Both seek our affections, and both want to be joined to us and have us on their side. We may choose whose side we will be on and whom we will serve.

This power of choice that God has given to us is described this way: "Many are inquiring, 'How am I to make the surrender of myself to God?' You desire to give yourself to Him, but you are weak in moral power, in slavery to doubt, and controlled by the habits of your life of sin....What you need to understand is the true force of the will. This is the governing power in the nature of man, the power of decision, or of choice. Everything depends on the right action of the will. The power of choice God has given to men; it is theirs to exercise. You cannot change your heart [that is not part of the will], you cannot of yourself give to God its affections [and that is not part of the will], but you can choose to serve Him [that is part of the will]. You can give Him your will; He will then work in you to will and to do according to His good pleasure. Thus your whole nature will be brought under the control of the Spirit of Christ; your affections will be centered upon Him, your thoughts will be in harmony with Him." SC 47,48.

In other words, as I choose Him totally, as I choose Him constantly, God's will and desires function in my life. A power outside of me, by a magnificent love affair, comes to dominate me; and I choose Him in love because I love Him who first loved me, and because He is a God of love. When I choose Him and invite Him in, the law of love—supreme love for God and love for my neighbor—is fulfilled in me. And we know that "love is the fulfilling of the law." Romans 13: 10. Again, it is an outside power coming in. This is Christ our righteousness.

"Through the right exercise of the will, an entire change may be made in your life. By yielding up your will to Christ, you ally yourself with the power that is above all principalities and powers. You will have strength from above to hold you steadfast, and thus through constant surrender to God you will be enabled to live the new life, even the life of faith." SC 48. It is choosing to submit in love to His love. It is making Him Lord, or Master, or King, or Ruler of my life.

We began this chapter with this quote: "It was possible for Adam, before the fall, to form a righteous character by obedience to God's law. But he failed to do this, and because of his sin our natures are fallen and we cannot make ourselves righteous. Since we are sinful, unholy, we cannot perfectly obey the holy law. We have no righteousness of our own with which to meet the claims of the law of God." SC 62. The quote continues on with the remedy for this inability. "But Christ has made a way of escape for us. He lived on earth amid trials and temptations such as we have to meet. He lived a sinless life. He died for us, and now He offers to take our sins and give us His righteousness. If you give yourself to Him, and accept Him as your Saviour, then, sinful as your life may have been, for His sake you are accounted righteous." The whole heart of Christ our righteousness is that willing, loving choice where we give ourselves totally to Him (and it must be a total surrender). "If you give yourself to Him, and accept Him as your Saviour, then, sinful as your life may have been, for His sake you are accounted righteous. Christ's character stands in place of your character, and you are accepted before God just as if you had not sinned."

Then she goes on and tells us how we must daily surrender and abide in Him. It is like marriage. Just because you are married does not mean you have to stay home. It does not mean you have to love that person. It does not mean you have to abide with that person. You can always choose to leave. Every day and every hour in marriage you are choosing whether to stay and maintain the relationship, or whether to leave and go to another lover. Likewise, everyday of the Christian life after conversion we make the choice of whether to stay (or abide as the Bible says) or to leave. Sanctification is giving our affections constantly to our heavenly Spouse instead of to some other lover. When I yield my heart to Him, He does His will in me, and He gives me His righteousness in sanctification as well as justification. As long as I desire His will to be done in my life, and ask Him to rule and dominate me, He takes over and controls my life. If the time comes when I am tired of His control and want to submit to another master, He says, "You may go." We have that freedom in all love affairs. The problem is that when I return to God and to His church, I think that somehow He does not love me as much as He once did. But He does. We have difficulty because our love is not exclusively for Him. We have been sharing it.

The very thing that causes us so much difficulty and makes us so sensitive about discussing our inability, our ineffectiveness, our deficiencies, our depravity, is the one point in life that turns us toward Jesus. The thing we think is the way of failure and of criticism is really the way of success. And amazingly, an understanding and acceptance of our inabilities is the one thing that leads us to Christ. "No deep-seated love for Jesus can dwell in the heart that does not realize its own sinfulness." SC 65. The more I try to make myself look good, in my human effort, or in doing my best, and thinking He makes up the slack, the less I need Jesus and the less I will love Him. "No deep-seated love for Jesus can dwell in the heart that does not realize its own sinfulness."

"The less we see to esteem in ourselves, the more we shall see to esteem in the infinite purity and loveliness of our Saviour. A view of our sinfulness drives us to Him who can pardon; and when the soul, realizing its helplessness, reaches out after Christ, He will reveal Himself in power. The more our sense of need drives us to Him and to the word of God, the more exalted views we shall have of His character, and the more fully we shall reflect His image." SC 65.

It is easy to misunderstand this. We do not want to be told how bad we are and we will hate the person who tells us. Tell me what I can do, and we like that; and we begin to think more highly of ourselves than we ought to. We cringe when we read from the Bible or the Spirit of Prophecy about our inability, about our proneness to failure, about our deficiencies, about the evil nature of man. We insist that there is some goodness in man that can be nurtured and made to grow. We think we are much better than that. Can I not develop that inherent goodness in me? And so we try, and we try some more, and we invent new gospels, new theories, and we search for Bible texts and quotations to prove our theories. But the world today is establishing beyond a shadow of a doubt, in the church and out of the church, that we are depraved people. Look at our selfishness, our self-centeredness, our neglect of our own children. We give them things but we do not give them ourselves. Look at our politics, our competitive natures, our vengeful spirits, our abuse of others, our envy, our jealousy, our seeking for the highest place. We, like Adam, blame others for our troubles. I have no problems with myself. All my problems are with my spouse, my children, my church, my neighbors, my boss. I am right and everyone else is wrong. I will do anything to justify myself. Everyone around me knows I am wrong, but I refuse to admit it.

The knowledge that God wants to give us, the knowledge from which we run and seek to escape, is the knowledge that leads us to Jesus. It is a knowledge that leads to a new nature, to a blessed love affair. It is a knowledge that will warm our hearts as we sense how precious we are to Him, that our value is not what we are but what He wants to make us. The precious price He paid, the restoration He will accomplish, the rebeautification of the soul—these make us valuable. We are priceless to Him, not because we are so good, but because of what He can do if He is allowed to work in us.

This very day, our Lover is asking, "Will you be Mine?" There is one thing we can do, which is to choose, and choose, and choose, and keep on choosing. Will you always choose Him? Is He supreme in your affections? Is He not the One altogether lovely? Is there anyone else in the universe like Him? Then choose Christ and live; and you will be crowned with success as you let Him come into your heart and work an entire transformation by His love and grace. May God grant you this glorious change that comes about by our choosing Him in love.

31

THE DEVOTIONAL LIFE

IN ORDER TO BENEFIT from what you have been discovering about Christ our righteousness, these principles must be absorbed more and more so that they become part of your everyday life, and so that your natural, legalistic tendencies will be pushed out of your system. I have learned that I must continually bombard my mind with the grace and goodness of the Lord and His righteousness, or I will revert back automatically to struggling to be righteous in my own self. I hope you will continue to study these things, and to pray without ceasing that the Lord will give you not only the theory, but the experience of receiving Christ and His righteousness. The Lord is giving us an abundant opportunity before probation closes to understand more about His grace and Christ our righteousness.

One of the biggest problems confronting Seventh-day Adventists is not the necessity of obedience, but how to obey. Those who have grown up in the church, and even those who are converts to it, have learned a great deal about what to obey concerning the moral law, diet restrictions, and so forth. The problem we have is in doing all these things. You can tell your children to do and not do certain things, but often they cannot. What do you tell them to do then? How do we obey? This is where we are so negligent.

Many will say that the way you obey is to try harder, but that is putting confidence in the flesh, which the Bible says will not work. Others say the way to obey is to pray more, which is still confidence in the flesh. Others say we must study the Bible more, or study justification by faith more. It is a deception when people come to believe that Christ our righteousness can be nothing more than studying more. Studying a subject more will never benefit you so far as becoming righteous is concerned. We can study and study the subject, and find it very intriguing, but it will only tickle our ears and our brain if we do not apply it to our lives. Christ our righteousness is more than something to study. It is an enabling power that does something for us.

Some believe the way to obedience is to teach people more about how bad their sins are. We think that by telling people how bad smoking and drugs are, they will stop. Many who know how bad these things are never do stop. Education does not necessarily stop people from sinning. It is true that you must have a knowledge of what sin is, but education will not educate them out of sinning.

Still others say that psychology, or psychotherapy, is the way to obedience. People are given a better understanding of their problem, looking at their background and how they got into this fix, explaining why they feel the way they do and why they do what they do. But experience has proven that you can understand all you want to about a person but everything will still not be all right. Many people have catalogued the whole history of their environment, their circumstances, their heredity and everything else, and they still go on the same way. They end up with lots of knowledge about themselves, but they do not obey.

Many have tried all these things for years and have come to the conclusion that none of them work. Thus, they conclude that you cannot be obedient. Some are able to achieve a superficial, external type of obedience, and they call that righteousness. This is a deception and hypocrisy, because it does not come from the heart. They do not delight to do His law. They do it because they have to, because that is the way to be saved.

Somehow the heart must be changed before there is genuine obedience. Righteousness by faith, justification by faith, Christ our righteousness, salvation by faith—whatever term you care to use—will succeed when it is the genuine article. There are all kinds of theories about Christ our righteousness and righteousness by faith; but the genuine article is the only one that will succeed.

Why do human beings fail in all their attempts to be righteous? In the book of Exodus, after God had given Moses His law and provided instruction on many things His people were to do and not do, the Bible says that "Moses came and told the people all the words of the Lord, and all the judgments: and all the people answered with one voice, and said, All the words which the Lord hath said will we do." Exodus 24:3. The Spirit of Prophecy comments on this. "Before there could be any permanent reformation the people must be led to feel their utter inability in themselves." PP 524. When you have prayed more, and studied more, and tried harder, and gotten more education, and understood more, you still are not obedient. All you discover is your "utter inability" to obey the Lord of yourself, and that is the right conclusion to come to. I cannot perform, but there is a Person can do it in me and for me.

The quote continues: "They had broken His law, it condemned them as transgressors, and it provided no way of escape. While they trusted in their own strength and righteousness, it was impossible for them to secure the pardon of their sins; they could not meet the claims of God's perfect law, and it was in vain that they pledged themselves to serve God." It was impossible, they tried in vain, and they could not meet the claims of God's law. The purpose of the old covenant was to show the people that they could not do what they had promised to do.

The quote continues: "It was only by faith in Christ that they could secure pardon of sin and receive strength to obey God's law. They must cease to rely upon their own efforts for salvation, they must trust wholly in the merits of the promised Saviour, if they would be accepted of God."

At the beginning of the Christian experience, and even after being in the church for several years, many people think that the burden of obedience is on them, and they keep on trying and trying; but ultimately all they learn is their utter inability to obey. When they finally come to the conclusion that they are unable to obey, many conclude that they are lost. That is not true. When we discover our inabilities, we are finally on the road to righteousness because we might trust Christ now instead of sinful self. This is an important point to come to along the Christian pathway.

People often come to see me, all discouraged because they discovered they cannot obey; and I always say, "Praise the Lord. Now you are making progress." They say, "You must be insane." And I say, "Then blessed are the insane." Many people do not know they cannot. Some go to church for fifty years and still have not discovered that they cannot. They refuse to believe it. It is progress when you have discovered that you cannot. The Lord has done you a favor, and somehow your mind has comprehended it, and we ought to thank Him for that.

The purpose of the old covenant was to teach them their utter inability to obey. They could not do it. The Egyptians thought they could serve their gods by appeasing them, and the Jews got the same idea. When they were led out by Moses, they tried it with Jehovah, but it would not work. The Lord was trying to teach them a lesson, and that was the main purpose for the old covenant.

It seems that the sinner is always saying like a little child, "Leave me alone. I want to do it myself. Just give me more time and I can do it." It is our nature to be independent, thinking we can do it. But the Bible asks, "Can the Ethiopian change his skin, or the leopard his spots? then may ye also do good, that are accustomed to do evil." Jeremiah 13:23. We have heard this many, many times, yet we believe it so little. We have been accustomed to doing evil, and we can no more do good than the Ethiopian can change his skin or the leopard its spots. When you discover your utter inability to do good of yourself, you are simply agreeing with the Bible. We should have agreed with it in the first place, but we are slow to learn.

Of himself the sinner is helpless to obey. Jesus said, "without Me, you can do nothing." John 15:5. There is no power in the sinner to do good unless he is connected to a power outside of himself. And that word *connected* is crucial. Jesus also said, "I am the Vine, ye are the branches: He that abideth in Me, and I in him, the same bringeth forth much fruit." John 15:5. The power is in the Vine. If you are attached to Christ, you will bring forth good fruit and much fruit. If you are not attached to Him, you will die. So unless you are connected to Christ in an intimate relationship, you can do nothing. Jesus is the source of all power when it comes to obedience. He said, "All power is given unto Me in heaven and in earth." Matthew 28:18. We all need to receive that power by being plugged into Him, so to speak.

Several years ago as I pastored a church, I discovered one winter's day that the furnace would not work. I turned on the thermostat and nothing happened. I went around and checked everything, but it just would not work. I checked some of the lights and they would not work, either. My logical brain concluded that there was something wrong with the circuit breakers. So I went back to the little kitchen and reset all the circuit breakers, then I checked the furnace and the lights again, but they still would not work. I decided on one more solution which was to go outside and check the fuse box. Sure enough, I found a fuse the size of my thumb that was burned out. I went down to the hardware store, bought another one, plugged it in, and pulled the switch down; and just then all the lights were burning and the furnace was going full blast. Why? The power had always been available, but we were not plugged in. That was all it took, and nothing more.

When you do wrong, you get after yourself and castigate yourself and go around with a guilty conscience for hours; and you ask, "Why did I ever do that foolish thing?" Imagine a man who has a lamp in his living room that does not work, so he gets angry with the light bulb in the lamp. Maybe he takes a ball bat and smashes the bulb to pieces, or maybe the whole lamp. Then he goes and tells people that someone sold him a bad light bulb. He never bothers to check the circuit breaker, or the fuse box, or to find out if the lamp is plugged into the wall. What would you think of a person like that? We do that spiritually all the time. We look at the lack of power in our lives and we say it is the fault of that sin. We think that the problem is our proneness to sin, and therefore somehow we must stop sinning. Somehow I must start doing right. The answer to getting the light bulb turned on is to get electricity to the lamp. The answer to living the Christ-like life is Christ in the life, or making contact with Him by faith. If I want to do right and stop doing wrong, the solution is to get the right power in my life. I must plug into the power, and then it comes into my life and He enables me to do what I cannot do. A light bulb of itself is helpless to give off light without the electricity. The Bible says that we are helpless. But if I abide in Christ and He abides in me, I can do all things, for He strengthens me.

Castigating and condemning ourselves because we have done wrong is not the solution. It is discovering that when you have done wrong and cannot do right that somehow you have separated yourselves from Christ. You have flipped the switch or pulled the plug. The source of power has been separated from you and you are not living the Christian life, because you cannot obey without Him. Faith is the channel of communication that connects us with the power of Christ.

When you find yourself doing wrong, don't get too upset about what you did, but realize that somehow the wires of your faith have been cut. Someone has flipped the switch off on your faith. Somehow you are not living by faith in contact with Christ.

For some reason it takes a great deal of wisdom to understand this concept. It is the lack of power in the life that makes us deficient, and not the fault of the sin itself. When I have sinned, I must *immediately* come back into communication with Him, and get plugged back in to the power. I must restore my abiding in Him.

The Spirit of Prophecy has much to say about this. "When we know God as it is our privilege to know Him, our life will be a life of continual obedience." DA 668. When we read this, we want to give up because we realize that we have not been able to continually obey. The question is not whether you can continually obey, but whether you can continue to know Him and abide in Him. How well do you know Him or how little do you know Him? Are you taking the time to know Him? That is the big problem. When we know God as it is our privilege to know Him, then our life will be a life of continual obedience. Knowing Him is the important factor. The result (continual obedience) will come automatically when I know Him.

"It is His grace that gives man power to obey the laws of God. It is this that enables him to break the bondage of evil habit." MH 115. What must I be concerned about? My evil habits? No, I must be concerned that I know His grace, that I thrive in it, that I bask in it, that I take hold of it by faith. His grace gives me power. If I am not functioning properly, I must connect to the power, and it is His grace that gives me power. It is this that enables Him to break the bondage of my evil habits. It is not trying harder, or praying more, or studying more, or getting a better understanding of myself. It is His grace, and we know so little about grace.

"When we seek to gain heaven through the merits of Christ, the soul makes progress." 1SM 364. It is through His merits, and not through our own struggles and attempts, that we make progress in the Christian life. Put the emphasis on the things that you can do, instead of on what you cannot do. We can acknowledge and claim His merits by continually beholding His spotless, unselfish life, and we can concentrate on knowing God, seeking Him with all our hearts. We can seek Him first every day, submitting our wills to the sovereignty of His love, which gets us plugged into the source of power; and we can learn as much as we can about His grace until our lives become permeated with grace. These are things that bless us and enable us to obey.

"Human effort without the merit of Christ is worthless. The plan of salvation is not understood to be that through which divine power is brought to man in order that his human effort may be wholly successful" RH, August 19, 1890.

Not partially successful, but wholly successful. This quote may sound confusing the way it is worded. It is really saying that we do not properly understand that salvation can only be achieved when divine power comes into us. When we are truly connected to that power, which is Christ, our human effort will gain the victory over sin. If that power is not in our lives, our human effort is useless.

"By His perfect obedience He has made it possible for every human being to obey God's commandments." COL 312. This also speaks of Christ's merits.

You must look carefully at these things. We think we understand them well, but do we? I must not look at myself, but at His perfect obedience. When I find myself imperfect, not obeying, I must look at His perfection, His obedience, His merits. That is where the power is. It is not in me. I must continue to look to Him, behold His merits, look at His perfection. I must behold Him.

"He came to show man how to obey, how to keep all the commandments. He laid hold of divine power, and this is the sinner's only hope." MYP 165. Jesus obeyed by laying hold on the divine power through a continual connection with His Father. We are to obey by a continual connection with Christ. It is this power that is so important, and the power is in Him, not in us. I must reach out by the hand of faith and plug into the power. I do this by thought processes. I choose to think about Him, I choose to read about Him, I choose to behold His righteousness and His merits and His grace. I learn to know Him. By doing this I am plugging into divine power. He has the power, and by gaining a knowledge of Him, seeking to first receive and understand His grace, and then imparting that grace to others. All these things make me a different person.

We are told that "you must take all—Christ, the fullness of all blessing, to abide in your heart, to be your strength, your righteousness, your everlasting helper—to give you power to obey." SC 70. God so loved the world that He gave Christ. You must take Christ as your everlasting Helper; and "everlasting" in this context means continuously—every second, every moment of the day. You must take Him as your everlasting Helper to give you power to obey.

All of these quotations point to something outside of self whereby you find the power and ability to do what God asks you to do. God never asks us to do something without providing the ability to do it. But to appropriate that power, I must plug in to Him by faith until the power functions in me. Then Christ works out His will inside of me. When we do not obey, it is evident that there is no vital connection with divine power. When I do genuinely obey, I am connected to Him.

We plug into Christ by our daily devotional life, where we allow our mind to focus on Jesus, trusting Him, looking to Him for all our needs, thinking about Him, talking with Him. This changes your life. It is the absence of a devotional life that disconnects us from Him. Having no devotional life is the secret of a sinful life. I have watched my life for a long time and have discovered that when

I have plenty of time for a devotional life, my life is much different, and I am much happier, and I am much easier to live with. When I neglect this for any period of time, my old life takes over and I am totally unlike Christ. Don't come around me then.

When people come to me and tell me how sin is overwhelming them, I simply asked them how long has it been since they plugged in. How long has it been since His power came into them through a vital connection with Him by faith? Every time they are overwhelmed with their sins, it has been quite some time. We can just drift along, hoping things will be different, but there is no other way to be different except by having contact with Him; and the more intimate the contact, and the more lengthy our time with Him, the better. The secret of the Christian life is to abide in Him.

What is it that accomplishes this changed life when you plug in to Jesus? Ellen White recommended that we frequently study the following verse, for here is where power is to be found: "Whereby are given unto us exceeding great and precious promises: that by these ye might be partakers of the divine nature, having escaped the corruption that is in the world through lust." 2 Peter 1:4. We should memorize this verse. Partaking of the divine nature is where the power is. The power is in divinity, not in self. And there is given unto us precious promises. It is by those promises that we are to partake of the divine nature, and thus to escape the lustful, selfish sins that have corrupted the world. The way I have divinity abiding in me, the way that power functions in me, is through faith in these promises. I must take these promises as though God had made them personally to me, and through these I connect up with God. I become a partaker of His divine nature in which there is so much power. You must do something with the promises.

In the book of Hebrews, we find what you have to do with the promises, or else they do not function in the life. Paul speaks of the children of Israel and how a certain promise did not work for them. "And to whom sware He that they should not enter into His rest, but to them that believed not? So we see that they could not enter in because of unbelief." Hebrews 3:18. Then Paul says, "Let us therefore fear, lest, a promise being left us of entering into his rest, any of you should seem to come short of it." Hebrews 4:1. He made a promise to them of a land of milk and honey, a beautiful place of rest, but they could not enter into it. They could not receive the fulfillment of the promise. Why? Unbelief, the Bible says. The Lord, through Paul, is saying that we must be careful, and even fear, lest by our unbelief we fall short of a promise that has been left to us. Promises are only effective when we have faith in the promises and in the One who promises. We must have faith in Him, and we must believe that He means to do well for us.

"For we are made partakers of Christ, if we hold the beginning of our confidence steadfast unto the end." Hebrews 3:14. We partake of that divine nature only as we hold our confidence steadfast. Confidence is trust and trust is an aspect of faith. If we hold steadfast our faith and confidence in Him, we will be made partakers of Christ. Notice that it says we *are* made partakers, not we *will* be partakers. With faith we are made partakers of Christ. Without that faith we are not made partakers. There must be a confidence in Him, or it does not function.

"Take heed, brethren, lest there be in any of you an evil heart of unbelief, in departing from the living God." Verse 12. We must be careful not to depart from the living God by unplugging from the power, or severing our connection with Christ.

Faith is the connector and faith functions by believing God's precious promises. As I trust His promises, something happens in me: I am made a partaker of divine nature. He makes the promise, I believe the promise, and a connection to the power is made by faith; and faith is a channel, or a wire that brings the power all the way from heaven to my life. Over this wire messages can be communicated which come through the devotional life. When the power comes, I am enabled to obey. It is believing those promises and applying them to my life that enables me to function. It is trusting God to perform what He has promised. Abraham believed the promise of God that he would be the father of a great nation, even though he got sidetracked a few times by taking matters into his own hands. It is only when I am connected to Christ by laying hold by faith on something He has promised that I begin to perform.

The big question in obedience is: Am I a believer? There is no doing without believing, there is no performance without faith. There may be performance without faith, but it is man's and not God's; and man's obedience is nothing but filthy rags. It will never be God's perfect righteousness upon which there is no blemish or stain. Without belief and faith there is no righteousness. Faith brings a connection to righteousness and power and enables the sinner to do what he has not been able to do.

Are you a believer? You say you believe our doctrines, but are you a believer in God's goodness to you, and are you a believer in all His promises made to you? Do you try His promises? Do you lay hold of them? Do you apply them to your life? Are you really a believer in God's love for you, that you are special in His eyes? Is your connection strong by having a strong faith in God, or do you have a loose or open connection? When we find ourselves in strange and difficult circumstances in life, we will discover that we really do not have much of a connection.

"But a belief that does not lead to obedience is presumption." MB 146. If I say I believe but do not obey, I really do not even believe. I do not believe if I do not perform. Poor performance means poor belief and a lack of confidence in God. "Obedience is the fruit of faith." SC 61. If I truly exercise faith in Christ, obedience will naturally result.

This is where we fail. We keep examining ourselves and wondering why we cannot seem to obey when the real flaw is that we do not believe. I have looked at my own heart too many times and been frustrated over and over again. Why can't I stop disobeying and start obeying? What is wrong with me? I scrutinize the causes for my bad temper, looking back at what may have happened that day, or what I had not done, and I just get more frustrated. I can see some logic behind this but it does not help me. And after a while, the Spirit of God in His patience asks me how long it has been since I sat down and had a good connection with the Lord. How long has it been since I really found a blessing in prayer, and that I knew I had made contact? Not just praying and reading, but I *knew* that God was speaking to me. How long has it been since I did more than have a morning watch going through the motions? When you have truly made contact with God, you feed your soul each day and go out feeling bolstered, encouraged, and strong; and all day long a verse, a song, or some precious thought goes through your mind over and over again.

I will never forget when one day, during my morning devotional time, I discovered a quote that says God's blessing will come by faith when we surrender to Him. That thought went through my mind for forty-eight hours: the blessing will come when we surrender to God. This is how God can communicate with us through the devotional life. When you go to bed at night and can still remember a text or quotation you read that morning, and it still means something to you, and you are still pondering it, and your soul still feeds on it, then you know that God is blessing you and making you stronger. But if five minutes after the morning devotion you cannot remember one thing you read or studied, that is not devotion. That is an empty ceremony and just going through the motions. Somehow you must make contact until an impression is made, and something that God communicates to you sticks with you all through the day.

We can get so wrapped up in trying to obey that we forget that it is faith that leads to obedience. Believing is also obedience, for believing is a good work. "And this is His commandment, That we should believe on the name of His Son Jesus Christ, and love one another, as He gave us commandment." 1 John 3:23. Here we see that God commands us to believe. To obey a commandment is good work. So believing is a good work. Jesus literally said that. "Jesus answered and said unto them, This is the work of God, that ye believe on Him whom He hath sent." John 6:29. This is the work that God requires, that you believe on Him whom He hath sent. In both cases the commandment and work are connected with believing, and we always thought that works and believing were separate. The Bible does not agree with you for it says that a good work is to believe.

When people in spiritual need come to us and ask what they should do, we tell them they must keep the Sabbath and do this and don't do that. The apostle Paul was not against the Sabbath, or tithing, or missionary activity; but he taught that if you want to be saved there is one thing you must do, and that is to believe. When the keeper of the prison Paul was about to escape from asked, "Sirs, what must I do to be saved?" Paul answered, "Believe on the Lord Jesus Christ, and thou shalt be saved, and thy house." Acts 16:30,31. Believing is a good work. Faith does something for men that other things will not do.

"But without faith it is impossible to please Him." Hebrews 11:6. It is impossible to please God without faith. You can do all the works you want to, but without faith they are all vanity.

Paul taught that "whatsoever is not of faith is sin." Romans 14:23. Whatever we do that is not an act of faith is an act of sin. Faith and believing are commands we can do. When we obey by believing we are becoming connected to divine power. When I believe and am connected to Him, then He produces good fruit and good results in my life.

Faith and believing come first, and these we can do. I believe Him because I am inspired by His love for me, by His trustworthiness, and by the testimony of others concerning His faithfulness. As I believe, I lay hold on Him, I plug into the socket, and power comes into my life to obey. I am connected to the One who can obey and I am no longer trusting in myself. Then obedience to all of God's requirements is possible because the Lord can do all things, and I can do all things through Him who strengthens me. We must make certain that our faith is in Him, and not in our own ability to obey.

Many people have joined the church because they have faith in the church. Many have joined the church because they have faith in the doctrines or the prophecies. Many had faith in the Bible studies they took, or the evangelist. But have you joined the church because you had faith in Jesus? You cannot live the Christ-like life by faith in the church or doctrines or the prophecies. You can only find the power by faith in Jesus. This does not eliminate teachings or doctrines at all. It makes them more important. But I must have my faith in Him, and not in just teachings. I must not segregate theories and ideas from Christ. I must have the truth that is found in Christ.

Only Christ can enable me to obey and no one else can do that. My confidence must not be in things but in a Person, not in ideas but in Jesus. I must serve and believe in the Son of the living God. In Him there is power, strength, hope, and righteousness. He said, "I am the way, the truth, and the life: no man cometh unto the Father, but by me." John 14:6. He is the door of the sheepfold, the blessed hope, and in Him are found all the riches of God. He said, "All power is given unto Me in heaven and in earth." Matthew 28:18. Therefore, if I am in Him, I can do all things; but without Him I can do nothing. Faith in Him produces righteousness in me.

"There are many who, though striving to obey God's commandments, have little peace or joy [they believe in His commandments or they would not strive to obey them]. This lack in their experience is the result of a failure to exercise faith. They walk as it were in a salt land, a parched wilderness. They claim little, when they might claim much; for there is no limit to the promises of God. The Lord would have all His sons and daughters happy, peaceful, and obedient. Through the exercise of faith the believer comes into possession of these blessings." AA 563.

It is not a matter of striving to do better or to do what is right, and it is not praying to do right. It is through the exercise of faith that the believer comes into possession of these blessings. These blessings include joy, peace, and obedience. The quote continues on: "Through faith, every deficiency of character may be supplied, every defilement cleansed, every fault corrected, every excellence developed." Do not kick yourself because you fail. Do not keep condemning yourself and criticizing yourself because you are failing. Go and look for the broken circuit. Find out where the switch is that is off, or where the blown fuse is. Get plugged back in! That is the secret of the Christian life. Through faith, "every deficiency of character may be supplied, every defilement cleansed, every fault corrected, every excellence developed."

This faith is not merely praying, "Lord, help me." It is laying hold on Christ, literally communicating with Him, and just reaching out and grabbing Him like the woman who touched the hem of His garment. When she did that, Jesus perceived that virtue had gone out of Him. She trusted that He would and could heal her, and that it was His desire to do that. Faith is trusting Christ by thinking of Him, by looking to Him, by abiding in Him, by walking with Him, by talking with Him, and constantly realizing that He is my only hope. This is the kind of faith that accomplishes great things.

This final quote gives us the how of obedience: "As the mind dwells upon Christ the character is molded after divine similitude. The thoughts are pervaded with a sense of His goodness. We contemplate His character and thus He is in all our thoughts. His love encloses us. If we gaze even a moment upon the sun in its meridian glory, when we turn away our eyes, the image of the sun will appear in everything upon which we look. Thus it is when we behold Jesus; everything we look upon reflects His image, the Sun of Righteousness. We cannot see anything else, or talk of anything else. His image is imprinted upon the eye of the soul and affects every portion of our daily life, softening and subduing our whole nature." TM 388.

As we behold more and more of the glorious character of Jesus, whenever we look at the church we see Jesus instead of all the problems that plague it.

When we look at our spouse, we see the image of Christ instead of their defects. Whenever you truly allow yourself to be temporarily blinded by beholding Him in morning worship, everything you see that day will have Christ superimposed upon it. We cannot see anything else, or talk of anything else, and all by looking in faith at Him until He imprints His image upon the mind.

Faith succeeds, because faith beholds. Faith trusts the One who has all power, all righteousness, all glory—the One who is able to do exceedingly abundantly above all that we ask or think. Look at Him. Behold Him constantly, and if you do not resist, you cannot avoid being like Him.

May the Lord help us to understand that He does not ask the impossible of weak human beings, and that He makes possible all things He requires of us. He would not frustrate us and torment us with constant failure. He would not be a loving Father if He did that. As He looks down upon us in our frustrating lives, in all our striving and attempts to be righteous, surely He longs to help and bless us.

May we see that there is only One righteous, the Lord Jesus Christ, and that all power is vested in Him. Apart from Him we are helpless, but with Him we can do all things. May the Lord help us to do that which we can do, which is to believe and trust His promises, behold His glorious character, and choose Him to rule over us in love. To every person He has given a measure of faith, and as we by faith lay hold on Jesus and trust in Him and His divine power, He comes to abide in us, and He makes us like Himself.

May God take away our striving to be better, and may He help our unbelief. May we maintain a precious contact with Him, sitting at His feet and plugged into that marvelous power that is able to transform us. May we so behold Jesus that as we turn away, His image is superimposed on all of life. This is my prayer for you, in Jesus' name.

32

PERFECTION

THE SUBJECT OF PERFECTION is closely related to Christ our righteousness. Your concept of perfection influences your understanding of Christ our righteousness; and conversely, your concept of Christ our righteousness will influence your understanding of perfection. Because there are so many misunderstandings about perfection, there are many misunderstandings of Christ our righteousness.

One of the major problems in discussing perfection is that it is much like discussing the soul. What do you mean by the word *soul?* In the Old Testament, only one Hebrew word for *soul* is translated into forty-three different English words.

The same thing is true of the idea of perfection. We must define what the word means. In the Bible, the reverse of the word *soul* is true. That is, in the King James Version, the two English words *perfect* and *perfection* are translated from many different Hebrew and Greek words. There are several cases where those many Hebrew and Greek words would be better translated into English words other than *perfect* or *perfection.*

For example, there are times when those many original language words would be more correctly translated as *complete, finished, integrity, exactness,* or any of several other English words and expressions. Therefore, when you read the words *perfect* and *perfection* in the King James Version, it may not mean perfect or perfection at all. So unfortunately, even the Bible adds to the confusion about perfection. Therefore, when you get into a discussion on the subject of perfection, you must ask, "What do you mean by perfection?" If you have not decided what you mean by it, then you are wandering around in the clouds somewhere.

There was a book published within our denomination some years ago titled *Perfection.* The book consists of several articles written by excellent Seventh-day Adventist scholars who present different views about the same subject. It is obvious that those who contributed to the book do not agree on the subject; but I think they agree more than we realize. Again, part of the problem is in defining what you mean by perfection.

One writer of that book wrote about absolute perfection, and by that he means the perfection of God. God the Father has never sinned. He does not have a sinful body, or sinful parents, or live in a sinful world. Does that make any difference? I think it does, don't you? He never has sinned! Of course these things make a difference. What is it like to live all your life in a sinful body? It is different than what can be produced in something sinless. The Bible teaches that we have been born of sinful parents, and we live in a sinful environment, and we carry about a body that Paul called "our vile body" in Philippians 3:21. Our bodies are called "corruptible" in 1 Corinthians 15:53. It does not matter how much you have been converted, you still have a corruptible body. Therefore, perfection in this kind of body has some problems. We have all sinned; therefore, to some extent our past experience has impaired perfection, and even our concepts of it. Since God is absolutely perfect with no background or history of sin, then there may be a difference between absolute perfection and human perfection.

Some will point out that Jesus said, "Be ye therefore perfect, even as your Father which is in heaven is perfect." Matthew 5:48. If absolute perfection is not possible, why did He say that? This is where we can be thankful that we have an inspired commentary. "He tells us to be perfect as He is, in the same manner." MB 77. It does not say in the same degree or to the same extent. There is a difference between degree and manner. In the same manner means "like this," or "in the same way." What, then, did Jesus mean about us being perfect even as our heavenly Father is perfect? "As God is perfect in His sphere, so man is to be perfect in his sphere." MM 112,113. God has a different sphere than we have. Ours is a limited one, and His is widespread.

Therefore, while we might not be able to be perfect in the same degree, we can be perfect in the same manner. This qualifies the meaning of perfection to some extent as it relates to man. You will think I am walking on both sides of the topic, but I defy you to read the Bible and the Spirit of Prophecy without straddling the fence sometimes. You cannot discuss the whole topic well without looking at every side of it. We must be most careful what we say and think about perfection, but most people are not sufficiently careful. This is a more involved subject than we assume it to be.

It is difficult for beginners to understand maturity. This is not a criticism; but many have a difficult time with the elementary things of Christianity. Try to talk to a young child about a retirement plan. There is little comprehension of such a thing. And often we may be in the church a long time but be quite juvenile in our experience and knowledge. Therefore, perfection, which is full growth, or maturity, is a difficult thing. But both the Scripture and the Spirit of Prophecy are most explicit about perfection. The biggest question we have is: Is perfection possible to any extent?

The Bible provides several answers. "Therefore leaving the principles of the doctrine of Christ, let us go on unto perfection...." Hebrews 6:1. (The margin of my Bible says "full growth or maturity.") "Now the God of peace, that brought again from the dead our Lord Jesus, that great Shepherd of the sheep, through the blood of the everlasting covenant, Make you perfect in every good work to do His will, working in you that which is wellpleasing in His sight, through Jesus Christ..." Hebrews 13:20,21. "I in them, and Thou in Me, that they may be made perfect in one; and that the world may know that Thou hast sent Me, and hast loved them, as Thou hast loved Me." John 17:23. "Whom we preach [meaning Christ], warning every man, and teaching every man in all wisdom; that we may present every man perfect in Christ Jesus." Colossians 1:28. "Let us therefore, as many as be perfect, be thus minded: and if in any thing ye be otherwise minded, God shall reveal even this unto you." Philippians 3:15. "Howbeit we speak wisdom among them that are perfect." 1 Corinthians 2:6. "Till we all come in the unity of the faith, and of the knowledge of the Son of God, unto a perfect man, unto the measure of the stature of the fulness of Christ." Ephesians 4:13.

The Spirit of Prophecy agrees with the Bible. "The Lord requires perfection from His redeemed family. He expects from us the perfection which Christ revealed in His humanity." CG 477. "God requires perfection of His children." COL 315. "If you make God your strength, you may, under the most discouraging circumstances, attain a height and breadth of Christian perfection which you hardly think it possible to reach." 4T 567.

With all this, we should cease to say we do not believe in Christian perfection. God does believe in it for mankind. The problem is that we look at ourselves and wonder how this can be possible. Yet we are told that we can attain to Christian perfection even "under the most discouraging circumstances." But only if you "make God your strength." Some kind of perfection is not only possible, but is to be expected. There is great disagreement as to what kind of perfection this is talking about.

Sometimes you can understand a difficult concept like this by eliminating what it is not. What is it that perfection is not? Commenting about the false doctrine of holy flesh, Ellen White wrote: "The teaching given in regard to what is termed 'holy flesh' is an error. All may now obtain holy hearts, but it is not correct to claim in this life to have holy flesh....To those who have tried so hard to obtain by faith so-called holy flesh, I would say, You cannot obtain it. Not a soul of you has holy flesh now. No human being on earth has holy flesh. It is an impossibility....Let this phase of doctrine be carried a little further, and it will lead to the claim that its advocates cannot sin; that since they have holy flesh, their actions are all holy... .The Scriptures teach us to seek for the sanctification to God of body, soul, and spirit. In this work we are to be laborers together with God. Much may be done to restore the moral image of God in man, to improve the physical, mental, and moral capabilities. Great changes can be made in the physical system by obeying the laws of God and bringing into the body nothing that defiles. And while we cannot claim perfection of the flesh, we may have Christian perfection of the soul. Through the sacrifice made in our behalf, sins may be perfectly forgiven. Our dependence is not in what man can do; it is in what God can do for man through Christ. When we surrender ourselves wholly to God, and fully believe, the blood of Christ cleanses from all sin. The conscience can be freed from condemnation. Through faith in His blood, all may be made perfect in Christ Jesus. Thank God that we are not dealing with impossibilities. We may claim sanctification. We may enjoy the favor of God." 2SM 32.

Here the idea of holy flesh is eliminated. Yet far too many look at the flesh to see how holy the heart is. The Lord looks on the heart, not on the outside. The Jews were interested only in the externals, but Christ was interested in what is on the inside; and perfection is of the heart, not of the flesh. Heart perfection will definitely have an influence on the flesh, but we will never find perfection in the flesh. We will have these corrupt bodies until resurrection or until we are translated. There might be occasional misdeeds of the weak flesh, but we must not make excuses by using this quotation and saying, "Oh well, I cannot be perfect anyway. I will do anything I want to." It does not say that. We cannot claim holy flesh, but we can have holy hearts that are rightly in tune with heaven. There should not be bondage to sin when the Son has made us free. An occasional misdeed is not bondage. That is just an encumbrance with these vile bodies that Paul calls the body of death. It seems to drag us down like a terrible weight. So we bear about in our bodies these types of problems.

What kind of perfection is perfection of the soul? How perfect can the soul be? What is a holy heart? Will it be as good as Adam's before he sinned? "Human perfection failed in Eden, the paradise of bliss." 5BC 1132. Sinless perfection in Adam and Eve failed when tempted. I am suggesting that you must have something better than they had. Is that too severe a thought?

Would we be well off if we had the perfection of the angels? The very next sentence in the above quotation says, "Angelic perfection failed in heaven." We are talking about sinless beings with sinless bodies that had never seen sin; yet when tempted, one-third of the angels fell, and both of our first parents fell. Their perfection was not a sufficient protection or guarantee against temptation. If you become as perfect as Adam before his sin, or even the angels before they fell, will that assure God that you will not sin in heaven? Never! Your perfection is not a ticket to heaven.

I used to teach flying in the Second World War, and I had a student named Vince who did everything perfectly. It seemed as though the other five students in that group would never learn to fly. Even after being shown a maneuver twenty times, those other students could not get it right. But Vince learned the first time how to do everything. This was my first batch of students, and I used to discuss Vince with the other instructors. They told me I should be very careful with that fellow, and that something terrible was liable to happen, even though it seemed that he did everything flawlessly. He did things so perfectly that I used to bump the stick with my hand when he was coming in for a landing to confuse him so he would have to go around and try again.

When my students finished my portion of their training, they all left and went to another school about two hundred miles away. After about six weeks we got news back from that school about one of my students. The runway was built so that there was about three feet of concrete sitting above the ground. The goal was to land within the first fifty feet of the end of the runway, so they had a long way to slow down in case they lost their brakes. The only one who seemed to be able to do that was Vince. But one day Vince came in to land and his plane was just slightly low, and he hit the wheels on the edge of the runway, and the wheels folded back and he went sliding down the runway on the belly of the airplane. All the rest of those fellows who had such a hard time doing things the right way never had an accident. The perfect one had the only accident. The imperfect ones had no accidents.

Who will be saved and go to heaven? You see, we do not have this figured out quite right yet. Do we? Heaven was not a safe place because many of the angels, with all their perfection, sinned. The same is true of Adam and Eve in their perfection. I don't care how perfect you become in your sinlessness, your perfection will not save you.

I want to go back to the previous quote (5BC 1132) and give you the entire context of the quotation. "The death of Christ upon the cross made sure the destruction of him who has the power of death, who was the originator of sin. When Satan is destroyed, there will be none to tempt to evil; the atonement will never need to be repeated; and there will be no danger of another rebellion in the universe of God. That which alone can effectually restrain from sin in this world of darkness, will prevent sin in heaven. The significance of the death of Christ will be seen by saints and angels. Fallen men could not have a home in the paradise of God without the Lamb slain from the foundation of the world. Shall we not then exalt the cross of Christ? The angels [who have never sinned] ascribe honor and glory to Christ, for even they are not secure except by looking to the sufferings of the Son of God. It is through the efficacy of the cross that the angels of heaven are guarded from apostasy. Without the cross they would be no more secure against evil than were the angels before the fall of Satan. Angelic perfection failed in heaven. Human perfection failed in Eden, the paradise of bliss. All who wish for security in earth or heaven must look to the Lamb of God. The plan of salvation, making manifest the love and justice of God, provides an eternal safeguard against defection in unfallen worlds, as well as among those who shall be redeemed by the blood of the Lamb. Our only hope is perfect trust in the blood of Him who can save to the uttermost all who come unto God by Him. The death of Christ on the cross of Calvary is our only hope in this world, and will be our theme in the world to come. Oh, we do not comprehend the value of the atonement!"

Any type of perfection that we have, or the unfallen beings on other worlds have, or the unfallen angels have, would not protect us from future sin. There is only one thing that protects us from sin and guarantees against future sin in the face of any temptation, and that is the cross of Christ.

How does the cross guarantee against future sin? First of all, the cross of Christ is one of the most unique types of righteousness, or obedience, that is found any place in the Scriptures. There is not one other act like it. "For as by one man's disobedience many were made sinners, so by the obedience of One shall many be made righteous." Romans 5:19. We understand that the death of Christ on the cross is that one act of perfect obedience, or righteousness. There is no righteousness like the death of Jesus. There is no perfection quite like the death of Christ. It is a different kind of perfection that we do not commonly think about.

The submission that was required at Calvary is most unusual. This is seen in the experience of Jesus in the Garden of Gethsemane. "And He went a little further, and fell on his face, and prayed, saying, O My Father, if it be possible, let this cup pass from Me: nevertheless not as I will, but as Thou wilt....He went away again the second time, and prayed, saying, O My Father, if this cup may not pass away from Me, except I drink it, Thy will be done....And He left them, and went away again, and prayed the third time, saying the same words." Matthew 26:39,42,44.

The Father tried to give Him the cup of our sins, and Christ prayed that this cup would pass from Him. But note in verse 39 that Jesus prayed, "nevertheless not as I will, but as Thou wilt." You must dwell on what was going on there. If Jesus took the cup of our sins, He would be separated from the One who had eternally loved Him. If He obeyed His Father, He would be separated from His Father; and He feared that separation would be eternal. By obeying His Father, He would have to leave His Father. If He loved us, He would take the cup. If He loved His Father, He would not take it. This was a terrible enigma for Him. And the only thing that carried Him through was that He knew that His Father could be trusted. He loved His Father, and He knew His Father loved Him, and so He always prayed that His Father's will would be done.

With all of the ramifications of this problem, to pray "not as I will, but as Thou wilt" is a most unusual submission. In other words, He would accept the separation, which He knew to be the Father's will, because the Father said so. And all the complications that seemed to enter His mind of eternal separation from His Father, in all the heartbreak that separation would bring Him, He submitted to the wishes of His Father. Have you ever seen such obedience? This submission, this yielding, this trust, this self-distrust almost seems to go beyond obedience. The One who was perfect in humanity so totally distrusted Himself that He would not follow His own logic or His own thinking. He simply submitted to whatever His Father willed. The cross of Calvary stands all by itself as the epitome of perfection and righteousness. This is a different kind of perfection. It is obedience, and obedience is righteousness. I suppose the best way to describe it is the self-denial and the total confidence of relying on someone else who is trustworthy.

This type of perfection is different. I would like to suggest that the whole Bible is filled with this, but we do not often see it. Christ presented the law in Matthew 22 where He talked about supreme love for God. This love toward God, according to Deuteronomy 6:5, is to be "with all thine heart, and with all thy soul, and with all thy might." This is total love for God. If all the heart and soul and might were wrapped up in love for God, what else would you love? He is an all-consuming affection. There is no room for self-love. God takes over all my plans, all my ideas, all my interests, all my thoughts. This is supreme love for God.

Also in Matthew 22, Jesus went on to talk about loving our neighbors as ourselves. What kind of love is this? "In the light from Calvary it will be seen that the law of self-renouncing love is the law of life for earth and heaven; that the love which 'seeketh not her own' has its source in the heart of God." DA 20. This self-renouncing, self-sacrificing love is the kind of love that Jesus had. And as we have stated so many times, "love is the fulfilling of the law." Romans 13:10. And the fulfilling of the law is righteousness and perfection.

Christian perfection is not an egocentric perfection. It is not looking to see how I am doing. It is what I am doing for others, and what do I think about them. And neither is it doing for others because I want to become perfect. It is doing for others because I love them and forget myself. This is found in many places in the Bible. "Who, being in the form of God, thought it not robbery to be equal with God: But made Himself of no reputation, and took upon Him the form of a servant, and was made in the likeness of men: And being found in fashion as a man, He humbled himself, and became obedient unto death, even the death of the cross." Philippians 2:6-8. In verses 4 and 5, it says, "Look not every man on his own things, but every man also on the things of others. Let this mind be in you, which was also in Christ Jesus." Do not worry about yourself and what you have, but be concerned about others and their needs. In the life of Jesus, this supreme love for God and consuming interest in the needs of others took over and guided Him in every step of life. He loves you and me so much so that He would even accept separation from His Father. That type of self-surrender, of yielding and submissiveness, is truly the perfection of Christ. This is the kind of perfection that we ought to look at.

Jesus said, "If any man will come after Me, let him deny himself, and take up his cross, and follow Me." Matthew 16:24. It is on the cross that we die to self. I would like to suggest that Christ is talking about Christian perfection in that verse. Deny yourself. We forget self, and take up our cross, for we die on the cross we carry. Self is forgotten, and we follow Jesus every step of the way. He leads, He guides, and I do His will. He is the only safeguard against sin.

"Kneeling at the cross, he [the sinner] has reached the highest place to which man can attain." 5BC 1133. We have visions and dreams that are way beyond the cross, but kneeling at the cross is in reality the highest place that we can ever attain. There is no higher place than to be on our knees, looking up and worshipping that marvelous One who sacrificed to such an extent.

We look to understand what our hands are doing to see if they are doing things as perfectly as we think they ought to. We look at what our eyes see and our ears listen to and our tongues taste to see if we are perfect enough. The Lord is telling us to look instead at the heart. Who has your heart? Who controls your thoughts? Who rules your life? Who dominates you? Are you gladly submissive to Him? Do you delight to do His law? Do you distrust self so totally that you must have Christ to lead you every step of the way?

It is that total distrust of self, that total confidence in God, and that total surrender to Him that is perfection. And there is a unique thing about this kind of perfection. It is easy for the worst sinners, and it is difficult for the best sinners. The bad sinners do not trust themselves because they know how weak they are, and they have been bad for so long. They have never been able to rise above bad sins. They have always been a failure. How desperately they need help, and so they gladly submit to the One who can help them. The good sinners, the ones who are proud of their goodness and doing quite well, externally, are the ones who do not need much help, and it is difficult for them to submit to someone else. They think more highly of themselves than they ought. Therefore, they do not submit. They say, "Let me try." And the Lord asks, "When will you discover that all your trying is nothing but failures?" He is waiting for us to learn that only in Christ can I accomplish anything. Even our best deeds are tainted with self, and yet we call our good works and our attempts at obedience *righteousness*.

When we submit to Jesus and He rules the life, life will be different. Jesus said that the greatest in His kingdom would be the ones who serve others. One of the finest parables on perfection is where Jesus talked with the rich young ruler. "Jesus said unto him, If thou wilt be perfect, go and sell that thou hast, and give to the poor, and thou shalt have treasure in heaven: and come and follow Me." Matthew 19:21. In other words, Jesus was saying if you really want to be perfect, deny yourself, not to obtain perfection, but because you love those poor people, and you want to see them fed and clothed. If you will be perfect, forget yourself. Then follow Him and He will show you what to do. Self-denial is the road to great success in the spiritual life.

Ellen White discussed how the Jews failed in achieving righteousness and perfection. "Now He points out to them the character of the righteousness that all who enter heaven will possess. Throughout the Sermon on the Mount He describes its fruits, and now in one sentence He points out its source and its nature: Be perfect as God is perfect. The law is but a transcript of the character of God. Behold in your heavenly Father a perfect manifestation of the principles which are the foundation of His government. God is love. Like rays of light from the sun, love and light and joy flow out from Him to all His creatures. It is His nature to give. His very life is the outflow of unselfish love….He tells us to be perfect as He is, in the same manner. We are to be centers of light and blessing to our little circle, even as He is to the universe. We have nothing of ourselves, but the light of His love shines upon us, and we are to reflect its brightness. 'In His borrowed goodness good,' we may be perfect in our sphere, even as God is perfect in His." MB 77.

Our sphere is that little neighborhood where we live, the office where we work, or the classroom, or the dormitory. That is your sphere. In that sphere we are to shed light and blessing on all around us. We can only give it as we receive it. We are told that when we give, "it shall be given unto you; good measure, pressed down, and shaken together, and running over, shall men give into your bosom. For with the same measure that ye mete withal it shall be measured to you again." Luke 6:38. The great givers are always great receivers. The small givers only get a small bit back. The channel of blessing becomes bigger as our hearts love people more and more.

How big a giver can God make you? I am not talking about money, for money is often meaningless in many ways. I am talking about encouragement, or a loaf of bread, or watching the neighbor's children, or the prayer at the bedside of someone who is sick, and visiting the dear lady in the rest home who has not had a visitor in two months. I am talking about all the common, ordinary things of life where we forget ourselves and go out to bless other people. All day long the Lord was doing this. And at night He filled back up the reservoir. Always, every day, serving mankind, forgetting Himself that others might be blessed.

I would suggest that the life of service, of total self-forgetfulness out of a great love for others, always lightening their load and always blessing them, has more to do with perfection than any other thing I know of. This life of service has a closer connection with the cross than any other type of activity. Distrust of self, and total confidence in God, makes us safe in heaven for eternity. The cross teaches that lesson. If Christ would not trust Himself under those circumstances, but only His Father, when can you trust yourself? Total trust in Christ is perfection.

How perfect can He make you? At one time the Lord promised Moses He would give the children of Israel flesh to eat until it came out of their nostrils. Moses reasoned with God by saying, "The people, among whom I am, are six hundred thousand footmen; and Thou hast said, I will give them flesh, that they may eat a whole month. Shall the flocks and the herds be slain for them, to suffice them? or shall all the fish of the sea be gathered together for them, to suffice them?" Numbers 11:21,22. In verse 23, the Lord rebuked Moses and said, "Is the Lord's hand waxed short?" Is God so weak that He cannot do what He promises to do? He said He would rain so many birds down from heaven that they would be all over the place. Did He do it? Yes, He did. What will He do with a human being who submits to Him totally? I can only imagine. If God can make out of dust a human being as complicated as you are, what kind of person can He make you? The Bible says, "Now unto Him that is able to do exceeding abundantly above all that we ask or think, according to the power that worketh in us." Ephesians 3:20. Never limit what God wants to do in man.

In that glorious kingdom above, when we gather there on the sea of glass, we will all be amazed at the others who are there; and we will stand there marveling at what God has done with weak human beings. None will take the praise to themselves. All the praise will be to Him.

May God help you this day to recognize that we can do nothing of ourselves. Without Him we are totally helpless. But I can do all things through Christ who strengthens me. This involves a unique relationship of total dependency on Christ and total distrust of self, and leaning on the everlasting arms for everything.

We have not yet witnessed what God wants to do with man. He is singling us out in these special last days to be an example and an encouragement to weak individuals of what God can do. May we so fully depend upon Him that we become huge channels of blessing to all mankind, so that they know that God is not only love, but powerful. May the Lord make you perfect in every good work through His Son, the Lord Jesus Christ.

Thanks

TURNING BILL LEHMAN'S SERMON series into this book was a tremendous blessing to all those who participated. Thanks go out to the following people for their unselfish devotion to this project:

Debra Pigeon for her tireless hours at the computer typing the sermons into manuscript form.

Stan Nelson who preserved the original sermon tapes from which this book has been transcribed; and for his generous donation towards getting the first edition of this book printed.

Jeannie LaPorte, Trish Turner, Betty Beam, DiAnn Randleman, and Julie Reynolds who proofread the manuscript and corrected a multitude of errors found in the first draft.

Bob Kent at HopeNet Resources International for his help with the publishing logistics of this book.

Special thanks to Nona and Rose Lehman for their support in this project. During those years that Rose was married to Bill, she saw him transformed from a former Air Corps pilot with a rough exterior and short temper into a man through whom the love of Christ radiated out to all around him.

Then, of course, we will have to wait until we meet Bill Lehman on the streets of gold to thank him for sharing this marvelous message of Christ our righteousness with those of us who needed it so much. A lot of saints will be looking Bill up to give him a big bear hug; for more than he knew, he touched the lives of many through his unselfish ministry to God's people.

—Dwight Turner, Editor

Be sure to ask for
Bill Lehman's other book,

The Matchless Charms of Christ

NOTES

NOTES

NOTES

NOTES

NOTES

NOTES

NOTES

NOTES